VOICES FROM THE CLASSROOM

Reflections on Teaching and Learning in Higher Education

Edited by
Janice Newton
Jerry Ginsburg
Jan Rehner
Pat Rogers
Susan Sbrizzi
John Spencer

Garamond Press

centre for the
support of
teaching

Printed and bound in Canada

A joint publication of Garamond Press
and the Centre for the Support of Teaching, York University.

Distributed by special arrangement with York University Bookstore,
York Lanes, York University, Toronto, Ont. M3J 1P3 Canada.

CSt
centre for the
support of
teaching

The Centre for the Support of Teaching was established at York University
in 1989 to provide advocacy for excellence and innovation in teaching and
to promote teaching that invigorates the learning environment for
students. The Centre coordinates a broad range of programmes and
strategies to promote reflective practice and scholarly dialogue on
teaching and learning among faculty and graduate students.
cst@yorku.ca
www.yorku.ca/cst/

Garamond Press
63 Mahogany Court,
Aurora, Ontario L4G 6M8
garamond@web.ca
www.garamond.ca

National Library of Canada Cataloguing in Publication Data

Main entry under title:

Voices from the Classroom: reflections on teaching and learning in
    higher education

Co-published by the Centre for the Support of Teaching, York University.

Includes bibliographical references.
ISBN 1-55193-031-5

1. College teaching. 2. Learning.
I. Newton, Janice, 1952-   II. York University (Toronto, Ont.). Centre for the Support of Teaching

LB2331.V64 2001   378.1'25   C2001-930157-X

Table of Contents

Acknowledgements

This book is the result of a community project initiated, designed and coordinated by York University's Centre for the Support of Teaching under the leadership of the Academic Director, Pat Rogers. A large number of people have contributed to the project's success along the way, most notably the members of the editorial committee: Jerry Ginsburg, Janice Newton, Jan Rehner, Pat Rogers, Sue Sbrizzi and John Spencer. John Spencer chaired the editorial committee for the first year. Janice Newton assumed the chair's role during John's sabbatical and continued in this role until the project's successful completion.

We would like to express our heartfelt appreciation to everyone who participated in the production and publication of this work. We thank each of the authors – faculty, students and administrators without whom this book would not be completed – for taking the time to share their thoughts, ideas and insights. In addition, we would like to thank the staff and associates of the Centre for the Support of Teaching who provided excellent support, guidance and feedback throughout the course of this project, especially James Brown, Susan Cohen, John Dwyer, Olivia Petrie, Gail Vanstone and Diane Zorn. We would also like to thank our publishers, Peter Saunders of Garamond Press and Michael Jackel of the York University Bookstore, for their belief in the value of this work and their advice and guidance in bringing it to publication.

Introduction

Responsibility, Respect, Research and Reflection in Higher Education

Janice Newton

Founded in 1959, York University is situated in one of the largest cities in North America. With a reputation for innovation in both teaching and research, York attracts students from a wide social spectrum to its two campuses. Many students are the first from their families to attend university; many are first-generation immigrants or refugees. All social classes are represented, as are a variety of groups with different disabilities. The diversity extends to different languages, sexualities, ages, religions and cultures. With more than 50,000 students in ten faculties, an ongoing challenge for faculty and teaching assistants at York is finding effective ways to teach and serve the needs of such a diverse student body.

This book is a project of York's Centre for the Support of Teaching and while its original intent was to encourage good teaching practices among faculty and teaching assistants at York, we hope instructors at other universities will also find it useful. The voices within these pages reflect the broad diversity of our community – the articles are authored by undergraduate and graduate students, teaching assistants, contract and full-time faculty, staff and administrators. Though the topics span a continuum from the theoretical to the practical, issues of equity, diversity and power form the foundation of our community's thinking about pedagogy.

The book begins with three articles written by students, graduate and undergraduate, who speak critically of their experiences in a university environment. Their voices provide a valuable reminder that if our task is to teach the students we have, we have a responsibility to begin by listening to and respecting what they have to say. Subsequent articles in Section I speak to the different ways that respect for student diversity and student concerns has been taken to heart and prompts our teaching community to reflect on teaching practices. In a fundamental way, the challenge of teaching on such ethnically and racially diverse campuses has enormously enriched our reflections on pedagogy. In this spirit, we believe that this book, though written by students and faculty from one university, has broader appeal to the university teaching community across North America. The challenges we face in the twenty-first century are challenges we have in common with many large urban campuses across North America. We offer this book as a contribution to reflections on pedagogy in university-level teaching for those in comparably diverse communities.

Effective teaching at the university level is not just about responding to demographic changes in the student body as it transforms apace with Canadian society. It is also about curriculum. We do not rethink our curriculum and pedagogy simply to appeal to the range of students in our classrooms. We rethink pedagogy and curriculum because the world of knowledge has changed. History is a good example. Do we introduce immigrant history into our curriculum simply because we now see immigrant students in our classes? That might be one impetus, but aside from the students in our classes, we have a responsibility to teach current understandings of knowledge in our disciplines. Canadian history did not unfold in the absence of women, immigrants, racial minorities or aboriginal Canadians. We should not teach it as if it did, regardless of who sits in our classrooms.

This points to the complex tensions between paradigm shifts within disciplines and transformations in pedagogy. If one does not teach in a discipline in which societal change is central to the curriculum, is rethinking pedagogy irrelevant or unnecessary? On the contrary, as many authors in this book will attest, the challenges of teaching in any discipline require us to engage students in the material. If we take our responsibility to promote student learning seriously, then we need to think about ways of teaching that appeal to the multiplicity of differences among students in our classes, from different learning styles or stages of intellectual development to different racial, gender or class experiences.

The articles in this book do not include only success stories. Articles on teaching can annoy when they talk about techniques or theories in glowing terms without talking about their drawbacks, or outright failures. If we are to progress and develop effective pedagogy in a university setting, we must develop a scholarly approach to our teaching practices. We must examine what works as well as what does not work and share the results of our reflections and research in teaching. A number of authors in this book write courageously about teaching experiences that backfired or had disappointing outcomes. The value of these discussions is that they echo, in a realistic way, the actual practice of teaching in university. Many of us have had similar experiences of trying new teaching strategies in our classes, only to be disappointed. It can be a challenge to find a collegial environment in which to discuss these experiences. A lucky few might feel comfortable turning to departmental colleagues – those who judge us for tenure and promotion, who eye our teaching practices and evaluations in relation to their own–to discuss their experiences; many do not. Without a collegial venue for reflecting on our successes and failures, the overall teaching environment is weakened.

We need to bring to our university teaching the spirit of scholarly inquiry that each of us brings to our discipline. In science, an experiment that fails to support a hypothesis is not wasted knowledge; it contributes to what we already know and helps to inform the direction of the next step in research. Experiments often have unintended results that turn out to be more valuable than the intended result. We need to think of our teaching practices in a similar light and use our research skills to assess our teaching practices.

Another important question recurs throughout the book: What are our teaching goals? If one takes this question seriously, simply covering the course material is clearly an inadequate goal. We need to link that goal with the crucial question, Are the students learning? Once we incorporate student learning into our teaching goals, a different set of priorities begins to emerge. We hope this book contributes to reflections about the relationship between teaching goals and the strategies used to achieve those goals.

The book is divided into eight sections. Section I, Power, Diversity and Equity in the Classroom, includes articles on power, gender, race, feminist pedagogy, heterosexism, disability, adult education and teaching English as a second language. Section II, Theories and Models of Student Learning, introduces several different theories of learning, including the Myers Briggs model, which associates learning styles with psychological types, the Gregorc model and the models of Perry and Belenky. Each of these articles provides useful perspectives on how theories of learning can inform our teaching practices. Section III, Course Design, introduces a range of issues that can be brought to bear when designing a course, including perspectives from the sciences and the humanities. Section IV, Working With Graduate Students, highlights two dimensions of the graduate learning experience: as students in a discipline and as apprentice teachers. Section V, Academic Honesty, focuses on an important but often overlooked dimension of university teaching. The articles discuss different ways to understand issues of academic integrity and stress the importance of teaching to prevent academic dishonesty in different settings, such as essay writing, laboratory experiments and the use of electronic sources. Section VI, Teaching and Learning Strategies, covers a broad range of teaching strategies, including lecturing, class participation, seminars, tutorials and group learning. Section VII, Assignments and Evaluation, offers ideas on a variety of assignments, including reading and research essays, as well as a section on grading and evaluation in different disciplinary contexts. Finally, Section VIII, Developing and Assessing Your Teaching, describes a variety of ways to obtain feedback on teaching performance from students and colleagues, and includes both the Teaching Evaluation Guide and the Teaching Documentation Guide developed by York's Senate Committee on Teaching and Learning.

We trust that this book will be useful both as a handbook, to be dipped into when one needs specific advice on a particular teaching issue, and as a broader reference source on university teaching. The works cited at the end of many articles offer a wealth of suggestions for further reading on specific topics. In these pages, both the novice teaching assistant and the seasoned professor will find ideas that are useful and stimulating. We hope that this book serves to remind us of our responsibility to teach the diverse range of students before us, to respect their unique needs and experiences as they embark on the path of higher education, to bring our skills as researchers to our teaching practices, and to engage in ongoing reflection on the task of university-level teaching.

Section I:
Power, Diversity and Equity
in the Classroom

This section is devoted to exploring the pedagogical implications of teaching a diverse student body. How can we teach in a way that promotes learning for *all* students? To do this, we must consider who the students in our classes are. What knowledge and experiences do they bring with them? How does this shape the balance of power in the classroom? In what ways does this enhance or interfere with the learning process? How should this knowledge influence our teaching practices?

We open this section with three articles reflecting students' perspectives on their learning experiences. In the essay by Markita Fleming *et al.*, we hear students discuss the different ways they have felt silenced or disempowered during their undergraduate experiences. The two articles that follow address graduate students' experiences. The perspectives offered in all three articles are very critical, challenging us to reconsider our pedagogical goals and revealing implicit biases that can occur in our teaching practices, classrooms and curricula. Further, these student voices remind us how vulnerable students can feel, even those whom we think are most likely to succeed. Listening to student voices is the first step in meeting the challenge of developing inclusive teaching practices. We must engage with the full implications of diversity and power dynamics in our pedagogical practices and keep returning to the task of clarifying our teaching goals – from first-year to graduate teaching.

The articles that follow are written by faculty and teaching assistants who take up this challenge. The range of issues they cover is quite broad, beginning with the cornerstone piece by Linda Briskin, "Power in the Classroom." Briskin outlines the different forms that power can take in a classroom, opening the way for us to consider how power dynamics can diminish a learning environment and create complex inequities within it. Subsequent articles focus on antiracist pedagogy, feminist pedagogy, heterosexism, disability, adult learning and English as a second language.

Our student body is diverse in many ways: men and women with a range of experiences from different cultures, with different first languages, some with learning disabilities or physical disabilities and some straight, gay or lesbian. Not all of this diversity is visible at first glance, nor do visual clues provide a sound basis for making assumptions about individual students. Each student brings an invisible quality to the classroom: a unique set of life experiences that, as the article by Leslie Sanders reminds us, can profoundly shape a student's interaction in a course. While reflecting on how diversity might shape our teaching practices, several authors caution against making assumptions about individual students. In the end, a recurrent theme emerges: Effective university teachers must respect the diverse needs and identities of students and create conditions in their courses in which all students can learn. In short, respecting diversity is the starting point of sound pedagogy.

Gender, Power and Silence in the Classroom: Our Experiences Speak for Themselves

Markita Fleming, Nadia Habib, Tina Horley, Sabynthe Jones-Caldwell, Marla, Kathie Moules, Lori Waserman and Samantha Wehbi

It never occurred to me that the classroom wasn't a neutral space. I always thought that we all received basically the same education. But in an economics course, the male students were given all the professor's time and attention, while the female students were repeatedly cut off. I was so angry and so alienated that I didn't know what to do or how to make myself heard and I didn't feel safe enough to ask questions. I eventually dropped out of economics altogether.[1]

As a man thinking about gender in the classroom, I was initially confronted by the dilemma that there seemed to be few examples of how gender relations influenced my own academic development. It occurred to me, however, that this was no accident. It is not just that men experience gender differently from women (in the classroom and elsewhere), but that we experience it largely as an "absence." It appears as something that is solely someone else's problem, or at best as a concern for the welfare of others.

The impetus to write this article arose out of our experiences as sixteen women and one man completing an assignment on gender in the classroom for a fourth-year seminar on feminist thought. Sharing our work revealed that our individual experiences were not isolated, chance incidents.

Although we had known that, for the most part, the classroom is not a neutral place, theorizing these experiences uncovered the deeply systemic character of discrimination. Depending on our gender, race, class and sexual orientation, we discovered that we are heard differently and hear differently; as a result, we take away with us more lessons than we are consciously taught.

We are angry. Audre Lorde reminds us that:

My fear of anger taught me nothing. Every woman has a well-stocked arsenal of anger potentially useful against those oppressions, personal and institutional, which brought that anger into being. Focused with precision it can become a powerful source of energy serving progress and change (1984, 127).

We want to share our experiences in the hope of breaking through the isolation that others like us might feel. We want to mobilize our "arsenal of anger" to effect change.

Whether they like it or not, students and professors bring into the classroom attitudes that reflect their gender, race and class. Gender, race and class are not neutral. They are systems of power and domination. They are reinforced by legislation, economics, cultural roles, social interactions, political systems and sexual taboos. They are also played out in the conventional teaching system. Female students are in a subordinate position and are discouraged from challenging professors and male colleagues. This is supported by a gender system that socially constructs a dichotomy of masculine and feminine roles, which we come to see as "natural." However, gender is not natural; it is not determined by biological sex but varies according to culture and shifts historically. Being aware of the social and historical nature of gender systems does not mean that the roles assigned to men and women can be escaped easily.

Women are struggling to break away from the gendered processes that silence them. In educational institutions, the success of such a struggle will depend on a new set of practices that includes and reflects the experiences of women and people of different races, classes and sexual orientations. It will also depend on challenging the traditional understanding of power in the classroom. It is assumed that power originates with the instructor and is directed towards a room of non-gendered, non-classed, non-raced "learners." The power relations in the classroom are hidden under the guise of liberal notions of democracy, truth, rationality, knowledge, science, individualism, objectivity and education. Contrary to popular belief, such notions do not create equality but are part of an ideology that perpetuates inequality. In fact, what is passed off as "neutrality" in classroom practices and "objectivity" in curriculum privileges the experiences and validates the intellectual concerns of white, middle-class, heterosexual men.

The problematization of these notions, which are deeply embedded in our society, would provide a radical critique of course material, teaching style, student interaction and the purpose of education. We challenge students to begin the process of naming their experiences in order to release the anger and despair that can be so debilitating when turned inwards against the self. We challenge the faculty to address the unquestioned assumptions that classrooms, curriculum and teaching practices are neutral. We challenge administration to respond to our concerns. We let our experiences speak for themselves in the following excerpts from the seventeen essays that were submitted on gender in the classroom.

Just Try Speaking Out

When four female students gave a presentation on the topic of the police and domestic violence, a male student challenged one of the speakers. He accused her of being a man-hater and of trying to crucify all police officers. She defended herself by saying that she was only trying to point out that often the police don't arrest batterers when they should. The debate turned into an argument. At one point the male student said, "I'm impressed by your enthusiasm but arguments are based on facts." Finally, the male professor intervened with the "facts," which clearly supported the female speaker's argument. His intervention implied that his input was necessary to validate her argument. The male student was not reprimanded for trying to humiliate and discredit the speaker by portraying her as an emotional, irrational woman.

In one of my classes, in which I was the only woman, I became so disgusted with the intellectual subservience and lack of vigorous thinking on the part of the students that, feeling I had little to lose except grades and much to gain in terms of personal integrity, I began to pose questions in each class. What I did not expect were the violent reactions of the male students. The professor did not have to answer my questions because the male students would respond before I had finished a sentence. The attacks were aimed at me personally rather than at the points I was raising. This pattern of attack became so vicious that even the professor referred to having to "hold back the wolves" in order to get in a word to respond to my questions. Later, a fellow student approached me. He wondered if I realized that I was jeopardizing my grades; he told me that a professor does not want to hear "some woman shoot him down in front of a bunch of men." By the end of the year I felt like I had just barely survived an experience of male academic violence.

I have found that female students react negatively to feminist students out of fear of being labeled a feminist or a lesbian. These fears are substantiated by some men's reactions to feminists. Upon learning that a particular female student was a feminist, a male student attempted to invade her privacy with questions such as "Do you shave your legs?" and "Do you sleep with men?" This initial attempt at intimidation was followed by sexist comments for the rest of the year.

I remember the last time I ever spoke in a women's studies class. A response by a male student was so degrading that I told him to shut his mouth. I expected the teacher to support me because this had been going on all year. The teacher did intervene; however, her comment was directed at my behaviour. She said, "I will not tolerate that type of behaviour in my class." I was silenced for the rest of the year. The male student proved that in the end he was still the more powerful.

What Constitutes Knowledge?

One of my courses centred around problems with urban planners, architects and those people working to "build communities." Another student, who was also a sole-support mother with a small baby, and I had just spent a year negotiating the city streets, parks and public buildings. We brought up accessibility as an issue that had a particular impact on women and children. Instead of responding by including such observations as valid and useful, the male professor responded by stating that gender had nothing to do with accessibility.

In a screen-writing workshop in which eleven students were women and nine were men, the male professor asked us to submit a proposal for a documentary on an issue of our choice. I submitted a proposal on women's ambivalent feelings towards motherhood. The professor's initial response to this proposal was that, in his opinion, "Motherhood is not an issue. All the women I have known have enjoyed it." The professor also expressed concern about whether the issue of motherhood would speak to a wide enough audience, yet the professor approved a proposal by a male student to do a documentary on plumbing. This male student was not asked if his issue spoke to a wide enough audience. For women, the legitimacy of the content of our work is often the focus of criticism. For men, the focus of the criticism is often only on the form, not on the content of their work. This particular professor was in no way intentionally biased. As a matter of fact, he always attempted to be as open as possible, but his perspective – white and male – kept him blind to issues that did not have primacy for him. In the three hours it took to briefly summarize our proposals, lessons were learned by the entire class about what is worthy of documentation and what is not. Such lessons further drive women and their lived experiences to the margins.

Most of my economics professors have never addressed the issues of race and racism and how they have an impact on economic relations. As a result, most of the class material is not relevant to my experience. Recently these professors have begun to talk about women in the economic market and it is assumed that I am included. However, their discussion on women in the economic market does not specify race; instead, women are treated as a homogeneous group. As a black woman I know I do not have the same experience as a white middle-class woman, nor does a middle-class woman have the same experience as a working-class woman. It is a problem for me when professors group all women in the same category, for as women, we are not solely defined by our sex, but also by our race and class.

My experience in the classroom is one of alienation. I find it hard to become empowered and excited when middle-class, educated concerns take precedence over other concerns. I feel the constant weight on my back of the lives of my illiterate parents. The women in the class assume I will want to form alliances with them without realizing that their comments about "welfare bums" make me hate them.

In a law course, one assignment was to apply a theoretical perspective to a social problem. The topic I chose was the use of law in the oppression of lesbians and gays; I approached it from a structural, critical perspective. The professor said he gave the paper a poor grade because the structural critique was not considered a theoretical perspective, and the lesbian and gay content was "personal and biased" and not from "authoritative" sources.

I was present in a class on deviance in which the professor spoke of the major deviants — murderers, rapists and homosexuals — without so much as a breath taken to delineate the three categories.

In a course focusing on an analysis of racism and sexism taught by a woman of colour, a few white women in the class complained that we were spending too much time discussing racism and not enough discussing sexism. They failed to see (although it was repeatedly stressed) that we were examining sexism from the point of view of women of colour, for whom an analysis of racism is central.

Whose Experience is Significant?

I have found that male professors are often unenthusiastic about discussing the issue of women in the philosophical and political writings of the "great male writers" even when these writers devote a great deal of attention to the nature of women and their role in the state. It is often the professor's opinion that these writers' views on women are less interesting than other lines of inquiry.

It was when I dropped out of economics and took up anthropology that I began reading and *discussing* issues about, and of interest to, me. For the first time I realized that I had been shoved through my years in school without a concept of my own history. In my high-school curriculum women did not exist, blacks played a part only in slavery … oh, and of course, the equal rights movement. Outside these isolated incidents blacks and women had supposedly played *no part in history!* This lack of information about me might have been one of the reasons for my lack of interest in my earlier university career.

In an economics course, the material was very male-centred. I was constantly asking myself how economics related to me as a non-white woman. Needless to say, that question was never addressed. I was made to feel that I was intruding on a very white, male space.

Theoretical assignments are those in which students are expected to research, repeat or memorize the theories of someone else. I find this type of assignment alienating because most of the theories I am taught are written by men about men, and if written about women they deprecate them. As female students we are deprived of exposure to theories that speak to our experiences. The education we usually receive reinforces our absence because its content validates only men. For instance, as a psychology student, it was not until this year that I discovered that a pioneer of the therapeutic technique of behaviour modification was Mary Cover Jones – a woman – and not just the men I previously had been led to believe were the founders. What a revelation that was!

The male model that views knowledge as "objective" prevents women (and men) from truly learning because it rejects experience as a necessary tool to synthesize theory.

I feel that what I have learned is incomplete. My education would have been much richer had I been exposed to the theories, research and life's work of female experts rather than only those of male experts. It is a loss for me that after four years of university I can name, at most, five female experts in my chosen field of study. My ignorance has only served to reinforce the powerlessness that I normally feel in the community outside the classroom.

Who Speaks With Authority?

The presence of a woman professor in a male-dominated discipline alters the dynamics within the classroom. Very often the male students do not give female professors the respect and attention they deserve. In a second-year economics course taught by a woman of a racial minority, the male students challenged her authority by constantly interrupting her during the lecture, most of the time to ask trivial questions in order to disrupt the class. I have noticed that there is a sharp contrast in how differently a white male professor's authority is accepted by his students.

When a male student in my class answers a question, a dialogue ensues between him and the teaching assistant. When a female student answers a question, the teaching assistant addresses subsequent remarks to the entire class, ignoring the specific source of the answer. This behaviour has caused the women in my class to withdraw their participation.

In my first year at York University, I rarely participated in class discussions and I never challenged professors because I feared the consequences. When I listened to the opinions and views expressed by male students, I admired their assertiveness and their ability to organize their thoughts coherently. Further, because the male students were more involved in the classroom discussion than were the women, the discussion tended to revolve around the issues that they found interesting.

In one of my classes, two students who received "A" grades on their assignments were asked to read their papers to the rest of the class. When the male student had the floor, he received the undivided attention of the class. However, when the female student read her essay, there was a perceptible change in the classroom environment. The noise level rose considerably. She did not get our undivided attention. She received a clear message that very few students were interested in hearing why she had received an "A." To gain control of the class, she turned to the professor for support. None was given. As women in the classroom, we are often left talking to ourselves.

Of the courses I have taken at York, women have taught only two. It is not surprising, then, that women have been largely absent from the content of these courses, both as authors of required readings and as subjects of discussion.

As an economics major, my classrooms have always been composed predominately of white male students. Their authority within the classroom has an overwhelming presence; their air of confidence seems natural. Most of the professors who teach in this discipline are also white men. Thus, it is not surprising that the female students (including me) are rendered silent in these classroom settings.

Who is Silenced?

As a female student, I have suffered from teaching practices and student interactions that have been discriminatory. The primary effect of these practices has been to silence me.

Women in my class remained silent for most of the tutorial sessions, afraid of sounding stupid. We have been conditioned to fear our own voices.

I previously viewed my silence as a flaw in my character, as my own inability to speak. It has been a liberating experience for me to realize that my lack of classroom participation is due to years of socialization and not to my own inadequacies. I have never really understood my academic self. I have always felt intellectually uncomfortable in discussion periods but reasonably confident when faced with tests and assignments. This process of examining my silence has validated my feelings of discomfort.

Teaching practices and student interactions silence women in the classroom. The failure of teachers and students to recognize and put an end to this further legitimizes the silencing of women. Through these practices I have been demoralized, degraded and intimidated.

A tutorial assistant, with whom I had taken a course two years earlier, asked what I had been doing lately. I replied that I was still working at the same job and still doing undergraduate work at York. Apparently shocked, she said, "Still?" and quickly ended the conversation, uninterested in anything else I was doing. I was dumbfounded that this woman, who had given her students the most rigorous and stimulating tutorials, a woman I had practically worshiped, had just clubbed me emotionally. I realized that she did not respect my struggles as a working-class woman putting herself through university. Each year I have been forced to spend a good part of my energy at waged work and the rest of my energy on three or four courses. It will undoubtedly take six years to receive a four-year degree, but there are few other choices open to me.

Classroom Interactions

Interactions in the classroom between professors and students and among students often reinforce sexist, racist, classist and heterosexist beliefs because differences among all the participants in the classroom are not questioned or recognized as pertinent to classroom interaction.

In one of my lectures a black male student from Jamaica spoke with a tone, dialect and body language that differed dramatically from that of the Canadian white male professor. When the student asked a question, he was ridiculed because of language. The professor responded to this student by mimicking his mannerisms and speech. "Well Richard my man," he began, and then did not respond to the question. In later classes, he singled out this student as a source of comic relief. As students we felt powerless to challenge him, for if a student of colour challenged the professor, the professor would assume that the student's colour was operating as a bias, and if a white student challenged the professor, the professor might view this as a tactic to undermine his position in front of this large class.

The insistence that the classroom is a neutral place hides dynamics that play themselves out in both subtle and unsubtle ways. It does not appear unnatural that male students speak more often and with more authority or that professors give more positive feedback to comments made by men. These dynamics are seen as natural because they reflect what happens outside the classroom.

One of my male professors frequently interrupts female students making presentations. He will even take over and give entire sections of the presentation for them.

My experience in one of my classes this year has proven to be so frustrating that I dread attending. The professor seems to want to facilitate class participation and discussion. He encourages questions throughout his lecture since the class is small, about twenty-five students. However, whenever I raise my hand to speak, he acknowledges me, and then looks at his watch. This automatically undermines what I have to say. When this first occurred, I thought that he was running out of time and was anxious to continue the lecture. But when it occurred a second time, I became agitated. I felt as though I had to make my point quickly. I began to notice that I was not the only victim of this type of reaction; other women in the class were treated in a similar manner. However, the men in the class were given ample time to speak and develop their points.

Teaching Practices

The teaching practices that I have encountered have limited the classroom in four ways: they have controlled the curriculum itself; they have limited the way in which this material is interpreted by controlling the content of classroom discussion and written submissions; they have controlled who has permission to speak about this material in the classroom; and finally, they have controlled who gets to be there at all.

My gender role at home is reinforced in the classroom. I have learned to be obedient to my professors as I am to my father. Further, I have not learned to question because my assignments have not allowed for any critical examination of the material.

Responding to Challenges about Sexism and Feminism

To make men aware of gender bias is to challenge implicitly their self-perception. Men tend to think that this implies merely a change in attitudes. However, it also challenges their privilege and the real power that they have over women. Many men not only resist changing attitudes but they also resist changing roles and giving up their privilege.

In one of my classes a professor made a remark about how the development of regulations regarding sexual harassment has created a situation in which unintentional gestures might now be misinterpreted. Further, he said something to the effect that he had better watch what he said "with all the feminists out there." This reinforced his sexism. He trivialized the need for a sexual harassment policy and although he perceived that there were many feminists "out there," he marginalized them as an alternative group whose opinions did not extend beyond their own circle.

A male student challenged me about taking a women's studies course. He asked why there were no men's studies courses, to which I replied, "All the courses are men's studies." There appears to be a resentment of women who take charge of their own destiny as well as their own education.

I often feel that I am discriminated against because of my choice to pursue women's studies. Derogatory remarks are made about the topic and my participation in it. I have become a tangible target for the free-floating hostility that perpetuates sexism and racism.

Learning Goes Back a Long Way

I recall that in grade eight, it was compulsory for girls to study home economics, while boys took industrial arts. I was interested in taking industrial arts, not in cooking and sewing, but when I approached my teacher about it, I was ignored. That year, the boys were allowed to come into our home economics class to taste the food we had prepared, but the girls were prohibited from entering the industrial arts class because of the potential danger of the machinery.

Throughout high school, I was always expected to take courses that would make me a better wife. Unlike the boys, I was never expected to take courses that would help me in my working life. I took courses such as home economics or art, while the boys took industrial arts or auto mechanics. Even in my physical education courses, the girls were folk dancing while the boys were training to become more physically fit. I did cross the barrier and take an electronics course, in which I was the only girl. The teacher was amused and did not treat me the same as he treated the boys.

I have found that men, more often than women, are able to justify longer hours of solitude for study. A woman's time is not her own. I have seen myself and other female students juggle our many responsibilities, constantly distracted by the demands made on our time. We're the ones who must pick up the kids from daycare or stay up nights with a sick child. Most of the household chores are our responsibility. We have to attend to these things before we can claim some time for ourselves.

Fighting Back

Three of the five women in one of my classes support one another in the pursuit of what has come to be called the "woman question." When one of the women makes a point, another backs her up and develops the line of thinking further or repeats it if it has been met with silence. The one male student who was monopolizing the conversation previously has now become very cautious about what he says. This is my first experience of a male student being limited in a traditional classroom environment.

Assignments that ask female students to theorize their experiences are empowering because they validate women as they are, not as they are seen by men or in relation to men.

Like society, the classroom environment is always gendered, raced and classed. The classroom not only reflects social structures, but actively seeks to socialize people into participating in them in a certain way. In this way, systems of oppression and privilege exist within the classroom and affect each person's learning, teaching, social interactions and self-concept.

We must continue our dialogue around difference and develop a critical conscious-ness that will problematize gender, race, class and sexual orientation into visibility.

Notes

1. This article includes excerpts from the essays of Howie Chodos, Lynn Daly, Markita Fleming, Gail, Michele Glemaud, Nadia Habib, Tina Horley, F.I., Sabynthe Jones-Caldwell, Catherine Kellogg, Penney Kirby, Marla, Carolyn Morris-Walker, Kathie Moules, A.R., Lori Waserman and Samantha Wehbi. The authors thank Professor Linda Briskin for her ongoing support. Reprinted with permission from the Lexicon, Wimmin's Supplement, Mar. 6, 1991, 7-10.

References

Lorde, Audre. 1984. *Sister outsider.* Freedom, CA: Crossing Press.

Fog and Frustration: The Graduate Student Experience

Jackie Buxton,
with the Teaching Assistants' Resource Group

At York University we have a Teaching Assistants' Resource Group, which works closely with graduate students from the wide range of disciplines and departments within the university. Operating in contradistinction to the assumption that teaching is learned through osmosis, the group provides a mechanism for confidential peer consultation and discussion of pedagogical issues. As well as attending to teaching strategies and techniques, the group offers assistance in understanding individual student differences and promotes sensitivity to human rights and equity issues. While the group provides a forum to foster teaching assistant development, it also offers a forum for the discussion of student learning at all levels, graduate and undergraduate. Reflecting on one's role as an educator necessarily involves reflection on one's experience as a student and our discussions and informal surveys of graduate students suggest that, by and large, students are more dissatisfied than satisfied with their experience in graduate school.

Given the diversity of both students and graduate programs at York, there is a multitude of specific differences, but our research indicates that there are a number of common issues and problems arising from the graduate experience that might be relevant to students in other graduate programs. These problems can be grouped under five main headings: the relationship between graduate and undergraduate work, the operation of the graduate classroom, issues of academic research and owner-ship, professional development and, most importantly, the meaning of a graduate education.

The first serious problem reported by graduate students concerns the perceived split between graduate and undergraduate work. Faculty members appear to believe that incoming graduate students somehow received an academic revelation in the summer between the completion of their bachelor's degree and the beginning of their master's studies, during which they read and comprehended the breadth and history of their discipline. Presumably, these same faculty would not assume this knowledge of their graduating students; yet somehow this knowledge is assumed to have been acquired in that four-month interval. But ever-increasing pressure for decreased degree completion times does not allow graduate students the extended opportunity to acquire this knowledge. Students admit their complicity in this state of affairs because they do not voice their ignorance in the classroom. This, however, is largely because they do not feel safe to do so. Issues of safety and risk in the graduate classroom are elementary pedagogical problems and must be addressed by faculty members.

This leads to the second area of shared concern: the graduate classroom itself. There is an assumption that graduate teaching differs from undergraduate teaching, but there seems to be little self-consciousness or theorization as to why this should be the case: undergraduate classes require thought and effort, graduate classes simply are. Faculty members continue to believe – in the face of all experiential evidence to the contrary – that a large table, some chairs and a few bodies will somehow produce a dazzlingly successful graduate seminar. The ways that graduate seminars are conducted range from the course director as tyrannical expert to the course director who views the seminar as a collegial cooperative experience. Obviously, the ways in which students learn are very diverse and not all teaching methods suit all students. Nevertheless, three salient points emerged from graduate students' comments.

First, graduate students do not learn from other students reading conference-format papers to the seminar group. Although this is a profitable experience for the paper-giver, it is far less beneficial to the other members of the class.

Second, students learn from reading groups, reading courses, discussions with supervisors and course directors, and from preparing conference presentations. They do not learn from class discussions unless the course director has a clear vision of the course, presents a particular stance or argument, and allows students to engage the instructor in that argument. Generally, many graduate faculty fail at this task because they are not skilled at facilitating discussion.

Third, students report that the single most productive ingredient in their learning is a faculty member who has the time and goodwill required for an intellectual exchange in the context of an interpersonal relationship. This, of course, is the ideal. Demands on faculty time and lack of credit for reading courses and supervision all point to a decrease in such involvement. That graduate students seek such collegial exchanges, however, suggests that something is not happening in the graduate classroom that should be happening.

The nature of the highly individualized and personalized student-supervisor relationship raises other problems that graduate students face. While this can be one of the most productive learning experiences, the relationship can give rise to some of the worst instances of professional misconduct in relation to human rights issues. The power imbalance in this relationship prevents many students from voicing their concerns, specifically with regard to racist and sexist attitudes and behaviour from those with whom they work closely. Fear, again, breeds silence.

Another ethical problem concerns the interrelationship of academic research and intellectual property. Students report cases of graduate classes that have been used by faculty members to conduct preliminary research. Other students have noted cases in which faculty members have seized research problems and first attempts and then developed and subsequently published them.

Perhaps the greatest concern voiced by graduate students centres on the issue of professional development. However optimistic it might seem given today's job climate, graduate students believe that they are preparing for careers, academic or otherwise. In some disciplines students collaborate fully with graduate faculty, developing funding proposals and writing scholarly papers based on research results. In addition, they are groomed for post-doctoral positions and academic jobs and introduced to faculty members at other research institutions and universities who share their interests. This situation, however, represents the exception rather than the rule. Most students must rely on more advanced graduate students for assistance in professional development. As a result, they feel that there is little or no adequate institutional preparation for subsequent job searches and research funding. Instead, the situation seems to be that of an institution intent on pushing graduate students ever more quickly through graduate school and propelling them ill-prepared into the job market.

This leads, then, to the final and most important issue: the question of the purpose of graduate course work. Should course work be relevant to the research endeavour of the student? Is it meant to prepare the student with a canon of necessary background material? Is it meant to train the student in modes and methodologies for learning, researching and analyzing? Is it to train students in areas in which they can later teach? Students infer these and other objectives from course work and comprehensive examination requirements, yet many faculty seem not to have reflected on these goals when they designed and executed these courses. As a result, students find that many of their graduate courses have little or no utility and flee to specialized reading courses when given the opportunity.

What, then, is graduate course work meant to achieve? The question is really a more specific instance of a much larger question: what does a graduate education mean? Clearly there is no one answer, but this should not prevent the posing of the question and the exploration of its implications. We suggest that faculty members teaching graduate students need to reflect not only on what we are doing, but also on why we are doing it.

This article was first published in March 1995 in Core 5 (2): 1–2.

"Dissertation Dementia": Reflections on One Woman's Graduate Experience

Anonymous

For long periods during the writing of my dissertation, I consoled myself with the comfort that – even if I was making no headway on my thesis – I had produced a definition of *dissertation dementia*. I imagined that dissertation dementia is that peculiar affliction located at the precise centre of three different sets of contradictions. The malady is created in the mad space between delusions of grandeur and the imposter syndrome, between fear of success and fear of failure, and between fears of abandonment and persecution mania. If this definition of dissertation dementia is humorous, the experience of it is anything but for the person enduring it. Moreover, from a more sociological perspective, the phenomenon reveals a great deal about the systematic organization of graduate teaching and graduate learning.

Graduate school is a gate-keeping institution: on one side, students enter as mere students; on the other, we emerge as fully accredited professionals. The organization of the graduate student experience relates as much to this gate-keeping function as to the intellectual requirements of the discipline at hand. It seems to me that the graduate student experience is systematically organized to produce anxiety, insecurity and a particularly unproductive form of competition and hierarchy.

Let's start with funding. Under conditions of scarce resources, money is key. I can recall a time when I was a member of my department's Curriculum Committee, which regularly met over the dinner hour. The casual assumption made by faculty members was that ordering in would be the most convenient way to feed ourselves. The food bill broke down at something like ten dollars per person, but that tiny sum represented a considerable percentage of my discretionary income on a teaching assistant's salary. I struggled to balance the expense against the benefits of professional development and networking. In practical terms, I could scarcely afford to be on the committee.

But money does not represent only money. The next year I held a Social Sciences and Humanities Research Council (SSHRC) fellowship, which – in addition to nearly doubling my income – provided an important psychological soother: I was part of that small group of "students who were funded." I discovered that students who were funded were a special groups of students: post SSHRC fellowship, mysterious faculty members nodded to me in the halls and I seemed to get more help from the bureaucracy. While assuaging a fear of failure, the approbation began to generate a certain fear of success: funding set me apart from my unfunded friends, who rightfully resented that they were not similarly recognized. This sets up a kind of horizontal hostility among a graduate student cohort, one to which I suspect female graduate students are particularly vulnerable.

Think about access to professional venues: publishing and conferences. A professor once recommended that I submit a course paper I had written to a refereed journal on whose editorial board he sat. The paper, in time, was accepted and published. I was tremendously appreciative of the assistance, yet was also vaguely troubled about the fairness of the mythical anonymous "peer review" that had led to my paper's acceptance.

Consider also access to teaching positions. In the spring of my first year in the PhD program, a senior graduate student whom I knew slightly called me and told me that he was turning down a teaching appointment at a nearby university. Would I be in interested in replacing him? I spluttered "Yes." He made a series of telephone calls and within thirty minutes I was on the phone to the department's acting head. Her quick call to my supervisor gleaned a positive recommendation and I was hired. This was a clear case of personal contact winning me access to a job that my supervisor's support clinched. Other graduate friends were again rightfully resentful that informal channels distributed perks through friendship and contacts, not through merit or competition – more horizontal hostility.

By the time I began producing my dissertation, I was part of an extremely privileged minority of students: I had published, I had presented several papers at conferences, I had held a couple of teaching appointments as a course director and I was "known" since I was one of those "students who was funded." I had assembled what promised to be a highly supportive committee, I had a clear dissertation proposal and a great topic to work on.

Despite this excellent beginning, the actual writing process was the hardest thing I have ever done. Someone once told me that writing is dead easy: you simply stare at a piece of paper (or a computer screen) until beads of blood form on your forehead, then you write. But even leaving aside the actual effort of writing, I found that the social relations that surround the writing process were almost unbearable. Students write in isolation: holed up in lonely rooms, struggling to produce a text that works at several levels: it must demonstrate professional competence, it must be "gateable," it ought to demonstrate intellectual brilliance, it must be "good," it must satisfy three (then more) committee members, it must be "acceptable," it must...

My strategy for coping with the isolation was to send regular notes to my committee members, reminding them that I was alive, reassuring them (and me) of my schedule and forwarding whatever other bits of news I felt relevant, in addition to circulating chapters as they were born. I later discovered that these packages were received as a barrage, overwhelming to my overworked committee members. Of course, I had picked supportive, young, progressive faculty who were being overused by other graduate students. They did not have the time to respond to my needs during the writing process. While they acknowledged receipt of my packages along the way, occasionally phoned me or wrote notes on the drafts and pointed out areas of concern, they basically encouraged me to keep going.

During the writing process, I was awarded a post-doctoral fellowship. By late August, I had "kept going" and had produced a complete draft. I was down to the wire in terms of taking up the post doc and so wrote yet another letter to the committee about what I needed from them. In the first committee meeting in over eight months, they presented a united front as they told me that my dissertation was not ready to defend and that I would not be able to take up the post doc. I was totally unprepared for this development since I felt that none of them had warned me that their concerns about the draft were as serious as they now seemed to be. In September, my frantic efforts to persuade the committee that the work was actually close to completion failed and I had to write to SSHRC to turn down the $54,000.

I nearly quit the program. In retrospect, I overreacted: it had been unreasonable of me to think that my first draft could be my last draft. But I felt like road kill on the academic highway. Despite all the approval I had garnered – funding, publication, teaching – I felt like a failure. My committee was unhappy with me (for being demanding of them) and unhappy with my work – a synergistic combination not easily resolved. I felt furious and frightened that I had not been warned that I might not finish in time. I felt shame that I had failed. I feared that all the little things that had smoothed my way so far had just been abruptly pulled out from under me.

The working relationship between me and my committee soured through this process. I took several months off to repair my ego and adjust to the loss of the post-doc fellowship. I had virtually no communication with my supervisor or other members of my committee, which meant that I was very frightened of them when I started working again. E.P. Thompson once wrote that one of the last remaining feudal relationships in the modern world is that between the graduate student and supervisor, and when my relationship with my supervisor took a painful turn, I viscerally felt the truth of this observation.

The complicated relationship between me and my supervisor was hard on many levels: I needed her intellectually, professionally and personally. Yet – through my not finishing – she withdrew her intellectual support since I had not demonstrated the competence I seemed to promise. Her professional support also lessened as I no longer seemed as bright or as collegial. Finally, she was unable and unwilling to offer the kind of personal support for which I hungered. In many ways, her response was reasonable. My needs were not really her problem, but were produced through larger administrative relations of ruling and institutional organization.

This is part of how dissertation dementia is organized. The very acts of graduate student confidence and hubris that had earlier been taken as clues that I was "hot" now appeared no more than delusions of grandeur. Where I had earlier seemed to promise success, I now seemed perilously close to failure. And I could not decide if I was getting any, not enough, or too much support from my committee: hence, my simultaneous fear of persecution and fear of abandonment.

In all of this mess, female students face particular challenges. Our work is often political and feminist, which makes us vulnerable when assessed against disciplinary conventions. This results in feminists flocking to the few faculty who support feminist research, overburdening already overworked faculty members. Women are often less skilled than men at negotiating the complicated issues of mentorship and competition. And, it is no surprise that in the uneven contest of egos and pocketbooks, women take longer to complete programs and drop out more frequently.

I have recounted dissertation dementia through my personal story, but I do not think that my experience is particularly unique – except to the degree that mine is probably among the least painful stories graduate students can tell. I think that the social relations of graduate school are systematically organized in ways that promote competition, hierarchy and alienation. While individual students and individual faculty members can and do strategize and negotiate the structural constraints that set the parameters to their work, the stark reality of the institution is that the gates are mainly to keep people out.

The author is now safely employed in a tenure-track job at a Canadian university.

Power in the Classroom[1]

Linda Briskin

"I have a problem with the notion that there is huge power imbalance in the classroom," he [Michael Bliss, a University of Toronto history professor] said. "It's not the reality. Professors are not doing their duty if they give bad grades (to an outspoken student) and students are not contributing if they don't speak up, if they hide behind what they think is a power situation." Mr. Robinson, on the same panel, disagreed. "That's a surreal view of the classroom," he said. "The reality is that there is a significant power imbalance. The professor has tremendous power." But others argued that, if there is any power imbalance in this age of political correctness, then it's on the side of the student. "When a student gets mad at a professor," continued Dr. Bliss, "it's amazing what they can do."

This interchange, reported in *University Affairs* in 1994, suggests a growing awareness of the relevance of a discourse on power to an understanding of the university classroom; at the same time, the comments reflect a limited understanding of the complexity and significance of the power relations operating in that classroom.

The following discussion takes up that complexity, examining the multiple practices that organize classroom power. The analysis challenges conventional approaches to classroom power in a number of ways. It recognizes both teacher and student power, distinguishing between power and formal authority; it rejects the binary paradigm of authoritarian classrooms dominated by teacher power and democratic classrooms based on sharing power; it disputes the possibility of classrooms as safe havens away from racism, sexism and homophobia and the view that sensitive teaching can make the problem of power evaporate; and it assumes that classroom power dynamics shape what is learned and thus cannot be avoided.

Understanding Power in the Classroom

When four female students gave a presentation on the topic of the police and domestic violence, a male student challenged one of the speakers. He accused her of being a man-hater and of trying to crucify all police officers. She defended herself by saying that she was only trying to point out that often the police don't arrest batterers when they should. The debate turned into an argument. At one point the male student said, "I'm impressed by your enthusiasm but arguments are based on facts." Finally, the male professor intervened with the "facts," facts which clearly supported the female speaker's argument. His intervention implied that his input was necessary to solidify her argument. The male student was not reprimanded for trying to humiliate and discredit the speaker by portraying her as an emotional, irrational woman.[2]

Dynamics of power shape, constrain, interrupt and facilitate both learning and teaching. They shape students' sense of entitlement to learning and to voice; they have an impact on teacher credibility and authority. Power is mediated, organized and expressed by and through "difference" – gender, race, class, able-bodiedness, sexual orientation, ethnicity, age – which affects the way students learn, the way teachers teach and interact with students, and the way students interact with each other and with teachers. As currently constituted, these power dynamics often produce exclusion, marginalization, disempowerment and silencing. They are always operating in the classroom environment and they not only impede learning, they are the site of some of the most important and deeply remembered learning. However, they have become so much a part of the common-sense practices of schooling, naturalized and thus seemingly not subject to intervention, that we don't even notice them (Ng 1991).

These power dynamics are part of a systemic and structural reality; they are not attitudinal, accidental or based on ignorance. To say that sexism, racism, homophobia, ableism or ageism are systemic is to say that they are embedded in the practices of institutions: policies, pedagogies, structures of knowledge and patterns of classroom interaction. As a result, teaching tolerance of "difference" is not enough. The implication of teaching tolerance is that difference will be overlooked, but such disregard makes discrimination based on and organized around difference invisible, and further, it makes the fact that difference itself, for example the meaning of gender, is constituted by and through power invisible as well.

Furthermore, the multiple dimensions of power in the classroom that operate on complex and interwoven lines of sexual orientation, age, ability, ethnicity and class, as well as race and gender, make the language of sexism and racism obfuscating.[3] It compartmentalizes oppressions, discursively suggesting that the experiences of sexism and racism are discrete, thus making it more difficult to see the ways in which these forms of oppression work with and against one another in producing both privilege and exclusion.

I prefer to focus, at least as a starting point, on the question of power itself. In her discussion of black women's experience, Patricia Collins (1990) argues for a move

from additive, separate systems approaches to oppression and toward...the more fundamental issue of social relations of domination. Race, class, and gender constitute axes of oppression that characterize Black women's experience within a more generalized matrix of domination. Other groups may encounter different dimensions of the matrix, such as sexual orientation, religion, and age, but the overarching relationship is one of domination (226).

She goes on to point out that "all groups possess varying amounts of penalty and privilege in one historically created system. In this system, for example, white women are penalized by their gender but privileged by their race" (225). I would go further than Collins; in her formulation, race and gender still remain somewhat distinct from one another. I suggest that we have to move towards an understanding of the ways in which gender is always raced, and race always gendered, class always gendered, etc.

To say that class is gendered means that, for example, men and women of the working class do not experience "class" in the same way. Women do not tend to do the same waged work as men, they tend to have a different relationship to unions, women are generally responsible for household labour in addition to waged work, women face violence in both the workplace and the family – all of these factors mean that working-class women experience their class position differently than do working class men. Simultaneously, gender is classed because women of different classes experience their gender in particular ways. For example, a woman who has the resources to hire someone to care for her children would experience the difficulties of household work differently than would a working-class woman who is herself responsible for child care. Not only does the recognition of the complex interrelation of "oppressions" challenge any hierarchy of oppression (Briskin 1990–94), it also makes clear that there is no abstract, ahistorical meaning to gender, class or race.

At the same time, focusing on power must not make invisible the historically specific ways in which gender, race, class or other oppressions operate. For example, Collins (1990) makes the point that

gender oppression seems better able to annex the basic power of the erotic and intrude in personal relationships via family dynamics and within individual consciousness. This may be because racial oppression has fostered historically concrete communities...[which] have stimulated cultures of resistance (226).

Concomitant with understanding the construction of gender, race, class, etc. as intertwining realities, recognizing that the subjective experience of "identities" is not static but relational and contextual, is critical to classroom practice.[4] Subjectivity is historically situated since the meanings of gender, race or class are always a site of struggle and are not based on conceptual abstractions. Subjectivity is relational because it is shaped and made meaningful in relation to other people. We don't each have an identity, or even multiple identities that we bring into the classroom; rather, we are constantly negotiating our subjectivities and producing ourselves in the classroom. Subjectivity is experienced, not owned. It is contextual since what is significant about each of us shifts depending on the situation and who is present and absent. The classroom, then, is constitutive of subjectivity, not just a site for its expression.

> By the end of semester, many of us began to understand ourselves as inhabiting intersections of multiple, contradictory, overlapping social positions not reducible either to race, or class, or gender, and so on. Depending upon the moment and the context, the degree to which any of us "differs" from the mythical norm varies along multiple axes (Ellsworth 1992, 16–17).

From such a perspective, student and teacher resistance to rigid labels, to being designated "the lesbian," "the woman of colour" or "the feminist" and being encouraged (or forced) to speak from such confining positions can be better understood.[5] Mimi Orner (1992) concludes that:

> Instead of framing the slipperiness of identity as a problem to be solved or an obstacle to be avoided, feminist poststructuralists regard the inability to fix our identities and to be known through them in any definitive way as a powerful means to "denaturalize" ourselves and embrace change (74).

Teacher Power, Student Power

Discussions of classroom power tend to focus on teachers who discriminate against students based on their race, class, sexual orientation, ability, age, ethnicity or gender. Research on gender and sexual harassment, on racial harassment and increasingly on heterosexism and homophobia has revealed the practices of teacher power. *How Schools Shortchange Girls*, the report of the American Association of University Women and the Wellesley College Centre for Research on Women (1992), is worth quoting at some length on the issue of racial dynamics in the classroom.

> Black boys tend to be perceived less favourably by their teachers and seem less able than other students…Black girls have less interaction with teachers than white girls, but they attempt to initiate interaction much more often than white girls or than boys of either race. Research indicates teachers may unconsciously rebuff these black girls who eventually turn to peers for interaction, often becoming the class enforcer or go-between for other students. Black females also receive less reinforcement from teachers than do other students, although their academic performance is often better than boys'.

> In fact, when black girls do as well as white boys in school, teachers attribute their success to hard work but assume that the white boys are not working up to their full potential. This, coupled with the evidence that blacks are more often reinforced for their social behaviour while whites are likely to be reinforced for their academic accomplishments, may contribute to low academic self-esteem among black girls. Researchers have found that black females value their academic achievements less than black males in spite of their better performance (70–71).

Table 1*: Gender Discrimination in the Classroom

DISCRIMINATION IN TEACHER CONTACT/
COMMENT AT THE SECONDARY AND COLLEGE LEVELS

- ignoring female students even when they clearly volunteer to participate
- calling directly on male students but not on women
- calling male students more often by name
- coaching men but not women in working towards a fuller answer
- waiting longer for men to answer questions
- interrupting female students
- asking female students questions that require factual answers while asking men questions that demand critical thinking
- responding more extensively to men's comments
- crediting men's comments but not giving authorship to women's comments
- making seemingly helpful comments that imply that women are not as competent as men

---

NON-VERBAL CUES

- making eye contact more often with men than with women
- nodding and gesturing more often in response to men's questions and comments
- assuming a tone of interest with men but an impatient or patronizing tone with women
- assuming a posture of attentiveness with men but the opposite with women

---

GENDER HARASSMENT

- Comments that disparage
  - women in general, reinforcing stereotyped views of women's traits
  - women's intellectual ability
  - women's academic commitment
- Comments that divert discussion of a female student's work to a discussion of her physical attributes or appearance
- Comments that refer to males as "men" but to females as "girls" or "gals"
  - using the generic "he" to refer to both women and men
- Comments that rely on sexist humour as a classroom device
- Comments that disparage scholarship about women
- Comments that address the class as if no women were present, such as "Suppose your wife..."

Drawn from Hall with Sandler (1982).

The literature on teacher power often makes the incorrect assumption that teachers are white males and that only teachers have power in the classroom. Here a more multilayered analysis is needed. By focusing only on teachers, power and formal authority are conflated and the complexities and complications of the operation of power in the classroom are made less visible. Power is a dynamic relationship; it is conditional, not absolute; it is situational, negotiated continually in interactional and local settings. Power cannot be given away or shared, so to speak, nor is there a fixed or static sum of power in any given context.

> "Power" is not seen simply as a fixed property of social structures and social institutions…Rather, it is treated as a dynamic relation which is negotiated continuously in interactional settings…Authority, on the other hand, is formal power granted to individuals through institutional structures and relations…Teachers have authority over students as a consequence of their ascribed role in the educational system. But in an interactional setting, this authority can be challenged by those without formal power (Ng 1991, 100–1).

Distinguishing power from the authority that is granted to teachers by virtue of their positions in institutional structures problematizes the complex and contradictory relationship between power and authority, revealing the ways in which authority is mediated by power and making visible the possibility that teachers and students both have power.[6] Two power axes, both of which involve student power, then, necessarily complicate an understanding of teacher authority and power (Briskin and Coulter 1992).

Students are always gendered, raced, classed, sexed and embodied subjects and thus bring differential privilege to the classroom, which is reinscribed in their interactions with each other.[7] Although such interactions, under the best of circumstances, can involve affirmation, just as frequently they involve competition, denial of the knowledge of the other and many techniques of silencing. One particularly disturbing effect of these power dynamics is the internalized self-devaluation and disavowal of their knowledge by many female students. This is expressed in the practice of prefacing their interventions with apologies or self-deprecating statements.

Power dynamics among students shape the learning of students, their participation, their risk taking and their sense of entitlement in the classroom.

> I always felt that I didn't belong in maths and science. Sometimes the boys would make jokes about girls doing science experiments. They always thought they were going to do it better and it made me really nervous. Sometimes I didn't even try to do an experiment because I knew they would laugh if I got it wrong. Now I just deaden myself against it, so I don't hear it any more. But I feel really alienated. My experience now is one of total silence. Sometimes I even wish I didn't know what I know (a Queen's University student quoted in Lewis 1992, 173).

Although student access to classroom power depends on race, class, gender, sexual orientation and ability, the meanings of these identities are continually being negotiated, are relational rather than static and will vary depending on the context. So, for example, the significance of gender to classroom-power dynamics is different in a mainstream course than in a women's studies course. Furthermore, Linda Eyre (1991) emphasizes that it is important to pay attention to "diversity of experience within sex groups"; so, for example, she notes in her study of coeducational home economics classes that "quiet boys, like girls, were humiliated and controlled by dominant boys" (213).[8]

Student exercise of power has an impact on the credibility and authority of teachers, affecting all women teachers and especially minority women and lesbians (Hoodfar 1992, Khayatt 1992, Ng 1991 and Ng 1993).

> Very often male students do not give female professors the respect and attention they deserve. In a second-year economics course taught by a female professor of a racial minority, the male students challenged her authority by constantly interrupting her during the lecture, most of the time to ask trivial questions in order to disrupt the class. I have noticed a sharp contrast in how differently the authority of a white male professor is accepted by his students.

Such biases also surface in student ratings of professors. For example, in a summary of research, Susan Basow (1994) points out that "most studies ignore the gender of the students in doing evaluations, the disciplines involved, and the fact that female professors are often judged on a double standard." When these factors are taken into account, evidence indicates that "female professors frequently receive lower ratings from their male students and higher ratings from their female students…[and] appear to be evaluated according to a heavier set of expectations than are male professors" (9). Basow reports on another study that shows that "in order to receive comparable ratings, female professors need to do more than their male counterparts" (10). This kind of data suggests that women and minority teachers function in a complex contradiction: they are both marginalized and privileged.[9]

Practices of Power

Complex common-sense practices, moments and sites of power inform the classroom in multiple ways: in patterns of authority and resistance, in struggles about expertise and experience, in controlling access to knowledge, in ways of assessing student knowledge, in the structure and organization of the classroom, in conversation patterns, in dynamics of validation and invalidation, in practices of self-disclosure, in body and voice language, in informal networks, and in personal comments (see Table 2).

Alliances and Bonding

Patterns of alliances and bonding are one concrete expression of these power dynamics. Bonding among male students (based on their power and to ensure its continuation) takes many forms; for example, male students are more likely to pay attention to and pick up on each others' comments, but overlook those made by women (Hall with Sandler 1982, 9). Female students seek alliances with male students in order to share in their power. This can take the form of attempting to distance

Table 2: Practices of Power in the Classroom

AUTHORITY • authority based on *experience*: whose experience is validated; what kinds of experiences are validated • authority based on *expertise*: whose expertise is validated; the privileging of experience over expertise or expertise over experience
RESISTANCE • resistance to the authority of experience or expertise: anti-feminism as a form of resistance • resistance to orthodoxies • resistance to power • resistance to identity politics
CONTROLLING ACCESS TO KNOWLEDGE • through the use of exclusive or inaccessible theoretical language • by discouraging questions
ASSESSING STUDENT KNOWLEDGE • types of assignments • grading practices
CONTROLLING STRUCTURE AND ORGANIZATION OF CLASSROOM • lectures • group work: obligatory; participation patterns • discussion structures: participation patterns
CONVERSATION PATTERNS • interruptions • who listens; who is listened to – by whom • who speaks; how they speak; how loud they speak • who speaks for whom • who asks questions; who asks questions to whom • who answers questions; whose questions are answered • who is silent; who is silenced • whose knowledge is validated
VALIDATION/INVALIDATION PATTERNS • patterns of bonding and alliances • patterns of censorship: moralism, political correctness, pigeonholing (insisting on "in character") • arriving late; leaving early • naming: knowing students' names; calling teacher by honorific (professor) or by name • self-invalidation: apologizing

SELF-DISCLOSURE
- who shares
- whose sharing is blocked or forced
- what kind of sharing is encouraged or discouraged
- the pressure to self-disclose
- confidentiality

"PERSONAL" COMMENTS
- harassment
- the "special" relationships (teacher's favourite, etc.)
- under- or over-attention
- commenting on physical appearance of teachers or students

BODY/VOICE LANGUAGE
- eye contact
- tone of voice
- attentiveness
- body language

PHYSICAL SPACE
- the claiming of physical space
- the physical organization of the room; size of the room
- who sits where and with whom

COMPOSITION OF THE CLASS
- based on gender, race, class, age, sexual orientation, ability, etc.
- teacher–student ratio

IN LARGE LECTURE HALLS
- attentiveness
- quiet

OUTSIDE THE CLASSROOM
- who socializes together at class breaks
- who shares information and cooperates and with whom
- who uses the teacher's office hours

themselves from other female students. Evelyn Fox Keller, famous for her work on women and science, wrote "I am even more ashamed to admit that out of my desire to be taken seriously as a physicist I was eager to avoid identification with other women students who I felt could not be taken seriously" (4).

Complex but understandable motivations underscore the practice of women seeking alliances with male students. Magda Lewis (1992) describes some of these dynamics in her discussion of "caretaking." In a debate about peace education in Lewis's university classroom that drew connections among patriarchy, violence and political economy, one of the female students said, "As you were speaking I was wondering and worrying about how the men in the room were feeling. What you said made sense to me, but I felt uncomfortable about how men took it" (174). Lewis comments:

> Such a protective posture on the part of women on behalf of men is a common drama played out in many classrooms...That such a dynamic should develop among the students was not a surprise. I know that, within the terms of patriarchy, women have had no choice but to care about the feelings of men. Women know that, historically, not caring has cost us our lives: intellectually, emotionally, socially, psychologically and physically...It became clear that as a collective social practice, for men, attentiveness to other than one's self is largely a matter of choice, whereas for women, it has been a socially and historically mandated condition of our acceptability as women (174–76).

Janice Newton, a political science professor at York University, describes a graphic situation that occurred during a film showing in a first-year political science course, which also suggests a potent pattern of accommodation on the part of female students:

> The film *No Way Not Me* explores the problem of female poverty in Canada from a liberal perspective: women make the wrong choices – they choose the wrong education; they don't plan for their careers; they have babies too soon, etc. The film does not in any way blame men for women's poverty.

> Within the first ten minutes of the film, I had to stop it several times to bring order to the class since the men sitting in the back rows were incredibly disruptive. When the film was over, I asked the class for their reactions to it. The men in the back rows spoke in quick succession about how they hated the film; how it attacked men; how poverty was really women's fault, and that women should stop blaming men. A number of male students talked about how women were to blame for getting pregnant because they dressed "sexy;" they were teases; they came on to men.

> After a number of men spoke (no women students volunteered to speak, and no men broke ranks to challenge these views), I intervened. I observed that only the men had spoken, and now it was time to hear from the women students. There was an uncomfortable silence; then the first woman spoke. She said she fully agreed

with the men, that if a woman had children it was her own fault and she should be forced to pay for them and raise them.

It was not just what she said, but how she said it that struck me. Her body language spoke volumes. She was sitting in the centre, just in front of the row of men. Before she spoke, she turned to look at them (seeking approval?), rather flirtatiously flipped her hair and adjusted herself in her seat. The overwhelming impression I had was that she was desperately seeking the approval of the men in the class.

I asked the class to cite evidence from the film where men were "blamed" for women's poverty – it drew blank stares and no one could come up with a concrete example. Finally, to my great relief, one brave woman disagreed. She challenged the idea that women were to "blame" for pregnancy and raised the point the film had made – about divorce and its impact on women's finances. Again, I was struck by her body language. She started out very tentative, and close to her seat, but when some of the male students from the back row challenged her, she turned and responded to them.

The male students said a number of very offensive things about women. They did not demonstrate any concern over whether they might offend their female audience (including the female professor), whereas the women who spoke all overtly demonstrated concern for keeping the approval of their male audience.[10]

Perhaps most disturbing is the complex bonding between students and teachers that reproduces discriminatory power dynamics. This takes the form not only of the expected bonding between male students and male teachers on the basis of their shared power, but also bonding between female teachers and male students, sometimes against female students.

I remember the last time I ever spoke in that women's studies class. A response, by a male student, was so degrading that I asked him to shut his mouth. I expected the teacher to support me because this had been going on all year. The teacher did intervene. However, her comment was directed at my behaviour. She said, "I will not tolerate that type of behaviour in my class." I was silenced for the rest of the year. The male student proved that in the end he was still the more powerful.

Although little background about what actually happened in the above example is available, it seems that the female teacher did not attempt to mediate the dispute and that the female student felt abandoned by her. Such actions by female teachers may reflect an implicit, if not explicit, recognition of the devaluation of women teachers and the difficulties they experience in exerting their expertise and authority. Bonding with male students might be a way to deepen their own classroom power. This suggests that female students have no "natural" ally in the classroom.[11]

Although beyond the scope of this discussion, it is worth noting that women's organizing inside classrooms could offer an alternative. Collective bonding by women can interrupt the practices of power:

Three of the five women in one of my classes support one another in the pursuit of what has come to be called "the woman question." When one of the women makes a point, another backs her up and develops this line of thinking further or repeats it if it has been met with silence. The one male student who was monopolizing the conversation previously has now become very cautious about what he says. This is my first experience of a male student being limited in a traditional classroom environment.

Conclusion: Problematizing Safety

The recognition of power dynamics challenges the common-sense notion of the classroom as a learning space, apart and safe from the outside.[12] Teachers have tended to have a distorted sense of what constitutes classroom safety and the limits of classroom safety, and of who feels safe in the classroom — perhaps projecting their own feelings of comfort.[13] Roxana Ng (1993) points out that "To speak of safety and comfort is to speak from a position of privilege, relative though that may be. For those who have existed too long on the margins, life has never been safe or comfortable" (210).[14] In discussing the lack of safety people of colour feel in antiracist workshops, Sarita Srivastava (1994) comments:

> The facilitator said only, "Safety is an on-going process, we all have to contribute to making everyone feel safe." These kinds of statements don't acknowledge that people of colour *cannot* be "safe" in such a context. They do not acknowledge that white people in this situation are generally safer, and that these different levels of danger are based on the power relations of racism. These statements also create an impression that the feelings of unsafeness are not systemic problems but rather individual problems that can be overcome (106).

Elizabeth Ellsworth (1992) speaks of classroom safety as a "repressive fiction [that has] the power to divert our attention and classroom practices away from what we needed to be doing…Acting as if our classroom were a safe space in which democratic dialogue was possible and happening did not make it so…We needed classroom practices that confronted the power dynamics inside and outside of our classroom that made democratic dialogue impossible" (107).

Once the "repressive fiction" of safety is dismantled and the limits of safety problematized, space is opened in which to develop techniques for creating safer, if not safe, classrooms. Amanda Konradi (1993) takes up the challenge of creating safer spaces in which to teach about sexual assault: "I believe that one creates safer spaces and/or builds trust by making parameters of participation explicit, removing or diminishing surprises, specifying power relations, working to level hierarchies, and distributing responsibility among everyone present" (17). Using concepts of power to deconstruct the everyday experience in the classroom reveals the classroom as a place of contradiction and difficult negotiation, where much is unsaid and power permeates all interactions. This deconstruction, however, leaves me quite optimistic. Creating a more politicized and less idealized basis for envisioning the alternative classroom allows for an understanding of both the limits and the possibilities.[15]

Notes

1. Unless otherwise indicated, all quotations in this article are taken from the article by Fleming *et al* in this section.

2. This article is part of a larger piece entitled "Negotiating Power and Silence in the Class: A Strategic Approach." I would like to acknowledge the way that this perspective has been clarified and deepened for me through interactions with the participants and audiences of workshops and lectures I have given at Dalhousie University, McMaster University, York University, and the Toronto Board of Education, at the Women's Fora of Goteborg, Linkoping and Uppsala universities, and at Kvinnofolkhogskolan in Sweden. The debt to the many engaged students I have had the opportunity to work with, especially in my fourth-year seminar on feminist thought, is acknowledged. I would also like to thank Rebecca Coulter, Harriet Friedmann, Nadia Habib, Didi Khayatt, Roxana Ng and Daphne Read for critical and instructive feedback on earlier drafts of this paper.

3. In an earlier discussion of classroom strategies, I counterposed non-sexism and non-racism with the more politically progressive "antisexism" and "antiracism" to emphasize the need for active interventionist strategies (Briskin 1990–94). However, I now find this language not complex enough to deal with the multiple and interwoven dimensions of power.

4. Bannerji (1991) calls for a focus on subjectivity rather than identity: "The social analysis we need, therefore, must begin from *subjectivity*, which asserts dynamic, contradictory and unresolved dimensions of experience and consequently does not reify itself into a fixed psychological category called *identity* which rigidifies an individual's relationship with her social environment and history" (98–99).

5. Denise Riley (1998) deconstructs the "crystallisations of 'women' as a category" to show that "women" is "historically, discursively, constructed, and always [relative] to other categories which themselves change…" (1–2). On this basis, she provocatively asks, "Can anyone fully inhabit a gender without a degree of horror? How could someone 'be a woman' through and through [and] make a final home in that classification without suffering claustrophobia?" (6). Further, "if indeed the label 'woman' is inadequate, that it is neither possible nor desirable to live solidly inside any sexed designation, then isn't that its own commentary on the unwillingness of many to call themselves feminists" (112).

6. This analysis is influenced by Foucauldian notions of power, in particular, Foucault's challenge to notions of monarchical power: "[P]ower must be understood…as the multiplicity of force relations immanent in the sphere in which they operate and which constitute their own organization; as the process which, through ceaseless struggles and confrontations, transforms, strengthens, or reverses them…Power's condition of possibility…must not be sought in the primary existence of a central point…; it is the moving substrate of force relations which, by virtue of their inequality, constantly engender states of power, but the latter are always local and unstable. The omnipresence of power: not because it has the privilege of consolidating everything under its invincible unity, but because it is produced from one moment to the next…Power is everywhere; not because it embraces everything, but because it comes from everywhere…[P]ower is not an

institution, and not a structure...it is the name that one attributes to a complex strategical situation in a particular society...Power is not something that is acquired, seized or shared...; power is exercised from innumerable points, in the interplay of nonegalitarian and mobile relations...[R]elations of power are not in superstructural positions, with merely a role of prohibition or accompaniment; they have a directly productive role...Power comes from below; that is, no binary and all-encompassing opposition between rulers and ruled" (Foucault 1978, 92–94). Although I find Foucault's formulations of power very relevant, I am concerned to embody this circulation of power; that is, to recognize, without reifying, the significance of structures of gender, race, class, able bodiedness, sexual orientation, etc.

7. So, for example, everyday inequities in talk patterns are carried into the classroom. Research shows that "men talk more than women, men talk for longer periods and take more turns at speaking, men exert more control over the topic of conversation, men interrupt women much more frequently than women interrupt men, men's interruptions of women more often introduce trivial or inappropriately personal comments that bring the woman's discussion to an end or change its focus" (Hall with Sandler 1992, 8). All these patterns are reinforced in the classroom.

8. Anne-Mette Kruse (1992) found a similar pattern in her study of coeducational and single-sex classroom settings.

9. An interesting parallel can be made to a discussion by Maria Mies (1983) of the contradictory position of women academics: "As women, they are affected by sexist oppression together with other women, and as scholars they share the privileges of the (male) academic elite" (120). She draws an intriguing conclusion: "The contradictory existential and ideological condition of women scholars must become the starting point for a new methodological approach." I might argue that the contradictory experience of women and minority teachers can be the starting point for re-visioning classroom practices of power.

10. I would like to thank Janice Newton for sharing this incident with me.

11. bell hooks (1998) points out the particular difficulties for black women who, because of the combined forces of sexism and racism, cannot count on the support of black men or white women: "The combined forces of racism and sexism often make the black female graduate experience differ in kind from that of the black male experience. While he may be subjected to racial biases, his maleness may serve to mediate the extent to which he will be attacked..." (60).

12. It might be that, even if achievable, the goal of classroom safety is problematic. Given the lack of safety in the world outside the classroom, it might be that providing safe havens will not equip students to deal with what they will confront. In their critique of the call for "connected education," which came out of the work of Belenky *et al.* in *Women's Ways of Knowing*, Victoria Steinitz and Sandra Kanter (1991), concerned about the needs of working-class and poor women, suggest that "Widespread adoption of connected education as an ideal model for women might well produce yet another generation of women who are ill equipped to advocate for themselves in the competitive, conflict-laden society where, unfortunately, we continue to live" (139).

13. Problematizing safety necessitates rethinking the thematic of safety in the discourses of feminist pedagogy. See Briskin and Coulter (1992) and Briskin (1990–94).

14. This resonates with the central insight of Elizabeth Stanko's (1985) work on violence, in which she argues that much of what society deems as "normal" behaviour on the part of men women experience as threatening.

15. For an exploration of a pragmatic application of this perspective, see "Negotiating power in the classroom: The example of group work" in Section V, Part 2.

References

American Association of University Women and the Wellesley College Centre for Research on Women. 1992. *How schools shortchange girls.*

Bannerji, Himani. 1991. But who speaks for us? In *Unsettling relations.* Toronto: Women's Press.

Basow, Susan. 1994. Student ratings of professors are not gender blind. *Women and CAUT News* 8: 9–11.

Briskin, Linda. 1990. Identity politics and the hierarchy of oppression: A comment. *Feminist Review* 35: 102–8.

———. 1990–94. *Feminist pedagogy: Teaching and learning liberation.* Ottawa: Canadian Research Institute for the Advancement of Women.

—— and Rebecca Coulter. 1992. Feminist pedagogy: Challenging the normative. *Canadian Journal of Education* 7 (3): 247–63.

Collins, Patricia Hill. 1990. *Black feminist thought.* Boston: Unwin Hyman.

Ellsworth, Elizabeth. 1992. Why doesn't this feel empowering? Working through the repressive myths of critical pedagogy. In *Feminisms and critical pedagogy,* Carmen Luke and Jennifer Gore (eds.), 90–119. New York: Routledge.

Eyre, Linda. 1991. Gender relations in the classroom: A fresh look at coeducation. In *Women and education,* 2nd ed., Jane Gaskell and Arlene McLaren (eds.), 193–219. Calgary: Detselig Enterprises.

Foucault, Michel. 1978. *The history of sexuality: An introduction.* New York: Vintage.

Hall, Roberta with Bernice Sandler. 1982. *The classroom climate: A chilly one for women?* Washington, dc: Association of American Colleges.

Hoodfar, Homa. 1992. Feminist anthropology and critical pedagogy: The anthropology of classrooms' excluded voices. *Canadian Journal of Education* 17 (3): 303–20.

hooks, bell. 1988. *Talking back: Thinking feminist, thinking black.* Toronto: Between the Lines.

Khayatt, Madiha Didi. 1992. *Lesbian teachers: An invisible presence.* Albany: State University of New York Press.

Konradi, Amanda. 1993. Teaching about sexual assault: Problematic silences and solutions. *Teaching Sociology* 21: 13–25.

Kruse, Anne-Mette. 1992. "...We have learnt not to just sit back, twiddle our thumbs and let them take over": Single sex settings and the development of a pedagogy for girls and a pedagogy for boys in Danish schools. *Gender and Education* 4 (1–2): 81–103.

Lewis, Magda. 1992. Interrupting patriarchy: Politics, resistance and transformation in the feminist classroom. In *Feminisms and critical pedagogy,* Carmen Luke and Jennifer Gore (eds.) 167–91. New York: Routledge.

Mies, Maria. 1983. Towards a methodology for feminist research. In *Theories of women's studies,* Gloria Bowles and Renate Klein (eds.), 117–39. London: Routledge and Kegan Paul.

Moses, Yolanda. 1989. *Black women in academe: Issues and strategies.* Washington, DC: Association of American Colleges.

Ng, Roxana. 1991. Teaching against the grain: Contradictions for minority teachers. In *Women and education,* 2nd ed., Jane Gaskell and Arlene McLaren (eds.), 99–115. Calgary: Detselig Enterprises.

———. 1993. "A woman out of control": Deconstructing sexism and racism in the university. *Canadian Journal of Education* 18 (3): 189–205.

Orner, Mimi. 1992. Interrupting the calls for student voice in "liberatory" education: A feminist poststructuralist perspective. In *Feminisms and critical pedagogy,* Carmen Luke and Jennifer Gore (eds.), 74–89. New York: Routledge.

Riley, Denise. 1988. *"Am I that name?": Feminism and the category of "women" in history.* University of Minnesota.

Srivastava, Sarita. 1994. Voyeurism and vulnerability: Critiquing the power relations of anti-racist workshops. *Canadian Woman Studies* 14: 105–9.

Stanko, Elizabeth. 1985. Ordinary experiences. In *Intimate intrusions: Women's experience of male violence,* 7–19. London: Routledge and Kegan Paul.

Steinitz, Victoria and Sandra Kanter. 1991. Becoming outspoken: Beyond connected education. *Women's Studies Quarterly* 1–2: 138–53.

University Affairs 1994: 7.

The University Classroom: From Laboratory to Liberatory Education

Teferi Adem

The Ontario Human Rights Code recognizes the "dignity and worth of every person" and provides for "equal rights and opportunities without discrimination." This legislation applies to all teachers, students and staff at any university in Ontario. Anyone who feels that they have been targeted or disadvantaged because of race or ethnic affiliation has the right to seek recourse under the law. York University's Centre for Race and Ethnic Relations interprets this legislation as the *sine qua non* and an essential pillar of the academic and scholarly freedom to discuss, explore, criticize and create our collective understandings of who we are.

Author bell hooks reminds us that it is difficult, if not impossible, to be disinterested in the pursuit and dissemination of knowledge. She warns against the "erasure of the body" that "encourages us to think that we are listening to neutral objective facts, facts that are not particular to who is sharing the information" (1994, 139). And she encourages teaching that relates to the life experience and history of our students.

I have found the writings of bell hooks particularly timely and valuable in my role as an advisor at the Centre for Race and Ethnic Relations. My ongoing task is to help ensure that no member of the university community is subjected to abuse, harassment, humiliation or degradation on the basis of race or ethnicity. That assignment might sound fairly straightforward, particularly since both the Government of Canada and the Province of Ontario have enacted clearly defined legislation to counter these violations of human rights. Moreover, the university for which I work is striving to promote diversity, an inclusive curriculum and a harassment-free classroom environment. And yet many university classrooms remain a "chilly" place for many students and teachers precisely because universities and teachers exaggerate their ability to provide education that is objective and neutral.

Academic institutions define themselves as laboratories for open and free enquiry. The classroom is imagined as a neutral and objective space rather than perceived for what it really is — in large part a reflection of the subjective cultural values and norms of the society in which it is located. Unfortunately, this illusion allows many teachers and students to collude in continual reification of a status quo that is as oppressive as it is exclusive.

Another factor contributing to dysfunctionality in university classrooms is the extremely limiting nature of the concept of "academic freedom" as it is presently understood. Certainly, if a learning environment is to be free from harassment and discrimination, some limits must be placed on freedom of expression. But this is not enough. If academic freedom is to represent any kind of human ideal, freedom of expression needs also to be grounded in a positive value system. Its *raison d'être* must be the liberation of all the personalities who participate in the educational enterprise.

These insights need to be applied to the difficult problem of challenging racism, ethnic stereotyping and the subtler forms of discrimination in our university class-rooms. University policies and disciplinary procedures are clearly important compo-nents of an antiracist program. But as long as they do not translate into a truly inclusive classroom climate, they function merely as negative constructs. Like the concept of academic freedom, they provide certain protection from blatant oppression but do little to improve interaction among people(s) with varied histories, emotions and outlooks.

The North American university is less a Medieval ivory tower than a microcosm of the diverse society in which we live. In our classrooms, we have students who belong to the dominant cultures (European descent) and those who belong to historically under-represented racial and ethnocultural backgrounds (First Nations peoples, those of African or Asian descent and many other ethnicities). If university education is to be relevant and effective for all of these communities, there are certain facts that all sensitive university teachers must confront and overcome in their classrooms:

- many students' ethnic and racial histories have been excluded from the curriculum
- minorities are typically marginalized in our classrooms and in campus life
- the life experience of marginalized communities generates barriers to effective classroom teaching and learning.

How educators — whether they are professors, teaching assistants, academic administrators or other teaching professionals — manage their classrooms will provide the key to whether their students will excel academically and become creative and collaborative members of the local and global community. Well-meaning university teachers often fail in their educational missions simply because they do not appreciate the complex and subtle dynamics operating in their classrooms, or have not taken the time to introduce basic norms and guidelines that encourage the participation and cooperation of *all* of their students.

I do not want to underestimate the profound difficulty of tackling the ideological supports of racism. The phenomenon is complex and requires a response that is subtle

41

and sophisticated. But I would like to suggest that a good starting place for deconstructing the supports of racism is to practise a kind of teaching that has been around for a long time and that has a proud history at this university, that is, *engaged and inclusive pedagogy*.

Engaged and inclusive pedagogy requires everyone, including the instructor, to participate actively in the learning experience. It also means providing a learning situation that requires participants to practise positive freedom by taking risks and by sharing insights and experiences. Engaged and inclusive pedagogy is teaching and learning that cultivates a healthy and healing relationship – one that encourages participants to bring their personalities and life experiences to the lecture hall and the discussion table.

When everyone participates as much as possible in the classroom – essays in this volume will show that even large lectures can allow for participation – and when individuals are present in body, mind and spirit, then mutual sharing, understanding and respect inevitably occur. In the modern multicultural and multiracial university classroom, engaged pedagogy implies giving little credence to the myths that support discrimination, such as

- racism no longer exists in our society
- all Canadian citizens have equal opportunities
- the pursuit of knowledge is always objective
- the classroom is a neutral laboratory.

But let's not mince words. No matter how progressive, engaged and inclusive the pedagogy is, it will never make a classroom neutral. At its best, it enables participants to begin to dismantle unnecessary power structures. And it generates an environment that encourages

- an appreciation of diversity and difference
- mutual respect and civility
- fairness and trust.

Engaged and inclusive pedagogy has always cultivated these norms. I would argue that it is not only a rational framework for teaching and learning, but that it is absolutely indispensable in our multicultural and multiracial environment. Until university teachers realize that they are not always impartial dispensers of wisdom – the concept was arrogant even in historically more homogenous environments – the chilly classroom climate will remain as uncomfortable for them as for their students.

University administrators play a critical role in the development of progressive teaching. Universities have been aggressive in promoting research but remiss in acknowledging innovations in teaching, in supporting research on inclusive pedagogies and in developing effective criteria for evaluating good teaching. Universities must begin to recognize and reward teachers who practise engaged and inclusive pedagogy.

Progressive teaching practices should not be regarded as a pedagogical cure-all. Teachers will always be confronted by the dilemma of their own authority and the need to wield it responsibly. Students cannot be expected always to bring every bit of their personality and their lives to the classroom. Such an expectation constitutes another form of oppression. And major roadblocks will always be there in the form of student apathy, teaching workloads and the lack of institutional or public support for the educational enterprise. But the biggest losers in any conceivable educational scenario will be teachers who continue to play the role of impartial dispenser of wisdom and students who allow themselves to be passive receptors.

This article is directed to all university teachers, some of whom might be new to the task of managing a multicultural and multiracial classroom. I'd like to close, therefore, by sharing a useful checklist for engaged pedagogy as it relates to race and ethnicity. This list is borrowed from the works of North American antiracism and race relations educators and supplemented by my own practical experience. My hope is that teachers will not view it as definitive.

The dos and don'ts in the checklist[1] on page 44 might seem somewhat simplistic to those who already have experience working in racially diverse environments. For example, it is patently more difficult to establish ground rules for mutual respect and to develop unbiased terminology than the simple recommendations here might appear to suggest. My intention in presenting the checklist – with all its limitations – is to encourage teachers in beginning the process of creating more liberating classroom environments and thinking about what it means to educate a diverse student body.

Notes

1. Adapted from "Working with special (diverse) populations," (1982) and Solar (1992).

References

hooks, bell. 1994. *Teaching to transgress: Education as the practice of freedom.* New York: Routledge.

Solar, Claudie, (ed.) 1992. *Inequity in the classroom: A manual for professors and adult educators.* Montréal: Concordia University, Office on the Status of Women.

"Working with special (diverse) populations." 1982. Boston: Community Resources Center.

Checklist For Engaged Pedagogy

DISCOURAGE

- qualifiers that reinforce racial stereotypes
- the assumption that all members of racial groups are the same, or even similar
- ethnic clichés
- racist or ethnocentric jokes
- patronizing behaviour or tokenism by race
- the expectation that students of non-European ancestry will respond for their entire ethnoracial group
- the avoidance of eye contact with students of non-European ancestry
- relating a student's academic difficulties with her or his ethnoracial background
- using a "colour code" to describe or interpret the actions of students

ENCOURAGE

- acknowledgment of the presence of racial diversity in your classroom
- taking responsibility for managing or monitoring ethnic and racial interactions
- the establishment of ground rules for mutual respect in the classroom
- choosing language and usage that do not reinforce bias
- giving equal respect to all races and presenting a balanced representation in visual aids and other media
- choosing texts and print media that avoid racial discrimination and stereotyping
- the expansion of your horizon by including contributions from non-traditional scholars
- the acknowledgement of and respect for *all* of your students' accents
- being patient with students whose first language is not English or French
- students to relate their learning to their personal experience.

Diversity in the Classroom: Engagement and Resistance

Carl E. James

The diversity to be found among today's university student population in terms of social class, gender, race, ethnicity, language,[1] sexuality and dis/ability poses significant challenges that require us to examine our pedagogical approaches if we are to make university education relevant and equitable to students. Much of this diversity in the student body is brought about by conscious efforts to remove barriers to university education. As a result, the new population of students enters with the expectation that the principles of access and equity will be reflected in the pedagogical approach to their education, and that their cultural interests and needs will be recognized and supported (Grayson and Williams 1994; Grayson, Chi and Rhyne 1994; James 1994a; Schenke 1993).

An antiracist approach to education attempts to meet the needs and interests of students by recognizing and validating their lived experiences and engaging them in dialogue that is premised on the "theoretical discourse of empowerment." In antiracism education as well, educators are prepared to acknowledge and question their relative power and privileged positions (Dei 1994, 1). In pedagogy and content, antiracism educators make explicit the contradictions and paradoxes that are inherent in institutions that promise equality and inclusivity while producing and reproducing inequalities based on race, class, gender and dis/ability. It is a critical approach to education that engages students in theorizing about social issues so as to produce transformative action. Working within this antiracist framework and reflecting on my own experiences as an educator working with students generally, and teacher candidates in particular, I will explore three issues: education in a diverse context, dialogical or interactive pedagogy and resistance.

Education in a Diverse Context

In his foreword to Paulo Freire's *Pedagogy of the Oppressed* (1968), Richard Shaull writes:

Education either functions as an instrument which is used to facilitate the integration of the younger generation into the logic of the present system and bring about conformity to it, or it becomes "the practice of freedom," the means by which men and women deal critically and creatively with reality and discover how to participate in the transformation of their world (15).

To engage in the latter function, the social, political, economic, cultural and historical contexts in which education takes place must be considered. The racial, ethnic and economic diversity reflected in our university classrooms (Found 1992, Ahamad 1987) must be met by course materials and pedagogical approaches that address the respective needs, interests and aspirations of the students that are in those classrooms.

In addressing diversity, we must address the issue of difference. As George Dei (1994) points out, we must ensure that the "politics of difference does not paralyse or compromise" (3) the goal of making education relevant to, and inclusive of, all students. The experiences of all must be validated, and differences must be critically analyzed and questioned. In particular, the experiences of marginalized groups —racial and ethnic minorities, women, the working class, disabled people, lesbians and gays —must be evident in the curriculum so that these students are not further marginalized by their absence.

As educators, we must be conscious of our power, authority and privilege in the classroom, as well as recognize how we influence the learning process. We must be conscious of the ways in which our roles and identities affect our interactions with students. This point has been examined by a number of professors whose work provides models for our individual responsibilities in this regard (Ahlquist 1992, hooks 1988, James 1994a, Mukherjee 1994, Ng 1994, Sleeter 1994). I will return to this point in the section on resistance.

Dialogical or Interactive Pedagogy

What we teach, how we teach and the questions we raise are certainly not independent of who we are. This understanding is critical in the teaching and learning process. As already pointed out, professors are not neutral, nor do the students see us as neutral. Therefore, we must also understand the students' perceptions and the factors that inform their perceptions.

A dialogical or interactive approach provides space for active class participation and for students to contribute to their own learning based on their experiences and expectations. It requires students to understand and see the teaching/learning process as one in which their participation is valued. It enables us as educators to learn about the students' experiences so that we might build on these experiences. It provides us with an understanding of the framework into which new information is being incorporated and of how that framework might be used to understand the new information (Sleeter 1994). It is also a way of inviting students to question, and to hear about their struggles with new or contradictory information so that it can be addressed. As well, it allows students to share with each other, and in bell hooks's words, "come to voice" (1988).

Getting students to articulate their positions in class is not always easy. Indeed, traditional schooling might have taught them that there are right and wrong answers, that teachers are endowed with the information and that their role is to listen, take notes and be ready to reproduce the notes in the examination. No wonder some are reluctant to talk in class. Many students might perceive the dialogical approach as intimidating. Some might fear being challenged or appearing uninformed or unintelligent. Those who participate might be perceived as "talking too much" and consequently might be criticized. Indeed, questioning students, questioning what they believe or have come to accept as "truth" or "fact," is always a problem.

The perception that truth and fact reside in the educator – the one with the knowledge – is pervasive. When educators attempt to challenge this notion, and therefore open the class for all to contribute their knowledge, some student might say, as I heard recently: "I did not come here to hear what other students' opinions are, I came to hear what you have to say because you have the information and the knowledge." Challenging beliefs about how knowledge is constructed and the value placed on knowledge is a significant factor in getting students to listen to and respect each other in class. They need to see themselves as also creating knowledge and contributing to the development of knowledge.

Students are sometimes reluctant to question things, not because they are unfamiliar with the issues being discussed, but because they have come to accept the idea that some issues are best addressed by "experts," such as the educator/professor, or by people whom they believe understand these issues because of their lived experiences. For instance, white students or male students tend to expect racial minorities or women to address issues of racism or sexism. However, it is necessary to encourage all students to address these issues. They have experiences with these issues as well, and it is important for them to engage in critical analyses of these subjects. It is crucial that students understand that they all bring insights and interpretations, which are informed by their particular identities and experiences. Often, on issues of race I have been asked, "What do you think?" before I could throw the question or issue out for discussion.

We must avoid making students, or ourselves if we are perceived as "having the experience," the only voices that are heard on such issues. In not encouraging other voices, we could be reinforcing sexism, racism, heterosexism or classism, in that, as bell hooks points out, we take the burden of accountability away from those who consider themselves exempt, while placing it on those who are perceived as having experiences with the issues.

Sharing one's ideas sometimes means taking risks. But doing so is influenced by the demographic makeup of the class and the speaker's perception of the extent to which her or his criticisms might be challenged. For example, I teach teacher candidates, and one of the things we talked about during the Christmas season was the different ethnocultural or religious celebrations at this time of year. I asked some of the candidates to return in January with what they had learned about the different celebrations. Kwanzaa was one of the celebrations they identified. During the first class, one of the students who had researched Kwanzaa volunteered to talk about what she had found out. She simply talked about what she had read. I then asked her what she thought about the celebration and the philosophy behind it. She replied, "It is okay." I asked about her perceptions of the relevance of such a celebration, and whether, like other groups, black people are entitled to have this ritual acknowledged in schools, particularly at this time of the year. She replied, "Everyone is entitled to their practices." This white female student did not wish to take a risk, particularly in a class with black students.

In questioning her I was aware of the risks and of her desire to avoid offending me or any of the racial-minority students. Nevertheless, I maintain that in an educational setting, it is important to encourage students to reflect critically on their positions and to question their own positions. The student would, of course, have a position about certain celebrations, for example Christmas, that occur at the same time. This student eventually will be working in multicultural classrooms so I think that it was appropriate to engage her in considering how she viewed or understood Kwanzaa based on the information she had, how she viewed it after her research and whether she had broadened or shifted her position.

Having this kind of dialogue in class sometimes produces tension and conflict. Our culture tends to avoid what is perceived as "conflict" or "confrontation." When it arises during classes, it is expected that the course director will *resolve* the differences or conflict and provide closure. The expectation is that individuals should be made to feel comfortable again. It is, however, not always possible to restore comfort or provide resolution or closure to discussions. But we can help students learn how to live with discomfort and manage tension and conflict, and to understand their sources. Sometimes this might mean engaging them in further discussions about the subject, having them raise questions and leaving them to arrive at what might be considered their own resolution and closure. Responsibility for seeking one's own closure is important to the learning process; learning does not begin or end in the classroom with that lesson or with that particular course director. Any discussion might be just the beginning of a long and difficult process in which students raise questions to be answered later, even after the course is over. Students should learn that unanswered questions do not always indicate ignorance but can reflect a critical and analytical mind.

Resistance

When we challenge or question traditionally held views, when new information interferes with individuals' understanding of events, when we provide information that individuals resist, when students are unfamiliar with the pedagogical approach taken in a course, or, as Roxana Ng (1994) writes, when both the course "content and the teacher represent authority in a power structure that marginalizes" white males

(43), then it is likely that students will resist. In essence, resistance will be a part of any classroom discourse in which, as Deborah Britzman (1995) points out, we willfully interfere with individuals' understanding, knowledge or sense of identity. Whatever form resistance takes, it is important to note both what is resisted and who resists (Ahlquist 1992, Britzman 1991, Tatum 1992).

When students attend classes because they want to know what is on the examination, then they expect the course director to take an approach that provides the materials in a lecture format so that they have in their notes what will be on the exam. When they come to find out what exactly the course director wants in the essay, or to discover the political orientation of the course director so as to submit work that will be approved, they will resist any attempts to engage in dialogue.

Individuals want to be liked and to maintain favourable relations with their peers and the course director; thus, they might be reluctant to respond critically to comments by either. Students wish to receive good grades so they might feel that challenging the course director will be to their detriment. Also, they might have difficulty separating criticism of an idea from criticism of an individual. An individual's idea is seen as intimately linked to the person; any criticism of the idea is seen, or received, as a personal matter — even as a putdown or rejection. Therefore, students resist engaging in critical discussions.

In the area in which I teach, attempts to get teacher candidates to comment critically on the educational system in Ontario are often met with resistance because students do not wish to see the flaws of the system. After all, it is where they intend to work after graduation; also, it is often the system through which they "made it." Criticisms sometimes even produce tears. For example, after a class in which we discussed the role of teachers and the extent to which they contribute to unequal educational outcomes for students, one student, who was very upset during the class and was, as other students said, "defending the system," explained to me after class, "I don't think my parents are what you guys are talking about." Both of her parents are teachers and she saw the discussion as a criticism of her parents, teachers in general and a school system that she felt were trying hard to address the needs and concerns of today's students. On this basis, she rejected the criticisms presented in class.

Sometimes resistance takes the form of silence. For instance, when I discuss employment equity and access to post-secondary education in classes, articulate, participatory students, usually white males, will disengage from the discourse, particularly in a situation where women or racial minorities are present (more so if they are the professors) or if the general sentiment in the class is one of support for equity programs. Their silence is very noticeable. If they are asked to comment, the response might be, "Everything has been said," or "I don't have anything to say." There are times when students will put forward their ideas and remain silent afterwards. Some might even leave the room. Such actions reflect students' attempts to exercise their power or their unwillingness to be challenged on their positions (Delpit 1998, Tatum 1992).

One might assume that members of marginalized groups would welcome the opportunity to participate in class discussions, particularly around issues that validate their experiences. As course directors, we would hope that by providing space for dialogue, students from marginalized groups, whose experiences traditionally have not been represented in class materials, would "come to voice" and provide their perspectives. But their participation in class is sometimes limited; they too use silence as a strategy of resistance. This might be a result of their skepticism or distrust of the institution's or course director's commitment to interrogating and changing the *status quo*. Or they might not wish to be made obvious in class, particularly if they are in small numbers. Although the student population has changed and reading materials no longer reflect a male, Eurocentric, middle-class bias, students are not convinced that it is safe to provide alternative viewpoints (James 1994b).

Further, marginalized group members might not wish to destroy the alliances they have made with other students or call attention to themselves. Consequently, they resist discussing issues that make them "realize or reflect on their experiences with oppression" (Ng 1994, 43) or matters that place dominant-group students on the defensive. For example, racial-minority students might resist any discussions that support employment equity or access initiatives to education by remaining silent or by arguing that the current system of meritocracy is effective in meeting the needs of all Canadians (Grayson, Chi and Rhyne 1994). For these students, maintaining positive relations with their peers and the integrity of their group with regard to their academic ability might be the basis for their resistance. They are protecting themselves.

Challenging students' viewpoints and presenting alternatives is sometimes met with resistance not only because students believe that "everyone is entitled to their viewpoint because we live in a democratic society," but also because they cannot live with, or are not prepared to live with, the proposed alternative. Furthermore, the alternative idea that is advanced might be dismissed or challenged because it might be perceived as untheoretical, self-serving, too radical or biased. In some cases, the identity of the person who presents the alternative viewpoint is factored into the interpretation of what is said, whether that person is a student or a professor. For instance, the viewpoints of women and racial minorities, who assert that inequality, sexism, racism and discrimination are responsible for the patterns of educational and occupational participation in our society, are sometimes resisted.

In commenting on the paradoxical situation of minority faculty members at universities, Roxana Ng (1994) points out that when students resist the teaching of minority faculty, the form such resistance takes is related to the fact that these faculty members are perceived in a "gendered and racialized" manner. In contrast, resistance to white male faculty members might take the form of challenging their course content or materials or engaging them in "intellectual debates."

> In the case of minority faculty, in addition to course materials, the person herself becomes a target. As a racial minority and a woman, I have no authority despite my formal position...The sexism and racism in this case is not only based on [stu-

dents'] attitudes toward minorities in general, it is about minorities in positions of authority whose knowledge and expertise is often questioned (43).

Conclusion

We see here a number of contradictions, conflicts and tensions that are inherent in the ways we engage students in the classroom. Evidently, there is no particular approach to teaching that will alleviate the problems we are bound to experience in the teaching-learning process. Probably Deborah Britzman (1995) said it best when she said that we "cannot teach anyone anything. We can only create conditions where they get to know how they learn, what they wish to learn, and understand what they think they are saying when they say what they say." Even as leaders in the classroom, we are not neutral. We come to our teaching with particular notions of what we wish students to know and how they should know it; we employ our understanding of the ways of knowing. Hence, there is the tendency for us to reproduce ourselves in the classroom. With this in mind, it seems appropriate that we use an approach to education that provides everyone with an opportunity to share her or his interpretation and knowledge. By so doing, we can provide space for dialogue and help students to manage their confusions, conflicts, tensions, doubts and ambiguities, which are inherent in any learning process.

If we acknowledge the risks involved in the teaching-learning process and that students come to classes with particular ideas and expectations of the courses, we can respond to their expectations by talking directly about our pedagogical approach in the first class. So in addition to distributing course outlines, we must say how we intend to conduct the class. Often students will forget, and weeks into the course we will hear complaints. When I have reminded students of what I had said at the beginning of the course, they sometimes respond as if they are hearing the information for the first time. Constant reminders and talking explicitly about the pedagogical approach as the course proceeds might be necessary.

Finally, it is important for us to model for students an approach to learning that acknowledges and respects differences and promotes equality. When we engage students in critical reflections and interrogation of issues, we are disturbing or interfering with their worldview and their sense of identities, even if they are voluntary course participants. Our responsibility, then, is to make the learning process as conducive as possible to dialogue.

Notes

1. In his study on the participation of different ethnic groups in post-secondary education, Ahmad (1987) found that there is a significant increase in the participation of racial minorities. At York University, Found (1992) showed that in 1991, some 54 different ethnic origins were represented in the undergraduate student population representing 22 major ethnic groups in Canada, including British (English, Scottish and Irish), Italian, French, Jewish, South Asian, Asian and African. While English was the first language of 67% of students, Italian and Chinese were the two most prevalent other "mother tongues." Nineteen per cent of students were racial minorities.

References

Ahamad, Bill. 1987. *Participation of different ethnic groups in post-secondary education.* Ottawa: Department of the Secretary of State.

Ahlquist, Roberta. 1992. Manifestations of inequality: Overcoming resistance in a multicultural foundations course. In *Research and multicultural education: From the margins to the mainstream*, ed. C.A. Grant, 89–105. New York: Falmer Press.

Britzman, Deborah P. 1991. Decentering discourses in teacher education: Or, the unleashing of unpopular things. *Journal of Education* 173 (3): 60–80.

——. 1995. Comments made at the seminar "Problematizing pedagogy." 19 Jan., York University.

Dei, George. 1994. Anti-racist education: Working across differences. *Orbit* 25 (2): 1–3.

Delpit, Lisa D. 1988. The silenced dialogue: Power and pedagogy in educating other people's children. *Harvard Educational Review* 58 (3): 280–98.

Found, William C. 1992. Who are York's undergraduates? Results of the university's 1991 comprehensive student survey. Toronto: Office of the President, York University.

Freire, Paulo. 1968. *Pedagogy of the oppressed.* New York: Seabury Press.

Grayson, J. Paul, Tammy Chi and Darla Rhyne. 1994. *The social construction of "visible minority" students of Chinese origin.* Toronto: Institute for Social Research, York University.

Grayson, J. Paul and Deanna Williams. 1994. *Racialization and black student identity at York University.* Toronto: Institute for Social Research, York University.

hooks, bell. 1988. *Talking back: Thinking feminist, thinking black.* Toronto: Between the Lines.

James, Carl E. 1994a. The paradox of power and privilege: Race, gender and occupational position. *Canadian Woman Studies* 14: 47–51.

——. 1994b. "Access students": Experiences of racial minorities in a Canadian university. Paper presented at the Society for Research into Higher Education, 1994 Annual Conference: The Student Experience. University of York, York, England.

Mukherjee, Arun. 1994. The "race consciousness" of a South Asian (Canadian, of course) female academic. In *Talking about difference: Encounters in culture, language and identity*, C.E. James and A. Shadd (eds.), 201–7. Toronto: Between the Lines.

Ng, Roxana. 1994. Sexism and racism in the university: Analysing a personal experience. *Canadian Woman Studies* 14: 42–46.

Schenke, Arlene. 1993. *Being "access"/doing change: Confronting difference in teacher education: A reading of teacher candidates' experiences of the faculty of education access initiative and consecutive program.* Toronto: York University.

Sleeter, Christine. 1992. Resisting racial awareness: How teachers understand the social order from their racial, gender, and social class locations. *Educational Foundations* (spring): 7–32.

—— 1994. White racism. *Multicultural Education* 39: 5–8.

Tatum, Beverly Daniel. 1992. Talking about race, learning about racism: The application of racial identity development theory in the classroom. *Harvard Educational Review* 62: 1–24.

Williams, Patricia. 1991. *The alchemy of race and rights: Diary of a law professor.* Cambridge: Harvard University Press.

Responsibility and Respect in Critical Pedagogy

Leslie Sanders

Certain issues in critical and feminist pedagogy trouble me, even though these approaches have had a profound impact on my own teaching practices. It seems to me that critical and feminist pedagogy both operate with a somewhat contradictory set of assumptions about students. On the one hand, they emphasize the knowledge and experience that students bring to their education, whether acquired from schooling or from life. On the other hand, they seem to assume that students need to be shaken out of ignorance and complacency, challenged in a way that disturbs their most deeply held assumptions about the world. However, when challenging our students, we ourselves often make assumptions about the nature of our students' experience and then teach to our presumptions.

I believe critical and feminist pedagogies do present important challenges to traditional ways of teaching, but I think that they also impose on students particular forms of participation in the educative process, and in so doing, can undermine the results they seek. The contradictions within these pedagogies particularly trouble me because they can be disrespectful of students.

I will illustrate what I mean with some examples. The first time I recognized these problems was over an incident that occurred some twenty years ago in a first-year humanities course on postwar culture. (Atkinson College, now Atkinson Faculty of Liberal and Professional Studies, where I have taught for more than twenty-five years, was devoted to "adult" students. Much of what I say is influenced by the fact that my career has been with adult students, although my comments do, I think, apply to younger students as well.) Filled with texts that vividly depicted the violence and inhumanity of Western culture and recent history, the course aimed, at least in part, at shaking out of complacency what the lecturing team arrogantly assumed were the (white, middle class?) conventional beliefs and experiences of a typical Atkinson class of the time.

One night we showed, with no forewarning, Resnais's film *Night and Fog*, a graphic depiction of Nazi concentration camps. Well, it turned out that a student in the class was a survivor of one of those camps, and the film was extremely traumatic for her. I was humiliated by my arrogant assumption that the film was "news," and twenty years later still regret the pain I caused her. Ten years later, I showed the film again in a similar course, although this time with forewarning. Several students, who had known little about the Holocaust, were physically ill after seeing it. Another student, whose uncle was a German soldier killed for his opposition to Hitler, spoke painfully to me of the uncle's diaries, still in his family's possession. He felt his uncle was dishonoured by the way the course instructors dealt with the Holocaust material. This experience again reminded me that we do not know our students; we do not know to whom we are speaking and we cannot and should not make any assumptions about "where they are coming from."

The danger of assumptions has also been made evident to me in teaching over the years an English course required of Atkinson students for whom English is a second language. These students come from all over the world and they have completed at least secondary education outside of Canada. I have come to understand that the course serves to introduce these students to the culture of the Canadian classroom. This culture is particular and it arises from the cultural and political practice of the dominant class in this country. It rewards speaking over silence; it demands questioning and critical analysis of material rather than uncritical acceptance (although, in truth, students rarely are encouraged to challenge the instructor's underlying assumptions). It penalizes lack of "participation" and simple memorization of material. It proposes that teacher and student are together engaged in making knowledge rather than privileging the knowledge and authority of the teacher and expecting the acquiescence of the student.

Yet many of our students come from cultural backgrounds that view education quite differently and as a result, their experience of education has been quite different from that of students wholly educated in Canada. For a variety of reasons, including strictures related to gender, these students might find the behaviour expected of them in the Canadian classroom inappropriate. Typically, we encourage them to learn Canadian behaviour, perhaps necessarily so, but I think that they have the right to retain practices with which they are more comfortable, as long as they can also meet the requirements of the Canadian system.

Another example comes from a more recent experience teaching a first-year humanities course called "Concepts of Male and Female in Western Culture." Approximately one third of the students were men and the men typically chose not to speak during tutorials. When I questioned some of them about their silence, they said that they wanted to listen to what the women had to say. They were thoughtful and hard working; they just chose not to participate in discussions. They did not feel silenced. They chose silence. Is this lack of participation? I don't think so.

I raise the issue of silence because it is a focus of radical pedagogies and is usually construed negatively. We often assume that the people who do not talk are "silenced" or unengaged in the course. I am certain that some people are, in fact, silenced in the classroom – by material and opinions that they find offensive, by curriculum that negates or obscures their history and experience. This kind of silence certainly interferes with those students' participation in their education and should be interrogated. But I am struck by the number of students who, in a course evaluation where I asked about tutorial participation, wrote, "I like to hear what the other students think," and "I prefer to listen."

A corollary to this kind of silence occurs when students feel that they have little experience when compared to others in a class. Again I draw from the humanities course "Concepts of Male and Female in Western Culture," in which students ranged in age from 18 to 65 and came from countries on every continent. Some students were just beginning their adult lives and some were fortunate enough to be emerging from a protected and peaceful upbringing. Others, however, were painfully attempting to repair lives that had been burdened, even shattered, in a variety of ways and the experiences they shared or which resonated in their comments truly "silenced" many of us – I include myself. Listening is an act of learning, too.

Perhaps related, when working in the Atkinson Essay Tutoring Centre, I have been told from time to time, by younger students in particular, that they feel they have no "experience" to bring to their essays. They therefore fear they won't "do well" because "everyone else in the class has 'traumas' of one sort or other to analyze" and "that is what the professor is looking for." Surely the disempowerment of such a student, who might not have the opportunity to connect course material to life experience, is as in need of interrogation as that of students whose lives provide them with an overabundance of difficulty. Placing experience at the core of our pedagogy is fraught with complication.

As well, there are responsibilities attached to eliciting certain kinds of participation. If we seek to "disturb" our students' views of the world, we should not be surprised if they do, in fact, become very disturbed indeed. Yet we are not therapists and we have limited time to give our students individually to talk out matters that arise for them should they come to us for help or guidance. Perhaps because I teach in areas where the material is very personal for many of my students, I might be particularly concerned about this issue, but I am sure that many of us encounter students with problems that are provoked or exacerbated by material in our courses. If a student is not prepared to deal with certain issues in ways we expect, certainly they also have the right to protect themselves, whether consciously or not, from the kind of self-examination or life change that dealing with the issue might imply at that point. I think we can open a space both for those who want to be disturbed and for those who choose otherwise.

For example, in a third-year humanities course, "Black Writers and their Worlds," I assign a "response" journal. Students are expected to submit a page or two of writing each week; they are instructed to respond, in whatever fashion they wish, to course materials, lectures or discussions. Journal entries have ranged from intensely personal commentary on private experience to critical analysis of particular texts. At the end of the course, some students end up with an intellectual diary and others with the germ of a variety of academic papers. I don't think that either is "better": each student chooses her manner of engagement in the course material.

I believe that we have to respect the ways in which students choose to engage in their education. I think we can fulfil our responsibility to present challenging issues and material and also respect individuals' rights and responsibilities as adults to pursue their education as they please. I fully support the principles of both critical and feminist pedagogy and offer my reservations in the hope that they will start dialogue and discussion about the ethical problems they raise.

Feminist Pedagogy: Paradoxes in Theory and Practice[1]

Kathryn McPherson

Over the past twenty-five years, feminist scholars and activists have challenged teachers to create a curriculum in which women's experiences and actions play a central role. Feminist pedagogy, as it came to be called, included more than just making course content gender balanced; it involved transforming how that content was transmitted, thereby making the classroom a site of social change. This article outlines three major elements of feminist pedagogy and, using examples from my own teaching of Canadian history, will consider some of the theoretical and practical strengths and limitations feminist pedagogy offers.

Early proponents of feminist pedagogy envisioned teaching methods that would subvert conventional relations of dominance and subordination in the classroom and thus outside of it. Building on critical pedagogy developed by educators such as Paulo Freire and on the feminist critique of Enlightenment thought, feminist teachers focused on three elements of classroom relations. The first was an emphasis on women's own experiences. Rather than trivializing students' experiences outside the classroom, those experiences were to be drawn on and validated. In this way, the conventional divisions between theoretically based knowledge and "the knowledge of everyday life" were to be dissolved. A second strategy of feminist pedagogy emphasized collaboration and collective learning rather than competition and individualism. Creating a "safe" environment in which all students had the opportunity to express themselves necessitated small-group teaching and small class size. Third, feminist pedagogy sought to transform relationships between teachers and students, reducing hierarchical relations between those two groups and democratizing relations in the classroom. As such, teachers were expected to "give away" power and authority to promote student-centred learning.

Validation of Experience

The question of experience is a particularly interesting one. In the discipline of history, instructors usually struggle to have students understand the past on its own terms, rather than from only the perspective of the students' own experiences. To balance the tension between questions generated out of contemporary politics and experience with answers generated in the past, the major research assignment in my third-year course "History of Women in Canada" is based on primary documents created by Canadian women. Students must locate a primary source and analyze whether the author's experiences and beliefs conform to or challenge what we think we know about Canadian women's history. In so doing, women's own words about their lives become the starting point for historical knowledge.

Students are also required to provide a methodological discussion identifying how they used the source, why the source was created and preserved and the degree to which we can generalize from that one woman's experience. In this way, students consider how we know anything about women's lives in the past and how that knowledge revises the conventional historical narrative. One option in this assignment is for students to create their own primary source by interviewing a Canadian woman aged 65 or older. Students who choose this option are most acutely aware of the importance of collaboration in academic research. If nothing else, the student depends on successful interaction with the interviewee to complete the assignment.

Collective and Collaborative Learning

To encourage students to work collectively, I ask them to prepare a preliminary methodological analysis of their primary source (based on a set of questions I provide) and to bring that two-page discussion to class. There, I ask students to pair up, read each other's analysis and raise questions or issues about each other's source. The pairs can conduct their discussion in the cafeteria, in the hall or in the classroom, but after half an hour, I ask them to reconvene and we spend much of the next hour in a large-group discussion about the nature of their primary sources. When students raise an issue, I ask the group if anyone else discussed that problem or concern. The first few years I tried this strategy, I did it in tutorials, but as the class grew I have continued these group discussions in the lecture. Because students are reflecting on their own research experience, and because the purpose of the exercise is to share ideas, students are willing to participate with even as many as 100 students in the class.

In my fourth-year seminar "Gender, Race and Ethnicity in the Canadian West," I have used a similar approach. Students are asked to bring to every class a two-page critical response about that week's readings. At the beginning of class, I ask students to exchange their response pieces and, once each student has read another's, I begin the discussion by asking students to comment on what they liked about their classmate's critical response. At the end of the seminar, I collect the response pieces and grade them on a pass or fail basis. This system of sharing written work has helped students communicate with each other and, because students get "credit" for having done the reading, there is less competition in discussion and a greater willingness to let less-vocal members of the group insert themselves into the debate.

Transforming Power in the Classroom

These small writing assignments achieve additional feminist goals. At a practical level, they ensure that students find an essay topic early in the term or do the reading for class, but at a pedagogical level they shift the focus away from the instructor and back onto methodological and theoretical questions generated by students themselves. Not only does this foster collaboration among students, it also places the instructor in the role of facilitator and resource rather than absolute authority. Students who choose the oral history option particularly benefit as they often have a great deal of time, energy and interest invested in the interview process (especially if they are interviewing a grandmother, aunt or family friend). Instead of writing a paper for a professor who "already knows the right answer," students focus on formulating the best explanation for their evidence. As such, the authority they bring to their writing often results in higher-than-usual-quality work for those students.

Having acknowledged the important contribution that feminist pedagogy can make to a course like mine, it is also important to recognize the limitations and contradictions inherent in feminist teaching methods. However much instructors emphasize collaboration and non-hierarchical relations, competition for grades and scholarships still exists. Rather than looking to be liberated by their education, many students expect their teachers to assert standardized grading schemes and due dates, while others do not like collaborative work and resent having to "waste time" talking to their classmates or, worse, having a grade depend on a group project. As well, many elements of feminist pedagogy are premised on small class size, but as enrolments increase, creating small-group work becomes less viable.

In the classroom, students' experiences vary tremendously according to cultural and social differences based on class, ethnicity, age and sexual orientation, and on students' experiences with sexism, racism, homophobia or class divisions. These differences can facilitate important interaction, but can also serve to marginalize minority students. For example, in a discussion of historical trends in marriage, students coming from a Euro-Christian tradition might see the connection between marriage, culture and patriarchy very differently than Muslim or Sikh students do. The latter groups might feel uncomfortable articulating a defence of traditional family structures to their white classmates. Seeking to validate women's experiences within the larger knowledge system, feminist professors often face the contradiction that some women's experiences are validated more than others. Just as women often feel that compared to the opinions of their male peers, their perspectives do not carry equal weight or get equal consideration, so too can women of colour or from cultural minorities be silenced or overwhelmed by the voices of white women.

As they try to balance the diverse needs and expectations of students, feminist instructors face further complications pertaining to power relations within the classroom. Some object to the expectation that as women they will "naturally" create a nurturing learning environment and insist that learning often is best achieved through challenge, not nurture. At the same time, feminist pedagogy encourages teachers to divest themselves of power, yet many instructors often feel they have little power to share. In large classes especially, professors who are female, gay, lesbian, from a cultural minority or merely young must often struggle to garner any authority or respect from students. For instructors addressing sensitive social issues in their courses, "giving away power" can leave classes open to racist, sexist or homophobic comments, which in turn can silence the very experiences feminist teachers were trying to nourish. As class sizes increase, the potential for these conflicts seems to grow exponentially.

Reflections on Feminist Pedagogy

My women's history course attracts students who are committed feminists, who are self-proclaimed non-feminists, or who take the course because it fits their timetable. Some students are seeking heroic tales of strong women in the past, others expect a historical critique of patriarchal relations, while others demand extensive analysis of class and racial cleavages among women. Meeting these demands necessitates recognizing that not all students expect education to be "liberating" and that some students will commit more energy to the course than will others.

Like their professor, students find adhering to feminist principles sometimes difficult. For instance, students who conduct oral interviews feel dismay when they discover that their heroic foremother was elitist. One student was bitterly disappointed to learn, contrary to family lore, that her much-adored grandmother had not been a missionary, but a missionary's wife, and as such enjoyed a privileged life in China as mistress of the manor, complete with numerous Chinese servants. Other students strive to reconcile their admiration for feminist foremothers with their recognition of the class and racial biases that those political leaders also espoused.

In the long term, such insights provoke students to think in more sophisticated ways about the interplay of gender, race, class and sexuality in specific historical contexts, and therefore to recognize the complexity of social relations and of historical changes. In the short term, however, students might find the course material and classroom setting challenging and even threatening, regardless of how much authority I share or how much nurturing I do.

As feminist instructors struggle to balance providing a nurturing, supportive environment with challenging the students intellectually or politically, they must also confront the reality that feminist pedagogy extends far beyond the classroom. Students approach feminist professors to discuss non-academic issues ranging from sexual assault to family violence and conflict to experiences of racism and homophobia. At the same time, feminist teachers, who are often in a minority in their departments or divisions, feel compelled to defend and promote female and minority students, as well as singular programs such as affirmative action, at departmental or divisional meetings, on scholarship committees and in the hallways. In this era of financial restraint, social conservatism and the "chilly" climate of the educational system, feminist teachers wonder if the emotional and psychological demands of feminist pedagogy contribute to their own stress and affiliated health problems.

Equally significant is the recognition that social change cannot be achieved only within the educational system and that the classroom is but one site where social relations might be transformed. However well-constructed or taught, an eight-month course cannot overcome completely students' previously held beliefs and attitudes, let alone well-entrenched systems of gender, sexual, racial or class privilege. Often we cannot even overcome our students' preconceptions of their instructors. Students who are uncomfortable with female authority figures or who resent non-white instructors will not likely have those sentiments erased, however revolutionary our pedagogy. Indeed, feminist pedagogy can reinforce some students' animosity towards us.

Feminist pedagogy is not as easy as its early proponents believed, but this should not dissuade us from seeking alternative teaching methods. Rather, it alerts us to the reality that not all students learn at the same pace, in the same way or with the same goals, and to the reality that political circumstances themselves change. Given the complexity of social relations in the present and in the past and given the evolving critique of social inequity, we must expect that pedagogical methods will be revised and reformulated. In the words of feminist scholar Margaret Conrad, "as historians, we are not easily hoodwinked into believing that there is a fixed and immutable feminist pedagogy" (1995, 120). As gender relations between men and women, and among women, change, so too do teachers continue to reevaluate what constitutes social power in the classroom and in the wider society. This challenge keeps many feminist teachers listening to what their students have to say and engaging in a critical appraisal of pedagogical approaches.

Notes

1. Research for this paper was completed for a longer paper, coauthored with University of Ottawa professor Ruby Heap; see Heap and McPherson (1995).

References

Conrad, Margaret. 1995. Keep it complex: Feminist pedagogies in a post-modernist, post-structuralist, post-colonialist, post-feminist world. In *Teaching women's history: Challenges and solutions*, Bettina Bradbury (ed.) *et al.*, 120. Athabasca, AB: Athabasca Educational Enterprise.

Heap, Ruby and Kathryn McPherson. 1995. What is feminist pedagogy anyway? In *Teaching women's history: Challenges and solutions*, Bettina Bradbury (ed.) *et al.*, 101–17. Athabasca, AB: Athabasca Educational Enterprise.

Teaching "Women and Men in Organizations": Feminist Pedagogy in the Business School

Pat Bradshaw and Catherine Ng

This article describes some of the experiences and insights gained from an attempt to use feminist pedagogy in a course entitled "Women and Men in Organizations." It was written as part of an ongoing dialogue between the course director and one of the students in the course. We evaluated the success of this teaching approach according to Carolyn Shrewsbury's three dimensions of empowerment, community and leadership.

At the beginning of the course, the instructor advised students of the course objectives:

- to examine critically the growing literature on women and men in organizations
- to help students explore the personal implications of the changing composition of the work force and to assist them in developing insights and strategies for dealing with these changes
- to assess the implications of change for existing organizations and identify possible future organizational changes
- to use the classroom as a forum for developing different ways of teaching, learning and interacting that take into account gender differences.

The course dealt with a range of topics, such as experiences of women in management, leadership styles of men and women, sexuality and sexual harassment, and the interface between work and family. The implications of each of the issues for managers and alternative organizational responses were outlined and evaluated. Assignments for the course included a critique of a classic management article replete with patriarchal assumptions, and a personal assessment paper in which students were asked to reflect on the course topics and explore the relevance of the readings in terms of their own experiences.

Fifty per cent of each student's grade was based on a written learning contract negotiated with the course director. In this contract, students defined their learning objectives, the resources they would use to accomplish their objectives, the evidence they would present to show they had accomplished their objectives and the criteria for evaluation, including the evaluator(s). The contract allowed students to work individually or in groups on topics of particular interest to them and to produce either written or oral reports based on different research alternatives, including interviews and library searches. The class was composed of forty-one students, only ten of whom were men.

Empowerment

Although total power sharing is impossible in a classroom setting (Shrewsbury 1987), the course director did attempt, through various teaching devices, to empower students, to foster their independence, to develop their critical thinking skills and to encourage their use of personal voice. While in general the class experienced successes and failures in this aspect of feminist pedagogy, the learning contracts were a positive step towards power sharing. One factor that contributed to the success of the contracts was that there were students in the class who had previous experience contracting with the professor about their learning goals and who were able to reassure others about the integrity of the process. Part of one student's learning objective was to conduct two classes early in the course. This early power sharing modeled empowerment and participation and, as the course progressed, other students also took over sections of various classes and defined the topics for discussion.

Unfortunately, the overall physical setup of the classroom worked against power sharing. Seats were banked in a horseshoe shape around the course director, positioned in the middle, who was forced by this setup to look up at the rows of students. This arrangement implicitly reinforces the message that authority is centralized and that expertise rests with a dominant figure, the professor. Further, the larger context of the business school, where the majority of courses do not value student empowerment, undercut student trust in such a change in teaching orientation.

Community

For the course instructor, creating a sense of community in the classroom meant facilitating a classroom dynamic that enhanced learning through feelings of connection and mutuality. However, traditional classroom dynamics of competitiveness, individuality and autonomy tended to dominate. Little trust was developed and, as a result, little sharing, nurturing or even discussion of personal issues occurred. As a result, the professor was unable to create a sense of community or to model new ways for students to interact.

Several factors could have combined to frustrate the course director's early efforts to establish a sense of community and cohesiveness. First, the class was too big to allow sufficient "air time" for all participants. Second, the composition of the class varied extensively over the first few sessions as students checked out this new "feminist" class. Third, the poor attendance of some students made the fostering of familiarity difficult. Finally, the issue of confidentiality of class discussions was not addressed at the beginning of the course. Some students were obviously concerned about this, although no one raised it as an issue until well into the course. An experiential "trust circle" exercise, one aspect of a process discussion in which few students participated, revealed the extent to which students had failed to develop a sense of community. Later, in evaluating the course, we realized that it is important to establish ground rules and consensus on how to handle sensitive issues early in a course.

The involvement of the minority male students in the course provides an example of how sensitive issues failed to be raised openly and constructively in class. In course evaluations, some women wrote that the course director discriminated in favor of the men "reacting as a protective mother to their statements," while others considered her "too hard on men." Had a greater sense of community developed, these concerns might have been voiced openly at the time and discussed in class.

While a general sense of community did not evolve, a handful of students consistently participated and offered generous insights. Small-group discussions drew out others and various pedagogical tools, such as experiential exercises, role playing, cases and discussions of films or debates, did involve different individuals at different times. Indeed, one woman wrote in her self-assessment paper:

> I have allowed emotions to surface that I would have rather suppressed. During the
> course I have gone from an "everything is fine" attitude to a "man-hating" attitude,
> to an understanding of everyone. My emotions have ranged from indifference, to
> hate, to anger, to depression, to a new confidence. I have come full circle and now
> I feel that it is going to be okay, because I realize the wealth of options I do have.

Clearly, the course had quite a profound impact on some of the students, evoking powerful emotions. But without a sense of community and a forum for expression and discussion, some students might have found their reactions difficult to handle. While the course director attempted to be accessible, on the whole, students did not call her or ask for emotional support, and the classroom itself did not provide a community of support.

Leadership

The course director found that negotiating the leadership role presented her with a series of tensions and contradictions. Striking a balance that would achieve the objectives of the course became an ongoing challenge, particularly because, as Carolyn Shrewsbury (1987) says, "leadership is the embodiment of our ability and our willingness to act on our beliefs" (11). Some of the personal paradoxes the course director experienced included the tensions between a facilitative versus a more directive mode, a structured versus an unstructured format, a co-learner versus an expert stance, and an emotional, personal versus an unemotional, impersonal approach.

The course director constantly questioned how to "lead" this type of class and what role to play at different times given the variety of needs and learning styles of the students. Slipping back into more traditional pedagogy as the impersonal expert who never displays emotion and keeps the course structured in a highly directive fashion was at times tempting and also helpful. However, staying in that mode would have been counter to the pedagogical goals of the course. In hindsight, had the course director discussed her personal and emotionally difficult struggles more explicitly with the students, she might have helped them reflect more effectively on the tensions they must balance in their own careers. Such sharing and co-learning might have advanced the course objective of developing personal insight and strategies for dealing with change and allowed the classroom to become a genuine forum for learning about gender issues.

Conclusions

Overall, the course director found her attempts to apply feminist pedagogy in a business school both frustrating and rewarding. Since writing this paper, she has taught the course again on several occasions. Nonetheless, the challenges outlined here continue to be relevant and she has learned to focus on two key areas of concern: the first has to do with structure and logistics and the second with more personal issues. In terms of structure it is best that the course have a limited enrolment (maximum of thirty) and that the classroom is a seminar room with moveable tables and chairs, providing an opportunity for everyone to make eye contact. Issues of confidentiality and ground rules for dealing with sensitive issues must be raised early in the course. Students need to be reminded of the importance of regular attendance and full participation. The course director needs to be available to students to discuss issues they are dealing with on an informal basis.

The course director must be mindful of the power and privilege she carries within the classroom context. While espousing empowerment might be an ideal, the reality is that the course director has a lot of power resulting from her position in the institution, her ability to evaluate and allocate rewards (such as reference letters), her expertise and her control over course design and philosophy, as well as other less obvious sources of privilege. For example, her being middle-class, middle-aged, white and heterosexual are not insignificant influences on her interactions with students. As the course director's sensitivity to issues of privilege and power have improved, so the opportunities for discussion of different realities and experiences have increased. This is a subtle area and one that requires constant awareness and learning at a personal level. Empowerment is easy to espouse, but very difficult to achieve, particularly within the context of a highly structured, bureaucratic faculty in which the rational, unemotional and linear are valued and the dominant discourse excludes and marginalizes what is being done in the class. We have all to some extent internalized a patriarchal, sexist and racist worldview and making these dynamics conscious is an essential ingredient of feminist pedagogy.

Writing this paper has provided both teacher and student with an opportunity for extensive reflection on the learning and teaching process we shared. Such revisiting, discussion and co-learning in a self-reflective way are another dimension of feminist pedagogy. The way we might conceptualize and write this paper tomorrow might be different as our understanding of the deep structures of power and the operation of unconscious privilege increases. The current dialogues about feminist pedagogy are very exciting and the emerging strategies for creating sites for resistance and transgression (hooks 1994) within the dominant culture help us reframe our teaching practices. We look forward to continuing to develop our approaches to teaching and learning within the spirit of feminism.

References

hooks, bell. 1994. *Teaching to transgress: Education as the practice of freedom.* New York: Routledge.

Shrewsbury, C. 1987. What is feminist pedagogy? *Women's Studies Quarterly* 15 (fall/winter): 6–31.

Empowering Students Through Feminist Pedagogy

Rae Anderson

Introduction

One of the key concepts in feminist pedagogy is empowerment, which in much of the literature has been related to giving individuals a sense of control. Ideally, the feminist classroom provides students with control over the processes of their own education. More importantly, however, this individual empowerment is fostered within a climate of collective interdependence and responsibility for the integrity of the classroom. One of the greatest strengths of the feminist classroom is its potential to become a place where students are able to debate in a relatively protected sphere and work through issues together.

The practice of feminist pedagogy requires ongoing evaluation by both students and teachers if this collective interdependence in the learning and teaching processes is to be fostered successfully. Reflecting on some of the contradictions that have arisen in my own teaching, this paper discusses some of the general principles of feminist pedagogy and shows how the classroom is a charged arena for contested meanings and interpretations.

Contradictions in the Feminist Classroom

These reflections on feminist pedagogy are informed by my experiences teaching a third-year anthropology course, "Women, Culture and Society." Of the fifty students enroled, typically only three or four have been men, but it is usual to have at least a dozen ethnicities represented. Students' ages range from the early twenties to the late sixties. As a third-year course with no prerequisite, the course attracts students from many disciplines (anthropology, geography, history, linguistics, physical education, political science, psychology, religious studies, sociology, visual arts and women's studies).

To take advantage of the diverse experiences of the students, I employed a number of teaching strategies that cultivated students' interdependence and encouraged them to work together to generate ideas that they might not have had by themselves. Lecture-listen-take notes, brainstorming, small- and large-group discussions, case studies, role-playing, critical analysis of films, and problem solving all had a place in our classroom. I encouraged students to review course content and suggest ways in which the curriculum could be enriched. Their contributions through class presentations were incorporated into the course and legitimated as "new knowledge." I solicited students' input on how they wished to be evaluated and tried to develop collaborative skills among students within structures that privileged and rewarded individual effort.

At the same time, I attempted to be sensitive to, and actively encourage, multiple perspectives in the classroom through my choice of required readings and by facilitating the voicing of different perspectives on issues such as able-bodiedness, race, ethnicity, gender, marital status, sexuality, profession, religion and life stage. All these categories of identity and their complex intersections inform our relational positions, including our positions as students and professors.

By such means, the feminist classroom challenges the conventions of a university education, which traditionally has relied on models of the teacher as authority. Yet our classrooms remain within the larger, inherently hierarchical, university system. However successful we are in sharing the pedagogical platform, shifting the axes of power in the classroom and blurring the boundary between student and teacher by understanding that we can all learn from each other, ultimately the instructor is required to assess, to rank and to pass judgement. At the end of the year, I considered how individual students had progressed in consciousness and knowledge of issues and how they rated in comparison with others in the class. I tallied up grades, adjudged and assigned marks. The political impact of this structure on students and teachers is profound.

Even the physical environment of the classroom can hinder the feminist challenge to conventional academic structures. The seating arrangement in a classroom with fixed desks, chairs and lectern can subvert attempts to encourage critical discussions in small groups. Much of the work in "Women, Culture and Society" revolved around small-group discussions, role-playing exercises and paired work after an introductory lecture. Fixed seating arrangements presented a constraint for this kind of classroom work and required careful thinking about what kinds of roles were possible for students and teachers within the classroom.

My goal in "Women, Culture and Society" was to encourage students to reflect critically on what feminist perspectives offer to the discipline of anthropology as well as for thinking about their own learning processes. Such a process leads, I believe, to empowerment for the student. That students can be empowered to take a leading role in their own schooling is, to my mind, one of the key goals of feminist pedagogy. This aspect of feminist pedagogy has much in common with the liberating mandate of Paulo Freire's critical pedagogy. And as Freire stated in *A Pedagogy for Liberation* (Shor 1987, 46) "I cannot proclaim my liberating dream and in the next day be authoritarian in my relationships with the students."

The notion of empowerment in the classroom includes "both a psychological sense of personal control and concern with actual social influence, political power, and legal rights" (Riger 1993, 280) and is linked with mastery, control and agency at the level of the individual student. Ideally, the feminist classroom enables students to feel an individual sense of control over the processes of their own education or of "leading forth" (from the Latin *educere*, to lead out). Empowering students has been a major focus in my own teaching. At the same time, however, it must be acknowledged that while my students might develop a greater personal sense of control over course content and structure, the challenge to the larger university structures may be slight.

Silencing in the Classroom

Despite our best efforts to facilitate an open forum for discussion, issues of silencing in the feminist classroom can still be potent. The following quotations are anonymous feedback I received at the end of the 1992–93 academic year from two students in "Women, Culture and Society." The juxtaposition of these comments startlingly reveals the complexity of social dynamics in the classroom.

> Student one: This course defies description. There was almost no week that we had an actual lecture. First term I had six pages of notes, second term I had three pages of notes. If I wanted to have a polite conversation with friends I could save $500.00. [The professor] saw fit to mark politics rather than the answer to exams. Personal feelings interfere with her judgement. This is *not* a feminist course in any way…In the interest of brevity I will stop here. If I didn't have the politics of the university as a concern and my academic future involved I would have made a formal complaint.

> Student two: I thoroughly enjoyed the class, particularly the class presentations at the end, which served to "wrap-up" all that we had learned through the course of the year. I particularly enjoyed learning about "difference," "ethnocentrism" and "relativity." It is all too easy to get wrapped up in our own personal worlds that we can forget there are other perspectives in which we can view things. Also the discipline of feminist anthropology I find to be very encouraging in its approach to wholeness as opposed to the fragmenting disciplines that are traditionally practised.

The first student disputes the integrity of "my" classroom as a feminist classroom, thus calling into question a single or essential definition of feminism. I obviously did not conform to this person's expectations of a feminist instructor.[1] The alleged lack of lectures and the implied lack of instructor guidance during discussion both point to a lack of identifiable conventional structure, ostensibly a sorry failing of the course. The internalized need on the part of some students to see the teacher as the expert repository of knowledge and, concomitantly, to see texts as authoritative perpetuates a system of learning that feminist classrooms challenge. The first quote also highlights the vulnerability the student feels in lodging a complaint for fear of possible academic repercussions.

The second passage affirms the diversity of experiences and multiple perspectives represented within the classroom. The student salutes the class presentations as drawing together in a very real way a number of theoretical issues with which anthropologists often engage during the course of their work.

These quotations exhibit different stages of intellectual understanding of the contributions of feminist research to the discipline of anthropology, as well as anthropology's contributions to feminism. The first quotation, with its suggestion of a "difference in politics," might be from someone who brings to the course an understanding, for example, that the apparent pervasiveness of male dominance in many societies represents a universal conspiracy against the sisterhood of women. There is a clear ideological rift between this view and one that understands, from the cross-cultural literature, that women's status and roles can differ tremendously along race, class and other modes of social organization. The second quotation acknowledges these kinds of differences and how such differences make a difference.

The notion of the feminist classroom as a harmonious place where gender hierarchies, racial discrimination and class differences have been eradicated is an ideal. However, a number of feminist researchers have pointed out that such harmony often has been gained only through the silencing of certain voices in the classroom (Maher and Tetreault 1993, 125). The charge, "This is *not* a feminist course in any way," points directly, angrily and sadly to that silencing.

The feminist classroom aims to offer a protected environment for contesting silencing and encouraging full participation and collective debate. However, achieving this and seeking, at the same time, to listen to the "silences" there might be in the classroom are not easily negotiated matters. I am thinking here of three other anonymous student comments on a question posed midway through the year. (There were only three such comments from forty-two student reaction papers handed in that day.) In answer to the question, "Are there any things or activities that make you feel uncomfortable in class?" one student responded, "Talking about race and racist issues. As a white woman I feel that my opinion is not valued as much as others'. People of colour are listened to more carefully." Another wrote, "Discussions which ask for personal opinions make me uncomfortable because I feel you can't (I can't) really express how you feel without having the other members pounce on you negatively." The third: "Sometimes I feel as if I can't say something because I don't want to offend people in class."

Evidently, despite my attempts to encourage students to discuss issues and collectively build understanding, some students still felt silenced in the classroom. Manicom (1992) writes of this contradiction:

> If voices are contradictory and multiple and inscribed with dominant relations of oppression, then these relations are going to exist in the classroom. Questions demand to be asked: Who shares? Whose sharing is blocked? What is shared easily and what with difficulty? When is sharing empowering and when is it disempowering? (376)[2]

Sensitivity and skillful, careful negotiation are required when one person's experience challenges, or even violates, another's in the classroom. An instructor needs to assist students in developing active listening skills and the ability to provide appropriate feedback through role reversal (looking at an issue from the point of view of another) and by jointly defining and clarifying problems or conflicts.[3] By bringing these anonymous comments into the open, I was able to offer the class an opportunity to discuss why some people were feeling silenced and to work together to build a safer classroom environment for all. In the process, we were also able to explore broader issues of societal oppression.

The feedback I have received from my students has required ongoing self-scrutiny, interpretation and accountability. The classroom has become a good place for me to begin "to learn how processes and things about which we are not aware can, despite our unknowing, have 'felt' effects" (Currie 1992, 357).

Feminisms in the Classroom

"Women, Culture and Society" assessed the relevance of such well-worn cultural constructs as relativism, ethnocentrism, male, female, difference, agency, resistance and power. Without essentializing, we drew on students' experiences as well as on selected comparative readings to negotiate conflicting understandings of these cultural constructs. One of the major organizing principles of anthropology has long been the concept of cultural relativism; that is, that human behaviour and practices arise in the name of culture, conventionally defined as a shared and monolithic category.

Tensions between the feminist agenda of actively reevaluating in order to seek social change, while acknowledging the analytical usefulness of cultural relativism, are no more palpable than when course content covers issues around the genital excision of women. The different voices in the classroom and in the readings – accepting, enraged, shocked, pragmatic, puzzled, defensive – challenged our ideas about cultural relativism and consensus. Singular notions of "feminism" have now been replaced by "feminisms." Third World feminisms are a clear example of this. Even within North America, the proactive expressions of feminisms are not homogeneous, and we need to acknowledge this and make efforts not to silence this difference as we debate our understandings of different social practices. The strength of the feminist classroom lies in its ability to work through such issues together creatively, to point to inequities, to debate in a protected sphere the precise nature of those inequities and to clarify the possibilities for change.

More importantly, feminist classrooms specialize in the collective processes of sense-making, although the structures within which they operate might not wholly support such processes. The value of rigorously integrating personal knowledge with the experiences of others and with comparative readings is also central to feminist pedagogy in anthropology. Thus, individual empowerment grows within the collectivity of the whole class. Feminist literature on consciousness-raising (Reinharz 1983) has debated the understanding of empowerment as political and collective, not just instrumental and individualistic (Reinelt 1994, 688). Student empowerment increases as a sense of community develops, where we can think of "community as a place, community as relationships, and community as collective political force" (Chavis and Wandersman 1990, 56).

Another concern of feminist pedagogy is to encourage reflection by students and teachers on ways to change oppressive practices within and outside of the classroom. Manicom (1992) suggests that the central question for those practising feminist pedagogy is, "Is what I am doing as teacher enhancing our capacity for transformative practice? In my particular circumstances, what kind of teaching and learning has the most potential to develop a collective capacity to engage in transformative feminist practice?" (383) These questions have relevance beyond teaching, for example, in such fields as research, writing, interpreting, mediation and administration.

Notes

This article is based in part on a paper originally presented at the Canadian Anthropological Association Annual Meeting, Vancouver, May 6, 1994, for "Women's Work in Canadian Anthropology." I would like to thank Mune Arrutia and Shelly Romalis for their helpful comments on earlier drafts of the paper.

1. Hoodfar (1992) writes as a minority teacher in the classroom: "My acknowledging the inequalities in power relations between students and teachers is seen not as an attempt to point out institutionalized inequalities but as my not being confident as a teacher or as compensation for my lack of knowledge. In making room for dialogue, I am seen not as a liberal teacher experimenting with or advocating a different pedagogy, but as someone lacking experience in controlling a class, or worse yet, as someone too lazy to deliver more conventional lectures" (311–12).

2. Several reflective studies discuss how the feminist classroom can operate to oppress students. Hillyer Davis (1995) and Weiler (1988) have looked at how their classrooms privileged feminist perspectives over other voices.

3. Ways in which teachers and students can begin such negotiation are examined in the article by Martindale, Shea and Major (1992).

References

Alcoff, Linda. 1988. Cultural feminism versus post-structuralism: The identity crisis in feminist theory. Signs: *Journal of Women in Culture and Society* 13: 405–36.

Chavis, David M. and Abraham Wandersman. 1990. Sense of community in the urban environment: A catalyst for participation and community development. *American Journal of Community Psychology* 18: 55–81.

Currie, Dawn H. 1992. Subject-ivity in the classroom: Feminism meets academe. *Canadian Journal of Education* 17: 341–64.

Haraway, Donna. 1992. Situated knowledges: The science question in feminism and the privilege of partial perspective. *Feminist Studies* 14: 575–99.

Hillyer Davis, B. 1995. Teaching the feminist minority. In *Gender subjects: The dynamics of feminist teaching*, M. Culley and C. Portuges (eds.), 245–52. Boston: Routledge and Kegan Paul.

Hoodfar, Homa. 1992. Feminist anthropology and critical pedagogy: The anthropology of classrooms' excluded voices. *Canadian Journal of Education* 17: 303–20.

Maher, Frances A. and Mary Kay Tetreault. 1993. Frames of positionality: Constructing meaningful dialogues about gender and race. *Anthropological Quarterly* 66: 118–26.

Manicom, Ann. 1992. Feminist pedagogy: Transformations, standpoints and politics. *Canadian Journal of Education* 17: 365–89.

Martindale, K., S. Shea and L. Major. 1992. Articulating the difficulties in teaching/learning feminist cultural theory. *Radical Teacher* 39: 9–14.

Reinelt, Claire. 1994. Fostering empowerment, building community: The challenge for state-funded feminist organizations. *Human Relations* 47: 685–705.

Reinharz, Shulamit. 1983. Feminist research methodology groups: Origins, forms, functions. In *Feminist revisions: What has been and might be*, V. Patraka and L. Tilly (eds.), 197–228. Ann Arbor: University of Michigan.

Riger, Stephanie. 1993. What's wrong with empowerment? *American Journal of Community Psychology* 21: 279–92.

Shor, Ira. 1987. *A pedagogy for liberation: Dialogues on transforming education*. South Hadley: Bergin & Garvey.

Weiler, K. 1988. *Women teaching for change: Gender, class and power*. South Hadley: Bergin & Garvey.

Other Recommended Reading

Women's Studies Quarterly 21 (fall/winter 1993). This issue is devoted to the theme of feminist pedagogy.

Belenky, Mary Field *et al.* 1986. *Women's ways of knowing: The development of self, voice and mind*. New York: Basic Books.

Briskin, Linda. 1990. *Feminist pedagogy: Teaching and learning liberation*. Toronto: Division of Social Science, York University.

—— and Rebecca Priegert Coulter. 1992. Feminist pedagogy: Challenging the normative. *Canadian Journal of Education* 17: 247–63.

Cully, M. and C. Portuges (eds.), 1985. *Gendered subjects: The dynamics of feminist teaching*. Boston: Routledge and Kegan Paul.

Gabriel, Ayala H. 1989. Politics, ideology, and scholarship: Teaching anthropology in women's studies. *Urban Anthropology and Studies of Cultural Systems and World Economic Development* 18: 111–20.

Lather, Patti. 1991. *Getting smart: Feminist research and pedagogy with/in the postmodern*. New York: Routledge, Chapman and Hall.

Luke, Carmen and Jennifer Gore. 1992. *Feminist and critical pedagogy*. New York: Routledge, Chapman and Hall.

MacDermid, Shelley M. *et al.* 1992. Feminist teaching: Effective education. *Family Relations* 41: 31–38.

Morgen, Sandra. 1990. Challenging the politics of exclusion. *Education and Urban Society* 22: 393–401.

Heterosexism in the Classroom

Leslie Green

Heterosexism is to sexual diversity what racism is to ethnic diversity. Whether rooted in hatred, fear or ignorance, whether overt or covert, heterosexism devalues the lives of lesbians, gay men and bisexual people. Unlawful discrimination, violence, harassment, etc., raise serious issues beyond the scope of this article, though, sadly, not always beyond the experience of our students. Here, however, I want to consider how instructors might satisfy more than just our legal obligations to ensure that the classroom is a secure learning environment for all, one that respects diversity while allowing for vigorous debate.

Invisibility and Stigma

Owing to their authority, instructors must take some responsibility for the climate in the classroom. Obviously, we must ensure that our own behaviour does not poison the atmosphere, but – and this more difficult – we must not allow the behaviour of others to do so either. It is always a delicate matter knowing when, and how, to exercise control. Heterosexism is easier to avert than to stop, but this can be trickier than averting sexism or racism.

The experience of gay students differs not only from that of the majority, but even from that of other minorities, for they are not only stigmatized but are also largely invisible. The stigma is evident: homosexuality provokes in many people feelings of disgust and more general anxieties about sex. Yet for gay people, sexuality plays the same roles that it does for straight people. To be hated, discriminated against or ridiculed on the grounds of one's capacity for love can be profoundly injurious. Consequently, many gay people keep their orientation secret, at least to some degree. This is particularly easy in a large, commuter university in which students' social lives are often conducted away from campus. But while invisibility might afford some individuals protection against direct homophobia, it brings costs of its own and reinforces the view that gay people don't exist.

75

Two other things can distinguish the situation of gay students. The university years are often their first opportunity to come to terms with their identity, to explore romance and so on. And second, because their parents are usually straight, gay students might at the same time experience considerable stress with their families of origin. While members of some other minorities can hope for family support in coping with the stigma of racial or cultural difference, gay students often have to construct their own support networks.

The combination of stigma and invisibility has important consequences that instructors need to understand. For one thing, the natural inhibition that even the prejudiced feel about ignoring or insulting marginalized groups in their presence is here considerably attenuated. For example, people who would never make racist remarks in front of Asian students feel free to say the most astonishing things in the (unrecognized) presence of gay students or colleagues. And gay students can be less apt to defend their own interests when that involves being open about their orientation, a step the costs of which they might not yet be able to bear.

The following suggestions, then, are derived from my own experience in confronting such issues in teaching a large, undergraduate course about sexuality. Though they are summarized as a handful of "rules," each obviously admits of exceptions and can be applied only with common sense.

1. Assume nothing. Do not teach as if you are in the presence of thirty or three hundred straight people. You are not. Between 5 and 10 per cent of your students are not straight; about one in four has a gay family member. After all, if you are a Christian you would hardly operate on the assumption that all your students are, too. The same principle operates here.

2. Respect the power of language. Our first concern is the matter of content. Plainly, one must avoid overtly homophobic terms such as "fag" and "dyke"; gay people might use these words with each other, but unless you are gay, you should not. Also avoid near-homophobic remarks that stigmatize effeminacy in men or masculinity in women. And where possible, use neutral terms such as "partner" instead of husband and wife, etc.

There is, however, no generally accepted term that covers lesbians, gay men and bisexual people. "Homosexuals" is widely regarded as offensive and dated, suggesting as it does a discredited medical model of sexual diversity. "Queer" has some currency among the young and radical, but can sound odd coming from the middle-aged and tenured; nor is it fully purged of its stigma. Many women think that "gays" emphasizes the male experience. Some bisexual people identify as gay, others do not. So there is no easy solution. Perhaps it is best to avoid general categories when you can, and when you can't, try "gay people." With individuals, ordinary courtesy should govern, as it would with proper names: if Margaret says, "Call me Peggy," you should; if she says "Call me Margaret," you should not call her Peggy. Likewise, if she prefers "lesbian" to "gay," use it. Under no circumstances insist on a label you think scientifically accurate or politically correct if to do so causes offense.

Second, there is a matter of style or tone. You and your students are entitled to hold, discuss or defend any scientific, moral, aesthetic or religious views about sexuality. In some courses, these views will themselves be the objects of critical discussion. But it is crucial to be able to pursue such discussion in a way that does not seek to undermine the self-esteem of others and does not cross the line from discussion into the realm of preaching, harassing or insulting. This line, however, is admittedly fuzzy, and its location is itself a matter open to discussion. My suggestion (it is nothing more) is that straight people should assume the line is a bit nearer than they are inclined to believe, and thus err on the side of sensitivity to others, while gay people would assume it is a little further than they are inclined to believe, and thus enter discussions with a presumption of their colleagues' good faith.

The best way to set the tone in class is by example. If, however, it becomes necessary to correct students in these matters, it should be done, in the first instance, privately. Young straight men, in particular, often feel a need to perform in class in ways that reinforce their gender identity. Homophobic remarks and attitudes are common in male adolescence (when "fag" is just a generalized term of abuse) but tend to moderate as young men become more comfortable in their own gender role and more secure about their own sexuality. But a public upbraiding never hastens this process if it is already delayed.

3. Review your discipline. Consider whether your own subject allows for a greater attention to the interests and concerns of lesbian, gay and bisexual people. Obviously the possibilities are greater in a course on "Sociology of the Family" than in "Quantified Modal Logic." But in practically every subject there have been important gay writers. Acknowledging that the philosopher Wittgenstein, poet Elizabeth Bishop, composer Benjamin Britten, writer Virginia Woolf, economist Maynard Keynes or mathematician Alan Turing were none of them straight can help break a powerful and imposed silence. There is often less need to enlarge the canon than there is to "out" it. As Eve Sedgwick (1990) writes, "not only have there been a gay Socrates, Shakespeare, and Proust, but...their names are Socrates, Shakespeare, and Proust" (52). Make that clear without making it an issue.

4. Be out. If you are lesbian, gay or bisexual, be out on campus to the extent that it is safe for you to do so. If you are straight, try not to be ostentatious about it, and if you are mistaken for gay don't be offended. This is harder than it sounds; merely acknowledging the existence of gay people, let alone defending them, leaves any instructor open to speculation about his or her own orientation, and could well attract hostility.

5. Do not out students or colleagues. No exceptions are allowed in the case of students, in view of the power relationship involved. They are entitled to their privacy and it is easy to underestimate the risks to which one exposes them in announcing

their orientation. That, too, is the best general policy with respect to colleagues (though here I am inclined to acknowledge an exception in self-defence: a closeted gay homophobe who is also in a position of power should not be allowed to persecute others from behind the closet door). In general, gossipiness reinforces stigma, so don't give in to it. When asked by others whether so-and-so is gay the best response is, "Why don't you ask him?"

6. Support your lesbian, gay and bisexual students, especially if they are just coming out. If you are straight, bear in mind that your own experiences as a student were probably very different. If you are gay, be prepared to listen, but exercise caution about being a friend and guard against support overload. If they want peer support, you can refer students to support groups that exist on your campus or in your community. On the York University campus, students can contact the Transgender, Bisexual, Lesbian and Gay Alliance. Off campus, students can contact Lesbian, Gay and Bisexual Youth Toronto or Lesbian Peer Support.

References

Sedgwick, Eve. 1990. *Epistemology of the closet.* Berkeley: University of California Press.

DisABILITY in the Classroom: The Forgotten Dimension of Diversity?

Sarah Clarke

I'm a perpetual student – or so they tell me, and with three degrees under my belt and a fourth on the way they could be right! My studies, punctuated by five years in full employment, span two continents, three disciplines and undergraduate through postgraduate education. I have experienced the highs and lows of a multitude of teaching formats: lectures, small groups, research seminars, "live" projects, laboratory work, simulations and case studies, and a variety of assessment methods: essays, reports, individual presentations, group projects, research papers, articles, reviews, dissertations and theses.

After all this I think I can put my hand on my heart and say what works...for me. And this is the crucial point: I'm a hands-on, practical person. I learn from pictures, images and metaphors. Give me a mix of small group projects and individual research papers any day. But how do YOU learn? Do you prefer to read or write, speak or listen? Do you like to mull things over one at a time or amass great amounts of information? Are numbers or words your thing? Which media trigger your creative ability – books, films, artwork or hands-on activities? I can guess, but how can I know? Do you see, do you hear, do you write, do you speak?

I recently attended a workshop on diversity in the classroom. We discussed how we might deal with issues of equality and discrimination, and how we could foster an atmosphere that was sensitive to the rights of all students to participate and learn regardless of their race, gender, sexual orientation, age or religion. We did not question whether our teaching was accessible, either physically or psychologically, to all students regardless of their (dis)ability. Interestingly, in *Tools for Teaching* (Gross 1993), a comprehensive resource book on teaching strategies, disability is singled out as something to be "accommodated," whereas race, ethnicity and gender are treated as issues of "[d]iversity and complexity in the classroom." I find it strange that this should be so, given the widely documented instances of discrimination experienced by people with disabilities in education, employment and society in general.[1]

Several years ago I was involved in a project to develop a computer-based training facility to be run by, and for, disabled people in Manchester, England. I was asked to convene a workshop to discuss and develop ideas for the scheme. It was attended by around thirty people, including representatives of governmental agencies, local health departments and non-governmental organizations run by and for disabled people. After seeking advice from many disabled people, I worked through a sign-language interpreter, prepared tape and braille copies of my presentation materials beforehand, arranged for note-takers and recorders and structured the day so that there was time for everyone to participate in the workshop by whatever means. This was an eye-opening experience for me and through it I was able to glimpse what a fully accessible workshop might look like. It struck me that few, if any, of the courses, lectures and seminars I had attended had incorporated the dimension of accessibility. Disability was certainly the forgotten dimension of diversity.

As a volunteer with the Office for Persons with Disabilities at York, where I assisted students with their research, proctored exams and acted as a note-taker, I further came to realize that the excellent and comprehensive services provided by such offices[2] do not, in and of themselves, necessarily make teaching more accessible. For example, I assisted a visually impaired student with a research project. The task was to write a paper based on fifteen self-selected papers and books. My role was to help identify material that would be read onto tape by another volunteer. It rapidly became clear that there was insufficient time for the task and that the results of this assignment would depend to a great extent on my ability to select, skim read, summarize and discuss with the student the relevance of each article to the topic of the paper. It would be too late to change our minds once the material had been taped. Considering the haphazard way in which I stumble across references for my assignments, it was clear that the student was at a disadvantage, and not for any lack of ability.

Another issue emerged when I was a proctor for an exam for the same student. On this occasion, I was asked to read the questions and write down the student's oral responses. Although twice the "normal" time had been given, it did not compensate for the inappropriateness of a written exam for this student: it was quite remarkable to watch an essay being formulated in "mid-air."

These experiences raise many questions about the degree to which our teaching styles, course structures, assignments and assessment procedures cater to the diverse learning styles and (dis)abilities of all students. While it might be impossible to anticipate every eventuality, unless basic accessibility issues are considered at the course-design stage and in the shaping of teaching techniques, it might be difficult to make ad-hoc, after-the-fact adjustments. Moreover, adjustments might be totally inappropriate; providing extra time and the assistance of a reader or note-taker or removing certain physical barriers will not necessarily enable students to participate fully in the learning experience in the classroom or to learn in a manner that is relevant to their particular learning style.

As instructors, what is our role in the classroom? I believe it is to facilitate students' learning: to launch students on a voyage of discovery that includes encouraging them to explore their particular learning styles and helping them to learn how to learn. This is perhaps the most useful lesson I have taken away from my undergraduate and graduate studies. It is in marked contrast with our tendency to prescribe how students should learn by formalizing virtually every aspect of the learning experience in the classroom. And yet the classroom is only one of many sites of learning: we learn from our peers, our family and friends, in the workplace, in groups, alone, on the bus, in the park. What this implies, therefore, is a need to move away from teaching styles based on total teacher control and towards methods that afford learners control over the way they learn (Herman 1981, 19). In this manner, the teacher is a facilitator of learning, a learning partnership is engendered between teacher and student and each has equal responsibility for learning.

Consequently, disability need not – and should not – be viewed as something to be accommodated, often at the last minute, as the need arises. A little forethought and flexibility will go a long way to creating an inclusive classroom atmosphere, sensitive to the learning styles of all students. There are many ways of bringing about this transformation. A simple first step is to use a variety of teaching methods, such as group discussions, lectures, projects, individual assignments and presentations, and an assortment of assessment options, such as different types of written or oral exams, individual or group papers or presentations and self- or peer appraisal. Along with this, it should be remembered that teaching materials should be available in, or easily translated into, different formats.

With increasing diversity in the classroom, there will be an even greater need in the future for students to choose from a wider spectrum of educational activity (Hiemstra and Sisco 1990). A potential route for dealing with this challenge is offered by Malcolm Knowles (1975), who has developed an approach predicated on a fundamental shift from teacher as controller to teacher as facilitator.[3] Underlying Knowles's "learning contracts" is the assumption that adults learn on their own initiative more deeply and permanently than they do when they learn by being taught. A learning contract between teacher and learner enables learners to blend the "imposed" requirements of the institution with their own personal goals and objectives, to choose their own ways of realizing them and to measure their own progress towards achieving them. According to Knowles (1989), "[learning contracts] are the most effective devices I have yet discovered for helping learners organize their learning in a systematic, individualised, self-paced, process-structured way" (45–50).

In a learning contract, the learner is required to negotiate with the teacher a set of learning objectives, the methods they will use to meet those objectives and the evidence on which they will be assessed and by whom. Some illustrations of the types of activities that learners might choose and the key elements of a learning contract are shown in Table 1. Most students (and teachers) will not have encountered this mode of learning before. Consequently, people should not be thrown into self-directed

Table 1. Relationships Between Objectives, Methods and Evidence

Competency Objectives	Methods for Learning	Evidence
KNOWLEDGE Generalizations about experience; internalization of information	Lecture, television, debate, dialogue, interview, symposium, panel group interview, colloquium, motion picture, slide film, recording, book-based discussion, reading, programmed instruction	Reports of knowledge acquired, as in essays, examinations, oral presentations, audio-visual presentations
UNDERSTANDING Application of information and generalizations	Audience participation, demonstration, dramatization, Socratic discussion, problem-solving project, case method, simulation game	Examples of utilization of knowledge in solving problems, as simulation game, proposal of action project, research project with conclusion and recommendation
SKILLS Incorporating new ways of performing through practice	Skill practice exercise, role playing, participatory case, simulation game, training group, non-verbal exercise, drill coaching	Performance exercise with rating by observers
ATTITUDES Adoption of new feelings through greater success with them than with old feelings	Experience-sharing discussion, sensitivity training, role playing, case method, simulation game, participatory case, group therapy, counseling	Attitudinal rating scales, performance in role playing, simulation game, sensitivity group, etc. with feedback from observers
VALUES Adoption and priority arrangements of beliefs	Value-clarification exercise, biographical reading, lecture, debate, symposium, colloquium, dramatization, role playing, simulation game, sensitivity training	Value rating scale, performance in value clarification group, simulation game, role playing, etc. with feedback from observers

Adapted from H. Kerwood, "Notes on Contract Learning," OBIR 6410 course notes, Schulich School of Business, York University, 1994.

learning with the assurance that they will work it out. Traditionally, students have been told what they are to learn, how they are to learn it and whether they have learned it. For some students it will be a stressful process to be asked to direct their own learning. Some exercises and strategies can help: exercises that build relationships between teacher and learner, skill-building exercises to develop the ability to diagnose individual learning needs, step-by-step descriptions of how to go about drafting a contract, and inviting learners to raise any unresolved questions about self-directed learning. Through these strategies many fears and barriers can be overcome (Knowles 1989 and 1975).

An individualized approach to learning opens up the classroom to students of all abilities, whatever their race, gender, sexual orientation, age or religion. At a time of increasing intolerance of individual differences, a flexible and open style of teaching can serve to enable all students, regardless of their (dis)ability, to participate fully in learning experiences both in the classroom and in society as a whole. I look forward to a time when disability is no longer the forgotten dimension of diversity.

Notes

I would like to thank Hazel Kerwood and members of the Centre for the Support of Teaching at York University for their helpful comments and assistance. The views expressed herein should be attributed only to the author.

1. See, for example, Barnes (1991) and Hahn (1985).

2. For more information about the support and resources provided at York, refer to the *Faculty Resource and Awareness Guide: Teaching Students With Disabilities* (York University, 1999), available from the Office for Persons With Disabilities.

3. Self-directed learning is an idea not only propounded by contemporary educators but also by philosophers of earlier centuries. "[T]o Socrates and Plato, teachers were mere midwives who might help youth give birth to his soul" (Berte 1975, 8).

References

Barnes, C. 1991. *Disabled people in Britain and discrimination: A case for anti-discrimination legislation.* London: Hurst and Co.

Berte, N.R. 1975. *Individualizing education through contract learning.* Alabama: University of Alabama Press.

Davis, B. Gross. 1993. *Tools for teaching.* San Francisco: Jossey-Bass.

Hahn, H. 1985. Disability policy and the problem of discrimination. *American Behavioral Scientist* 28 (3): 291–318.

Hiemstra, R. and B. Sisco. 1990. *Individualizing instruction.* San Francisco: Jossey-Bass.

Herman, R., (ed.) 1981. *The design of self-directed learning.* Toronto: Ontario Institute for Studies in Education.

Kerwood, H. 1994. Notes on contract learning. OBIR course notes, Faculty of Administrative Studies, York University.

Knowles, M.S. 1975. *Self-directed learning: A guide for learners and teachers.* Chicago: Associated Press, Follett Publishing.

——. 1989. Everything you wanted to know from Malcolm Knowles (and weren't afraid to ask). *Training* 26 (August): 45–50.

York University. 1999 (revised edition) *Faculty resource and awareness guide: Teaching students with disabilities.* Toronto: York University, Advisory Committee for Persons with Special Needs and Division of Student Affairs.

Teaching Students with Learning Disabilities

Marc Wilchesky and Margaret Willis

Individuals with a range of intellectual abilities who receive, process or express information in ways that are different from those used by most other individuals are described as having "learning disabilities" (LDS). University students with LDS can have average or above-average intellectual abilities, yet experience difficulties in one or more of the following areas: perceiving, listening, speaking, reading, writing, calculating or spelling. They might lack skills in organization and some can experience problems with social interaction. However, to succeed academically, many students with LDS have had to become expert problem solvers, compensating for the obstacles to their learning by being persistent and developing creative coping strategies. In our experience at York University, many students with LDS are among the most highly motivated learners on campus – otherwise they would have given up long ago.

Students with LDS often develop unique ways of learning effectively, yet they share the frustration of coping with a disability that is virtually invisible and often misunderstood. A learning disability is a weakness in the central processing system that should be considered along with the strengths and talents of each individual. It is NOT a form of mental retardation, emotional disturbance or laziness.

The cause of LDS is not clearly understood but is generally presumed to be an identifiable or inferred central nervous system dysfunction or difference. Causes can stem from genetic factors, biochemical variations, maturational lags in the development of various psychological processes, events in the perinatal period or other events resulting in neurological impairment.

What Factors Indicate the Presence of Learning Disabilities?

Students with learning disabilities usually have areas of difficulty that contrast markedly with other areas in which they excel. Some might be able to express themselves well orally, but have extreme difficulty articulating their thoughts on paper (hence, their written assignments can lack organization and contain poor spelling, improper grammar and inappropriate punctuation). Others might be proficient at mathematics, yet be unable to read at a satisfactory rate and experience comprehension problems under time-limited conditions. Often students with LDS demonstrate their capability to understand abstract ideas in discussion, but seem to have limited ability organizing their thoughts on standard-format examinations. Because of auditory processing difficulties, some students with LDS have difficulty following a sequence of complex instructions or class lectures. They might be unable to take lecture notes effectively because of language processing problems or fine-motor coordination difficulties.

While these manifestations do not automatically signal that the student has an LD, if you notice a student experiencing some of these difficulties, it might be helpful to advise them of the support services available on your campus. Rather than suggest that they "get tested for learning disabilities," you could encourage them to meet with a counselor to discuss the nature of their learning problem. This would be a first step towards determining the type of suitable support. At York University, students who indicate to an instructor that they have a learning disability are encouraged to make an appointment with the Coordinator of the Learning Disabilities Program. We should, of course, respect the wishes of those students who prefer to "go it alone."

What Can the Instructor Do?

By the time students with LDS have reached post-secondary education, they already have a good grasp of what works best for them. As the teacher, your work is greatly simplified if you allow yourself to become the learner of the student's needs by taking a few minutes to inquire what methods of teaching and learning have been effective to date. Once a learning difference or disability has been identified and diagnosed, students can be taught in the regular classroom setting with no disruption to the learning situation.

Methods used to teach those with differences in learning styles are not really unique. Instructors must become more conscious of *how* success is achieved in communication with individual students with LDS and apply this in the larger class setting. Occasional verbal comprehension checks at the class's end will verify that the method has succeeded and that the learning disabled student has received information accurately. Generally, these good teaching strategies benefit all parties involved in the learning situation.

Once the strategy has been established, the instructor can meet the student's needs in a way that will enhance the whole class's learning experience. For example, if Lee needs to have all assignments spelled out on paper, the whole group will gain clarity when written assignments accompany your orally presented explanation. If Pat needs three months' lead time for the tape-recording of class reading materials, the whole class might benefit from the professor's early organization and selection of course readings. If Leslie requires paraphrasing of a course task, everyone in the group might benefit from the reworded explanation. If Jesse can focus better on class discussions without noise from the halls, all students might be less distracted with the lecture-room door closed. If Casey can grasp an exam question only by hearing it, maybe the whole class would comprehend the task better if it were read aloud. If Alex needs assistance with organizing data, perhaps the whole group would gain from a review of essay structure.

Helping a student with different learning needs usually requires only minor adjustments, yet the awareness of the problem and the ensuing changes can make or break that individual's ability to participate successfully in the post-secondary academic setting. On occasion, the only thing students with LDS might need is extended time for an essay or exam as their processing of information can be extraordinarily time-consuming. You might be asked to accept written material that has unusual spellings if a student with an LD has not had the opportunity to use a spell-checker or the assistance of an editor or tutor. Some students are unable to sequence letters in standard formats and need help with orthography. Others confuse words and need help sorting out homonyms. These students should not be asked to submit first drafts of any work unless the instructor has patience and tolerance for deciphering unusual letter sequences or concepts. Individualized assistance from an on-campus writing instructor or a private tutor can help such students submit organized, orthographically standardized works. At York, writing centres provide individual assistance in critical skills, assignment analysis and writing instruction for students.

Generally speaking, good teaching practices for students with LDS are good teaching practices for any student. With this in mind, a few suggestions are offered here.

1. Provide a detailed course syllabus several weeks prior to the beginning of class that outlines the expectations, topics, technical vocabulary and evaluation procedures for the course.
2. Choose well-organized texts with "reader aids" and available study guides.
3. If possible, begin each class with a review of material previously presented and an outline of topics to be discussed. Summarize important points at the end of class, perhaps using the chalkboard, overhead projector or written hand-outs.
4. Try to speak clearly facing the class and make use of audio-visual aids to emphasize important points and to explain unusual terminology. Writing and printing on the chalkboard or overhead projector should be large and legible.
5. Permit the use of tape recorders in class.
6. Allow time for questions and clarification.
7. Provide study questions that indicate the relative importance of course content as well as the format for possible exam questions.
8. Encourage students to form study groups (See Coulthard; Section VI), share class notes and get assistance when needed.
9. Explain all class assignments clearly, both orally and in writing, noting deadlines. Allow sufficient time for completion and time extensions where necessary.

10. Allow reasonable accommodation[1] in evaluation procedures, such as: extra time to complete exams; a reader to read exam questions to the student; use of a word processor with spell-checker; separate exam room free from distraction; alternative format evaluations if possible.

Notes

1. The Learning Disabilities Program at York will recommend the appropriate accommodations based on a review of the student's psycho-educational report and will assist faculty in the implementation of alternative evaluation procedures. All tests and exams can be written under the supervision of the Learning Disabilities Program provided that sufficient notice is given.

Avoiding the Retrofitted Classroom: Strategies for Teaching Students with Disabilities

Nancy Johnston

For nearly two decades, advocacy organizations, students and university teachers have been working to remodel post-secondary institutions because they agree that equal access to education for students with disabilities is a right, not a privilege. The inclusion of persons with disabilities under human rights codes and under employment equity legislation has prompted institutions of higher education to improve the physical access to campuses for students with disabilities, particularly for those with mobility impairments, medical disabilities and visual impairments. Guaranteeing that students can enter a library or lecture hall has been, and continues to be, a primary focus of human and financial resources.

Spurred by complaints and requests from individuals, advocacy organizations and campus advisory committees, administrators have hired architects and contractors to retrofit or upgrade campus facilities. Freight elevators have been refurbished for passenger use, entrances have been equipped with automatic door openers and washroom stalls have been enlarged for wheelchair access. Despite the expense and the sometimes inadequate results of retrofitting existing campus buildings, no one would deny its importance as a preliminary step to making campuses more physically accessible. Nonetheless, retrofitting is obviously inappropriate in the planning of new buildings where equal access for all students can be incorporated into architectural plans before foundations are laid.

As university teachers, we can be more proactive in creating an equitable educational experience for students with disabilities. Our increased disability awareness is essential to the integration and success of our students. Rather than simply retrofitting the classroom, or addressing isolated concerns as they arise, we can sensitize ourselves to disability issues when we design our courses or prepare for the first class. By making ourselves aware of disability issues and the rights of our students, we can better facilitate a teaching environment that ensures the full participation of all students. Pedagogical and curricular foundations can be laid with the needs of students with disabilities in mind.

We can begin by addressing a number of questions related to course development, classroom management, student rights, resources and faculty support services.

1. In what ways can I make my course more accessible to all students?

You will not have to make a special case for students with disabilities if you build some flexibility into your course requirements. Review all your course materials. Are there hidden academic or educational barriers that might affect persons with specific disabilities? For instance, if you use films and video, do you know if they are close-captioned for hearing-impaired students? Are scripts of these films available? If field trips or oral class participation are emphasized, can you accommodate students with mobility impairments or students who are hard of hearing? If not, are there alternative course materials or assignments you could assign that would still enrich the learning experience?

2. Is my teaching environment (classroom, laboratory or lecture hall) physically accessible to students with mobility impairments?

Examine your teaching environment before classes begin. This will help you anticipate student difficulties before they arise. Visit the classroom and lecture hall to assess whether the arrangement or number of desks will permit the easy movement of a wheelchair or scooter. Have wheelchair-accessible tables been provided in the lecture hall? Such a visit can serve a dual purpose. If you incorporate innovative teaching techniques, such as small-group learning, in your classes, you will be able to ensure that the classroom is appropriate for your other pedagogical practices. In addition, a nominally accessible classroom that no longer accommodates the free movement of a wheelchair or scooter – perhaps because of too many chairs or bolted tables – could be a fire hazard. Contact the appropriate support service office as soon as possible to correct any problems.

3. How can I facilitate a good teaching environment for students with disabilities?

From your introductory class, you can create a teaching environment that allows students minimal anxiety about disclosing their learning needs. Respect students' decisions about whether to disclose the nature of their disabilities and accessibility needs, either with their instructor or the appropriate support service officer. To facilitate this process, you can incorporate information about special services for students with diverse disabilities into your first introductory lecture or course hand-outs. Since many students with disabilities might be justifiably reticent to expose the nature of a medical problem or disability before their peers, announce your willingness to meet privately or during your office hours with those students who request some accommodation of their physical or learning disabilities. Be prepared to refer these students to the appropriate special needs offices for professional services and counseling.

4. What else can I do to facilitate the full participation of students with disabilities in the classroom?

Many common strategies used to facilitate better learning opportunities for students with disabilities improve communication for the entire class. Students with learning disabilities and hard-of-hearing students are not the only ones who benefit when you improve classroom communication. For instance, speaking slowly and carefully ensures that all students understand classroom procedures. Facing students when you speak, especially when using the board, promotes more attentive engagement. Encouraging students to speak one at a time in class discussions develops their interactive skills. Clarifying your class requirements by providing oral and written outlines ensures that all students are equally aware of class fundamentals. As well, adopting inclusive strategies will prevent you from drawing unnecessary attention to the accessibility needs of particular students. Familiarize yourself with some of the common assistive devices, such as FM systems or the support role that note-takers and oral or sign language interpreters can play in the classroom. Most special needs offices have educational and introductory materials for students and university teachers. If you can demonstrate some familiarity and comfort with disability issues, your students can emulate your behaviour and interact appropriately with individuals with other learning needs.

5. What are my students' rights?

Under the Ontario Human Rights Code, and in most academic plans or mission statements, students with disabilities are entitled to equal access to support services necessary to obtain an equitable education, and to become integrated members of the campus community. For example, the mission statement, senate policies and academic plans of York University and most academic institutions encourage, at least in principle, equal access to education for all individuals. To qualify for these services, students are obligated to provide any requested confidential documentation to the appropriate special needs office. These offices are frequently responsible for informing instructors of services and special devices that can be arranged for their students.

Inquiries also might originate in the classroom. As university teachers, we are obligated to comply with all reasonable requests from students for accommodations that will enable their full participation in the classroom. Students commonly request:[1]

- extension of deadlines when the need is substantiated by medical documentation
- willingness to use assistive devices or auxiliary aids (for example, instructors might be requested to wear portable fm systems by hearing-impaired students)
- permission to audio-tape lectures
- permission to use oral and visual language interpreters and manual or computerized note-takers in the classroom.

University teachers will need to contact the appropriate special needs offices for assistance if students request

- adaptive testing environments that require special equipment or facilities
- video-taped lectures
- special seating or wheelchair-accessible tables
- adjustments to lighting or ventilation.

6. What resources are available for students and teachers?

For specific information on diverse disabilities issues, you should contact your institution's special needs office, faculty support services, student affairs office or library. Publications distributed by the federal and provincial governments, the Canadian Hearing Society, the Advocacy Resource Centre for the Handicapped in Toronto and various charitable organizations can provide suggestions and guidelines for teachers. Reference materials for university teachers, such as Barbara Gross Davis's *Tools for Teaching*, also offer information on academic accommodations for students with disabilities.

Conclusion

Accessibility is based on the rights of students, not an appeal to a sense of charity or ethics. When students request special services, they are exercising their basic right to educational access under provincial legislation and under most universities' academic plans. As the title of this article suggests, we should strive to find a solution to the "retrofit" model of teaching students with disabilities. Too often students have to wait for us to find a solution to their "problem." Too often they do not take courses or drop courses when they are uncertain that their needs will be met. To provide an equitable education, we should take the initiative and familiarize ourselves with relevant services, policies, adaptive equipment and academic procedures. As university teachers, we are required to comply with all reasonable requests by our students for accommodation. As committed instructors we can assume this challenge willingly and with imagination.

Notes

1. Adapted from the *Faculty Resource and Awareness Guide: Teaching Students With Disabilities* (York University 1999), developed by ACCESS York (Advisory Committee for Persons with Special Needs) and the Division of Student Affairs. The guide provides a comprehensive explanation of support programs and services, practical guidelines for supporting persons with disabilities, and lists of organizations and support offices available at both the Keele and Glendon campuses.

References

Davis, Barbara Gross. 1993. *Tools for teaching.* San Francisco: Jossey-Bass.

York University. 1999 (revised edition). *Faculty resource and awareness guide: Teaching students with disabilities.* Toronto: York University, Advisory Committee for Persons with Special Needs and Division of Student Affairs.

Adult Students

Leslie Sanders

What constitutes good teaching? What attitudes, strategies and methods best promote student learning? These are matters for inquiry and debate. It is clear, however, that generic approaches can disadvantage certain groups of students who might have particular needs. Addressing these needs most probably will also assist all your students; however, the experience of "adult" students will certainly be enhanced if you keep a few things in mind.

General Background

Adult students come to university with a variety of educational experiences. Many have had rigorous and very traditional early schooling; others might have had their schooling prematurely or even severely disrupted. However, their current studies often are bolstered by a life of reading and personal inquiry and their commitment to education is usually intense. Adult students might be among your very best students, and can be strikingly more sophisticated than their younger classmates, or their lack of background might render studies difficult for them. It is likely that even the very best will have some of the concerns suggested below.

Previous Schooling

By virtue of their presence in the classroom, adult students have already invested a tremendous amount in their education. Typically, they are sacrificing much to be in school; they also are quite conscious of putting themselves on the line, of risking failure. Those who have been out of school for a number of years might have forgotten certain aspects of "school culture." They might be unfamiliar with academic conventions or have inefficient study habits. They may have lost the knack of sitting examinations or be hypersensitive to correction (for example, of their grammar in essays) or evaluation. Especially in a mixed-age class, adults can feel reluctant to voice confusion or uncertainty. Anxieties may be linked to earlier painful school experiences or to setting extremely high personal goals for themselves. As well, adult students can bring with them attitudes derived from the more rigid educational systems of previous years or of other countries. These students might need encouragement to participate in the less authoritarian, more exploratory, climate that is often typical of our classrooms.

Life Experience

Adults readily bring to bear on their academic work not only their previous schooling, but also a wealth of life experience. In courses where relating course material to "real-world experience" is important, they particularly stand out, and instructors often find their worldly wisdom stimulating. However, where younger students might need prodding to relate theory to practice, adult students at times need prodding in the other direction, and instructors should be prepared to assist them in making the practice-to-theory connection.

Undertaking Assignments

Extremely important for adult students is in-class discussion of what your assignments require. Their ignorance about these issues signals their length of time out of school, not incompetence (essay writing and exam taking are not, after all, "natural" – or even commonplace – activities). Adults will greatly appreciate tips on how best to approach research, write essays or prepare for exams. You might also encourage study or writing groups and allow class time to arrange networks. It is often quite difficult for adult students to meet outside class time and often they must rush from class to work or family responsibilities.

Independent Study

Literature on adult education typically emphasizes adult appreciation of independent study and more open-ended assignments than conventionally expected from under-graduates. If instructors are clear about what sorts of research or analysis an assignment requires (for example, whether scholarly journals must be consulted, what sorts of theoretical analysis must back up a workplace study and so on) adult students will readily pursue their academic interests independently and to great effect. In fact, they might find immediate applications for course work; for example, in the form of articles for local or workplace newsletters. You can enhance their experience by having them consider audiences for their work beyond the instructor.

Flexibility

Flexibility is crucial for adult students because life emergencies must take priority in their lives: family illness, workplace deadlines, shift changes and work-related travel all on occasion interrupt even the most organized and dedicated adult students. Under these circumstances, adult students will appreciate your flexibility in office hours and deadlines and the possibility of make-up tests and examinations.

Adult students bring to their studies deep interest, great enthusiasm and excitement. They also often bring with them insecurities, tentativeness and very crowded schedules. Yet they take immense pleasure in their education and their pleasure will be your immediate reward.

English-as-a-Second-Language Students

Leslie Sanders

Like other large urban universities, York University is fortunate to have a large number of students from all over the world. Some have come to Canada for their education; others have recently settled here. Some students, whether born in Canada or elsewhere, speak French, Canada's other official language, as their native language. These students for whom English is a second language (ESL) have a broad range of educational backgrounds and their English fluency varies. Often very good students, they might have difficulty expressing what they know, especially in courses that require essays and essay-type examinations. Some, accustomed to a more authoritarian school system, might be reluctant to speak out in class, sometimes because they feel self-conscious about their English, at other times because public dissent and argument are not customary in their cultures.

There are several strategies you can employ to help ESL students in the classroom and to elicit their best work, in spite of linguistic interference. Write difficult words on the blackboard and take the time to define them. Students' facial expressions might suggest which words they do not understand. If asked in a non-threatening or non-judgemental fashion, students will come forward with what they need to know. Asking is more effective when there are several ESL students in the class. In any case, try to make sure that students understand your explanation. Often, students will claim they understand rather than draw more attention to themselves by asking for a protracted explanation. You might speak to them outside of class to confirm that the matter has been clarified. As well, whenever you can, illustrate concepts that might be difficult for ESL students as graphically and concretely as possible through visual aids and blackboard work. Outlining the key points on the blackboard at the beginning of the class creates a framework ESL students can us to help follow the lecture.

A number of strategies that are helpful for many students are especially helpful for ESL students. In tutorials, ask the students what they missed, or didn't understand, in the lecture. Drawing the whole class into a reconstruction of the lecture can be instructive for everyone. ESL students also benefit from some instruction in strategies for classroom and seminar participation. This might include guidance on what the purpose of such participation is, what kinds of points one might pick up on or introduce and how one responds to points made by others. You might suggest phrases to use when seeking clarification (for example, "What are you getting at?" "Are you saying that...") and ways of interrupting or getting points across, and so on. Encourage ESL students to speak in class, but be sensitive to whether the students simply need encouragement or whether your insistence that they speak causes intolerable discomfort.

Whenever possible, allow students to submit drafts of essays to you for advice and comment. Encouraging students to work with the appropriate writing instructors or tutors can also be enormously helpful. At York, for example, we have four centres that offer individual writing instruction to students: the Computer Assisted Writing Centre, the Centre for Academic Writing; Atkinson Essay Tutoring Centre and the Glendon Writing Workshop. For more general advice or assistance with particular problems, assistance is available to faculty and teaching assistants through academic advisors in each faculty. The ESL Program is coordinated through the Faculty of Arts Academic Advising Centre.

If, in your view, the expression in a paper discredits its ideas, have the student rewrite it before you mark it. Students learn by working at improving their expression; correcting work in the hope of a better grade is time well spent. Students learn nothing from a paper full of red marks, especially if there is no reward for making the corrections.

Try to become sensitive to your own reaction to people whose English is heavily accented or hard to understand. Do you become distracted or frustrated by the expression and inattentive to what the speaker is trying to say? Try to concentrate on what the speaker is saying; politely ask for clarification if you are not sure. Be prepared to rephrase the answer that an ESL student has given. This provides a model to the speaker of how the answer might better be presented and also supports the speaker's participation by getting the information into the discussion.

Communication among people of different languages and cultures often runs into difficulty. Try to ensure that students understand your instructions; for example, avoid colloquialisms and irony when communicating things that you want the students to understand.

Try to become aware of the cultural assumptions and information we bring to everything we do. Don't rely on culturally specific references for your analogies and explanations, or, if you do, check to see that students understand the references. Instructors often comment that the lack of familiarity with cultural context can handicap ESL students as much as or more than difficulties they might face as ESL speakers. It is worth taking this into account and feeding into lectures and discussions relevant cultural information that might help ESL students to understand better the context of the discussion. Where possible, encourage ESL students to relate assignments and discussion to their own backgrounds. This validates their experience and can be informative to others in the class as well.

Section II:
Theories and Models of
Student Learning

Another crucial dimension of student diversity involves differences in learning styles or stages of intellectual development. The four articles in this section draw attention to the research on student learning and intellectual development and the ways it might inform university-level teaching.

The article by Clarkson focuses on different psychological types and how these influence ways of learning. Why does one learning strategy work best for some students, but not for others? How can you encourage particular kinds of learners to improve their learning? The Ginsburg article directs our attention to the different ways people process information. Each person tends towards a particular learning style, and these styles can vary significantly from person to person. An awareness of these differences in learning styles can help us respond more effectively to students' needs.

This section does not attempt to cover the full range of literature on how people learn, but the articles do raise two important issues for university teachers. First, they lead us to self-reflection: what is my own personality type? Do I have a preferred learning style? Where would I fit in these schemes? Second, they lead us to wonder how our particular learning style is reflected in our teaching. If we tend to teach to our own preferred learning style, what constraints are we imposing on students who do not share our preference? This returns us to the issues of equity raised in the previous section. With an understanding of how different people learn, including ourselves, we can expand our repertoire to include teaching strategies that appeal to different types of learners.

The article by Westcott provides a different kind of focus. Rather than asking us to reflect on different learning styles, Westcott draws our attention to the literature on growth and change in human intellectual development. What stages do people go through as they develop intellectually? How can we, as teachers, design our courses to encourage students' progress through these stages of intellectual development? These questions require us to reconsider our function as teachers in a particular discipline. As important as it is for us to lead students to learn the content of a course, we must also consider how to lead them to higher stages of intellectual development so that they can make informed judgements in a disciplinary context. Thus, while we focus on the content of each of our courses, these articles also enjoin us to help students become capable of making judgements in the face of uncertainty and to see themselves as meaning-makers within the context of our discipline. As Westcott says at the end of her article, like a compass, these questions do not provide a map of how to get there, but they orient us to ask crucial questions about the process of learning.

The final article by Rogers addresses the despair that some faculty feel in the face of students' apparent poor academic performance. Rather than blaming students, Rogers argues that it is within our power to transform students' attitudes towards learning. She argues that changes in course design, curriculum and teaching strategies that are informed by theories of learning can encourage deeper levels of learning for students. The articles in sections VI and VII provide a range of teaching strategies and assignments that address these concerns.

Teaching Styles/ Learning Styles: The Myers Briggs Model[1]

Austin Clarkson

The differences among students in their responses to my teaching has always been a matter of interest and concern to me throughout my career as a teacher. Why is it that some students respond so enthusiastically, while others can be so indifferent? I became more aware of the one-sidedness of my style of teaching when I began to teach in the Atkinson Faculty of Liberal and Professional Studies, which provides evening degree programs to part-time students. Many of my students were themselves teachers in elementary and secondary schools and challenged my preconceptions about how best to organize and present a course. As I was already familiar with the psychology of C.G. Jung, I started to analyze my teaching style in terms of his theory of psychological types. When the first program was offered in Toronto to qualify people to administer the Myers Briggs Type Indicator (MBTI), an instrument based on the typology of Carl Jung, I signed up.

I have been working with the MBTI for more than ten years and it has become an invaluable tool for me in understanding personal interactions, including those in the educational environment at all age levels. Of the various systems for analyzing teaching and learning, the MBTI appears to me to be the most sensitive, widely tested, best-validated and extensively applied indicator. In some courses, I introduce the concepts of the MBTI briefly to explain why students tend to prefer one type of presentation or assignment over another, why some have more problems with deadlines than others, why some like to work in groups and others prefer to work alone and so forth. When time permits, I distribute the short MBTI self-scoring form to students who wish to take it and then discuss the results the following week. I also explain my own type and reveal how I have learned to capitalize on my strengths and compensate for my weaknesses as a teacher.

Many students find it a source of great relief to discover that their problems in learning are not unique and that they share ways of functioning in educational institutions with other students. But one must allow for the fact that some individuals take exception to any form of psychological typing and have a justifiable resistance to being pigeonholed and told how they are likely to behave.

The MBTI is based on a dynamic, transformative model of the psyche that admits a continual development of conscious self-awareness of oneself and others. It should never be thought of as a means of labeling people and placing them in boxes. Jung's typology is based on the idea that energy typically flows along paths determined by one's preferences at a given time and in a given situation. It is as though one sets out on a journey from a particular point of departure, a particular point on the compass, and that as one matures and becomes more aware of how to deal with the functions with which one is less adept, one travels around the compass of the types. Thus, working with types is a means of showing students how to become aware of their particular patterns of preferences and how they can capitalize on their newly acquired awareness in terms of their own dynamic process.

Research conducted within the framework of the theory of psychological types has shown that the psychological type of the instructor and the student profoundly influence teaching and learning. Practical application of the theory shows that the student's type relates to the three principal aspects of educational achievement: aptitude, application and interest. Furthermore, psychological type affects the student's learning style and studying environment, handling of deadlines and responses to various types of assignments and testing formats. Type also determines teachers' preferences in the organization of a course, presentation formats and ways of interacting with students. Of course, many other factors affect the interaction of teachers and students, but the psychological type of the instructor is pervasive in setting the tone of the classroom learning environment.

Awareness of individual differences in styles of teaching and learning makes it possible for instructors and students to adapt strategies for instruction and study accordingly. When teachers are aware of their teaching styles, they can understand more readily why their teaching is more successful with some types of students than with others. If students are aware of their own learning styles, they can take steps to build on strengths and anticipate where difficulties might arise. Gordon Lawrence (1979) argues that the match between a student's learning style and an instructor's teaching style is a significant factor in the student's progress:

> It is crucial to explain why certain instruction works with some students and not with others. The fact that a student prefers sensing perception over intuitive perception, or prefers an active, extroverted approach to studies over a reflective, introverted one is not just an interesting curiosity. It is information that some teachers have used to make dramatic improvements in the effectiveness of their instruction (5).

A number of authors describe differences in psychological type and their implications for teaching and learning. The Myers Briggs Type Indicator identifies the basic preferences of people in regard to the reception of information (perception) and the processing of that information (judgement), so that the effects of each preference, singly and in combination, can be established and put to practical use. The MBTI identifies four separate indices that direct the use of perception and judgement. The preferences affect not only what people attend to in any given situation, but also how they draw conclusions about what they perceive. Individuals tend to favour one pole of each of the four indices over the other pole; the preference on each index is independent of preferences for the other three indices. The four indices yield sixteen possible combinations, called "types." Each type is denoted by the four letters of the preferences (for example, ESTJ, INFP).

Extroversion (E)—Introversion (I) identifies the direction of the overall flow of energy. In extroverts, energy typically flows towards the things and people of the outer world. In introverts, energy typically flows towards the inner world of thoughts and imagination.

Sensation (S)—Intuition (N) identifies the functions of perception. Sensate types take in information predominantly through the five senses. Intuitive people prefer to take in information through intuition (the "sixth sense").

Thinking (T)—Feeling (F) identifies the means of judging. Thinking types depend on objective, impersonal reason for making judgements. Feeling types depend on empathy and subjective values for making judgements.

Judgement (J)—Perception (P) identifies whether the principal function is a judging (thinking or feeling) function or a perceiving (sensation or intuition) function.

The following summaries indicate the style of teaching and learning associated with each of the eight functions.

Extroverts work best with others in groups, need to talk about the topic with others to develop their ideas, write with little planning, benefit from discussing their drafts and develop ideas best when writing quickly, impulsively and uncritically.

Suggestions: Dictate a first draft into a tape recorder or give a talk on the topic, make an outline after writing the first draft, select important ideas from the rough draft and revise after getting some oral feedback.

Introverts work best alone, uninterrupted by people and events, and benefit from advance notice and time for reflection. Much of the first draft of a paper is written mentally. They pause frequently to plan and are in danger of getting bogged down in planning. They are reluctant to ask for advice.

Suggestions: Connect theory with practice by adding descriptions of immediate experiences. Test ideas with another person to see how others react. Keep on the lookout for examples from others to test your own experience.

Sensate learners appreciate audio-visual aids and live demonstrations and benefit from having ideas and facts repeated. They do not think symbolically and need time to understand and answer questions and thus are at a disadvantage in time-dependent testing. They benefit from a didactic approach and find memorizing relatively easy, but tend to be slow to generalize from examples to concepts or from reading material to real life. They are at their best with concrete information presented in sequential, step-by-step fashion. These people can be overwhelmed by too much data (facts or theories). They prefer detailed, factual, concretely verifiable material and need explicit, detailed, specific instructions, especially in the early stages of a topic. They can be blocked by directions that are too general and not concrete enough. First drafts of papers tend to be a compilation of facts with little concern for connection with a central theme or thesis.

Suggestions: Try to "read between the lines." In revising, explain the implications of the theme, add or rewrite topic sentences to make large-scale connections, summarize what has been demonstrated, sort out irrelevant facts from the relevant, imagine new possibilities, ingenious solutions and future possibilities, and gather more data than you think are absolutely necessary.

Intuitive learners prefer self-paced learning and courses that let them study on their own initiative; they benefit from an inductive approach. They feel academically superior to other students and expect to achieve higher grades. They like examinations that include essay questions rather than multiple choice and like abstractions and conceptual complexities. They think symbolically and are intrigued by symbolic and subtle interpretations. These people develop a unique, original approach to even commonplace things; they trust first impressions and hunches. They work best with general instructions and generate ideas without difficulty. They ignore the mechanics of essay structure and writing style; first drafts are full of generalizations unsupported by analysis of concrete examples or cases.

Suggestions: In making revisions, simplify, check facts, correct mechanical errors and provide concrete examples and details essential to the reader's understanding before dealing with the interpretation of complex events. You might be blocked by searching for originality; don't ignore the straightforward way of doing things. Read the instructions very carefully, notice what needs attention now and DO IT NOW. Be patient and keep track of essential details.

Thinking learners prefer objectivity and logical order and so appreciate structured courses with clear goals. They like to categorize and analyze according to basic principles and organize into clear structures with logical rationale; they prefer patterns and to follow outlines. This type of learner has a gift for incisive critical analysis, logical organization and brevity; they focus on clarity of content rather than on audience appeal. They are dogmatic, enjoy relating intellectual disputes and can be blocked without clear, objective standards. Drafts of papers are often dry, lacking a sense of personal relationship to the subject.

Suggestions: When revising, add vivid examples from personal experience that reveal the value of the topic and will interest the reader; try to be persuasive and arouse enthusiasm for your topic. When criticizing other people's theories do so with some feeling for their position, thus avoiding scorn and sarcasm; try to be conciliatory.

Feeling learners prefer working on group projects. They are more likely to report interference in their studies by their social life. They relate the topic to their personal value system, focus on communicating values to the reader rather than on the intellectual content and write from the heart. Organization and style are based on the need to move and persuade the reader; they are not interested in disputes but in communicating the subject matter. These people overlook controversy and emphasize personal convictions. Structure follows flow of thought and feelings, not logical outlines.

Suggestions: Revise by clarifying thoughts and checking facts and references. Prepare an outline from the first draft and make a logical structure; don't overstate points for emphasis. Check your analysis of the issue for flaws in the argument and internal consistency among ideas; uphold your position against others'.

Judging learners work efficiently according to schedules and get assignments in on time. They would benefit from study-skills courses and prefer to learn from material presented in an orderly way and through workbooks, lectures or demonstrations. They are disturbed by last-minute information and like to limit topics at once and set manageable goals; they plan their approach and may stick to the plan rigidly. They make stylistic and organizational decisions quickly without reflection, even arbitrarily; they prefer not to put a project aside to gather more data, generate more ideas or do more research. They set realistic goals for themselves and try to meet those goals by planning their time and work schedule systematically.

Suggestions: Allow more time to reflect and be spontaneous. In making revisions, expand and clarify; you may focus too soon or cut too much in revision. If inadequate data are collected, writing could be slow and painful.

Perceiving learners are more likely to report starting too late on assignments, letting their work pile up and having to cram at the end. In experiential situations they are seen as more open and more effective in identifying issues. They favour flexibility and spontaneity, need deadlines to get finished, like broad topics and have trouble focusing. They have difficulty deciding on a specific approach or dividing material into manageable sections. First drafts are long and thorough, but usually contain too much material and too many ideas. These people tend to be perfectionists and to procrastinate. They tend to gather information indefinitely and have trouble limiting themselves to meet deadlines.

Suggestions: Reduce the scope of the topic to the portion sufficient to develop and demonstrate the thesis; abbreviate and focus by cutting down the number of examples and ideas. Assess realistically the amount of time you need to complete the task and begin accordingly.

While a sensitive instructor needs only a few class sessions to begin identifying learning types, the real reward comes with watching students respond to a teaching approach tooled to student needs.

Notes

1. Workshops, courses and further information on the Myers Briggs Type Indicator are provided by the Ontario Association for Application of Personality Type, PO Box 84, Thornhill, Ontario L3T 3N1.

References

Jung, Carl G. 1971. *Psychological types*. Princeton, NJ: Princeton University Press.

Kolb, D.A. 1976. *Learning style inventory: Technical manual*. Boston: McBer.

Lawrence, Gordon. 1979. *People types and tiger stripes: A practical guide to learning styles*. Gainesville, FL: Center for Applications of Psychological Type.

Myers, I.B. 1980. *Introduction to type*. Palo Alto, CA: Consulting Psychologists Press.

Myers, I.B. and M.H. McCaulley. 1985. *Manual: A guide to the development and use of the Myers-Briggs Type Indicator*. Palo Alto, CA: Consulting Psychologists Press.

The Gregorc Model of Learning Styles

Jerry Ginsburg

Several years ago I attended a talk at my daughter's high school concerned with learning styles. The theoretical model the school counselor chose to develop – the model used in the school to advise both students and teachers – was the one devised by Anthony Gregorc. After describing the four learning styles delineated by Gregorc, the counselor gave members of the audience a test to identify which style best characterized their approach to learning. The results were surprisingly satisfying and illuminating. Most people found that the learning style ascribed to them "fit" in an intuitively satisfying way and shed light on the factors that influenced their learning. Did one find comfort in "authorities" or bridle at them? Did one prefer dealing with abstract theory or concrete situations? Did one try to solve problems using rigorous deduction or intuition? Gregorc's categories lent coherence to the audience's responses to these learning issues – as well as to others having a more tart edge, such as whether one tended to be innovative or stodgy and rule-bound.

Although I am not an expert in learning styles,[1] I thought other teachers might find value in a brief summary of Gregorc's model. His schema has certainly stirred some questions in my own mind regarding whether my way of teaching favours a particular type of learner. I believe it does, and I suspect that most university instruction does. Moreover, I have come to appreciate that the learning style we privilege has significant weaknesses as well as strengths. Perhaps reflecting on this will allow us to grow as learners and thinkers as well as teachers.

Gregorc's model of learning styles focuses on two key aspects of how people process information: 1) whether they prefer to work on a concrete or abstract level and 2) whether they tend to analyze issues in a sequential or a "random" fashion (for example, by adopting a holistic approach or by emphasizing one's intuition, instincts or emotions). These dimensions give rise to four types of people/learners:

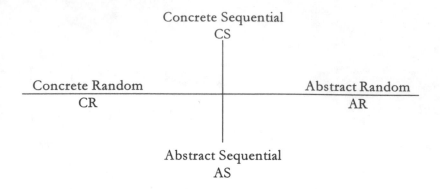

As you will see in the capsular descriptions below, Gregorc's "types" are distinguished not only by how they learn but by other attributes as well (for example, how an individual dresses, whether one is punctual, etc.). These ancillary characteristics are intriguing in and of themselves and could have relevance to teaching if they helped one identify the different types of learners in one's classes. It will also become apparent that many learning characteristics can be given either a positive or negative gloss; for example, a preference for sequential analysis might be seen either as facilitating the teasing apart of issues or as discouraging unconventional "lateral" insights. These conflicting implications should, perhaps, give us pause in promoting a particular learning or thinking orientation.

According to Gregorc, **concrete sequential** (CS) learners enjoy dealing with the physical world revealed by their often acute senses. They like hands-on experiences and find satisfaction in real products and results. Favouring step-by-step linear analysis, they tend to proceed in a methodical and deliberate way, seeking proof via their senses. They tend to focus on details and to be precise and accurate in their work. CS learners use terms in a literal sense and might find theoretical or metaphorical notions confusing or wasteful. They are good at planning their time, feel comfortable following instructions and like to work within structured environments. On the sartorial front, CS people tend to be meticulously dressed and colour coordinated. On a negative note (assuming one likes neat dressers), they might have trouble understanding feelings, choosing from many options and taking new approaches. Additionally, they might suffer from being excessively conformist.

Abstract sequentials (AS) share the deductive approach to problems of CS learners, but feel more comfortable dealing with theories and models than with the "real world." This combination of traits yields a person who is intellectual, logical and analytical. AS types love to debate, often with precise, polysyllabic language, and are inclined to be absent-minded. Rather than concentrating on physical objects and material reality, the AS individual focuses on knowledge, concepts and ideas. These are patient learners who feel most comfortable when they follow traditional procedures and have time to learn material thoroughly. Like CS folk, AS individuals tend to be neatly dressed but to prefer moderate colours. Drawbacks include a tendency to be sarcastic and opinionated, traits that can make it difficult for an AS type to participate cooperatively in group discussions. AS people might have trouble verbalizing emotion in a constructive way and, like CS sorts, can experience difficulty writing creatively and taking a risk. (The latter quality is, apparently, the flip-side of their preference for synthesizing work of a conventional nature that has evolved incrementally.)

Learners of the **abstract random** (AR) variety feel most at home in an abstract world of feeling and emotion. Rather than viewing situations in a two-dimensional, deductive manner, they are prone to seeing web-like, multidimensional patterns. Their thinking leans towards the emotional, psychic and perceptive and they employ fantasy and metaphoric language more effectively than other learners do. AR learners are appreciative of the arts, colour and nature and are good at absorbing entire themes. They find great satisfaction in personal interactions and are particularly effective at empathizing with people and sensing shifting moods within a group. Given their "artistic" temperament, it perhaps is predictable that ARs like to dress in bright colours that are not necessarily coordinated. Like other learners, AR people have their shortcomings. They tend not to be on time because they see routines as boring. Their need to evaluate affairs on their own terms can make them appear stubborn. Their holistic orientation can make it difficult for them to recall specifics, give exact answers, memorize material or work step by step on a project.

Concrete random (CR) learners inhabit a world that is concrete in its activity and yet still illuminated by rather abstract intuition. Like their AR relatives, CRs gravitate towards three-dimensional patterns and put a premium on their instincts, often leaping from fact to theory without being able to show how they reached their conclusions. CR individuals use language that is dramatic and colourful, but they tend to leave sentences dangling. They prefer to work independently and are more responsive to practical demonstrations and personal proofs than to the words of an outside authority. CRs are very curious; they are also prolific, unconventional thinkers who like to create new ways of doing things. Preferring a hands-on approach to learning, they enjoy experimenting. In terms of weaknesses, CR people have difficulty meeting time limitations, finishing a project if a new idea hits or choosing one answer. They do not enjoy preparing formal reports and find it frustrating to listen to a lecturer without being able to interact. (And how do CRs dress? "Variably.")

As the preceding descriptions suggest, people's learning styles will significantly influence how they react to different pedagogical strategies. The following chart summarizes some of the more pertinent implications.

Table 1: Summary of the Gregorc Model

Characteristics	Concrete Sequential	Abstract Sequential	Abstract Random	Concrete Random
Prefers classes featuring:	Field trips, computer-assisted instruction	Extensive reading, lectures, slides, debates	Group discussion, movies and records, short readings or lectures leading to discussion	Independent projects, games, short presentations
Prefers assignments:	With exact directions and examples, likes hands-on experiences	That involve analysis, where one works alone and can learn material thoroughly	That involve interpretation and artistic expression, likes working with others	That are self-directed, hands-on and use trial and error
Relationship to authority:	Likes teachers who are "in charge"	Respects "referent" authority (biggest names in field)	Desires a teacher who is a guide and who refers to personal experiences	Accepts many different authorities
Feedback expectations:	Expects feedback on what one is doing wrong, not on what is right	Expects corrective feedback from "significant others," wants to excel	Expects approval responses, likes non-verbal feedback	Both corrective and approval oriented
Preferred questions:	"How does this work?"	"Why is this?"	"How can we interpret this?"	"How many different ways can I...?"
Situations likely to be difficult:	Answering "what if" questions, interpreting abstract ideas, understanding feelings	Writing creatively, taking a risk, dealing with open-ended problems, dealing with emotions	Memorizing, dealing with authority, going step by step, turning work in on time	Choosing one answer, avoiding being side-tracked by a new thought, doing formal reports
To "stretch," these students need to learn to:	See the whole, consider the process by which results are produced	Be less perfectionistic, consider non-traditional approaches	See the parts of the whole, adhere to time limits	Recognize when change is impossible, prioritize

Gregorc's model, even considered superficially, has very serious implications for university teaching. It seems to me incontrovertible that most university instruction is geared for abstract sequential learning. We emphasize the development of analytical skills and focus most classes on theoretical and conceptual issues; we eagerly give "corrective feedback" and often, if inadvertently, encourage perfectionism; we rely more on lectures than group discussions and in our small groups we feature the cut and thrust of debate over the exchange of feelings and spiritual insights. All this might seem natural enough, but Gregorc's schema should give us pause. We should consider whether our teaching methods are making it difficult for non-abstract sequential learners in our classes to progress. Even more crucially, we should ponder whether, as learners and teachers, we ourselves manifest the limitations of the abstract sequential approach. More often than not, I suspect that we do.

Notes

1. Unfortunately, when I say I am not an expert in learning styles, I am not being modest. The summary of Gregorc's ideas presented here is based on quite a small pool of information: the materials provided by the high-school counselor. These include the counselor's own summary charts as well as others photocopied (apparently) from Butler (1984), Gregorc (1985) and Wheeler (1980). A six-part article, "Open letter to an educator," by Gregorc was also used. (Despite strenuous efforts, I have been unable to identify the journal or, more likely, informal newsletter in which this multipart epistle appeared.)

References

Butler, Kathleen. 1984. *Learning and teaching style: In theory and practice.* Columbia, CT: Learner's Dimension.

Gregorc, Anthony. 1985. *An adult's guide to style.* Maynard, ME: n.p.

Wheeler, Daniel. 1980. Learning styles: A tool for faculty development. *POD Quarterly* 2 (3–4): 164–74.

Student Development: From Problem Solving to Problem Finding

Page Westcott

The Hidden Curriculum

Faculty members are usually hired for their subject-matter expertise, and for many of us, commitment to our discipline looms large in our identity. It is not surprising, then, that we may focus on subject-matter content goals more than on student development or the processes of liberal education goals, such as critical thinking, understanding of others, tolerance for ambiguity, and ethical responsibility.

The past twenty years have produced important empirical research to guide university practices and the student's involvement in subject matter is now recognized as providing conditions that can also support social, intellectual and ethical development. (Pascarella and Terenzini 1991, 114; Chickering and Reiser 1993, especially Chapters 12, 13). In a foreword to a large study of undergraduate institutions, Trow (1977) discusses this tension between specialized knowledge and the processes of liberal education and states that "the best education can be found where that tension has not been resolved" (iii). Furthermore, Chickering and Reisser (1993) suggest that

> if we start thinking about content as a vehicle for encouraging learning and personal development, our selection of readings and writing assignments, performances, laboratory experiences and other learning activities will be enriched. We need not give up our objectives concerning particular areas of knowledge and content (348).

But, as Chickering and Reisser also note (350-3), there can be a considerable gap between the formal curriculum (which includes the development of critical thinking skills) and "the hidden curriculum" (Snyder 1970), a practice, all too prevalent today, whereby too much information is presented and the student copes by paying selective attention to parts of the content that can be memorized. When faculty and students collude in such practices, the result is an overemphasis on the reproduction of existing information and the inhibition of students' ability to make judgements and think independently.[1]

Instead, Knapper and Cropley (1985) urge university teachers to promote life-long learning goals by helping adults develop a clear sense of themselves as meaning-makers, undaunted by complexity, and able to recognize differences as legitimate. Yet, these are the very characteristics that a fast-paced society and the hidden curriculum in universities discourage.

Contradiction and Paradox in Learning

Less than twenty-five years ago adulthood was considered a plateau, a holding pattern. This static image of self-sufficient adulthood contributes to the practices of the hidden curriculum in that learning is seen as the unproblematic assimilation of information and the emphasis in education as providing objective information and solutions to problems.

Psychological theory contributed to the plateau image of adulthood, often treating the adult years as unmarked territory between adolescence and old age. In texts of the 1960s and 1970s, Piaget's formal operations in adolescence were considered the end-point of cognitive development. In the same period, Kohlberg's research on the development of moral judgement indicated that the highest stages relied on formal operational thought (Gilligan 1981, 143). For both cognitive and moral development, the theoretical end-point assumed an adolescent individual who was distanced from on-going life, and engaged in solving hypothetical problems by means of formal abstract principles. Numerous scholars now recognize that this image of human development and of reasoning was limited and limiting.

The image of adult development now current in psychology portrays adults peering into contradiction and paradox using dialectical processes (Riegel 1973), finding unrecognized problems (Arlin 1975), and recognizing multiple viewpoints and standards in solving "ill-defined" problems. Ill-defined problems are open; strategies for finding solutions to ill-defined problems must transcend hypothetico-deductive processes of formal operations and use imagery, metaphors, dialectical operations, empathy, and other processes involving disciplined imagination and reasoning. Ill-defined problems abound in a changing society that is fast-paced and complex. Solutions that worked before must be reassessed in terms of current conditions; the individual meets unfamiliar situations more often. Being alive to the reality that situations can be interpreted in multiple ways, and being aware of one's own taken-for-granted beliefs and procedures is at a premium, but few adults are accustomed to such cognitively effortful activity.

Langer's (1989) research program explored mindlessness and mindfulness in various contexts. She demonstrated that adults have a propensity to be "mindless," to do what is effortless and what has worked in the past (9). Her research warns us that rigidly following set rules and being mindful are incompatible. Our thinking can be trapped too easily in old categories and our behaviour can become automatic or limited by a single perspective. How can these considerations be reflected in our teaching practices?

Uncertainty in Undergraduate Education

Many researchers agree that it takes conscious awareness of some anomaly or incongruity for us to surrender our ordinary mindlessness. When we can tolerate the tension of a mindful focus on an incongruous event, the possibility of new ideas is born. Consequently, developmental psychologists often favour the slogan "support and challenge" to describe conditions that facilitate development.

It is easy for faculty to underestimate the degree of uncertainty that undergraduates experience. By the time we begin teaching, faculty are experts in selecting, reading, comparing and interpreting articles in their field, and with this expertise we lose conscious awareness of the many processes that support decision-making. In listening to students describe difficulties with course assignments, it struck me that they often seem to believe that they should be able to do them alone without experiencing any uncertainty. Many processes in a field of expertise become effortless, and this makes it important for faculty to explain to students that is natural for them to experience uncertainty. In supporting effortful learning of students who are novices in the field, I try to honour uncertainty, and make room for it in class.

The incongruities or anomalies experienced by university undergraduates often concern their personal epistemology – questions such as What is knowledge? How can I know? However, the student's experience of incongruity is grounded in a specific event, not in abstraction. Puzzling through such an event requires focused thought, effort, and emotional resilience.

In interviews investigating epistemological uncertainty among six undergraduate and graduate students from York University, Trevor Warren (1993) used probes such as: "What has stood out for you in your academic career?," "How do you account for competing claims in important issues?" and "Has your view of the world ever been challenged, or a familiar pattern of meaning failed you?" Rather than allowing the interviews to become abstract and general, he asked individual to describe their own experience and the feelings that accompanied the event. Five of the six students reported negative affect, feeling devastated, overwhelmed, powerless, frustrated, depressed, resentment, or scared.

Warren's discussion of his results identifies a sequence of meaning-making: following the particular experience the students reflected, either seeing personal or more general implications of the unsettling experience, or denying any such implications. Following reflection came a mental search for new foundations, and this identified what was important. After this, the person might feel a new sense of purpose and meaning. Warren comments that "perhaps the most interesting and surprising outcome of this whole voyage was that all informants ultimately, in some emancipatory sense, regarded epistemological uncertainty as a form of empowerment" (13). Though we cannot know from this study how representative the described struggle is of students in general, the important point is that the struggle happens, and is worthwhile.

Evolving Interpretive Frameworks in the Undergraduate Years

William Perry's research on (male) undergraduates at Harvard College sheds light on students' varied and contradictory perceptions of their course work. Perry's interviews reveal a pattern of change over the years in the "coherent interpretive frameworks through which students give meaning to their educational experience (Perry 1981, 177)." The interviews also show that epistemological uncertainty is a transition event in the evolution of the frameworks.

The work of Belenky and her colleagues (1986) extends Perry's interpretive frameworks and shows that they are not unique to those male interviewees at that place and time. The interviewees for this study came from three "invisible colleges" – family agencies to which the women addressed parenting questions – and six diverse academic institutions at the late high-school or college level (Belenky *et al.* 1986, 12).

Of the 135 women interviewed, four were described as locked in a position of "silence." These were the youngest (teenagers) and most disadvantaged in the group of 45 interviewees located through family agencies. The four were seen as "representing an extreme in denial of self and in dependence on external authority for direction (24)." This position was not found among undergraduates by either Belenky and her colleagues or by Perry in his study.

Building on the work of Perry, Kohlberg, and Gilligan, as well as their own coding systems, Belenky *et al.* found similar issues to those Perry had identified two decades earlier. And like Perry, they found the development of thinking about thinking processes or "metathought" to be critically important to adult development.

In the discussion that follows, the headings show Perry's term followed by a parallel term from Belenky *et al.*, and the sequence of positions is from dualism as the least complex to more inclusive and adequate ways of knowing.

Dualism/Received Knowledge

In this stage, students seek simple answers and certainty. Knowledge, values, and people are divided into two absolute categories of right and wrong. The decision as to which is which is based on an appeal to an external Authority, such as a tradition, a person or "the majority must be right" rule. Students do not consider themselves to be meaning-makers.

None of the interviews showed Perry's men as predominantly in dualism at the end of their first year. However, many of the women in the Belenky study were. Although, they had confidence in their ability to listen to others and reproduce information, they looked outside of themselves for the source of knowledge and were intolerant of ambiguity. But this dualism/received knowledge perspective quickly changes in intellectually challenging environments, or as students (are encouraged to) leave (Belenky *et al.* 1986, 43; Clinchy and Zimmerman 1982). As Belenky *et al.* state: "Reliance on authority for a single view of the truth is clearly maladaptive for meeting the requirements of a complex, rapidly changing, pluralistic, egalitarian society, and for meeting the requirements of educational institutions which prepare students for such a world (43)."

Dualism Modified by Multiplicity/Subjective Knowledge

The discovery that some questions have no single authoritative answer legitimizes uncertainty and creates a free zone in which everyone is entitled to his or her own opinion, according to Perry's men. In this personalism, a term Perry preferred, "an opinion is related to nothing whatever – evidence, reason, experience, expert judgement, context, principle or purpose – except for the person who holds it. All that Authority cannot prove to be Wrong is Right (85)."

Belenky *et al.* (1986) emphasize that the change from external authority to subjectivism or subjective knowledge is "particularly significant for women when and if it happens." They "encountered women from sixteen to sixty for whom the discovery of subjective truth was the most recent and personally liberating event of their lives (54)." Almost half of their 135 interviewees were predominantly subjectivist in their thinking. The majority of them did not come from supportive achievement-oriented backgrounds and few were attending prestigious colleges. Education was not seen as a transition event for these women; for many, their educational experiences had seemed irrelevant. Unlike Perry's men, who had a rights orientation in setting themselves apart from authority through their subjective opinions, many of these women came to trust their gut feelings and their experiences of life after bad experiences with failed authorities.

Belenky *et al.* described advantaged women in prestigious schools as "hidden multiplists." Unlike the advantaged men's vigorous claim "I have a right to my opinion," women of similar background make "a modest inoffensive statement 'It's just my opinion.'" Belenky's interviews revealed that women are likely to value a connection to others, and fear that holding a different opinion will cut her off from others. (In many instances this is a very real fear.) The women might be reluctant to make private thoughts public and be listeners to friends and teachers rather than full participants. Families and others are not likely to encourage them in risk taking (64).

Relativism Discovered/Procedural Knowledge

As students encounter faculty who insist that they provide evidence to support opinion, and grade on that basis, they consciously cultivate an analytic approach and evaluate evidence (at least in the courses and disciplines where this is required). In this stage, reasoned reflection begins to replace received knowledge and subjectivism. Perry (1981) defines relativism as

> Diversity of opinion, values, and judgements derived from coherent sources, evidence, logics, systems, and patterns allowing for analysis and comparison. Some opinions may be found worthless, while there will remain matters about which reasonable people will reasonably disagree. Knowledge is qualitative, dependent on contexts (80).

Students think more, going beyond the atomistic opinions of earlier perspectives and recognizing other systems of thought and alternative ways of knowing. Initially students may view this attention to evidence as simply providing what some faculty want; they need the course credit. Out of the need to conform, some learn ways to be independent.

In relativism discovered, students realize that all knowledge, in the academy as well as in life, is relative. Anxiety about there being no absolutes to grasp on to, a new sense of freedom followed by a yearning for old certainties, and an expanded conception of meaning-making and one's own agency are some of the realizations that preoccupy students who discover relativism. A quiet student walked out of class with me once close to the end of term, saying: "So there is always going to be some alternative, some ambiguity, right? So I might as well make friends with it, right?"

Belenky et al. use the parallel term of procedural knowledge, which emphasizes the student's conspicuous activities in effortfully considering ways to know. The meaning of an event is relative to the purposes of the knower as well as to the event's context.

Commitments in Relativism/Constructed Knowledge

The most inclusive framework in Perry's scheme involves choices that are commitments in relativism. What marks this last part of the intellectual journey is that choices are based on meanings originating in the individual (agency) rather than externally (92). Questions concerning "what are adequate grounds, given the lack of an absolute standard?" and "how can you make an assumption that is worthwhile?" preoccupy the student.

The acceptance of personal knowledge (Polanyi 1958) and knowing oneself as a meaning-maker reveals possibilities of ethical responsibility and choice of action. For Perry commitment means choosing to invest oneself in something in full awareness of relativism. Intellectual, social and ethical growth of the kind needed in our complex, fast-changing society is not a simple process of maturation or of gaining experience. Its first requirement is that we unlearn simple conceptions of knowledge and how we know. Such unlearning does not happen all at once. Adult thinking may be sophisticated in one domain and dualistic in another. Perry tells us that development is recursive, we may face "the same old issues" but "do so from a different and broader perspective (97)." Adults who do not review a commitment or scrutinize anew the evidence for a particular belief return to processes described as dualism/received knowledge.

With the recognition of the relativism of all knowledge, responsible commitments may be made based on empathic and objective ways of knowing (Belenky et al. 1986, 137). Commitments in relativism are a powerful form of thinking where personal choices and caring about others are part of making meaning, and it is recognized that such choices and values will continue to be needed and continue to be modified. "It is in the affirmation of Commitments that the themes of epistemology, intellectual development, ethics, and identity merge (Perry 1981, 97)."

Conclusion

Perry's inductive study was pioneering work. He was the first to recognize relativistic thinking as positive adult development. Some undergraduates discover relativism and are able to go beyond reliance on external authority and superficial subjective knowledge to an intellectually and ethically demanding and caring orientation of personal responsibility. The essentially creative act of coming to make sense of the world in new ways entails making connections and differentiations that are new for the individual. Respectful institutional climates that give time and encouragement to reasoned reflection on complex matters have been shown to foster the development of these cognitive processes.

Human selectivity and interpretation is involved in all our enterprises. But under pressures to "cover material" and "keep up," we may forget that, and our students may never learn it. The non-trivial consequences are a narrowed conception of knowledge and of human possibilities. I think of the ideas in this article as a compass which, of course, cannot tell us how to get from here to there, but I hope it is of value in keeping us oriented to the ever-present human processes involved in learning. This article offers some ideas about adult development and discusses the positive changes that, with effort, can happen to undergraduates and keep on happening to faculty.

Notes

1. See also the discussion of deep and surface learning by Rogers, *Using Theories About Student Learning to Improve Teaching*, in this Section.

References

Arlin, P. 1975. Cognitive development in adulthood. *Developmental Psychology* 2: 602-6.

Belenky, M. F., *et al.* 1986. *Women's ways of knowing: The development of self, voice, and mind.* New York: Basic Books.

Chickering, A. W. *et al.* 1981. *The modern American college.* San Francisco: Jossey-Bass.

Chickering, A. W., and L. Reisser. 1993. *Education and identity.* 2nd ed. San Francisco: Jossey-Bass.

Clinchy, B. and C. Zimmerman. 1982. Epistemology and agency in the development of undergraduate women. In *The undergraduate woman*, P. Perin (ed.), 161-81. Lexington, MA: Lexington Books.

Gilligan, C. 1981. Moral development. In *The modern American college*, A. Chickering *et al* (eds.), 139-57. San Francisco: Jossey-Bass.

——. 1986. Remapping development: The power of divergent data. In *Value presuppositions in theories of human development*, L. Cirillo and S. Wapner (eds.), 37-61. Hillsdale, NJ: Erlbaum.

Kegan, R. 1982. *The evolving self.* Cambridge, MA: Harvard University Press.

Knapper, C. and A. Cropley. 1985. *Lifelong learning and higher education.* Netherlands: Croom Helm.

Langer, E. 1989. *Mindfulness.* Don Mills, ON: Addison-Wesley Publishers.

Pascarella, E. T. and P. Terenzini. 1991. *How college affects students.* San Francisco: Jossey-Bass.

Perry, W. G. 1970. *Forms of intellectual and ethical development in the college years.* New York: Holt Rinehart and Winston.

——. 1981. Cognitive and ethical growth. In *The modern American college*, A. Chickering *et al* (eds.), 76-116. San Francisco: Jossey-Bass.

Polanyi, M. 1958. *Personal knowledge.* London: Routledge and Kegan Paul.

Riegel, K. F. 1973. Dialectical operations: The final period of cognitive development. *Human Development* 16: 346-70.

Snyder, B. 1970. *The hidden curriculum.* New York: Knopf.

Warren, T. 1993. A phenomenological study of epistemological uncertainty. Honours BA Thesis, York University.

Using Theories about Student Learning to Improve Teaching

Pat Rogers

A typical challenge at the post-secondary level is finding ways to respond to the tension between students' desires to "get the grades" and the teacher's wish that they would "get learning" (Weimer 1990). It is not uncommon for faculty to be frustrated by students' insistence on a recipe-book approach to teaching and by their resistance to engaging in critical dialogue about the material they are asked to learn. Faculty try to meet students' questions with more questions, but students want answers and they want them immediately. As instructors, we know that if we submit to this kind of pressure, students might do well on the assignment or pass the test. We also know that this approach to learning is unlikely to lead to long-term success. What we long for in our students instead is for them to approach learning with the intention of understanding rather than memorizing the material. However, at the same time, we may not realize how much we are complicit in our students' behaviour.

A few years ago, I was invited to help a large (10,000 to 15,000 full- and part-time students) comprehensive university develop strategies for responding to its students' apparent lack of success in the mathematical sciences. The university (I'll call it Problem University) had experienced a recent and alarming increase in failure rates. According to many instructors, a number of factors ranging from poorly thought-out exam schedules to societal problems had contributed to this increase. But the strongest factor was believed to be the deterioration of problem-solving skills among first-year students.

The task I was given was to assess the attempts that were being made to improve student success and to begin informing faculty and staff about current theory and practice in problem-solving instruction. In this article, I present my assessment of the situation at Problem University as a case study. My conclusion was that the faculty were, despite good intentions, teaching in a way that promoted the very behaviour they sought to change. I will show how an understanding of students' intentions in their approach to learning can inform curricular and instructional transformation and suggest solutions to the problem that are within each faculty member's power to effect.

Case Study: Problem University

In attempting to define the scope of the problem at Problem University, I conducted a series of interviews and focus-group discussions with students, faculty members and tutors (for the most part senior undergraduate students hired by a central university facility to provide additional help to students in particular courses). My discussions with faculty revealed four major themes. Most centred around student deficits of one form or another: students' resistance to engaging in the process of problem-solving, the impact on learning of students' time constraints, students' lack of preparation in important basic skills, and also the lack of support for teaching at the university. Three of these concerns relate directly to the topic of this article and are described below in more detail, incorporating, where relevant, the student and tutor perspective.

Students' Resistance to Problem Solving

Students' resistance to engaging in the problem-solving process was the dominant theme in all discussions. According to faculty, "students focus on memorizing formulas and procedures to get answers"[1] – the prevailing impression is that "students expect to be told a formula or procedure rather than trying to figure it out for themselves." The tension between what students need and what they want is very strong. Students have "little experience in constructive independent thinking" and do not believe they are capable of it. They don't understand the need for explanation or justification and are more secure dealing with situations where there are "right or wrong" answers or a template to be filled in. Tutors agree. They complained of frequently being confronted by students who were unwilling to devote any time to solving a problem for themselves before demanding answers.

Comments from students shed light on why they adopt this approach to learning. For example, several students lamented that some courses are "just memorizing." In such a circumstance, students say, they remember the material for the test but "after the test, they just forget everything." Assessment schemes that base the entire grade on tests and exams add to their need to adopt this approach: "all you can do is memorize," they despair.

On the other hand, many students evidenced a very different perspective: they expressed a strong preference for challenging courses and a desire for faculty to encourage more problem-solving. They detailed several teaching practices that they found useful in promoting and encouraging their engagement in problem-solving. These included:

- solving problems at the board (my own experience with this strategy suggests that pairs at the board works best and is less intimidating for most students)
- "[getting] students to do things right there" (for example, one professor in a very large class has students do problems in class while he walks around;

students find this challenging and it helps them understand the material: "in this course, memorizing wouldn't be enough," they assert)

- working with other students in small groups
- giving students the final answer but not the full solution
- reducing the amount of content to be covered (for example, in one course, students complained that there was so much material covered in class that there was no time left for solving problems).

Students' Time Constraints

Faculty talked a lot about the difficulty they experienced in getting students to read and prepare for class. Tutors added to this a concern about students who come to the tutoring centre only on the day before a test. Students agreed and complained of time-management problems. Their lives were filled with "work, work and more work and almost nothing else." Many students are returning to school after a long break and are simultaneously holding down a job and taking care of a family. They simply have "too much to do in too short a time." For this reason, arranging to meet and work in groups off campus, while desirable in many eyes, would be almost impossible.

Students' Lack of Preparation

According to faculty members and tutors, another big problem is that students lack important critical thinking and learning skills. They have poor communication skills, little familiarity with mathematical or scientific language and are inexperienced with group work. Students complain of this, too. However, they suggest that professors have a responsibility to provide explicit training in these skills.

Understanding the Problem

According to the faculty at Problem University, the most serious barrier to their students' success is their apparent resistance to engaging in problem-solving. However, as I will show, it is within the power of these same faculty members to change this behaviour. An important first step is to understand the reasons behind students' resistance to solving problems. Two theories from the research on student learning are helpful: the first defines students' intentions in their approaches to learning tasks (Marton and Saljo 1984) and the second describes the stages in the development of their understanding of what learning involves (Perry 1970).

Surface and Deep Approaches to Learning

Students with a surface approach to learning reduce it to rote memorization. They expect to demonstrate their knowledge of the course material by reproducing it in its original form at a later date; for example, on the final examination. This contrasts sharply with the deep approach to learning, in which students attempt to make sense of what is to be learned. For them, the learning task involves thinking, looking for connections and trying to make meaning by playing with ideas and concepts.[2]

There is abundant evidence that the first-year students at Problem U are adopting a surface approach to learning. Such an approach is sadly very common in post-secondary education. It is more common in science than in arts and more common in those who do not plan to go to graduate school. As the faculty are acutely aware, this approach to learning is disastrous for students because, although they can achieve short-term success (by obtaining high marks on exams through memorizing facts), their ability to retain information in the long-term, to fully understand a concept or to grasp a complex argument is severely impaired.

> For example, a study of a first-year undergraduate economics course found that few students had understood a range of key economics concepts. Indeed the quality of understanding of several concepts was actually poorer by the end of the course than before the course started. Results on a conventional exam revealed none of this failure. (Dahlgren 1984)[3]

The good news is that students' approaches to learning can change. As it is, most students vary their approach depending on the demands of the specific task. Students' conceptions of the nature of learning itself underlie their approach to learning. Several developmental schemes have been proposed to describe the stages in students' intellectual development. The most useful model for our purposes is Perry's (1970) model.[4]

Stages of Intellectual Development

Students in their early college years – and Problem U's students are certainly no exception – are for the most part at the dualistic stage of intellectual development: they see the world divided into right and wrong, good and bad, expert and novice. Their focus is on what to learn and how to learn it. Students with this conception of learning are unlikely to engage in deep learning. Indeed, they will be quite resistant to any task that demands thinking and understanding because associated with their conception of what learning entails are strongly held convictions of what constitutes good teaching. Dualistic students expect to be fed "right" answers by experts who tell them what to do and reward them for following the rules. They see the teacher as bearing all of the responsibility in a course, including selecting material, presenting it and testing what students have learned (that is, memorized) – a teaching practice that has been termed "closed" (Gibbs 1992, 6).

There is considerable evidence to suggest, however, that students who consistently adopt a surface approach to learning do so because they have experienced "closed" teaching throughout their schooling. On the other hand, studies have documented increased sophistication in students' conceptions of learning when they experience more open-ended learning tasks (Gibbs 1992, 6). On a practical level, my experience with an open-ended exploratory approach to teaching math-avoidant elementary teacher candidates supports this finding. This suggests that a solution to the problem at Problem U could lie in the hands of the teachers.

Course Characteristics That Promote Surface Learning

Many studies involving thousands of students across a wide range of disciplines have identified the course characteristics that are likely to foster a surface approach to learning (Gibbs 1992, 9). These include:

- a heavy workload
- excessive quantity of course material
- a lack of opportunity to study course material in depth
- a lack of choice of topics
- a lack of choice of study methods
- an anxiety-provoking assessment system
- assessment methods that tolerate regurgitation.

All of these characteristics are typical of first-year courses in the mathematical sciences[5] and there are echoes of them in the comments quoted earlier in this paper. Of these characteristics, probably the most influential is the assessment system – often this allows students to get by despite taking a surface approach even when other features of the course promote a deep approach (Gibbs 1992, 10).

Course Characteristics That Promote Deep Learning

According to Graham Gibbs (1992, 10–11), the course characteristics associated with fostering a deep approach to learning include:

- *Motivational context*. Deep learning is more likely to occur when students' motivation is intrinsic and they experience a need to know. One way to achieve this is to present students with problems and let them learn what they need to know in order to solve them. The actual problem to be solved in this situation is less important than the learning that occurs through the process of solving the problem. Providing a positive, supportive emotional climate for learning is the key to establishing the motivational context for the risk-taking that engaging in such a learning task requires.

- *Learner activity*. Students need to be active rather than passive in the learning process if deep learning is to occur. Deep learning is associated with doing but doing is not enough by itself – activity must be planned, reflected upon, processed and related to abstract concepts.

- *Interaction with others*. It is easier to negotiate meaning and manipulate ideas when working with others than when alone. Small groups in class and outside of class are important ways to engage students with each other.

- *A well-structured knowledge base*. New knowledge must be built on existing concepts and experience and taught in integrated wholes rather than bits and pieces. Students also need time to reflect on new knowledge so that they can integrate it with their existing understanding and connect it to what they already know.

Moving Towards a Solution

Countering Student Resistance to Problem-Solving

In the previous section I argued that the behaviour students exhibit at Problem University in response to problem-solving is characteristic of a surface approach to learning and arises from dualistic concepts of the nature of learning. I also described the role that course design, teaching methods and assessment play in supporting or challenging a surface approach. This section describes approaches that are more likely to foster a deep approach to learning and, as a result, improve students' problem-solving skills.

The most fruitful response to students in a dualistic stage of development is to support them (so that we don't lose them) and at the same time to challenge them to move to higher levels of intellectual development. One way to support dualistic students is to provide them with some of what they expect, that is, a high degree of structure and clear instructions. However, we also need to challenge them to consider different viewpoints and think for themselves. Active learning and student interaction are vital elements of a course designed to promote deep learning. They are also important components of the Kolb experiential learning model (Kolb 1984), which provides a framework for selecting and sequencing learning activities to encourage students to take a deep approach to their learning.

Kolb contends that learning involves a cycle of four processes, each of which is essential for learning to be complete. Focusing on the experience of the students in this model, the phases in the cycle can be described as

- personal involvement in a specific experience (*concrete experience*)
- reflecting on the experience from many viewpoints and seeking to find its meaning (*reflective observation*)
- drawing conclusions and explaining (*abstract conceptualization*)
- actively experimenting, making decisions and applying new knowledge to different situations (*active experimentation*).

Used as a guide to instructional design, the Kolb model assists in the selection of activities that support different phases of the cycle. To illustrate how this model can be applied in a specific situation, I have outlined an instructional sequence I have used in my own teaching (see Table p.126). The example is chosen from an upper-level course in abstract algebra with a class size of about thirty students. The sequence described occurred about four weeks into a twelve-week course and many of the remaining weeks were guided by the questions and conjectures that arose during this session.

Kolb contends that each phase in the experiential model must be included in any learning experience. Svinicki and Dixon (1987, 146) provide useful guidance in choosing appropriate activities for each phase of the cycle depending on the degree of active learning the teacher chooses to provide. Sample instructional sequences for a range of disciplines are also provided. However, the value of active involvement in a course must be weighed against a variety of other factors. In choosing an appropriate sequence of teaching and learning activities, a teacher might first take into consideration whether the learning objectives require development of factual knowledge, for which a lecture approach is as good as any other,[6] or higher-order thinking, for which more active learning approaches are essential. Which activity you ultimately choose will also depend on a variety of other factors, including the physical constraints of the classroom, the timetable (in the case of field or practical work), the time available and

Sample Instructional Sequence Based on the Kolb Experiential Learning Model

Topic: Lagrange's Theorem (the order of every subgroup of a finite group divides the order of the group)	
Experiencing	Students, independently or in pairs, work with a specific finite cyclic group (different groups for different students) to find all of its subgroups.
Reflecting	Students categorize the subgroups of their particular finite group and make initial speculations on the sizes of subgroups that are possible.
Explaining	Whole class pools its results (on the board or on chart paper). After more reflection and discussion, as a class we attempt to describe what we see, explain it and make generalizations and conjectures. Some conjectures are easily refuted because they do not fit the displayed data. For others, proofs can be attempted. This results in a "need to know" more algebraic ideas in order to prove Lagrange's Theorem. These conjectures can become the basis of further experiential exercises in following classes or a lecture can be given on the material if preferred or if time is scarce.
Experimenting	Even before a proof of the general theorem is attempted some students might observe that we have verified its validity only in the case of cyclic groups. Students might then be motivated to test their conjectures on non-cyclic finite groups and finite non-commutative groups, and the cycle continues.

the extent of instructor preference for, or experience and comfort with, active learning and student interaction in class.

Another important factor to consider in designing learning experiences for deep learning is the nature of the expectations of dualistic learners. Because they respect only the authority of the teacher and do not believe they have anything to learn from peers, we must anticipate and prepare for student resistance to active learning and to small-group work in particular. The introduction of group work must therefore be gradual and limited at first until the students begin to see the benefits of taking a more active role in their own learning and the value of engaging with their peers. As students become accustomed to simpler strategies, more complex collaborative learning strategies can be introduced.[7]

Responding to Students' Time Constraints and Lack of Preparation

Much of what I said above also relates to the impact of students' time constraints and background preparation on their success in learning. When students are actively involved in the learning process, they are learning important study skills and tend to find the time to work on a course.

If students are ill prepared, then they should be taught the skills they need – not in remedial courses, but within their required courses and through an approach that promotes a deep, process-oriented approach to learning rather than rote memorization. For example, reading exercises, such as those described in Rogers (1992), can be used in a variety of ways to teach students the skills of asking good questions, explaining their ideas clearly and convincingly, understanding the meaning of a definition and cooperating with each other to understand a concept or a proof. The use of such strategies might entail reduced coverage but in the long term it will produce more effective learners who will also be capable of learning material on their own.

When students find that they have little time to study, they will prioritize more meaningful and immediate tasks over activities that can be postponed. So faculty need to help students choose different priorities by making it hard for them to ignore the demands of their courses. For example, the teacher who lectures on assigned reading material teaches students that they do not need to prepare in advance. Instead, teachers could make it essential for students to come to class prepared by basing the class on the assigned readings through questioning or assigning problems, by springing pop quizzes or by asking students to give presentations at the board.[8] In another example, if students complain that they cannot find the time to work together in small groups, then faculty can assist them by setting aside time in class to help them form small study groups to meet at mutually convenient times to discuss the course material.[9]

Conclusion

I have argued that much of what instructors despair about in their students' approach to learning is within their power to transform. Knowing more about learning theories and students' intentions in the approach they take to learning provides instructors with a conceptual basis for making curricular choices. I have also described a model that provides instructors with guidance in choosing and sequencing learning activities that are best suited to their particular teaching style and most appropriate for helping students achieve the learning objectives of the course.

Early reports from Problem University suggest that faculty are introducing more active learning approaches into their teaching and are pleased with the results. As the situation has slowly improved and faculty have gained more confidence in their own convictions, they have developed their own strategies for making students more responsible for their own learning and more responsive to the goals of the course.

Notes

1. Throughout this section I am either paraphrasing or quoting directly from transcripts of my interviews.
2. In this section, I borrow extensively from Gibbs (1992, 1–11).
3. As quoted in Gibbs (1992, 3).
4. Perry's model has been criticized because it relies exclusively on interviews with male students. Another scheme (Belenky *et al.* 1986), based entirely on women, provides a richer and more complex analysis. For more details about the Perry scheme see the article by Westcott earlier in this section.
5. See, for example, Tobias (1990).
6. See, for example, the author's article "Improving Student Learning in Lectures" in Section VI.
7. Several strategies for easing students into group work are described in Section VI and in Rogers (1992). *The Journal of College Science Teaching* is also worth browsing.
8. See also the articles on reading in Section VII.
9. See Katie Coulthard's article on study groups in Section VI for guidance on how to do this.

References

Belenky, Mary Field *et al.* 1986. *Women's ways of knowing: The development of self, voice and mind.* New York: Basic Books.

Dahlgren, L-O. 1984. Outcomes of learning. In *The experience of learning*, F. Marton, D. Hounsell and N.J. Entwistle (eds.). Edinburgh: Scottish Academic Press.

Gibbs, Graham. 1992. *Improving the quality of student learning.* Bristol: Technical and Education Services.

Kolb, D.A. 1984. *Experiential learning: Experience as the source of learning and development.* Englewood Cliffs, NJ: Prentice-Hall.

Marton F. and R. Saljo. 1984. Approaches to learning. In *The experience of learning*, F. Marton, D. Hounsell and N.J. Entwistle (eds.). Edinburgh: Scottish Academic Press.

Perry, W.G. 1970. *Forms of intellectual and ethical development in the college years: A scheme.* New York: Holt, Rinehart and Winston.

Rogers, Pat. 1992. Transforming mathematics pedagogy. *On Teaching and Learning* (May): 78–98.

Svinicki, Marilla D. and Nancy M. Dixon. 1987. The Kolb model modified for classroom activities. *College Teaching* 35 (4): 141–46.

Tobias, Sheila. 1990. *They're not dumb, they're different: Stalking the second tier.* Tucson, AZ: Research Corporation.

Weimer, Maryellen. 1990. Teaching tensions: Confronting opposing forces in today's classrooms. *AAHE Bulletin* (May): 9–13.

Section III:
Course Design

This section is devoted to course design. The first two articles raise issues that can be applied to course planning in any discipline. The article by Rehner and Spencer provides a practical outline of steps to take in designing a course, emphasizing the need for clear, reasonable course goals to guide the planning process. The range of issues to consider extends beyond content goals to include critical skills and attitudes you also want students to learn, and how to design activities to meet those goals. This article is useful for first-time teaching faculty, but some of its insights also might be instructive for more seasoned faculty.

The Bazley article asks us to ponder the relationship between course content, critical skills and style of teaching in designing a science course, and emphasizes the importance of using feedback throughout the course to assess whether you are meeting your course goals. These themes could apply to any discipline.

The Ginsburg article provides a wonderful counter-point to the idea of a well-planned course. Like all good plans, even well-organized course plans can go astray. Ginsburg's example of how a history course evolved provides a humble and poignant reminder that however well we might think we have planned the perfect course, every course develops its own dynamic and we must be prepared to respond appropriately. Rigidly sticking to one's plan despite student discontent and frustration does not enhance the teaching or learning experience. The key is to adapt the course plan with your goals for student learning in mind.

The remaining two articles speak to issues of course planning in specific disciplines, but also raise important issues that apply more generally. Fenton's article on teaching goals in science urges us to reflect on the tension between covering the "facts" of a discipline and finding ways to develop students' curiosity for the unknown. The excitement of science lies in the latter, and Fenton urges us to keep our teaching goals focused on students' learning the passion of scientific inquiry, a suggestion that is useful in other disciplinary contexts. The final article, by Adolph, discusses the tension between teaching content and form in an English class. Both are important, but Adolph ponders the best way to get students engaged in the quintessential *practice* of the discipline. These two articles remind us that an important goal in our course planning should be for students to learn not just the facts of the discipline, but also the excitement that each of us feels as a practitioner in our discipline.

Course Planning: From Design to Active Classroom

Jan Rehner and John Spencer

As critical skills coordinators, we are often asked to provide guidelines about course design that will help integrate content, skills, assignments and classroom activity. There are no magic formulas or rigid rules for course design, but we hope these guidelines might make the link between content and skills more explicit. Essentially, teaching critical skills is not a discrete activity, but a means of teaching content in active and student-centred ways.

To design an effective course, you need to consider a full range of issues, all of which should be interrelated with your course goals. Thus it is best to clarify your content and critical skills goals first and then to design assignments, consider classroom activities and obtain feedback to reinforce those goals. Other facets of course design include the kind of climate you wish to establish in the classroom and the appropriate workload. The following outline will guide you through the process of course design in a linear fashion, but be aware that planning is often a recursive process. In other words, clarifying one part of the course could cause you to reconsider a previously defined aspect.

A key objective of this exercise is for you to make explicit each of your course goals and the relationship of each assignment, activity and evaluation format to those goals. Making these goals explicit to your students is a key component in developing their critical skills.

Process Guide for Designing Your Course
What Are Your Course Goals?
A. Content
In determining your content goals, you will probably want to decide the following:

- the theoretical issues and abstract concepts that you want your students to understand
- the basic information and facts that you want your students to know

- required texts
- appropriate supplementary texts.

In considering content goals, you might start with the theoretical issues that you want your course to emphasize and then choose texts that illuminate those issues. Alternatively, you could start with some texts you want to include and then determine the theoretical issues raised by those texts. It is useful to consider the word "texts" in it broadest definition; in addition to books and articles, you might want to use music, film, painting, architecture, primary documents and so on.

B. Critical Skills

After clarifying your content goals, consider what skills your students need to develop to enhance their learning of the content. You might begin by listing all of the critical skills you would ideally like your students to develop and then prioritize that list to help you limit the critical skills goals to a manageable number. Your critical skills goals might focus on the development of some of the following:

- reading effectively: in addition to books and articles, other kinds of texts such as film, painting, music and so on
- comprehension: the ability to paraphrase or summarize ideas and translate them into your own words
- analysis: questioning strategies and generating ideas; the ability to connect theoretical issues with course texts and concrete situations
- strategies of argument: dissection of ideas; integration of ideas
- appropriate use of evidence: ability to judge the value of an idea, procedure and so on, using criteria appropriate to your discipline
- formulating and testing hypotheses
- discipline-based research.

In choosing the critical skills important to your course, it is preferable to begin at a basic level and build towards more complex skills. Until you have met with your class, you should not assume that students already have certain skills because they might be novices in your discipline. Remember, however, that one course cannot effectively teach *all* the critical skills a student needs to succeed at university. Focus on two or three skills most relevant to your course and your discipline.

C. Attitudes

Although often overlooked, it is worthwhile to make explicit those attitudes you wish to encourage in your students. These attitudes might include an appreciation of the subject or discipline and more generally, intellectual curiosity, self-reflection and a spirit of tolerance and open-mindedness. As with all your course goals, you need to develop activities that will foster these attitudes and you need to model them in your own interaction with students, texts and ideas.

What Assignments and Activities Can You Design To Accomplish Your Course Goals Effectively?

A. Formal Assignments and Assignment Design

In this part of your course design you should decide how many and what kinds of assignments you want your students to complete. Again, the guiding principle is to link your course assignments to course goals, which necessitates considering assignment variety, sequencing and format.

Adding variety to your course assignments is crucial as it allows you to focus on the development of a range of critical skills, appeals to different student learning styles, makes the course more interesting and enhances the opportunity to build from simpler to more complex skills. In addition to, or in place of, the traditional analytical essays and exams, there are many assignments you can choose from, including the following:

- writing journals, précis, abstracts, reaction papers, reviews or collaborative essays
- participating in field trips
- conducting library or laboratory research
- reading strategy sheets
- conducting interviews
- solving problem sets.

Many of these assignments are discussed more fully in Section VII of this book, "Assignments and Evaluation," and in various issues of *Core*, the newsletter for York University's Centre for the Support of Teaching. In addition, the centre might be able to put you in touch with members of the York faculty currently using some of these assignments in their courses.

B. Classroom Activities

Student-centred activities in the classroom provide students with the opportunity to learn critical skills strategies and apply them to course content. A comfortable rhythm in the classroom necessitates balancing variety with patience and reasonable limits. For example, trying a new activity every week will probably make the classroom too frantic; it is wiser to choose three or four activities that the students can become comfortable with over time. After choosing the mixture of activities that best meets course goals, you must explicitly communicate their purpose to your students. To help you determine which activities might best promote your critical skills goals, Section VI of this book, "Teaching and Learning Activities," discusses a range of such activities from which you can choose. It includes discussion and explanations of

- lecturing, questioning and assessment techniques
- group work
- case studies
- methods to improve class participation.

C. Evaluation

Evaluation should stem from and reinforce course goals. First you should determine the kind of evaluation most appropriate to your course. There are a number of assessment models to choose from, including self-assessment, peer evaluation and professor evaluation. Again, the Centre for the Support of Teaching has resources available to help you determine which assessment models can best serve your own and your students' needs. At this point you should also think about the distribution of grades among various formal assignments and classroom activities. Although often overlooked, it is wise to decide on a course policy for late papers, the granting of extensions and the grading of any rewritten assignments before the course begins.

What Is an Appropriate Workload for Your Students?

There are a number of institutional constraints to consider in determining course workload. These include the year level; the established standards in your department, division or college; the number of student contact hours; the lecture-tutorial ratio and class size. Given these constraints, the need to balance content and critical skills goals, and your own available time and energy, it is necessary to be realistic in defining your course goals. It might be helpful to consider this issue metaphorically: the question is not "how much gold is there in the hills?," the question is "how much will your bucket hold?"

This outline provides a useful starting point for designing your course and for using some of the resources available at through York's Centre for the Support of Teaching. However, the design process is ongoing in that you will likely reconsider your course as you teach it, as you consult with your colleagues and as you interact with your students. Much of this book was designed to help you decide on particular assignments and strategies for classroom participation and activities.

Developing and Teaching a Science Course: A Junior Faculty Member's Perspective

Dawn R. Bazely

When I taught my first upper-level biology course, I realized the limited practical use of my prior, extensive experience preparing tutorials, laboratory demonstrations and short field courses. Planning and delivering a half- or full-year course demanded a breadth of vision much greater than that required for, say, planning eight one-hour tutorials in animal behaviour.

I found it helpful to break down the process of course planning into three basic components, which are presented in the following diagram.

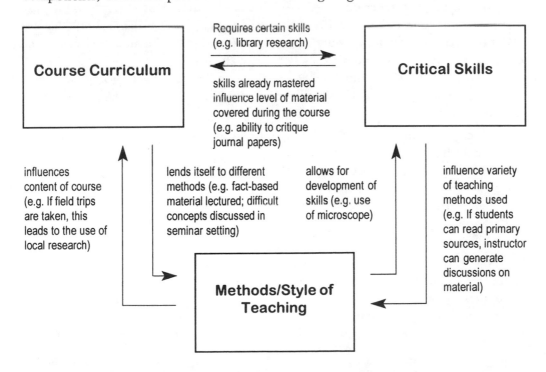

Judgements must be made about all three areas. With regard to "course curriculum," one must decide on the body of academic information to be included. The area of "critical skills" raises three issues: the skills beginning students need to have to cope with the subject matter, how to gauge the skills one's students already possess and how to determine what additional skills they need to develop. Finally, one must settle on the "methods and style of teaching" to use – whether to have tutorials and/or laboratory sessions, whether to use overheads, what marking scheme to employ, etc.

These three areas interact with each other. For example, the content of my fourth-year course in plant ecology required that students already had particular skills (such as, the ability to understand certain statistical analyses). On the other hand, the skills students possessed influenced the level at which I was able to teach the course (for example, familiarity with reading journal articles rather than only textbooks). Additionally, the nature of plant ecology required that the course involve field trips, and the use of field trips to local forests resulted in my use of Ontario research for examples in my lectures.

Once I had constructed this model of the teaching process for myself, course planning and development became easier. In thinking about course content, I drew on my experience as a plant ecologist as well as on various texts. In thinking about my classroom teaching style and methods of delivering information, I drew upon memories of my own teachers, remembering what I liked and disliked, and also on ideas from publications such as *Core* and *The Teaching Professor*. (For example, as a student, I disliked lecturers who used overheads because I could never keep up with note-taking, so as a teacher I decided to use the blackboard.) However, it was the third component of course planning, deciding on the critical skills students should have in order to learn most from my course, that I have found to be the most interesting and challenging part of course design.

I made a list of the skills I believe third-and fourth-year biology students should have developed or be in the process of developing. I feel they should have the ability to:

- locate primary literature (that is, journal articles) and to evaluate material critically
- locate recent literature and use it in a research essay
- participate freely and with confidence in scientific discussions
- give effective short (ten-minute), well-structured and coherent presentations and talks
- discriminate truth from unsubstantiated claims in printed material.

This list probably had more influence on my course design than anything else, apart from some obvious curricular decisions about what a course in plant ecology should cover. In their research essays, I required students to include at least some references from recent journal articles. We occasionally had tutorials instead of lectures in which we discussed specific papers, often presenting opposing points of view. Prior to these discussions, I assigned one or two students to prepare critiques of their research essays for presentation to the group.

There is an invisible component in my course planning model that I have found invaluable and that has the potential to improve all aspects of course design. This is student feedback. Initially, I solicited verbal feedback, but in some courses I eventually designed my own surveys. Of course, I sometimes got feedback in the form of complaints, for example, that the workload was too heavy, and I gave these complaints serious consideration. But I received other feedback that was positive. For example, one student said that she finally realized what research in biology was all about and why journal articles were interesting and valuable.

In conclusion, I am sure that, if asked, many new faculty would acknowledge that their lack of formal training in teaching can make planning and teaching a course for the first time an enormous challenge. I completely agree. My model for course planning has worked for me, and I hope it will be of use to others.

The Dialectic of Course Development: I Theorize, They React...and Then?

Jerry Ginsburg

I am not a dialectical kind of guy. I don't like to learn on the fly, to grow through experimentation and interaction. I prefer to attack problems in a sequential fashion, moving logically from premises to conclusions. Given my temperament, I naturally hewed to a deductive procedure when I set out, two sabbaticals ago, to develop a new third-year course in nineteenth-century American political history. I carefully identified my teaching goals and pedagogic assumptions. Then, with Cartesian elegance, I derived a perfect course structure. Unfortunately, it survived only three weeks of class. Perhaps recounting why it had to be modified – not once, but repeatedly over the next ten years – will shed some light on the messy way that courses actually evolve.

In organizing my course I relied on what seemed a self-evident truth: that students learn more when actively engaged in the education process. From this principle I drew two conclusions: that discussion-focused courses are superior to lectures (since lectures encourage spectatorship and reliance on authority) and that having to "process" readings results in greater understanding than merely doing them. (I have since learned that my first deduction underestimates the potential of the lecturing process. But being a university professor I was unburdened by any formal knowledge of teaching when I set out to design my class.)

The course I developed from these two premises had two novel features, both related to the "processing" of the readings. To encourage students not to get bogged down in historical minutiae, I asked them to produce, on a biweekly basis, a four-by-six-inch card identifying the central thesis of each work contained in the hundred pages of reading per week. To stimulate lateral thinking and to allow room for the students to pursue their own interests, I also asked them to define an interesting research problem flowing from the readings. The idea was that on alternate weeks, the students would pursue these research problems, generating a two- to four-page mini research paper in the process. As a reward, they would face no final examination or long end-of-term essay.

By week three it became apparent that the students could not begin to do the amount of work required. So we compromised. I modified the requirement to five note cards and one or two longer essays per term. The result was a set of undistinguished semi-long essays and a remarkably close-knit class (the students being bonded both by the still-heavy reading demands of the course and the excellent discussions that resulted when they came to class genuinely prepared).

Over the next few years I tinkered with the assignment mechanism. Having found that insecure students could pack a mind-numbing number of words onto a four-by-six-inch card, I began to require that their "summaries" be turned in – preferably typed – on normal-sized paper. The bigger problem concerned the mini research program. This was a decided bust. In its place, I inserted a series of class debates, a shift inspired by the galvanizing effect of an unplanned debate in a previous class. In the new format the students, divided into teams, had to participate in one debate per term. A wide array of topics keyed to the readings gave most a chance to pursue a subject of genuine interest. We held the debates during the one-hour meetings of the course, with the two-hour weekly meetings still devoted to discussion of the readings.

This revised format was only moderately successful. The summaries – boosted to nine or ten per semester – continued to promote critical reading and excellent class discussion. But the debates proved a mixed bag. At their best they were highly engaging, but at their worst they were excruciating. Watching two teams of nervous students burrow determinedly through disorganized notes, oblivious to the opposition and the audience, was not an elevating experience. Clearly, a new format for the short days was needed. What I didn't anticipate was that it would evolve as a result of a quite separate change in the weekly essays.

By the seventh year of the course, these papers had been refined in three ways. First, in response to repeated appeals, I now provided the students with lists of questions – "summary emphases" – to guide their assessment of the readings. Indicative of the growth of the course, these questions became quite challenging. For example, in dealing with the reconstruction of the post-Civil War South, rather than asking the students to summarize the legislation involved, I would require that they decide whether it was fundamentally liberal in nature. A second change in the essays concerned their length. To encourage concise writing and also to minimize my burgeoning grading chore, I required that the students limit their responses to my questions to no more than two type-written pages, or five hundred words. (The students soon realized this limitation was not the gift it seemed. In response to their complaints regarding the amount of time it took to write the sharply focused – and reasonably polished – essays now being demanded, we jointly decided to reduce the number they owed me to six per semester.)

The final change in the papers concerned the introduction of a new ungraded element called the "enlightenment." As a postscript to their essays (which could be informally written and of any length), the students were asked to address the following question: "If history is supposed to enlighten your life, what enlightenment did you draw from the readings for the week?" My objective was to encourage reflection on how the knowledge the students gained through school enriched their "real" lives, a linkage that can be pretty obscure when studying the dead-and-gone world of the nineteenth century.

To my delight, some of the responses I received were just wonderful – sensitive, thoughtful and full of life. I was so inspired that on occasion I read some of the commentaries to the class (without attribution, though the writers were often happy to be recognized). These, it turned out, generated superb discussions. Students were constantly amazed by what members of the class took from the readings. "You mean you liked the articles on the antebellum economic system? You found they *illuminated your life*?" "Actually, yes. That reading on apprenticeship in particular made me think about how little pride I feel in my job, how little connection to the products I sell." And away they would go.

It became apparent that I had stumbled upon a way to structure my short classes. I would read aloud the most poignant "enlightenments" and let the discussion proceed where it would. (Is this still history? I'm not sure. Would I like my colleagues hanging over my shoulder in class? Oh, I don't think so. Are the students learning? Of that, I'm confident.)

Finally I had the perfect course…except for one minor problem. Sometimes students more or less dropped out of the course after completing their mandatory six assignments per term. Adding a participation mark had little impact on this phenomenon. So this year I reluctantly added a final examination worth 20 per cent to encourage attendance. The student response, by March, was an unsettling mixture of hysteria and despair. They simply didn't have time to do all the readings as closely as the course demanded. Adding a final exam had not eliminated the root problem but simply highlighted it.

I have a new plan for next year, but I've finally come to the realization that it won't end my quest. Try as I might, I will never be able to develop the perfect course. Even if my design for next year does not reveal an unexpected failing (like my final exam scheme), it will inevitably become ineffective in the face of change – in my students, in the material I am teaching, in myself. This is not an easy lesson for a logical/sequential person and in many areas I continue to resist it. I still have little time for thoroughgoing relativism and believe that even in history there are Truths, not just perspectives that evolve through time. But when it comes to course development, it seems inescapable that "progress" is dialectical and never ending. One tries, the students respond, and then, if you care, you amend and move on.

Lord, I hate to learn on the go.

Beyond Bare Facts:
Teaching Goals in Science

M. Brock Fenton

To students and non-scientists, science seems to be dominated by a multitude of facts that must be retained to demonstrate one's grasp of a topic. Challenging students to recall facts or use them to solve problems provides a convenient and objective way of assessing student performance. This approach is particularly attractive when classes are large and students expect prompt return of graded material. Scientists justify their emphasis on "facts" by comparing scientific facts to the vocabulary one needs to learn a language. There is some truth to this, but reality is a bit more complex. Most scientists are not in the game because of the facts they can accumulate. They are scientists because of what they do not know. Curiosity drives their enthusiasm for science.

Here I suggest three ways we might change our teaching of science to inspire such curiosity in our students.

Science and the Unknown

The lure that draws people into science and keeps them there is the unknown. The answers to many basic questions in science continue to elude us, providing a challenge to future generations of investigators. Science teaching can be more dynamic if instructors identify areas needing study in the future. Speaking about the things we do not know and how we might explore them will help students understand the excitement that keeps scientists active.

Science and Writing

Employers are often critical of the inability of science graduates to write effectively. Unfortunately, multiple choice and similar examination techniques – though facilitating the objective assessment of students, particularly in courses focusing on factual material – do nothing to develop a student's communications skills. Requiring science students to write short essays could help. Essays of three hundred to five hundred words can be graded in a way that offers qualitative and quantitative feedback to students without imposing an unbearable burden on the instructor. Topics can include such things as the history of a subject ("outline three factors contributing to the development of…") and the work of prominent scientists ("discuss Dr. X's recent contributions to…"). In addition to other benefits, such assignments quickly help students learn to make effective use of the library.

Science and Speaking

As students progress beyond first and second year, more and more science courses should include oral presentations as part of their requirements. Brief (five- to ten-minute) student "lectures" can be used to introduce laboratory or tutorial sessions, giving students the opportunity to research topics, prepare material and make spoken presentations. Public speaking will become an integral part of the careers of many of our graduates, so we should take steps to ensure that they get an early start in this area.

Each of these approaches exposes students to factual material. But placing the facts in a more enticing context can result in a more enjoyable and effective learning experience.

"Why Didn't He Just Say It?": Getting Students Interested in Language

Robert Adolph

It is your Tuesday 10 o'clock in "Intro Lit," and the reading is selections from *Walden*. The lecture seems to go well. First a summary of the high points of Thoreau's life: the stifled romance, the journeys to Cape Cod and Maine, the fateful night in the Concord jail, the relationship with Emerson and the Transcendentalists, the support of John Brown, and finally, to liven things up, the deathbed zinger when, on being asked by a pious auntie if he'd made his peace with God, Brown replied that he never knew they'd quarreled. The students like it; at least, they take lots of notes. Then a summary of the experiment at Walden Pond as an inversion and redefinition of the American Dream of Success. You get more specific, bringing in Thoreau's advocacy of voluntary poverty, civil disobedience and environmentalism. You mention the influence of all this on Gandhi and the 1960s. They are still with you, though you notice that the Moral Majority types are uneasy. Good – that means you are still getting to them. It's still going well.

Then it's discussion time. You start talking about the style of *Walden* and it doesn't go well at all. They lose interest right away. Most of them, you soon discover, have not made it past the first few pages. It's not that they don't want to and it's not that they don't like Thoreau's ideas, though, of course, they have no intention of practising them. It's just that, well, the style is too hard, though curiously, they don't want to talk about style, the very thing that is causing them problems. It all seems so irrelevant, they say, and not worth the effort, and why do we have to learn all those horrible words like symbolism and metaphor? All this, we know all too well. But my purpose here is to recall something so obvious that it has been forgotten, as the obvious always is: namely, that we must teach our students that language and style are the heart and soul of literature.

Now some of their alienation could come from *Walden* being an old book, as Thoreau himself scornfully referred to the Bible. Like Huck Finn confronted with Widow Douglas's required reading on Moses and the bullrushers, they don't take stock in dead people. Nor do they catch Thoreau's allusions to literature or history; in fact, they don't understand why there must be allusions at all. Maybe, you start to think, they are some sort of exotic species, lost not only to history and old books but to the printed word altogether. Mellowed out on their Sony Walkmans, their sensoriums, as the barbarous dialect of the McLuhanites would have it, are visual, electronic, oral and tribal rather than linear. Or, as our dialect would have it, they don't know how to read.

The students, of course, don't see it this way. Literature should either entertain or "say something," and we like to think the literature we teach does both. "But," they ask of Thoreau, "if he had something to say, why didn't he just say it? Why did he have to make it so hard?" In other words, what is literary language?

Now how do you answer their question about the nature of literary language? Well, you've done your homework and keep in touch with critical theory. If you are of a certain age you were probably brought up a New Critic and as an undergraduate imbibed the concept of literature as complex patterns of ambiguity, irony, tension, tone and point of view. When Brooks and Warren went out of style you might have dabbled in rhetoric, transformational grammar and sociolinguistics. Swarms of Marxists and feminists warned you how class, race and gender biases infect all language, reading and critical discourse. From myth critics, semioticians, psychoanalytic critics, structuralists and postmodernists, you learned that literary language exists as elaborate ciphers, signifiers of half-hidden archetypes, structures, instincts, codes and ideologies. And now, according to the post-structuralists and Reader Response people, anything goes. And so, your worries are over. It doesn't really matter what Thoreau said after all, but what you could have said he might have said.

Unfortunately, though, Grand Theory won't help you in your Tuesday 10 o'clock. At any rate, you can hardly send them barefoot through the likes of Chomsky, Barthes and Derrida, so how can you get them interested in language and able to talk about it? You might ask yourself at this point, what is *their* theory of literature? After all, when we think of literature we assume a dualistic understanding of language. One kind of language, lucid and requiring no analysis, gives us the Message or Useful Truth. The other kind – "style" – is stuck onto the Message as ornament, presumably to make it go down better, but more often than not obscuring it. The Message is more important than style; it is the "it" in "Why didn't he just say it?" Hence the perception that stylistic analysis is irrelevant and perverse.

Can we return, as the phenomenologists say, to the thing itself? Or is Northrop Frye right when he says that we cannot teach literature, only literary criticism; that is, facts or ideas *about* literature? The problem is that literature is two very different things at the same time. Antihumanistic post-structuralist theory and recent experiments in non-referential or concrete poetry notwithstanding, literature is still, at least in "Intro Lit," "about" something other than itself. This something – not Messages but values, passions, ideas, bicycles, sexism, butterfly wings, war, the sun, the moon, the stars – is conveyed through a very different something – language. If we emphasize one without the other we are not returning to the thing itself of literature, and Frye is right.

Frye is wrong, though, if, on the one hand, we avoid teaching style as a subject by itself, as "devices" to be discovered, defined and catalogued with no reference to anything but themselves. Hence the failure of introductory courses based on Grand Theory — rigorous linguistic or rhetorical approaches that might be fascinating intellectual exercises in their own right but end up frustrating the students by keeping them from the literary *Ding an sich*. Equally bad is the opposite, the teaching of literature without reference to language but purely as Great Ideas or Answers to Questions or artifacts of cultural history or social sciences or playthings of solipsistic deconstructors.

When we ask, "What does this word (or line, or paragraph or novel) mean?" we are really asking, to be sure, "What are its contexts?" — cultural, historical, biographical, political or whatever. And we are also asking, with our students, "Why didn't he just say it?"

Literature is not, or is not principally, the transmission of information, but is usually perverse, setting up formal impediments so that its total significance can never be summarized or paraphrased. The effect of these linguistic impediments on perceptive, open readers is that, first, they see things in a fresh way in what the Russian Formalists called "defamiliarization"; second, as a result, there seem to open up endless vistas of meaning and interpretive possibilities; and third, every detail in organically unified texts seems to relate to every other. These are the true pleasures of the text, and they all depend on language. Thus, while no interpretation will ever be "right," some are superior to others, and those that ignore language will be no good at all. This, it seems to me, is what we must demonstrate in our teaching.

In "Intro Lit" we should *begin* with style, rather than save it for the end, after the Message. I like to sneak up on a text from behind by choosing a specific stylistic item that seems to me to reach out into the heart of a text's meaning, both internally and in relation to its contexts. I concede that my choice of foregrounded stylistic item and significant meaning is purely intuitive. Take, for example, a sentence at the start of *Walden*: "I have travelled a good deal in Concord (Thoreau 1966, 2)." It is quite possible to spend an hour or so on that word "travelled," which in its context connotes spiritual journeying as well as walking around and generates Thoreau's central comparison between, on the one hand, the physical, pointless movement of the American Dream of Success, and on the other hand, his redefinition of success as a spiritual traveling to new frontiers of the imagination. I get them into all this by asking, "Why 'travelled'? Why not 'strolled' or 'walked'?" Then we all explore the related lexical set, common in *Walden*, of various terms referring to travel, movement and so on.

After a while, if we have all been doing our work, the text begins to resonate, and you've won. Then it is time to ask *them*, "Why didn't he just say it?" They will be able to answer with some precision. Then they'll *want* to know about the topical references, allusions and so on. If all goes well, the students will see that the "meaning" of a text is not the Message but a kind of vibration between all parts of the text together on one side, and whatever the reader brings to it on the other. They might even develop, to use a Transcendentalist phrase, original relations to the universe. As Thoreau put it, reading must not be astrological – merely utilitarian – but astronomical.

Choosing the text is half the battle in "Intro Lit." Almost any bit of writing can be seen, in some sense and in some context, as "literature." What, then, shall we have our students read? *Walden* is particularly fortunate here, because it so deliberately throws up stylistic impediments with the express purpose of defamiliarizing the reader. Most obviously through his wealth of brilliant puns, Thoreau deliberately tips language upside down and turns it inside out so that we will slow down our reading and see things in fresh ways. And Thoreau is also completely explicit about what he is doing, and its connection with his deconstruction of American civilization. At the end of *Walden* he sums up, in a few extravagant sentences on the subject of extravagant expression, all that I have tried to say about the essential playful flamboyance of literary language, its ability to get us to see things in a fresh way and its opening up of new vistas of meaning beyond itself. In Thoreau's mind, all this is inevitably associated with the possibilities symbolized by travel on the American frontier – for Thoreau, of course, the physical frontier serving only as an image, as the physical Concord did, for the finer frontier, at once more spiritual and profoundly subversive:

> I fear chiefly lest my expression may not be *extra-vagant* enough, may not wander far enough beyond the narrow limits of my daily experience, so as to be adequate to the truth of which I have been convinced. *Extra vagance!* It depends on how you are yarded. The migrating buffalo, which seeks new pastures in another latitude, is not extravagant like the cow which kicks over the pail, leaps the cow-yard fence, and runs after her calf, in milking time. I desire to speak somewhere *without* bounds like a man in a waking moment, to men in their waking moments; for I am convinced that I cannot exaggerate enough even to lay the foundation of a true expression (214).

References

Thoreau, Henry David. 1966. *Walden and civil disobedience, Owen Thomas (ed.).* New York: Norton Critical Editions.

Section IV:
Working with
Graduate Students

Often overlooked in thinking about university-level teaching and learning are the issues that relate to graduate teaching. Here we consider two dimensions of that learning experience. Graduate students learn as students in a discipline, but at the same time, they are also apprenticing to become teachers. In each case, much of that learning hinges on successful relationships between faculty members and graduate students. Leyton-Brown's article addresses the relationship between graduate student and supervisor, offering guidelines for a successful supervisory relationship. The next two articles focus on teaching apprenticeship relationships. As a graduate teaching assistant, Dionne discusses how teaching assistants can have a productive working relationship with the course director. The Green article has the same focus, but Green's perspective is that of a faculty member working with teaching assistants on a course. Finally, the Elson article offers tips and suggestions for the international teaching assistant in dealing with language and cultural differences in teaching.

Graduate Supervisory Practices

David Leyton-Brown

The research experience is the heart of graduate education and the supervisory relationship is essential to the quality of that experience. Recognizing and respecting the differences among practices in different disciplines, and among individual learning and supervisory styles, the relationship between the graduate student and the faculty supervisor is perhaps the most important academic determinant of the quality of the graduate student's education. Especially at the doctoral level, the quality of supervisory practices can facilitate or discourage successful completion of the degree program, can accelerate or delay progress towards completion of that program and can have a powerful influence on the academic quality of the dissertation itself.

Different types of supervisory relationships will be more or less appropriate for different personalities and styles (of the student as well as of the supervisor). Some students want and need close direction, while others wish to be left largely to their own devices, taking the initiative to seek feedback from the supervisor only at times of their own choosing. Some supervisors are more comfortable and effective when being quite directive, while others encourage independent initiative and approach. Nevertheless, while students must be willing to seek a supervisor with a compatible style and to speak out if the pace or intensity of supervision does not seem suitable, in general the greater responsibility must rest with supervisors to be sensitive to the learning styles of their students, and within the boundaries of their own styles and abilities, to shape their supervisory practices accordingly.

Different types of supervisory relationships also might be called for at different stages of the student's program of study. Again allowing for disciplinary variations and individual preferences, the needs of students can vary and different practices might be suitable at the various stages of initial definition of the research topic, design of the specific research project (that is, the dissertation proposal), training in research methodology, actual conduct of research to acquire data, analysis of that data, initial

147

writing of draft chapters of the dissertation, revision of draft material, bringing the project to completion and preparation for defence.

Research has shown that the quality of supervision is one of the most important variables accounting not only for the quality of the dissertation produced, but for the completion rate and the time to completion of doctoral study (See CGS 1990, OCGS 1991, Fletcher and Stren 1992 and Bowen and Rudenstine 1992). This and other research also has shown the effectiveness of certain supervisory practices in enhancing the quality of the supervisory relationship, and thus of completion times and rates, and of the academic quality of the dissertations produced (SSERC 1983).

The quality of a supervisory relationship is dependent on recognition and acceptance by the supervisor and the student of their responsibilities to each other. Various universities have attempted to draft policies addressing the legitimate expectations students and supervisors have of each other, and to outline principles of effective supervision (York University 1992, University of Guelph 1991). The efforts of supervisors and students can be made more productive if each is conscious of the following principles.

Guidelines for Supervisors

The supervisor's principal task consists of helping students realize their scholarly potential. This can be accomplished only in a relationship that offers insights born of experience and furnishes the requisite challenges, stimulation, guidance and genuine support. The student has a right to expect the supervisor to bring to the relationship expertise, accessibility and support. The supervisor must offer substantive and procedural assistance with the design, planning and conduct of feasible research projects, introduction to the network of scholars in the area of specialization and support for the presentation and publication of the research results. At the same time the supervisor must ensure that the scholarly standards of the university and the discipline are met in the student's work. It is the responsibility of the supervisor to:

1. Conform to basic principles of academic integrity and professionalism in the development of a mature and objective relationship with the student. It must be recognized that there is a power imbalance in the supervisory relationship and care must be taken to ensure that there is not even inadvertent infringement on the rights of the student.

2. Be reasonably accessible to the student for consultation and discussion of the student's academic progress and research problems. The frequency of such meetings will vary according to the discipline involved and the stage and nature of the student's work. In the natural sciences, student and supervisor will work together in the laboratory daily, while in the humanities and social sciences, especially when the student is away from the university doing archival or field research, there could be months between formal meetings. Nevertheless, there is consensus in the literature that student – supervisor meetings should normally occur at least once a month and never less than once each term. Such regular meetings are especially important to guard against the prolonged drift that can

result if a student is at an impasse in research, analysis or writing and feels reluctant to approach the supervisor until the task is complete. Even where both parties prefer a loose supervisory relationship, the student will benefit not only from constructive criticism of draft material, but also from assistance in working through the inevitable problems that can temporarily stall any major scholarly enterprise.

3. Give timely responses to submitted written work, with constructive suggestions for improvements. Some research is prescriptive about a maximum permissible turnaround time for comments on draft chapters or parts of chapters (for example, two to three weeks). Exit surveys of graduating and withdrawing students now being conducted at various universities point to widespread student dissatisfaction with delayed supervisory response to submitted material as one of the most common, but easily remedied, complaints, even from successful students.

4. Make satisfactory arrangements for the supervision of the student when on leave or sabbatical, or on extended absence from the university. This does not mean that the supervisor need step down from that role, but that arrangements must be made for the student to receive the necessary supervisory contact and feedback during that absence – for example, through regular electronic communication or an enhanced role for other members of the supervisory committee. It is important that these arrangements be more than an informal understanding between the student and supervisor and also that they be known and approved by appropriate academic authorities such as the director of the graduate program.

5. Encourage the student to set realistic and attainable goals for the various stages of the dissertation project and be aware of the student's progress in working through those stages. Many universities have found it helpful to mandate a minimum of a progress report meeting once a term or once a year, in which the student describes the accomplishments of the past term or year and defines goals for the next term or year, and the supervisor comments on the appropriateness of the progress made and the subsequent goals set and advises changes in the overall plan as needed.

6. Ensure that the student is aware of university, faculty and program requirements and standards to which the dissertation is expected to conform. These will include everything from research ethics and expected scope of original research to deadlines and page formats and should not simply be taken for granted for students encountering them for the first time.

7. Assist the student with attempts to acquire external funding (for example, scholarship and research grant applications), including meeting appropriate deadlines, and to engage in scholarly development (such as conference presentations and publications).

8. Offer supervision and advice appropriate to the stage of the student's work, helping the student to establish and modify a suitable timetable for completion of the various stages of the dissertation project:

- At the proposal stage, assist the student with selection of a suitable and manageable topic and approach.
- At the research stage, assist the student with initial research design and subsequent modification, with alleviating current and anticipated problems, with interpretation and analysis of findings and with bringing the project to completion.
- At the writing stage, assist the student with appropriate and timely feedback on individual draft chapters and with revision to the draft dissertation as an integrated whole.
- At the oral defence stage, advise the student on preparation for the examination and assist the student to interpret and comply with any changes recommended by the examining committee.

9. Respect the intellectual property of the student and appropriately acknowledge in published material the contributions of the student, including consideration of joint authorship of publications (York University 1995). Where the student's research comprises a component of the supervisor's research program and joint publication is envisaged, it must be recognized that the responsibility for use of data and for publications is held jointly by the supervisor and student. It is useful and important to endeavour to clarify at the outset of the supervisory relationship expectations regarding the responsibility and publication credit for work initiated, designed and researched by the student, but supported financially or otherwise by the supervisor.

10. Maintain responsible standards of personal conduct, with particular recognition of the unacceptability of any form of racial, sexual or gender harassment.

11. Conform to graduate program and faculty grievance and appeal procedures in the event of a supervisory relationship that is unsatisfactory for any reason. It must be appreciated by all parties that when a supervisory relationship has broken down, it does not necessarily reflect fault on either the student or supervisor. When a supervisor and student can no longer work productively together, it might be necessary to seek a new supervisor.

Guidelines for Students

As observed above, a supervisory relationship involves two parties and both supervisor and student are responsible for making that relationship work effectively. The student is not a passive recipient of the supervisor's supervision, but an active participant in the supervisory relationship, with responsibilities that must be fulfilled. By entering into a doctoral program, the student has made a commitment to devote the time and energy necessary to engage in research and write a dissertation that constitutes a substantial and original contribution to knowledge in a field. The supervisor has a right to expect the student to bring to the relationship ability, initiative and receptivity. The student must seek advice when needed and be receptive to that advice when given. It is the responsibility of the student to:

1. Conform to university, faculty and program requirements and procedures for completion of the degree, with regard to such matters at research ethics, registration and graduation requirements, dissertation style and quality standards, etc.
2. Develop, in conjunction with the supervisor and supervisory committee, an intended timetable for completion of all stages of the dissertation and work to realize that timetable, meeting appropriate deadlines. It has been found that such a timetable breaks the student's dissertation project of unprecedented scale into manageable components. Far from locking the student into a rigid routine, the timetable can facilitate progress by setting a series of intermediate objectives against which reality can be measured and expectations revised.
3. Meet regularly with the supervisor to review progress and interact with other members of the supervisory committee as appropriate. The frequency of such meetings will vary according to the discipline involved and the stage and nature of the student's work. The preparation of a report on progress for regular meetings with the supervisory committee has been found to make these meetings more focused and productive. The student must inform the supervisor about problems as well as accomplishments, or the supervisor cannot be expected to respond to them.
4. Keep the supervisor and graduate program office informed of where the student can be contacted and respond appropriately to all communications received.
5. Give serious consideration to and respond to the advice and criticism received from the supervisor and the supervisory committee. Resistance to supervision is one of the most serious problems reported by faculty members in unsatisfactory supervisory relationships.
6. Recognize that the supervisor and other members of the supervisory committee have other teaching, research and service obligations that might preclude immediate responses. While the student is entitled to expect timely response to work submitted, the student must realize that it is not reasonable to expect the supervisor to drop all other responsibilities in favour of making that response.
7. Recognize that where the student's research comprises a component of the supervisor's research program and joint publication is envisaged, the responsibility for use of data and for publications is held jointly by the supervisor and student. In such cases, the dissertation, or draft papers, together with a copy of the raw data, should be made available to the supervisor prior to submission for publication.
8. Conform to basic principles of academic integrity and professionalism in the development of a mature and objective relationship with the supervisor, the supervisory committee and other scholars. The entire master's or doctoral program, including research and writing of the thesis or dissertation, should be conducted under the strictest rules of ethics and academic honesty.

As in any interpersonal relationship, the key to success is effective communication. That communication, and that supervisory relationship, is more likely to be effective if both supervisor and student are mindful of the responsibilities that each owes to the other and of their mutual expectations. The guidelines presented in this article can help to make those responsibilities and expectations explicit and to provide a foundation for effective supervisory practices on the part of both members of the supervisory relationship.

References

Bowen, William G. and Neil L. Rudenstine. 1992. *In pursuit of the Ph.D.* Princeton, NJ: Princeton University Press.

Council of Graduate Schools (CGS). 1990. *Research student and supervisor.* Washington: Council of Graduate Schools.

Fletcher, Joseph and Richard Stren. 1992. *Report on a survey of recent and current doctoral students at the University of Toronto.* Toronto: University of Toronto.

Ontario Council on Graduate Studies (OCGS). 1991. *Doctoral graduate rates in Ontario universities.* Ontario Council on Graduate Studies.

Social Science and Engineering Research Council (SSERC). 1983. *Research student and supervisor: A guide to good supervisory practices.* Swindon, UK: Social Science and Engineering Research Council.

University of Guelph, Faculty of Graduate Studies. 1991. *Responsibilities of advisors, advisory committees and graduate students.* Guelph, ON: University of Guelph, Faculty of Graduate Studies.

York University, Faculty of Graduate Studies. 1992. *Graduate supervisory principles, policies and practices.* Toronto: York University, Faculty of Graduate Studies.

York University. 1995. *Task force on intellectual property.* Toronto: York University.

Working Together: The Teaching Assistant– Professor Relationship

Annie Dionne

This article aims to help teaching assistants (TAs) and faculty members maintain good working relationships. It combines insights gleaned from other TAs as well as from my own teaching experience. Typically, TAs work on a course that a professor has designed. The professor lectures to a large number of students, while the TAs work with students in smaller groups as tutorial leaders and marker/graders. But not all of us work in ideal circumstances – teaching what we like and working with people we like. I will discuss the four aspects of the TA – professor relationship that are most significant in keeping that relationship a positive one. I hope that these suggestions will be useful even for TAs and professors in less than ideal situations.

Developing a Relationship Based on Mutual Respect

The first and most important characteristic of a good working relationship is mutual respect. Respect is an extremely complex issue that affects all other aspects of any working relationship. When I spoke with other TAs, the issue of mutual respect came up repeatedly and TAs agreed overwhelmingly that a lack of respect by either party had adverse effects on the overall learning environment for students.

Professors must openly demonstrate their respect for the work of the TAs with students by showing confidence in their roles and abilities. Failure to do so undermines the TAs' authority with students. TAs face students on a one-to-one basis, providing assistance and guidance on assignments and course material. In a fundamental sense, the TAs are professors' "front line" representatives with students and if they are to be effective, they need professors' support and trust. Students quickly notice when such confidence is lacking. They begin to question the authority of their TAs and are likely to question grades and other decisions made by their TAs. The classroom dynamic, in both the lecture and the tutorial, can mirror any lack of respect between the professor and the TA. At a minimum, students could lose faith in the quality of the teaching they receive in that course.

153

Equally important is the respect a TA must show for the professor. Typically, professors are responsible for the lectures, but they also have ultimate responsibility for the course and its overall quality. Often, they must work with novice TAs, some of whom might be ill equipped to deal with the complexities of the university classroom or have insufficient background to teach competently in a particular subject area. TAs who question a professor's authority, knowledge or judgement in front of students undermine the credibility of the professor and ultimately that of the course. Some students undoubtedly will exploit such a situation to personal advantage. Students might pay more attention to the internal dynamics of the teaching staff than to the course material.

This is not to suggest that legitimate intellectual disagreements or critical commentary are to be discouraged. Indeed, many professors expect their TAs to participate in critical discussion and to encourage the students to do the same. In the best courses, lectures are not meant to be dogma and tutorials are laboratories for critical thinking. But if critique is undertaken without respect, the authority of the TA or the professor will be undermined.

These insights can be summed up in four recommendations. First, air any serious disagreement about course organization, content or teaching styles privately and with discretion. Second, never, under any circumstances, demonstrate a lack of respect for one another's decisions or judgements in front of students. Third, try to discover ways to reinforce each other's roles and status as teachers engaged in an important enterprise. Fourth, remember that teaching is not a personality contest and that it helps if the teaching staff show mutual appreciation.

Communication

Communication is clearly a critical aspect of the teaching assistant – professor relationship and, by implication, the teacher – student relationship. Positive communication will maximize the involvement of each party. It is particularly important for the professor to encourage TAs to express their opinions on assignments and course material. Not only will the TAs feel more like partners in a joint enterprise, but they will also be able to provide the professor with valuable information on how the students are learning in the course. The TA often has a closer link to students and a better sense of how they might react to and perform on assignments.

With open communication, the TA and professor can depend on each other for information that will lead to the success of the course. Some of the contributions a TA can make have been mentioned already, but professors also can play a significant role by sharing their expertise with TAs and by communicating their deeper understanding of the course's subject matter. In large courses with several tutorials, the professor is the appropriate locus for the exchange of information on developments throughout the course. When TAs and professors collaborate, course consistency is maintained, teaching is improved and a positive and enjoyable relationship is maintained.

Five recommendations follow from this discussion. First, professors and TAs should ensure that the lines of communication in their courses are always open.

Second, TAs can help professors adjust their teaching by providing timely information on what is taking place in their tutorials. Third, as the academic year progresses, professors can be flexible in adjusting the course design and assignments in response to feedback from TAs. Fourth, while professors clearly have final authority for all decisions, they should solicit information and encourage input from TAs. Fifth, in courses for which TAs are not required to, or cannot, attend lectures (for example, because of contract requirements or timetable conflicts), professors can help ensure uniformity and mutuality by providing copies of lecture notes or communicating the themes under development.

Setting Clear Goals

Setting clear agendas and expectations is another aspect of a good working relationship. It is vital that professors meet with teaching assistants before the beginning of a course to outline the goals of the course. This models clear course organization and goal setting, providing TAs with guidance in their capacity as apprentice university professors. It also minimizes possible discrepancies between sections of the course and disagreements over what should or should not be done within the course.

Professors should also clearly articulate the TAs' responsibilities in the course. It is especially important, when working with new TAs, to provide guidance on how to conduct tutorials and fulfill course responsibilities. Not only does this give TAs important clues on how best to frame and provide information to the professor, but establishing clear goals and expectations makes forming a good teaching team more likely. Both parties have a better sense of what can and cannot be done within the confines of the course. Without such clarification, the possibilities of discrepancies and conflicts increase dramatically.

Five recommendations follow. First, professors and TAs should meet prior to the beginning of the course to discuss overall organization, course goals and the division of labour. Second, professors should articulate clearly their expectations of TAs and the boundaries of their responsibility. Third, professors should take this opportunity to encourage their TAs to provide feedback and input into the course. Fourth, TAs and professors should discuss possible areas of flexibility in the course, where the TAs might contribute to ongoing course development or development of course assignments. Finally, professors also might suggest appropriate ways for TAs to provide this feedback and input.

Conclusion

Respect, communication and clear agendas create better working relationships. When any one of these aspects of the working relationship is missing, it can have serious negative repercussions for the teaching staff and the students who have to sit, watch and carve out their own agendas.

Astute readers will appreciate that my advice has concentrated more upon the responsibilities of the professor than on those of the TA. The reason for taking this approach is one of economy. A few simple principles reflected in a professor's behaviour towards a TA can foster an atmosphere in which effective teaching and learning can take place in a course. Further, since a TA is often in an apprenticeship role, responsibility falls on the professor to ensure the development of the TA's skills as a teacher. The corresponding responsibilities of a TA – particularly a novice TA – would appear to be more open ended, relating as they do to the entire spectrum of scholarly preparedness, teaching competence and collegial experience.

The responsibilities of the TA also must be understood within the context of other competing demands. How, for example, does one calibrate the demands of professionalism with the limitations of a teaching assistantship (governed, at my university, by strict contractual regulations)? How does one balance the oppressive and often conflicting demands of a teaching position with the imperatives of writing a thesis? How can universities better support teaching assistants in the balancing of these duties and professional responsibilities? While these questions remain outside the scope of this article, they are germane to the discussion at hand and I would be remiss in not acknowledging them. Hopefully, however, the information and recommendations provided offer a starting place for teaching assistants and professors to begin collaborating in the wonderful enterprise that is university teaching.

Working with Teaching Assistants

Leslie Green

Tutorial Life

Tutorial sections in a large course have the potential to be among the best or the worst learning experiences of our students. A good tutorial engages their interest, stimulates discussion and exploits the tension between the course director (CD) and teaching assistant (TA) in a productive way to broaden the perspectives of the students. A poor tutorial alienates them and plods along with dwindling attendance and discussion, and the tension between course directors and teaching assistants degenerates into rivalry or even open conflict. The following suggestions might help ensure that tutorials work well.

Suggestions for Course Directors

1. Plan Your Division of Labour

First, there is the question of how the tutorials will relate to lectures and course materials. There are many options here, but I have found the following most effective. In lectures, I spend a certain amount of time expounding the subject and discussing, but not summarizing, the required readings. At the same time, however, I argue a case, a particular perspective on the material. The developing tension – between my own views and those represented in the readings – is what I encourage TAs to develop and explore in their meetings. This ensures that lectures, readings and tutorials each contribute a different perspective on the course.

Second, there are questions about the division of powers and responsibilities between the CD and TAs. Who is to grade assignments, consider requests for extensions, plan tutorial content, etc.? Here, the most important thing is for everyone, including the students, to know clearly and in advance who will do what. Confusion is easily avoided if the CD circulates a memorandum to the TAs before their first meeting, discusses it with them and then checks regularly during the term to see whether adjustments are needed.

2. Stay in Touch

In addition to complementing lecture material and guiding discussion, TAs help bridge the gap between the CD and students. In a large class, the TAs are an important two-way conduit for information, reactions and views between students and CD. But this in turn requires close and regular contact between the course director and the teaching assistants. Here, the aim is to strike a balance between intrusive supervision and loose anarchy. In some cases, close contact might develop naturally out of the working relationship; more often it must be planned by setting regular meetings whose agendas allow for discussion of successes, failures and common problems.

3. Observe All Formalities

Course directors must be familiar with, and guided by, contractual arrangements with their TAs. Of special importance is the CD's obligation to ensure that the work expected of the TAs can be done in the time agreed. TAs are valued members of the teaching team and their position gives them needed experience (and financial support), but it is for them still, and properly, ancillary to their studies.

Suggestions for the Teaching Assistant

1. Plan Ahead

Just as a good lecture must be planned, so must the tutorial. Obviously, TAs need to have done the readings in advance; I generally recommend that they stay two or three weeks ahead. But in any case they should also try to work out in advance the main issues and problems raised by the material and to plan some discussion questions or exercises based on that.

2. Get To Know the Students

In a large class, the course director will probably get to know few students. Here, the tutorial must compensate and TAs must quickly master the knack of learning names. This sounds trivial, but it is in fact central to helping the students feel rooted in the course, for students who go nameless generally go unnoticed in other ways, too. Simple methods include taking roll call in early meetings, asking students to introduce themselves (or, better, each other) or in the first few weeks having them state their names before speaking. And students should also be encouraged to refer to each other by name – never say, "The point that was just made over there."

3. Be Animator and Umpire

While TAs will inevitably spend a certain amount of time answering questions about readings and lectures, defining terms, etc., they also have a central role in animating and regulating discussion. Even when the students themselves present material or lead discussions, TAs need to ensure that particular students or issues are not being unfairly excluded and to ensure that the discussion begins and ends on time and remains on point throughout.

Considerations as simple as these help ensure that tutorials fulfil their potential.

Issues for International
Teaching Assistants

Nick Elson

Most advice that is relevant for teaching assistants (TAs) in general is also relevant for international teaching assistants. This article provides some additional suggestions for international TAs who may not be familiar with Canadian cultural assumptions and experiences, or with the language. Some attention to these areas will make the experience of teaching and working with students more rewarding.

Teaching and Learning Styles

If your educational experience was in a formal and disciplined context, you may find the situation here in Canada somewhat different. Teachers and students in Canadian classrooms often have quite informal relationships, and the forms of address are sometimes quite casual. In a tutorial format, take the opportunity, when checking names in the class, to ask individual students how they prefer to be addressed.

The main purpose of tutorials or seminars is to encourage sharing of ideas, information, and opinion on issues related to the course material. Sometimes these discussions can get quite lively. Try to aim for a balance between complete control of the class that discourages participation, and no control that leaves the class with little sense of direction or purpose. Be prepared to intervene on occasion, restate the ideas coming out, encourage those not participating to have their say, and bring the discussion back to the relevant issues.

Take whatever opportunities there are to observe Canadian TAs and professors to see what kinds of classroom strategies they employ to achieve their objectives. Try these out in your own classroom and adopt those that seem to work best for you.

Language

If English is not your first language, it is reasonable to expect that this will influence how you use English in your work as a TA. The keys to making the most of your language ability are preparation and planning for how to make communication in the classroom as effective as possible.

- At the beginning of the term, make it clear to students in your classes that you encourage them to ask for clarification of any points you make that are not clear, whether spoken or written. Take whatever opportunities you can to meet with students informally, after class or by appointment, to discuss the course and get informal feedback on what more you can do to help them improve their learning in the course.
- Use visual aids as much as reasonably possible. These include the chalkboard, overhead transparencies, class handouts, films and videos.
- Encourage students, when they are making their points, to use visual or concrete aids, so that any problems you might have with what they are saying are minimized. It is reasonable to assume that if you are having difficulty understanding what they are saying, so are others in the class. Do not hesitate to ask students to rephrase, or elaborate on their comments. Use questions such as "Do you mean...?" "Can you expand on that?" or even "I don't see what you're getting at, can you put it another way?"

Effective pronunciation involves much more than just "saying the sounds correctly." Stress, rhythm, and tempo are also factors. This suggests that some "rehearsal," especially of lectures, can be beneficial. Try out parts of your lecture, or read selections of class material to friends or colleagues, in order to get feedback on where they think you might have difficulty. In most cases, speaking difficulties can be reduced to one or two specific elements, such as speed of delivery (tempo) or stress patterns. Practice these, and watch recorded lectures that offer models to copy. Sometimes audio or video-taping part of your lecture, then examining your delivery can help you to be objective about your performance.

Section V:
Academic Honesty

INTRODUCTION TO SECTION V

Academic honesty can be one of the neglected elements of course planning, yet when a problem arises, we might deeply regret not building this consideration into our overall teaching goals and strategies. The five articles in this section offer quite different perspectives on the issues of academic honesty that one might consider during course planning. The first, by Parry, outlines the classic arguments for the importance of academic integrity in an academic setting, primarily emphasizing the unfair advantage it poses for dishonest students. Parry also outlines steps one can take to prevent academic dishonesty, including ways of informing students of the penalty process that can ensue from dishonest acts.

Brown's article casts a different light on the issue. He emphasizes the various perspectives that inform academic understandings of plagiarism and the ways that conventions can vary among disciplines. As faculty members, our perspective will likely differ from that of students, and our views might differ by discipline. Brown reminds us that students might lack an orientation to the academic environment and to the variety of writing conventions among disciplines. He urges us to treat the proper use of sources as an important critical skill that should be a teaching goal in our courses.

The Newton article discusses research based on interviews with students who have plagiarized, exploring their accounts of why they did so. Newton's research reveals that students plagiarize for a variety of reasons, but often the problem is rooted in weak essay-writing skills. Consequently, a variety of strategies is needed for dealing with students who plagiarize. The article offers advice for preventing plagiarism and ensuring that students understand the mechanics of referencing. The prewriting assignment at the end of the article is designed to improve students' essay-writing skills and could be adapted readily to courses in many disciplines.

The final two articles discuss academic honesty in distinct settings. The Delaney article provides useful tips for ensuring academic honesty in scientific labs; the Watson article encourages us to reflect on the implications of the widespread availability of electronic sources and to discuss with students how to properly reference these materials.

Academic Dishonesty

Hugh Parry

What is Academic Dishonesty?

Academic dishonesty refers to cheating of any kind that secures for the student an unfair advantage in his or her academic career. The most prevalent forms are receiving illegal help on exams or in-class tests, and plagiarism. Plagiarism means trying to pass off – in an assignment, an essay, a thesis or an oral report – someone else's work as one's own. A bought essay is the clearest example. But if students borrow *any* words verbatim or merely paraphrase an argument from a book or any other source, they are guilty of plagiarism if the precise extent of the debt is unacknowledged. Any such unacknowledged borrowing is an offence, but plagiarism in a university course essentially applies to *graded* assignments that count towards the student's final standing in that course.

Why is Academic Dishonesty a Serious Offence?

Universities exist in general as centres of learning. They seek to promote, through instruction, individual inquiry and the exchange of ideas with others, a love of learning and the development of such attendant skills as thinking critically and expressing oneself coherently and persuasively to the best of one's ability. University study is also about the ranking of a student's achievement, in individual courses and overall, measured against university standards. Such ranking will play a part in competition for entry into special areas (law, education, medicine, etc.) or post-graduate study and in competition for certain jobs. Academic cheating violates the principle of honesty in which learning must be rooted and seeks an unfair advantage over students who earn their grades and standing honestly.

How Can it be Prevented?

Universities are teaching, not punitive, institutions. Our primary aim should be to prevent cheating by educating students about it. Every course syllabus should include a prominent statement on the university's definition of cheating in general and plagiarism in particular, and its policy in the case of infractions. Instructors should discuss details of the issue in class early in the academic term and return to the matter later at least once, perhaps before the first major assignment or test.

What Points Should be Stressed?
A. The General Meaning and Seriousness of Cheating
B. Some Specific Details about Plagiarism

Concrete evidence of unacknowledged verbatim borrowing will establish guilt beyond doubt. But even in the absence of incontrovertible proof, a clear and compelling case of guilt also will be made when the possibility that certain words or ideas are the student's own exceeds credulity. The following kinds of defences are usually inadequate: "I *thought* the idea was mine; I forgot I heard it in X's lecture or read it in Y's book," or, "The idea was mine. It's a coincidence that Z makes the same point – I have never seen that article." A student must expect to be examined orally to defend such assertions. Lies quickly become transparent.

"I had a friend help me with the grammar, sentence structure, etc. But she/he merely tidied up my style – the language and ideas are essentially my own." This perhaps is a grey area; to receive such help *can* be educational and by no means plagiarism. But even when the friend has contributed only minor adjustments, the precise extent of the help must be acknowledged explicitly. A student's writing in different parts of the same essay, in other essays, in tests, etc., could be scrutinized to determine the likelihood that the help received was minor or substantive. Similarly, any cooperative work with another student that influenced the form and content of each assignment must always be acknowledged. Instructors should make it clear to students what assistance they consider legitimate, and the proper method of acknowledging such assistance.

In sum, the student must acknowledge sources for an oral report via full disclosure at the time of presentation and for a written assignment via explicit acknowledgement of the source of paraphrases, appropriate quotation marks in the body of the essay, necessary footnotes and full bibliographical information at the end. All references should provide a clear and unambiguous guide for the reader to re-locate the sources used to write the essay.

C. The Chances of "Getting Away with it"

To be charged with cheating is not, of course, to be guilty. At York University, the procedures governed by the Senate Policy on Academic Honesty give an accused student every chance to rebut the charge, with or without legal representation, at several levels, from the department to the dean's office to committees of the faculty and senate. A wrongful accusation is unlikely to succeed, but the chances of "getting away with it" must also be regarded as remote.

Procedures

To ensure that students receive fair and equitable treatment among different departments and among faculty members, it is important that instructors follow university procedures in cases of academic dishonesty. Since specific regulations can vary by faculty, it is important that you request a copy of your faculty's current policy on academic dishonesty when cases arise.

Penalties

The consequence of a finding of academic dishonesty will depend on the nature of the offence and the record of the offender. Penalties can range from an oral or written warning, a grade of zero on a paper or test or a grade of F in the course, to suspension from the university or the rescinding of a degree, diploma or certificate. A finding of guilt can be entered into the student's official transcript and remain there until removed after a successful appeal. In light of the seriousness of these penalties, our time is well spent instructing students on how to avoid academic dishonesty.

Plagiarism and Student Acculturation: Strangers in the Strange Lands of our Disciplines

James Brown

> It goes without saying that not all transmitted words belonging to someone else
> lend themselves, when fixed in writing, to enclosure in quotation marks.
> – Mikhail Bakhtin, *Discourse in the Novel*

I was walking back from a meeting about the revised procedures for academic dishonesty when I ran into one of my students from the Faculty of Arts Centre for Academic Writing. She was interested in talking about plagiarism too, but her perspective was so different from mine that I experienced a kind of culture shock.

She was one of about forty students whom I had seen last semester at the centre. The only commonality among these students is that they are all highly motivated. To book a one-hour appointment with me or one of the other instructors at the centre, students generally have to call about two weeks in advance. We then work on whatever aspect of their academic writing needs attention; this could be anything from analyzing the assignment and planning appropriate research to learning to correct a pattern of grammar errors. Many of the students who use the centre are already good writers; they simply wish to continue to improve. They might need to learn alternative strategies to cope with the new demands placed on them by the increasing sophistication of their ideas as they progress through their courses. Other students are weaker writers, and for some the motivation has been extrinsic – they've been getting disappointing marks on their writing assignments.

This particular student was a bright, mature, upper-level student. As we walked along, she started to tell me about her most recent concerns about academic honesty: "I just got an essay back – I'm relieved I wasn't accused of plagiarism. I've been worrying ever since I turned it in." What she'd been worrying about was this: She had had to write an essay that involved interpreting Plato's allegory of the cave. She wasn't satisfied with her understanding of it from *The Republic*, so she'd read Barron's notes. She knew that her interpretation was informed by that source; she'd considered but rejected citing it and including it in her bibliography. She'd never seen a source like

Barron's in any academic paper and thought her work would be downgraded if she included it in hers.

This situation seems to me to occupy a grey area. If a student in one of my courses raised this issue, I'd ask her about how closely dependent she was on Barron's explanation. If, as was the case here, Barron's had just served to give her a general context for interpreting the passage and she had made no specific use of the ideas or language, then I'd tell her not to bother citing it. In other words, I would classify what she got from Barron's as "common knowledge" instead of "paraphrase/summary." However, if a student raised the same issue during essay tutoring, I would have told her to explain the situation to whoever was going to mark the essay and to get the instructor's advice. I know that reasonable people differ on this and that another instructor might tell her to cite the relevant part of her essay as a paraphrase of Barron's.

We generally do not expect to see sources such as Barron's in the bibliographies of our students' essays, but that could be because we think about student writing on the analogy of our own, and this, like analogies in general, does not run on all four legs. When we tell students either that they should (or should not) include a source like Barron's in their bibliographies, we are translating the conventions from our own writing situations to the students'. Different instructors might translate differently — just as there could be different views on whether the analogy "on all four legs" above should be cited to Coleridge. Certainly not all of the situations in which students might be accused of plagiarism are as ambiguous as this one. There are, however, considerable complexities in students' use and documentation of sources. My experience is that, even in the most extreme and seemingly obvious cases of plagiarism, there's some mixture of misunderstanding, lack of orientation to an academic environment and lack of skill.

Some students have no sense of the rules for using sources and even have trouble "hearing" them when explained, because such rules just do not make sense of their experience of writing. Many of our students come to us with a background in "school" writing such as this: You are assigned a topic; you collect information about that topic from such sources as encyclopedias and you "write up" your research. In effect, these students have been paraphrasing, but they have never heard the term or been expected to document their sources.

Such students are initially confused by any expectation that they cite sources. They will often respond with "Well, then every sentence needs a footnote, because everything in my essay has been said before." You've heard this from students, and you probably have some response to it. The question is, how do such students hear your response and how are they affected by it. Their vision is that somewhere in that vast library there must be some dusty book with essentially the same idea. When we tell them about plagiarism, especially if we try to frighten them into academic honesty by discussing the seriousness of its nature (and penalties), what they hear is an unreasonable expectation on our part that they check all those books to make sure that the idea is not in there — clearly an impossible task. What they might conclude is that the whole concept of documentation is unreasonable (or, at least, incomprehensible to them).

Most students have discovered that it is a good idea to include some direct quotations and that they need to cite those. They will ask, "how many footnotes should I put on each page?" They mean, "how many direct quotations" and the reason that "footnote" means "direct quotation" is that they just do not know that paraphrasing — with a citation — is a legitimate option. They then "spice" their (unacknowledged) paraphrases with a sprinkling of acknowledged direct quotations. Their sense of the writing process is one of changing the language in which the information is expressed because that's the only contribution that they can conceive of making. On this assumption, they cite only the direct quotations (not the paraphrases) — the paraphrases are "theirs," only the direct quotations are "borrowed."

In response to what they see as the ambiguity of writing in university, they often translate the rules we give them into approximations that make sense from their perspective. One variation of this is a "rule" that I've heard from a number of students: "if you change every third word, you don't need a footnote." Again, the assumption here is that the only contribution a student can make is language change: a "borrowing" of ideas — being inevitable — needs no acknowledgement. All of this has a certain internal consistency; it's just not the one for which we are looking.

The other complicating factor is that we, as instructors in our various disciplines, are not all assigning the same kinds of student writing nor looking for the same things within it. Even conventions of citation vary; these are intimately connected to methodologies and, in a larger sense, to the ways in which different disciplines generate knowledge. So, for instance, most disciplines have abandoned footnotes for some form of parenthetical documentation. History has not — probably because it employs so many explanatory footnotes that there's little advantage in treating documentary citations differently. This is a minor example at the level of mechanics, but larger rhetorical patterns and even the modes of discourse that are typically assigned in student writing vary widely among disciplines. For instance, many of the assignments I see from psychology courses are "expository" and require strategies to gather, select, organize and paraphrase information from sources. Essays assigned in English courses are much more typically "argumentative" and these require a different attitude towards sources and raise different problems for students in making decisions about what needs to be documented and how.

I think, too, that students are seen differently within different disciplines and that the assignments they are given reflect this variation. Psychology seems to see its undergraduate students as needing first to acquire the basic knowledge of the discipline and so uses short-answer tests and expository writing. Generally, psychology students are encouraged to think critically and write argumentatively about the knowledge of the discipline only when they reach its upper levels. English students are more typically treated as apprentice "literary critics" at the first-year level and are asked from the first class to construct and argue for their own interpretations of the primary texts. This range of variation in what "counts" as academic writing can be very confusing for a first-year student taking, among others, a course in English and one in psychology. Of course, not all writing in psychology courses is expository, nor is all writing in English argumentative, but this variability makes things more, not less, complicated for a student.

What all this suggests to me is that we need to consider use of sources a "critical skill" and that we need to teach students the practices appropriate to our various courses and disciplines. In the context of this complexity, providing a general explanation of what constitutes plagiarism – while exhorting students to refrain from it – is probably not sufficient. Devoting some class time to a presentation in which you give some discipline-specific examples of what needs to be cited is more helpful. Setting up some kind of interchange around an actual piece of academic writing, that is, generating a context in which students can encounter some of the problems of using sources and providing a forum in which they can raise questions, is better still. Finally, designing a writing assignment to which students can apply their understanding of documentation and then responding to their attempts is probably best.

For my humanities and English classes, I give this short presentation when I assign the first essay. Some version of this might be useful in your courses as well. I say that the "information" in their essays can be divided into four kinds: their own ideas, common knowledge, paraphrase/summary and direct quotation. Only the latter two require some form of documentation. I then spend some time giving examples of what kind of thing would fall into each category, based on that assignment. For instance, in my courses, the first type is made up of students' own interpretations of the primary texts, so I produce some oral interpretations as examples. I also give examples of relevant direct quotations and paraphrases from both primary and secondary sources, and I show them on the board how to document each.

Common knowledge is a tricky area and will probably need discipline-specific examples to clarify. The concept really depends on some notion of a "discourse community" – it is only among the members of such a community that this knowledge is presumed to be common. This is a clearly defined concept when, for example, you're writing a journal article: the discourse community is made up of the readers of that journal. Its application is not so obvious in regard to students writing essays in university courses. Are they supposed to judge the "commonness" of a particular piece of knowledge against the knowledge of their fellow students in the class, against that of the instructor or against that of the typical member of their society – that famous fiction "the common reader?"

My experience is that opening up the complexity of this issue of audience is useful in itself. If you do the marking in your course, it doesn't matter too much what advice you give them about conceiving their audience, as long as you observe a couple of caveats. First, remember your own advice when you mark their work and don't be surprised if you get a lot more explanation than you probably want after you've told them to write for the common reader. Second, be cautious about presenting your advice as something that can be generalized to writing situations in other courses – we don't all agree on this, though each one of us becomes *de facto* the final arbiter when we mark our own students' work. Finally, the best general advice on this issue is probably "when in doubt, treat it as a paraphrase and cite."

You should also recommend that your students register with a writing program if they are available on your campus. They can probably best learn to document sources through discussing their drafts-in-progress with a writing instructor. (The Faculty of Arts Centre for Academic Writing offers a short non-credit course in documenting sources; the Computer-Assisted Writing Centre has a program called "Using Sources" that students in courses registered with the centre can use.) Students will more likely follow up on these opportunities if you present documenting sources as a complex series of skills and suggest that these are best developed, like all writing skills, in the context of their academic work-in-progress.

Plagiarism and the Challenge of Essay Writing: Learning from our Students

Janice Newton

Most of us have encountered plagiarized essays at some time in our teaching careers, and we might assume that dishonesty leads students to do this. In one common form of plagiarized essay, the student has done the research and written most of the essay, but leaves out crucial quotation marks or footnotes. In contrast to other forms of academic dishonesty, such as a purchased essay or submission of someone else's work, this type of plagiarism always strikes me as especially curious. Invariably, I can discern some measure of intelligence in students' selection of the unacknowledged facts or ideas they copied. Why would they fail to acknowledge their extensive research after they had done so much work gathering together relevant material? Rather than thinking of these students as simply dishonest and deserving of punishment, we need to try to understand what leads students to do this and how we can help transform them into competent and confident essay writers who do not need to resort to such ruses to succeed in university.

To understand this problem, I believe we should start by listening to our students and learning from them. By taking their perspective into account, we can significantly improve our ability to teach our students the basic mechanical skills of proper referencing and improve their essay-writing skills in the process. Drawing on my experience over the years and interviews with a number of students who have been charged with plagiarism, I have identified four common factors that faculty can address: sloppy research methods, reliance on inappropriate reference guides, misunderstanding of the logic and rules of referencing and weak essay-writing skills.

Research Methods

I routinely ask students about whose work I have suspicions to bring all their research notes to my office so we can discuss the entire essay-production process. Sometimes I discover that the student has collected photocopies or taken copious notes from library sources, but with absolutely no reliable way of tracing the source or page number. I think of these students as enthusiastic vacuums who suck up all the relevant

171

material they can find, without understanding the need for retrieval and verification of sources. Many have admitted to me that they realized the information for proper citations was missing while typing the final draft, but at 3:00 am before the deadline date, they simply decided it was not worth it to track down the sources. These students understand the logic and mechanics of referencing, but decide to leave the citations out, hoping that no one will notice.

Careless students are easy to identify (from a quick glance at their research notes) and easy to help. I show them how to collect the relevant bibliographical information when they are searching for sources on the library's online catalogue; they can even use this from home at 3:00 am if they have a computer and a modem. I offer them a one-page hand-out that they can take to the library to guide them in collecting the proper information. Using a sample of my own research notes, I demonstrate that good research notes can be used years later if they distinguish quotations from paraphrases and record page numbers and full bibliographical information. Finally, I require them to undertake the tedious task of tracking down their sources and redoing the assignment. If the timing is right, I will also make a note to myself to ask to see their research notes while the next essay is in progress, just to make sure they have mastered the habit.

Choice of Reference Guides

Another common problem is students' reliance on inappropriate sources for instruction on how to reference. Almost half of the students I interviewed acknowledged that they *knew* they were probably not doing it right, but instead of consulting their tutor, the reference text required in the course or the course hand-outs, they turned to unsuitable sources for help: friends, parents or old hand-outs from high school. In these cases, the advice they got or remembered was often misleading.

Recommending that students buy a reliable, university-level reference guide is crucial, but it is also important to ensure that the students know how to use it. When I first required my students to buy the *MLA Handbook*, I discovered that many had no idea how to use it. Several students took the textbook approach – reading it starting on page one, hoping to find the answer they were looking for. This is like reading a dictionary from page one, hoping eventually to encounter the word you want to spell. Without understanding the concept of a reference source, I was not surprised that these students gave up on the *MLA Handbook*. Now I require them to bring it to class and I explain how to use the index and how the different sections work, and highlight the most useful sections so they can readily find what they need.

Understanding the Rules

Students charged with plagiarism often claim they misunderstand the rules for proper referencing. The most common reason I have encountered is students' belief that certain types of sources are somehow "exempt" despite explicit instruction to the contrary. The range of such exemptions varies according to the student. Some believe that course texts, government documents or readings from other courses do not require referencing. Some students claim that they are only required to reference limited types of sources: direct quotations but not paraphrases; statistical facts but not other people's ideas or words. A few claim that if they include references in the bibliography, it is not necessary to reference the ideas used in the body of the essay. Several worry that they will have "too many" footnotes, so they arbitrarily include some but leave others out. Each of these mistaken notions of "exempt" sources reflects a fundamental misunderstanding of the logic of proper referencing.

I have trouble finding these explanations credible, because I always cover these issues explicitly in course hand-outs and lectures. Nonetheless, despite the abundance of material available for students to learn proper referencing, a significant minority of students seems to resist learning. When asked, many acknowledge that they ignore the lectures and hand-outs because they believe they already know how to do this. An astonishing number of students lack the competence to reference, but nonetheless feel confident that they know how to do it.

Conducting classroom research to assess my students' prior knowledge and ability to reference, I discovered shocking results in two of my second-year classes (350 students). When I administered a short, unmarked assignment, only 10 to 15 per cent actually had a satisfactory working knowledge of skills I considered necessary for this level. In contrast to teaching new material, where students might listen more closely precisely because they *know* they know so little, when we teach familiar material, we must find ways to encourage them to assess the adequacy of their prior knowledge critically.

One solution is to integrate key components of proper referencing skills into a course assignment, letting students know they will lose grades if they do not properly master these skills. (See the sample prewriting assignment on page 174.) When you deduct grades for problems in referencing, you can allow students to do an error analysis and correct their mistakes to recover the lost grades. This way, you can be satisfied that even the students who did not get it right the first time actually learn the proper method by correcting their own errors. The chance to reduce the grade penalty offers an added incentive to learn. Lecturing on this topic might never be enough. Some students might require the additional impetus that comes from one-on-one instruction or written assignments.

In sum, as these problems arose in my interviews with students, I learned to alter the way I teach. First, I emphasize that no "category" of source is exempt from referencing: books, quotations, statistics, paraphrases, government documents, speeches and course texts all must be cited. Second, I explicitly encourage students to collect complete bibliographical information while researching. Third, I encourage them to line up an appropriate authority to consult when in doubt: the tutor, the hand-out, the course reference book or the appropriate writing centre. Fourth, and perhaps most importantly, I continue to emphasize the connection between referencing and essay-writing skills in general.

PREWRITING ASSIGNMENT

NAME:_____   TUTOR:_____

> ____ACCEPTABLE
>
> ____NOT ACCEPTABLE: You must make an appointment to speak with your tutor or the course director about your essay, otherwise 5% will be taken off the essay grade. If you wish further guidance in preparing the prewriting guide or in planning your essay, arrange to speak with your tutor.

1. Which set of concepts have you chosen to focus on in your paper?

2. Which theorists will you be using?

3. Using proper citation methods outlined in the mla Handbook, prepare a bibliography of the course material you expect to use below. Be sure to distinguish the articles you plan to use as well as the texts themselves.

4. Summarize in a nutshell the main point or argument you hope to develop.

5. ISSUES: On the left side of a page, list the specific points or themes you expect to discuss in your paper for your main point or argument to be convincing. On the right, briefly indicate how you think each point relates to the concept under discussion. Note: This section must be detailed for the assignment to pass.

6. What relevant counterpoints will you need to respond to for your paper to be convincing?

7. What further research or information is needed to make your paper coherent and plausible?

8. REVIEW OF DOCUMENTATION RULES: Review the departmental guidelines for proper referencing.

    a. Under what circumstances are you required to put words in quotation marks? Demonstrate a proper quotation and endnote from one of your sources.

    b. How does the substance and presentation of a paraphrase differ from a quotation?

    c. Demonstrate proper presentation and reference of a paraphrase from one of your sources.

    d. Do you have any outstanding questions about how to document the information you use in this paper – handling quotations, paraphrases, footnote format, bibliography format, etc?

9. POSSIBLE PROBLEMS: What possible problems do you foresee in completing this assignment? What do you (or we) need to do to solve them?

Essay-Writing Skills

The difficulty some students have in mastering the technical skills of proper referencing is often rooted in weak essay-writing skills. Students who lack confidence (or who have poor essay-writing skills) might find the expectations of proper referencing daunting when applied to their writing process. They experience a credibility gap, finding it hard to believe that you expect them to acknowledge every source – that would mean *everything* in their paper would be referenced. This attitude is premised on a profound lack of self-confidence and bewilderment as to how to develop their own ideas in an essay. Many of the students I spoke with were distressed when I pointed out that they had to acknowledge their sources. A common puzzled response is, "But then my entire essay would be all quotations or paraphrases. Nothing comes from me."

These students are very frustrated because they know, on the one hand, that they must do research, but on the other hand, they have been asked to develop a thesis and an argument. They are often capable of the former but terrified and bewildered at the prospects of doing the latter. I am convinced that many students, lacking the confidence and the skills to develop their own analysis or argument, deliberately retreat to plagiarism in the desperate and naive belief that other people's ideas will be mistaken for their own arguments.

An example illustrates this point. In one fourth-year class, students prepared research papers on a current federal policy of their choice. The essay question asked them to evaluate the policy in light of different theoretical issues we had studied in the course. One student's essay thoroughly and competently surveyed the literature on pornography policy, but lacked adequate references. The paper was further flawed because it displayed a total absence of argument throughout. The student had simply failed to assess the evidence or make judgements as to the relative significance of the material she had collected. When I called her in to my office, we discussed the problems of referencing briefly. She lamented, "How can I reference everything? The whole essay comes from sources." I agreed that this is how the essay appeared to me, and changed my tack.

I explained that the absence of her argument and judgement of the evidence was striking. After all, people had blown up video stores over this issue! I spent the rest of the hour praising her research skills, for she had collected relevant and crucial material. Paragraph by paragraph, I encouraged her to explain the implications of this evidence for the essay question. I was not surprised, given her research, that it took little effort on my part for her to start making the judgements that led her to develop a cogent thesis. At this point she burst into tears and lamented that no one at university had asked her to think and develop her own argument. Since no one had cared what she thought about the topics in her essays, she had lost interest in writing essays. Essays had become boring exercises in expressing other people's ideas. This was the last essay she would write, and she cried because she felt she had missed out on a whole dimension of learning. She said she longed to go back and rewrite all those "B" essays with her new understanding of how to relate her arguments and ideas to the research material. By talking about her own ideas, she quickly learned the importance of maintaining the distinction between other people's ideas and her own.

What can we learn from this student? I don't think she was at all unusual except in the frankness with which she disclosed her feelings. It is our job to help students through this difficult transition from repeating other people's ideas to developing their own and I think we should expect the bulk of this transition to occur in the first and second years of university. When we insist that our students openly declare their use of sources, it becomes glaringly apparent that it is now their turn to say something. I am convinced that far from being a technical or mechanical issue, teaching proper referencing is intimately bound up with teaching students about thinking and developing their own ideas, arguments and judgements. Once students have clearly set out another person's ideas, they can then ask, "so what? Why is this significant? How does this help answer the question?" In short, teaching proper referencing can be yet another means to challenge and encourage students to think for themselves. If we keep this goal in sight, spending time teaching our students how to reference properly can be rewarding and worthwhile.

This is a revised version of an article that was first published in 1994 in Core 4 (7): 1.

Honesty in the Laboratory

Paul Delaney

I usually try to work on the principle that everyone is basically honest. Yet it seems that I am forever needing to remind students (and myself) about academic honesty and the penalties involved when this code of conduct is broken. I have been involved in only a few serious (read that to mean prosecuted) cases, but for the laboratory courses in which I am involved, rarely a week goes by without reminding some students of the definition of plagiarism.

Perhaps laboratory assignments are more open to plagiarism than other assignments are. It would seem to me very simple to see whether two or more students have collaborated, above and beyond the law, in handing in remarkably similar essays. It is far more difficult to decide if the work submitted is created by the student and not, say, by an essay-writing service. In science, though, especially at the lower levels, experiments and exercises are of a necessarily "canned" nature and results are not unique and are often predictable. For this reason, it is harder to be sure that certain material has been completed by the student who submits it rather than by committee. After all, 2 plus 2 is 4, and if everyone reports this as the answer to a certain question, it does not mean that the students have necessarily collaborated to the point of plagiarizing.

For many years I have been developing laboratory exercises in the Natural Science program, attempting to make them useful to the students as a way of demonstrating aspects of the scientific method as well as highlighting certain concepts in the course. What can you do in two hours with a limited budget and a large number of students, especially when the majority of the students are deathly afraid of arithmetic and scientific equipment and are only in the laboratory at all because it is a required component of a required course? To my mind the laboratory experience is essential if we are to give non-science majors some appreciation of science. However, I freely admit that I am not as happy with my results as I would like to be. I think my laboratory exercises are better now than they were when I first started teaching the course, but they still lack the excitement of real science. (If at first you don't succeed, try, try again…)

So what have I done to keep academic dishonesty to a minimum, while maximizing the students' opportunity to experience science? For one, I don't let students leave the laboratory session without handing in their completed lab assignments. This increases student concentration during the assigned period, forces them to prepare in advance of doing the laboratory exercise and cuts down any compilation of answers *en masse* after class at Tim Horton's or wherever. I keep attendance records for each laboratory session and don't allow any free-wheeling transfer between sections. The section to which a student is assigned at the commencement of the term is the section that student must attend throughout the term, unless given written permission by me to do otherwise. No graded material is returned to students until everyone has completed the given laboratory exercise.

Nonetheless, some students can be very tempted to circumvent the system. If one year's laboratory exercise is the same as, or very similar to, one from a previous year, then a surprising number of copies find their way from one year's class to the next. Hence, I have found I need to modify the exercises on a yearly basis to make them sufficiently different from year to year. For some exercises this is easy to do, while for others, it simply cannot be done. In such cases, and also to assess whether students have understood the concepts examined in the labs, I have initiated a laboratory exam. But this has met with limited success and some student anxiety.

I cannot say that plagiarism has been entirely eliminated by my use of laboratory hand-in sheets. The myth persists that collaboration in science means one person working out the answer while the rest copy. When all is said and done, there is no substitute for vigilance in the laboratory session. This is where I find that TAs can be particularly helpful. The TA who cruises from station to station, questioning students about their results, and who gives a clear statement at the beginning of the lab that academic dishonesty is not tolerated, will likely succeed in impressing upon students the need for individual work. The personal touch goes a long way but does require commitment and perseverance. It is my experience, though, that the courses that are evaluated the highest are those in which TAs have gone the extra mile (kilometre) and were teachers, not just supervisors or chaperones.

A final point is that when exercises are designed that are truly individual, then of course the problem of plagiarism is diminished. I have developed term projects, in addition to the laboratory exercises, that have a strong individual component. These projects require some trial and error that can be done to some extent in groups, but that largely requires individual effort. These term projects also involve considerable library research, which provides additional scope for individual differences. The success of these projects and the enjoyment the students have derived from doing them has, in my mind, made up for some of the shortfalls in the laboratory environment.

In short, we need new ways of getting students into the experimental spirit. Traditional methods, such as laboratory exercises, still have their place in the curriculum, but are fraught with problems that require our vigilance and willingness to teach rather than police.

Electronic Plagiarism: A Cautionary Tale

Elizabeth Watson

I recently underwent an electronic epiphany while working at a public workstation in the library. A student next to me was searching a database that indexed articles and included an extensive abstract in the record. He downloaded the information onto a disk, plugged in his portable PC and called up an essay he was in the midst of writing. He then copied the complete abstract into the text of his essay. I remarked upon how well he was adapting to this technology. I also asked how he was planning to cite the abstract. He admitted that it had not occurred to him to reference the fact that he had not written this paragraph of his essay. We had a brief discussion on the ethics of incorporating someone else's work into an essay without citing it, but I was unable to persuade him that this was plagiarism.

The nature of digital technologies permits the rapid and accurate copying of information. One cannot dispute the benefits of these technologies, but I wonder how many of us are aware of their misuse and abuse. Copyright issues are important, but in this brief article, I would like to alert everyone to the potential for plagiarism.

When one considers all of the possibilities, such as electronic journals, electronic bulletin boards, full text files available via the Internet and online from commercial vendors, databases available in libraries on CD-ROM or through CiteLine, it becomes clear that this is an issue of immediate concern. In any hand-outs and in all discussions about plagiarism, we need to help the user understand that electronic materials, as well as print materials, must be referenced. In addition, we should stress that referencing electronic sources is a way of sharing information so that others can have access to these still relatively unknown resources.

The rules for proper referencing of electronic sources are beginning to be standardized and you should ensure that the style guide to which you direct your students includes a section on electronic sources. For example, the fourth and subsequent editions of the *MLA Handbook for Writers of Research Papers* (Gibaldi

1995) include instructions for referencing electronic sources. Typically, citation of electronic sources follows standard referencing formats modified in two ways:

- After the publication title, insert "type of medium" information. This refers to the nature of the source: cd-rom, online sources or e-mail.
- At the end of the citation, insert "availability" information; this often replaces the place, publisher and date information (Li 1993).

In general, modify the standard format to include additional information about the electronic source, giving enough information for the reader to locate the source. Finally, for those electronic sources that are relatively ephemeral, making it impossible for others to locate the original source, you might ask your students to append a copy of the original passages cited at the end of their essay.

This article was first published in Core 4 (2): 6.

References

Gibaldi, Joseph, (ed.) 1995. *MLA handbook for writers of research papers*, 4th ed. New York: Modern Language Association.

Li, Xai. 1993. *Electronic style: A guide to citing electronic information.* Wesport, MA: Meckler.

Section VI:
Teaching and Learning Strategies

This section focuses on strategies that one can use in a course to enhance learning. Since there is such a variety of contexts in which one can teach, we have divided this section into three parts: 1) Lecturing, 2) Class Participation and 3) Seminars, Tutorials and Small-Group Learning. However, this division is somewhat artificial because many of the articles are relevant to more than one context. For example, the articles on class participation could be relevant to a lecture-based course or a small seminar. Readers are encouraged to seek out relevant ideas from all the parts, rather than focus exclusively on one part. In addition, articles from Section VII, Assignments and Evaluation, will also prove useful to these different teaching contexts.

Part 1, Lecturing, begins by addressing the question, Why lecture? The articles caution us about assuming that a lecture is always the appropriate teaching strategy and they outline circumstances when it is appropriate. The Green and Kehoe articles outline crucial steps one can take to ensure that lecturing is successful. As Kehoe points out, though some might be naturally gifted lecturers, the skills of good lecturing can be learned. The Rogers article focuses on the benefits and drawbacks of lecturing as it affects student learning and both the storage and retrieval of information. To overcome these drawbacks, Rogers offers useful suggestions on how to create the conditions for active learning, even in large classes. Indeed, these suggestions would be useful in smaller classes.

Part 2 focuses on class participation. The lead article, "Dead Silence...," discusses how the think-write-pair-discuss technique can be used in a variety of class sizes to encourage more thoughtful and broad-ranging participation. Bradshaw's article asks us to consider the entire class as a group and the need to devise appropriate strategies to support the development of good group dynamics and participation. Bradshaw argues that we must be mindful of how group processes develop and she suggests active intervention to encourage students to take responsibility for their own learning. Laurendeau's article explores how teachers respond to students' comments and whether these responses encourage or discourage intellectual engagement. Finally, for those who are curious about how computer technology can promote communication and interaction among students, the Craven article surveys the pros and cons of educational applications of different types of electronic communication. From MOOS to newsgroups to listservs to computer conferencing, Craven concludes that they all share the potential to promote student writing and thus enhance learning in a course.

Part 3 focuses on teaching small groups of students. We open with an article by Coulthard that provides detailed instructions for creating a small-group experience in a large course by creating study groups. Drawing on a review of research on group work, the article includes advice on how to set up and maintain successful study groups, how to solve problems that groups typically encounter, warm-up activities and using groups in class. Though written for mathematics classes, the ideas in this article are relevant to any discipline. The article on warm-ups by Schlesinger outlines several strategies for beginning a seminar and encouraging good group dynamics from the outset. Articles that follow address formal group activities in a variety of disciplines, including economics (Handy), languages and linguistics (Vizmuller-Zocco), sociology (Bischoping), urban studies (Caulfield), and administrative studies (Nath). McKenna's article offers suggestions for helping students learn to do class presentations, including a list of guidelines for students. The article by Ungar addresses the way seminar leaders use office hours. Ungar encourages us to use this time for more than just crisis management and suggests alternate ways that office meetings can promote positive learning for students. Most authors note the benefits of using group work, whether inside or outside of the classroom, to promote a sense of community among students and to diminish student anonymity. Indeed, the Handy article highlights this point as a central benefit of group work. Other issues that arise in these articles include different ways to organize groups, planning discipline-appropriate group activities and the problems of grading group work. A wonderful variety of group activities is also suggested, from scrapbook presentations in a course on genocide to a field walk for a course in urban studies.

Whether one considers the entire class as a group or divides a large class into smaller groups, understanding group dynamics is important. Several articles in this section discuss the different stages that groups go through and how instructors can help students move through these stages to become collectively productive. The final article, by Briskin, returns to the important theme of power in the context of group work in a classroom setting. Briskin offers a critical perspective on the assumption of the neutrality of randomly organized small groups; indeed, she argues that gender and racial power dynamics can be reinforced in small-group work. To challenge this problem, she concludes that we must be proactive and interventionist in addressing issues of power and group dynamics.

Effective Lecturing
Techniques

Leslie Green

Just as the lecture hall is a physical symbol of a university, the large lecture – one instructor addressing a room full of students – is emblematic of university teaching. And its special role is justified: a good lecture is an efficient and potentially inspiring way to teach. But lecturing also has its special problems. Unlike a seminar discussion, where the "chemistry" of the group influences its success, the large lecture depends much more on the instructor, who has greater control and thus greater responsibility. Lecturing can be one of the more theatrical modes of teaching, and not all academics do well on stage. The "performance" side of lecturing certainly can be learned: maintain eye contact, speak clearly, modulate your voice, do not rush. But I will say nothing about that here. (I have found Joseph Lowman's 1984 book, *Mastering the Techniques of Teaching*, a goldmine on this and many other subjects.) Nor will I treat the matter of devising lecture content: that varies too much by subject and my own experiences in the arts, social sciences and law might not be of wider value. I do have, however, four suggestions that will improve almost anyone's lecturing.

Decide Whether to Lecture

The question, "How should I do this?" is sometimes illuminated by asking, "Why am I doing this?" Yet the decision – if one can call it that – to lecture is often made by the time slot, the shape of the room and the number of students: three one-hour sessions in a large room with seventy or more means a lecture. This is a mistake.

As the word itself suggests, lecturing began with reading aloud to an audience, one that was short on books. Some lecturers preserve this monkish tradition: they just read or summarize the texts. But since students can read faster than lecturers can speak, and since there is no longer a shortage of books, that approach seems to be a colossal waste of resources.

Instead, lecturing can provide a means of presenting a subject in a focused and engaging way, when a) you have a distinctive perspective on the material – an approach, an argument, a vision that you want to communicate, one that is not yet available in books and articles, not even your own, or b) your material ranges more widely than students can be expected to read for one course, but it can be synthesized. Here, your expertise rests in knowing what to present, what to omit and how to situate and evaluate scholarly disputes. If neither of these scenarios holds true, you should replace or supplement the traditional lecture with other techniques of instruction. After all, not everything that goes on in a lecture hall is lecturing: the hour can also — or instead — be taken up with discussion, demonstration, exercises, tests, audio tapes, videos, etc. Lecturing has an important role to play in university teaching, but it is not suitable for everything.

Communicate Your Expectations

Having decided to lecture, you need to communicate your purposes and expectations to your audience. Students are understandably frustrated when they do not know what to expect. This is particularly true of first-year students, who have probably never before sat through a lecture. They need to know what will happen from week to week, why it will happen and what their own responsibilities are. Thus, by the second week of class, they need a syllabus and lecture list showing at least:

- the time and place of lectures
- the instructor's name, office location and office phone number
- the course description and aims
- the basis of evaluation and any formalities relating to late work, attendance, etc.
- a dated or ordered list of lecture topics (I often organize each lecture around a question that I'll try to answer that day)
- a list of readings required as preparation for each lecture or recommended for further work.

Instructors sometimes try to make do with less, but this is very risky. In particular, "winging it" from week to week, announcing readings and topics as you go, seeing where the spirit moves you, does not make for good lectures. (I am not denying that this might work in small reading groups or graduate seminars.) A student should never walk into a lecture hall wondering what the hour will bring and should never leave a lecture wondering how the material covered fits with the aims of the course.

Have Good Lecture Notes

Unlike a seminar woven out of the threads of class discussion, a lecture should follow a planned pattern, even if it allows for variation. Good lecture notes — ones that contain all the main points that you will make, in their proper order, including any quotations or examples fully worked out — are thus essential to a good lecture.

This is surprisingly controversial. People teach with everything from no notes, through scribblings on old envelopes, to flow charts, boxes of index cards, point-form summaries and even fully drafted, paragraph-form, printed and bound lectures. (My own practice leans towards the fully drafted end of the scale, though in truth my notes are not yet bound.) The medium is irrelevant, but the existence and content of the notes is vital. Their length obviously varies with the degree of compression — for a forty-five-minute lecture I have on the lectern between four and six typed pages, never more. Any quotes are typed out with page references. (If you prefer to take the books, try yellow sticky-notes to mark passages.)

The point of fully prepared notes is simple: they anchor the talk and, as far as possible, eliminate last-minute uncertainties and decisions. Having thought it through enough to write it out, you will know it enough to lecture on it. Because this might seem obvious, it is worth considering why some doubt it. Resistance to full lecture notes is of two kinds: the rational and the romantic.

Rational resistance is based on the fear that full notes are time-consuming to prepare and that they make lectures too rigid. Both fears are justified. I have learned to live with the first and thus with the fact that August must be partly given over to writing or revising lectures. I mitigate the second by not *reading* my notes, and by revising them — sometimes radically — before giving the lectures again.

Romantic resistance is based on the notion that only when free to move with the spirit, thinking aloud, can one deliver the lapidary insights of a Socrates. Only then can students experience the true genius of the Great Man (as this character so often is). Romantic resistance usually rests on self-deception, and students see through it. They like August, too.

Give Good Lecture Notes

Students expect to leave a lecture with a good set of notes. Within limits, this is a perfectly reasonable hope. If the lecture is such that a prepared and attentive student does not know what to write down, cannot distinguish core points from peripheral or cannot spell unusual or technical terms, then the lecture is just not working. (Of course, students need to do the preparation, and actually take notes, as opposed to making tapes for later listening.)

Instructors sometimes fear that giving good notes requires spoon-feeding and summarizing texts and readings, thus reducing all to the lowest common denominator. This is exaggerated. The sense in which a good lecture simplifies and orders the material is not one of spoon-feeding, but of preparing a carefully planned menu.

Two things are prophylactics against intellectual indigestion. Most important is to *give an outline of the points and arguments to be covered.* This can be done by preparing a one-page hand-out showing headings and key points, by putting the same material on the board or overhead transparency or by incorporating it into the beginning of the lecture. The idea is not to give a substitute for the lecture; a satisfactory outline does not need to be elaborate. If there are eight key points, six crucial arguments and eleven technical terms, you will certainly not be able to lay them out in a convenient summary. On the other hand, you will probably also not be able to get through them in forty-five minutes.

Second, it is helpful to put on the board or hand-out a list of *key words* for that day's lecture, in roughly the order in which they will be heard. It takes some practice to get the list right: new technical terms, foreign or unusual words, symbols, formulae and proper names all need to be included. Writing this down as one goes is a poor substitute: it makes for a messy and interrupted presentation, usually forcing one to turn one's back on the audience.

On the point of key words, there is a delicate question of how to cope with varying language skills among students. (I once sensed unease when I said, "every contract purports to change normative relations." I naturally thought my explanation of the term "normative relations" had failed to take hold. Alas, a good fifth of the three hundred students could not use the verb "to purport.") My own practice is never to "talk down," but to try to avoid misunderstandings where I can. I also have some fun with etymologies, which, in my disciplines, often helps with arcane terms.

There is, of course, more to good lecturing than that. But those four suggestions yield, I think, the fastest returns: make an active decision about whether to lecture, make your expectations clear through the syllabus, have good notes for yourself and lecture so that the class can take good notes. That will go far to ensure that our lectures earn their central place in the university curriculum.

References

Lowman, Joseph. 1984. *Mastering the techniques of training.* San Francisco: Jossey-Bass.

Improving
Large-Class Lecturing
Dalton Kehoe

Universities everywhere are currently under pressure by funding agencies to stretch their resources and accomplish more with less. What this has meant for teaching is increasing class size and a growing focus on large-group lecturing as the mainstay in our repertoire of teaching techniques. This trend has met with resistance from many academics concerned about a decline in the quality of education that we are providing to undergraduate students. They contend that large-class lecturing is simply not as effective as discussion for teaching undergraduate students. I am not convinced that this is necessarily the case.

Numerous comparative studies indicate that carefully structured and well-presented lectures are as effective as other forms of teaching when the educational goals are transmitting information and providing explanation (Davis and Alexander 1977, Brown and Atkins 1988). Moreover, larger class size *per se* has not been found to disadvantage students in terms of information learned. However, the same literature reviews also make clear that lectures should be augmented by other forms of teaching if a full range of educational objectives are to be achieved, such as teaching students to apply information, develop problem-solving skills or change attitudes. To accomplish this, small-group discussion, clearly focused assignments and encouraging students to read complex material on their own are necessary complements to the lecture process.

If the trend to larger undergraduate classes is inevitable (and it seems to be), then simply resisting the use of large-group lecturing is far less responsive to concerns about educational quality than 1) insisting on the resources to create a variety of means for teacher – student interaction to complement lecturing in large classes and 2) focusing on improving the quality of information transmission in our lectures.

The focus of this article is on the latter point. My intention is to review some of the basic techniques for effective lecturing in large classes (one hundred or more) and to suggest that we need to see effective lecturing for what it is – not the mysterious art of a few gifted "naturals," but a set of thinking and communication skills that can be acquired and applied by anyone willing to make the effort.

What follows is an overview of what I believe are the most important of these skills. I have organized them into four sections that reflect the model of large-class lecturing as predominately a one-way form of communication that is structured and transmitted by the teacher so as to create a context within which students can easily gain access to substantial amounts of factual and analytical material and motivate themselves to understand it.

PLANNING → PRESENTATION → STUDENT PERCEPTIONS

← ← FEEDBACK ← ←

I will begin with several key elements of planning an effective lecture and then proceed with an overview of several aspects of effective presentation. In conclusion, I will review several key concepts from the research literature on students' perceptions of lecturers and recommend an end-of-lecture approach to obtaining useful feedback about student understanding.

Planning the Lecture
Intentions

The plan for an effective lecture begins with the lecturer's intentions. In their review of the teaching literature, Brown and Atkins (1988) note that lecturers intend to 1) cover a topic, 2) generate understanding and 3) stimulate the students' interest (7). These are not necessarily complementary goals and to achieve all three in any lecture requires planning and preparation.

The most commonly expressed goal of lecturing is full topic coverage. However, when covering as much as possible is a lecturer's main goal, students are cast into the role of passive recording machines. Almost inevitably their interest flags and they find it difficult to understand the point of the lecture while being bombarded with information. The typical result is summarized in this anecdote from research on large-class teaching at Oxford Brookes Polytechnic by Ward and Jenkins (1989):

> I also found that the [classes] that I got on better with were the ones where [the instructors] didn't try to pack in everything they could on the subject. They made the basic points, or the important points, and made sure by the time you left the lecture you understood them. You might come out and think, "Well, hang on a minute, we only learned about two things." But that was a good foundation for you to then go away and look at whatever seminar sheet or hand-outs. That's a lot better than coming out totally confused by the wealth of information they try to cram in, and they cram it in such a way that you can't possibly listen and take notes at the same time, 'cause they are just rabbiting on.

An effective lecture requires the thoughtful balancing of coverage with explanation and illustration to create the possibility of engaging student interest long enough to achieve some level of understanding. In deciding what to cover in a large-class lecture, remember that "less is more." A few concepts, well illustrated with apt examples and presented with a clearly stated purpose, provide the key to an effective lecture.

Structuring the Lecture

The "classic" lecture structure is the most common. It divides the lecture into broadly related sections, each of which is then divided into subsections. In a well-planned presentation, each section should unlock understanding of the larger subject; contain its own main points, examples and qualifications; and conclude with a brief summary.

Research suggests that the classic structure is easiest to plan and is best for providing an orderly overview of topics. In addition, it also seems to be the format from which students find it easiest to take notes. However, perhaps because it is so common a form, I believe that it is also the easiest to botch. Because the classic format requires the same kind of thinking needed to write an expository essay, lecturers often view the lecture as simply written text to be read out loud. Using this approach, they create order, but almost inevitably cover too much material too quickly. Indeed, when lecturers use their "on-the-page" structure as their lecture guide, they rarely think to use, as well, the basic tools of explanatory clarity (Brown and Atkins 1982, 22–23) to provide an orally based structure for their listeners as they go along. The result is that students regularly lose the flow and, consequently, their understanding suffers and their interest flags.

To make the classic form effective, first structure the topic. Be clear about what you want to leave in and leave out and then structure your explanation. To accomplish this, Brown and Atkins outline four communication techniques to provide the clarity of explanation that makes it easier for students to follow a presentation:

1. Signposts: Use statements that signal the direction and structure of a lecture. This is best done as an overview at the beginning of the lecture, for example, "Today we will cover the following approaches…I will show the strengths and weaknesses of each and present examples of their application…" Students will have a much easier time following if you let them know where you're about to go.
2. Frames: Use these verbal markers to delineate the beginnings and endings of topics and subtopics; for example, "Let me now turn to the next approach…"
3. Foci: Use statements that highlight and emphasize the key points in each section. Students want to know what's important. Tell them.
4. Links: Periodically link sections of the lecture together; for example, "So you can see that the first two approaches are complementary," or link them to the experience or previously acquired knowledge of the audience, such as previous lectures or readings. The closing statement of a lecture should also act as a link.

Without care in structuring your explanation as you present it, your efforts to structure the larger topic effectively are likely to be lost on your listeners. I suggest that it would be useful to 1) prepare your lecture in note form, with clear headings for key sections and subsections and 2) build the techniques for clarity of explanation right into your notes. You may or may not read them exactly as written, but they are there to remind you when they need to be used.

Creating a Lecture/Reading Outline

In a large-class lecture course, the most powerful guidepost you can create for students is a detailed lecture and reading outline. By writing descriptive lecture titles, attaching exact readings to each lecture and by sticking to the outline, you create a sense of topical order and flow that students easily follow as the term progresses. In fact, if you have to deviate from the outline, be sure to explain why, as well as when and how you will return to it.

The Text and Lecture Content

In a large lecture course, the text is often the one thing that holds everything together for students. Thus, in structuring lecture topics, I believe it is crucial to connect them consistently and effectively to the course text.

The lecture should be used to heighten particular text points, to personalize them in terms of your academic interests and research work and to enliven them with illustrations that are appropriate for your particular audience. If chosen carefully, the text can provide coverage, while you focus on generating interest and in facilitating understanding of key concepts. In courses that use kits of readings, your lectures will create the conceptual connections ordinarily provided by a text author, specifically by using key aspects of the readings to illustrate your presentation.

Presenting the Lecture

Openings and Closings

The most important moments of a lecture are the opening and closing minutes. Your opening sets up the audience for what is about to happen; it is a critical signpost. The most effective lectures start with an overview of what you will say, beginning with a statement that describes the importance of the topic and its linkage to what has gone before or will be coming. In addition, I believe openings should be used to convey your enthusiasm for the topic, underscoring for your students the sense that each lecture is an important event.

Your closing summary is equally important; however, your goal here is more specifically focused on assisting with understanding. To appreciate what they've just heard, your audience needs to be reminded of several key lecture points and how they are linked to one another, how they are connected to the larger subject matter they represent and, most importantly for them, how those key points relate to the readings and the next lecture.

In preparing lectures over the years, I have become convinced that the creation of opening and closing statements is best left to the end. Indeed, I often don't see all the implications of what I've written until I see it all together as a single unified piece of work.

Telling a Good Story

Generally, first- and second-year students enter the lecture hall with little experience in conceptual thinking or in the use of formal language. Until we make an effort to "concretize" abstractions by grounding our explanations and examples in plain language that is closer to their own experience, our best efforts at clarity of explanation will literally go over their heads. When this happens, students struggle mentally, trying to create meaning out of the unfamiliar words they've just heard. Instead of facilitating their understanding of the topic, this struggle usually results in their missing the next things we have to say. So while you move ahead, they will end up stuck trying to interpret previous points you've made.

Attention Span

An often unrecognized but essential fact of lecturing life is the length of our students' attention span. It is not fifty minutes. Classroom research indicates that fifteen to twenty minutes is the most we can hope for before the minds of most of our audience wander off to other things. The effective lecturer changes pace at around the twenty-minute mark to help students refocus their attention and re-engage their thinking processes.

Typical pace changers might include a video clip, a short experiential exercise or a brief question-and-answer period. A number of authors (Andresen 1990) suggest using "buzz groups," both to refocus attention after the twenty-minute mark and to enhance understanding of the material being presented. This technique involves asking students to discuss a clearly structured question with their neighbours (usually in pairs or threesomes) for a short period of time (not longer than five minutes). The lecturer then asks for feedback on discussion outcomes and processes it for clarification before moving on.

Involved Note-Taking

Another way of engaging students while lecturing is the use of what Deukin (1973) calls semi-notes. He describes them as "hand-outs covering the entire lecture but having all the most important parts replaced with blank spaces." Their use encourages attention, while at the same time discouraging student attempts to take dictation as you speak or to copy verbatim material you've put on the blackboard or on the overhead projector. Students know they must listen so that they can identify key concepts to fill in the appropriate blank spaces, but since the rest of the material is on the hand-out, they are freer to think about what is being said and to make supplemental notes on key examples or illustrations. For the past few years, I have experimented with the use of semi-notes in my third-year classes, with excellent results.

Using Audio-Visual Aids

For large-class lecturing there is probably nothing more important for effective presentation than the proper use of audio-visual technology. Without a doubt the most frustrating situation for a large group is a barely audible speaker stolidly reading from notes or working on a green chalkboard with thin, white chalk. If we are to be responsive to the needs of increasingly large classes, we must do so in a way that allows our words and our persona to fill the ever-larger spaces within which we must work. Audio-visual tools can help us do this.

Microphones are an essential tool in large classrooms. The ability to project your voice above the natural noise of having a hundred or more people in the same space at the same time is fundamental to effective presentation. Unless you have trained yourself to do this over the years, amplification is the only way. A good microphone allows you to speak in your natural voice and permits a wide range of volume modulation without your having to make unreasonable efforts to project your voice. Indeed, it permits a kind of vocal intimacy usually achieved only in small-group tutorials.

Microphones are easy to use and come in a variety of types, from lectern-mounted to wireless lapel-clipped. A few minutes of conversation with a technician from your institution's audio-visual facility will be adequate to familiarize yourself with their use.

The *chalkboard* is still the most widely used audio-visual tool, but it has been found to be least effective in large lecture halls. Given the lighting and construction of most lecture halls, thin white chalk is easily visible only from the first few rows. I recommend that if you are going to use chalk, purchase the thick, yellow variety and use the blackboard to note key points only. In this way, what you write is more likely to be seen and understood.

The use of the blackboard for extensive mathematical proofs or complex drawings in large lecture halls also has been found to be a common source of frustration for undergraduate students. Unless the lecturer has extremely clear handwriting or excellent drafting skills, students often can't read or comprehend what is being presented. I recommend that you use the semi-notes approach outlined above to solve this problem. Handing out incomplete drawings, charts and notes gives students enough structure to comprehend what you are presenting, while at the same time providing enough involvement to maintain their attention.

I believe that the *overhead projector* with prepared acetate sheets is far more effective than the chalkboard for presenting written and drawn material to a large class. It commits you to structuring your explanation effectively before entering the lecture hall and ensures that what you present can be clearly seen by all. Moreover, you are free to face the audience while you present, using the points on each acetate as mental cues to what you want to say next. By using key point phrases and a simple "reveal" techniques (using a sheet of paper to uncover one phrase at a time) you can build up a complex argument and keep student attention focused.

An additional advantage of using clear acetates for presenting drawings, charts or key points is that you can make additional notations on the acetates as you proceed. Again, the basic structure is present to support the learner's need for order while you're adding new material.

Computer-based presentation programs create the ultimate "overhead" for large-scale lecture-hall presentations. I have been experimenting with one type – Powerpoint for Macintosh – in my lectures over the past two years. This program allows me to project any type of text on a wide variety of attractive backgrounds in full colour. The appearance of the text on screen is controlled so that you can create "builds" or "reveals" by adding text through key strokes. There is also a wide variety of ways that text can be moved onto the screen.

In addition, there is an extensive clip-art library in the program, including mapping and statistical table presentation subprograms. Moreover, the colour of the background, text, slide titles, drawings and so on can be fully manipulated. With a little practice you will be able to create more than enough visual interest to sustain the intellectual interest you are trying to stimulate in your students.

In some institutions, the audio-visual facility can assist in providing access to equipment that will project computer-based presentation programs onto a back-lit projection screen. Depending on the room in which you are lecturing, you also might be able to make use of the blackboard and a regular overhead projector at the same time, as well as incorporate videotape or movie segments into your presentation.

All of this might seem excessively technological; however, I urge you not to dismiss it without at least finding out what is possible at your institution and requesting a demonstration. Presentation programs are easy to learn, even for those with limited computer experience. Moreover, they make pedagogical sense because they represent an accessible technology that takes advantage of your students' communication backgrounds. Your audience has been raised on television, where colour and moving text and images have been used for decades to capture and keep their interest. Presentation technology allows you to engage this video experience in the classroom.

Student Perceptions

A study by Sheffield (1974) outlined several of the key factors students perceived to be important in characterizing effective lecturers. Students (and lecturers) who participated in the study stressed that highly rated lecturers who successfully engage students share four general characteristics. They

- communicate their love of the subject matter
- display obvious care for their students
- prepare appropriately
- focus on conveying principles rather than on imparting details.

The first two characteristics reflect enthusiasm for the work of lecturing in one's discipline; the latter two reflect a commitment to lecturing practices such as the ones I've outlined above. Surely these characteristics reflect a series of commitments to quality presentation that are within the reach of anyone who intends to lecture as part of an academic career.

Feedback

Finally, I want to describe briefly two methods of gaining immediate and valuable information on the effects of your work in the lecture hall.

The first simply involves paying close attention to the reaction of students whose faces you can observe in the rows closest to you. While you are lecturing, locate several responsive faces in your audience and periodically note how their facial expressions change as you progress through your material. You will be able to gauge whether they are following your lines of reasoning, or whether you need to reiterate a certain point by using an additional example. It seems patently obvious, so much so that we often forget to do it (or don't want to do it).

Another fast feedback method to help you assess the students' understanding and determine your clarity is the "One-Minute Paper."[1] In the last few minutes of your lecture, hand out a half page containing one of these questions: "What was the clearest point for you in today's lecture?" or "What was the muddiest point for you in today's lecture?" Ask students to take one minute to answer and pass their responses back to you.

Before the next class, review these responses and begin your next lecture with clarifying remarks. The effect on student interest levels is dramatic. When they realize that you are willing to respond to their concerns, they become much more involved with what you have to say. The effect on you might be dramatic too. After all, your students might tell you things you don't want to know, but might need to learn, about your lecturing. A willingness to be open-minded is vital.

Conclusion

As a technique, fast feedback could be the most dramatic form of learning you can engage in to improve your lecturing, but it shares a common theme with all of the other techniques, practices and thought processes reviewed above – a willingness to learn and experiment.

I recognize that pointing out what to do is a far cry from helping lecturers with how to actually do it. One sure way to help yourself with "how" is to go and watch highly rated lecturers in action and talk to them about what techniques work well from their point of view. I am certain that you will find your colleagues ready and willing to help; indeed, you might find them to be an inspiration.

Notes

1. For more information on the use of the One-Minute Paper and related classroom assessment techniques, see the article by Rogers that follows, and Section VIII, Part One, on Classroom Assessment.

References

Andresen, L. 1990. *Lecturing to large groups* (SCED Paper 57). Standing Conference on Educational Development. Australia: University of New South Wales.

Brown, G. and M. Atkins. 1988. *Effective teaching in higher education.* London: Methuen.

Davis, R. and L. Alexander. 1977. *The lecture method: Guides for the improvement of instruction in higher education.* East Lansing, MI: Michigan State University Press.

Deukin, G. 1973. The use of semi-notes in lecturing. *RUUE Bulletin, University of Western Australia* (May). Quoted in Andresen (1990), 11.

Sheffield, E., (ed.) 1974. *Teaching in the universities: No one way.* Montréal: Queen's University Press.

Ward, A. and A. Jenkins. 1992. The problems of learning and teaching in large classes. In *Teaching large classes in higher education: How to maintain quality with reduced resources*, Graham Gibbs and Alan Jenkins (eds.), 23–36. London: Kogan Page.

Improving Student Learning in Lectures

Pat Rogers

The lecture is the most pervasive forum for student learning on university campuses. When you consider that the majority of classrooms and lecture halls are designed with masses of chairs and tables (usually bolted to the floor) all focused on a single location – the lectern – this is hardly surprising. Yet despite the constraints imposed by the physical environment, there are pedagogical advantages to lecturing as a mode of instruction. There are also limitations. In this article,[1] I offer suggestions for overcoming some of them. In practical terms, I describe the "One-Minute Paper," a simple technique developed by a physics professor at the University of California at Berkerley (Wilson 1986) that can be used to improve student learning and encourage active participation in lectures.

For teachers, lecturing has the advantage of being comfortable – in some measure because it is the method that most of us experienced ourselves when we were students. It is an extremely efficient way of getting across and synthesizing a large amount of material in a short space of time. It allows maximum control over pace, content, organization and use of time, and the lecturer is assured that the students have been exposed to a common core of material.

Years of research have shown that the lecture method is no less effective than other teaching methods (see, for example, Bligh 1972). Indeed, support for lecturing abounds – it is recommended for specific purposes such as introducing a new section of material, providing a historical background or context, connecting new concepts to previous material, providing an overview, demonstrating a skill or technique and summarizing major concepts, to name but a few.

Several limitations of the lecture method have been cited in the literature (Bligh 1972). Many of them stem from factors that affect student learning. Although there is no consensus on what constitutes good teaching, there is general agreement that effective teachers organize their material and classroom time in ways that promote student learning. What, then, do we know about learning that might affect how we plan and deliver a lecture?

Failure to remember is more often a problem of retrieval than a problem of storage, yet in its traditional uninterrupted form, the lecture places more emphasis on storage than on activities that facilitate the retrieval of information. Retention of lecture material can be increased greatly by giving learners practice in memory retrieval during the lecture. As well, studies show that we tend to remember best what we hear in the introduction and in the conclusion of a presentation and that the average attention span is between fifteen and twenty minutes. Lecturers can turn this knowledge to advantage by stating the most important points at the beginning or the end of a lecture and by dividing the lecture period into smaller units. This means, for example, that a fifty-minute lecture might be designed to contain three beginnings and three endings. In the intervals between the units, the lecturer can provide students with much-needed practice in memory retrieval.[2] Below I describe several of the ways in which the One-Minute Paper can be used to support this lecture structure.

The One-Minute Paper is a technique that can be used by instructors to obtain feedback on what students are learning. It can be introduced in small seminars or in large lectures and in first-year or upper-level courses. In its simplest and most widely used form, the One-Minute Paper asks students to respond anonymously to the following two questions: "What is the most important thing you learned in class today?" and "What question remains uppermost in your mind?" Following are a few of the ways the One-Minute Paper can be used in lectures:

- Used at the end of the lecture, the One-Minute Paper provides the instructor with valuable information for planning the next class. After giving students a few minutes to answer one or two pertinent questions on the lecture they have just heard, the papers can be collected and scanned after class and the major trends noted. In a large class the papers can be sampled; for example, by looking at every tenth paper. Instructors who use this technique find that it motivates students to take the task seriously if instructors provide feedback to students in the next lecture on the overall pattern of responses to the questions asked. It also shows students that instructors take the exercise seriously and that they respect and value student feedback.

- In a course with tutorials as well as lectures, the information gleaned can be passed along to tutorial leaders, thereby giving them advance warning of issues that might be explored in the tutorial. A variation of the One-Minute Paper, which is particularly useful in this context, is the Muddiest Point, in which the lecturer asks the single question, "What was the muddiest point in my lecture today?"

- Used during a lecture, the One-Minute Paper is an excellent way to break the lecture period into smaller segments. Responses to the One-Minute Paper do not have to be gathered and analyzed on the spot by the instructor. They can be collected verbally by having students form small groups. In their groups, students identify one or two common themes that can then be reported to the whole class. This provides active student involvement in the class, gives all students an opportunity to contribute to the discussion and increases the range of students willing to volunteer answers to questions during the lecture. This method works particularly well in two-or three-hour lectures.

The One-Minute Paper and its variation, the Muddiest Point, are just two examples of classroom assessment techniques that can be used to obtain feedback on, and improve, student learning in lectures. For other techniques, see the articles on classroom assessment in Section VIII and the author's article "Dead Silence...A Teacher's Nightmare" next in this section.

Notes

1. A version of this article first appeared in 1991 in Core 2 (1): 1, 4. Its publication inspired two unsolicited contributions to *Core* by Aldridge and Merrens, which can be found in Section VIII of this volume. For more information about this and other classroom assessment techniques see Cross and Angelo (1988) and the two papers by Newton in Section VIII.
2. See Murray (1978) for a discussion of the research on student learning and its implications for the lecture method of teaching.

References

Bligh, D.A. 1972. *What's the use of lectures?* Toronto: Penguin.

Cross, K.P. and T.A. Angelo. 1988. *Classroom assessment techniques: A handbook for faculty.* Ann Arbor, MI: National Center for Research to Improve Postsecondary Teaching and Learning.

Murray, Harry G. 1978. Ten ways of improving the lecture method of teaching. *The Ontario Psychologist* 10 (2): 7–19.

Wilson, R.C. 1986. Improving faculty teaching: Effective use of student evaluations and consultants. *Journal of Higher Education* 57: 196–211.

Part Two: Class Participation

Dead Silence...
A Teacher's Nightmare

Pat Rogers

Fed up with asking, "Any questions?" only to be greeted by silence? Heard that students learn best when they participate actively in the class, but not sure how to make it happen? Want to begin group work, but not sure where to start? Tired of hearing from the same students every time you ask a question? Concerned about the students who don't participate? Think-write-pair-discuss (TWPD) provides a solution to all of these problems and more. It is a simple and effective way to improve student learning and at the same time, according to Gareth Morgan of the Schulich School of Business at York University, "change the energy in the classroom."

The next time you ask your students a question, ask them to *think* about it quietly for a few minutes on their own, then tell them to put their thoughts on paper (*write*). After a minute or two, depending on the complexity of the question, ask them to turn to the person (or persons) next to them (*pair*) to *discuss* what they have written (here you find out why some people call these "buzz groups"). After another five minutes or so, bring the class together. You can handle this stage in several ways. Ask each group to contribute one answer to the question or choose individuals to report their group's discussion. If the class is small, you can go around the class collecting responses from each student. You can be certain that the answers you get will be richer and more thoughtful than before. You also might decide there is no need to collect responses, because while they were talking you were circulating among the groups.

Veena Gokhale, formerly a teaching assistant in environmental studies at York University, has found that TWPD provides a good transition to discussion:

> It helps the students to start interacting with the person next to them and encourages a friendlier atmosphere that prepares the ground for discussion. The other reason I like TWPD is that it leads to reflection and to writing in class. It gives students a pause, as it were, to sort out their ideas. The writing part helps to clarify thoughts.

TWPD provides support for those students who are unsure about their ideas or who are anxious about speaking in front of the class. It increases participation and involves all students in active learning. It allows you to draw on student experience and knowledge, gives immediate feedback on student learning and allows students to assess their own understanding. It is also an excellent way to begin experimenting with collaborative learning in the classroom. TWPD can be used to:

- discuss an assigned topic
- solve a problem
- relate theory to students' own experience
- make lists of questions, comments or ideas
- to find out what students already know about a topic.

Nonetheless, the technique has drawbacks. The biggest is that it takes time. You might need to prune your syllabus, leaving out some optional topics. You might experience some anxiety about your ability to control the class. You also might have to be prepared for the unanticipated response or question and allow yourself the luxury of learning from your students! Someone once said to me, "The best way to cover the curriculum is with a blanket." TWPD allows students to uncover the curriculum while helping them develop independence and teaching them the value of learning from each other.

This article was first published in November 1993 in Core 4 (2): 5.

Evoking and Provoking Student Participation

Pat Bradshaw

When I reflect on how to encourage students to participate actively in classes, I realize that I use a combination of strategies ranging from subtle evoking to unvarnished provocation. Underlying these strategies is an awareness of group dynamics and stages of group development, a philosophy of power sharing and an enthusiasm for my subject matter. I would like to share some of my tactics in order to engage your participation in an exchange of ideas and reactions.

Class participation and the energy and focus of class members are influenced by the stage of development of the group. Researchers who study groups suggest that there are four developmental stages: forming, storming, norming and performing (Tuckman 1965).[1] Member confusion and uncertainty characterize the *forming* stage. Group members attempt to get acquainted and to establish ground rules for acceptable behaviours. During the *storming* stage the group is characterized by conflict as group members resist control by the leader and show hostility towards each other. After the conflicts are resolved the group moves to the *norming* stage, in which members become more cohesive, develop relationships and find mutually acceptable ways to solve problems. These feelings of camaraderie enable the group to move to the stage of *performing*, in which the group devotes its energy to getting the job done.

Being aware of these stages enables me to adjust the strategies I use to encourage student participation. For example, when a class is in its forming stage I attempt to ensure broadly based participation from all students. This allows everyone to feel included in the class and moves the group through the confusion stage more quickly. If I am not successful at facilitating the group through this stage and we get stuck at the forming stage, the class continues to be characterized by distrust, partial participation and a certain level of artificial pleasantness, which inhibits the group from fully engaging with the course content and challenging and interacting with one another. I believe that a group is most fully in a learning mode when it gets to the performing stage.

Evoking

Some of the subtle strategies I use to encourage student participation and movement through the forming stage are structurally embedded in my course design and reflect my personal style. They include:

- giving participation grades as a symbolic indicator of the importance of getting involved
- assigning readings that are topical and designed to hook people's interest
- engaging in exercises during the first couple of weeks in which I contract with the students about expectations, roles and the importance of participation
- setting norms early so students see that I am serious about valuing their input
- drawing on various pedagogies that will appeal to different students' interests and strengths, including films, speakers, role playing, debates, experiential exercises and cases
- trying to make eye contact with students who don't speak much in class
- using small-group discussions so quieter students will feel more comfortable joining in
- "cold calling" on students who don't speak up
- using a short wait time after I ask a question in hopes that quieter students will formulate a response; I give them the floor immediately after they raise their hands
- explaining the stages of group development and stressing that it is important for each student to speak up for the whole group to build trust and to move out of the forming stage. I facilitate this with ice-breaker exercises in the first few sessions in which I insist that students speak in sequence. A simple ice breaker involves having all students introduce themselves and describe their hobbies, work experiences, educational backgrounds or other personal information.

Provoking

Once the group has moved through the early forming stages and some basic level of trust is established, I use more aggressive strategies for provoking participation. This can be difficult without an awareness that the group could be entering the storming stage and an understanding that often the group's hostility is articulated by a few students and is directed at the authority figure, the professor. Some of the strategies I use at this point include playing devil's advocate, taking extreme positions or introducing controversial topics. This allows the storming to be acted out in the context of the course content, and if handled non-defensively establishes the norm that disagreement with the professor will not result in punishment or disapproval.

If the class is actively storming I might re-explain the stages of group development and describe the characteristics of a storming group. I can then legitimate the challenging behaviours and support the group in its efforts to move towards the norming stage. My power-sharing philosophy in the classroom is tested by my reactions at this stage of the group's development. Falling back on a power-over or traditional teaching approach at this point usually prevents the group from moving out of the forming stage and could cause it to fall into a mode of trying to "play the game," as I define it, in order to get their grades and get out of the course.

If the class is still not active, I will stop and "process" the group. As a process facilitator I take time away from the course content and lead the class in discussion and reflection on the dynamics of the group. For example, I might describe the behaviours and communication patterns I see in the group and then ask students (in the total group or in subgroups) questions such as what dynamics they observe, what is going on with them, why they are not involved and what can be changed to facilitate their more active involvement. In the next session, I must follow up on their suggestions so that the students realize their input is valued and valuable.

In cases of extreme lack of involvement, I leave the room and ask the class to come and get me when they have completed a discussion of the group dynamics, including my role. Leaving the students alone to debrief and to critique my style is a terrifying process for me but one that vividly illustrates my belief in student empowerment and my trust in them to live up to expectations (they do). With the professor out of the room the group is at liberty to storm in private and those students who are hesitant to give feedback in front of the professor gain space and safety to express their opinions. On my return a spokesperson for the group gives me a summary of their discussion and their suggestions for changes to make the class a more effective learning community.

One advantage of this intervention is that the students feel more ownership and more responsibility for implementing the changes as the initiators of the ideas. Process discussions with or without the professor in the room start the class moving towards positive relationships, agreement on acceptable ways of solving problems and other behaviours typical of the norming stage. Once cooperative working norms are in place the group can move to the performing stage and maximize the learning experience.

When a set of negative norms has been established I use different strategies. For example, when group discussions are dominated by a few vocal students, I do not leave the class alone and I do not confront the students explicitly. Instead I use the following games to surface the dynamics, since I believe awareness will lead to change in the norms and broader class participation.

- Each student gets three tokens or small pieces of paper, which they have to trade in after each contribution they make to the class discussion. Once their tokens are used up, they cannot speak again. This technique ensures that all students have an opportunity to speak.
- In small seminars, I have used a ball of string to chart the dynamics of the discussion. Each person who speaks is given the unraveling ball so we get a visual representation of who is speaking to whom and how often.

These types of interventions clearly illustrate the class norms and are followed by a discussion of the process of the class. I once stopped a class and had groups of students formulate a joke to share with the whole class. While these exercises can be time consuming, they usually break the norms enough to get discussion going again. When all else fails, I become very quiet and wait; if I wait long enough during the ensuing silence and don't panic, I usually find someone will make a valuable contribution. At times such as these, however, I wonder if a good old-fashioned lecture wouldn't be easier!

Previously published in February 1994 in Core 4 (4): 2.

Notes

1. See also the article by Schlesinger, "Stages in Group Dynamics," in Section VI, Part 3, of this book.

References

Tuckman, B. 1965. Developmental sequence in small groups. *Psychological Bulletin* 63: 384–99.

Resistance in the Classroom

Paul Laurendeau

L'activitié ne supprime pas la contradiction: elle en vit. Au moment même où elle travaille à la réduire, elle la porte en elle; elle ne la domine, elle ne crée une unité plus haute qu'en la faisant renaître plus profoundément.
– Henri Lefebvre

Most of us consider being resisted as a traumatic experience. We feel it destabilizes our social image and jeopardizes our credibility. Consequently, we try to avoid such situations in ordinary social life. For example, to take friends to a movie we consider fantastic or to get them to taste a wine we see as the best vintage ever, only to discover our opinion questioned afterwards by the Françoise Truffaut or the wine taster of the group is very hard to take. It is quite unlikely that we would not fight back. It is natural to want to protect our self-image. Despite the fact that the capacity to laugh at ourselves or to be genuinely self-critical is seen as a highly positive sign of personal credibility, the need for self-protection is stronger. We simply do not see ourselves saying something like, "Yeah, you're absolutely right. That movie I loved is actually ridiculous and meaningless!" or "Gee, it's so true. That wine I was keeping in my cellar just for this occasion tastes like ammonia!"

As instructors, we bring these spontaneous self-protective reflex reactions to the classroom. Already strong within each of us as "ordinary citizens," these reflexes often can be strengthened by the existence of three realities that make the teaching situation radically different from that of ordinary social life:

1. Some instructors believe that they have to demonstrate that the information they bring to their teaching is genuine and reliable. They fear that resistance could prove them wrong.
2. Instructors can feel that they are being put on the spot and fear that resistance could make them look weak. They feel that any sign of hesitation or instability

they show will be magnified by the asymmetric organization of the learning environment.

3.   Instructors are academics, working in an institutional universe where struggle and contradiction are omnipresent. Colleagues at conferences, journal editorial boards and anonymous evaluators from granting agencies are all bodies that they constantly have to persuade. Resistance in the classroom can be experienced as yet another challenge to their professional expertise.

My aim in this article is to demonstrate that any attempts by instructors to bring the self-protective attitudes of their ordinary lives to bear on the classroom situation and to eliminate resistance are futile and inappropriate. The arguments I put forward here are founded on the premise that the classroom is a place where instructors have neither the ethical right nor the objective capacity to impose any form of power over students. Further, I believe that instructors must abandon forever any conception of themselves as controlling or manipulating students and see themselves instead as modest instruments in the hands of the people they serve.

Objective Conditions of Resistance in the Classroom

The causes of, and conditions for, resistance in the classroom are often different from those in ordinary life. In the classroom, I see three sources of resistance: confusion, objection and subversion. Regardless of its source, I believe that each and every manifestation of resistance must be viewed by the instructor as an important call from the student and is likely the most sensitive moment of communication during the lecture of the day.

Confusion, as Peter Sinfield wrote for the band King Crimson in 1969,

> ...will be my epitaph
> As I crawl a cracked and broken path
> If we make it we can all sit back and laugh
> But I fear tomorrow I'll be crying.

No doubt this verse might be our students' refrain, for they are completely bamboozled by our teaching far more often than we dare imagine. Confusion is the first source of resistance in the classroom – the most common and the most sincere. When students start to resist, our first approach should be to consider that they are confused and are simply cueing us to the need to provide clarification.

Objection: "Objection, your honour!" This one is crucial. The students understand; they have the picture, but they *do not agree*. By simply questioning what we state, let's admit it, students can make us feel our whole academic discipline begin to shake on its foundation. If we silence objection, it might disappear from sight like a small flame we blow out. But resistance grounded in objection is actually more like the flame from a barbecue briquet. From the moment it has caught fire, the heat remains, growing and increasing in intensity even though we see nothing. If we do not handle this form of resistance well, we might be roasted by the flames of our own clumsy dirigisme.

Subversion: Resistance grounded in subversion is not directed towards our material or our theoretical conceptualization, but towards us. For example, a particular student formed a dislike of me and did everything he could to undermine me and ruin my lectures. He complained about me in any way he could and fought me using every possible means, strategizing interactions with me like a guerrilla. This rare form of resistance is a very mysterious phenomenon to experience. We feel very puzzled and worried about the situation, but usually do not want to investigate its profound causes. We adopt a "wait and see" approach, probably the best reaction to such an unexplained misunderstanding. To date, being openly hated by a student has happened to me twice during my eight-year career, once by a female student and once the male student in the situation described above. Both memories are still vivid. I felt sorry and powerless. I took a low profile vis-à-vis both individuals and waited for better days. That these things happen, nobody would deny.

It is important to stress that the objective conditions of resistance in a learning context are both quantitatively and qualitatively different from those we experience in our social lives. The relative levels of confusion, objection and subversion we generate in our personal lives might well vary, but in the classroom the frequency of these parameters is predictable: confusion is frequent, objection varies (and is up to the instructor) and subversion is rare. As for the qualitative aspects of these phenomena, objection is not confusion, objection is not subversion and an objection is nothing but an objection.

In clear terms, when students object, it is not because they "did not get it" or want to "mess around and nail us" or "tear us apart." Rather, they object because our teaching and their resistance are on the right track. In such situations, the ball is in the instructor's court. Such manifestations of resistance are crucial moments. Any temptation to trivialize or disregard them, or to manipulate them in any way to serve the instructor's agenda, should be firmly rejected. The only attitude to adopt in front of this form of resistance is modesty, receptivity and genuine respect.

Academic Status of Resistance

What, then, are the strategies proposed here for dealing with resistance? Well, if resistance in the classroom is an extraordinary phenomenon compared with what is experienced in ordinary life, instructors will have to address it with extraordinary procedures. The foundation of the strategy I propose can be formulated as follows: confusion is objection, subversion is objection and an objection is not only an objection.

In this model, objection is seen as the spinal cord of resistance in the classroom. If students are confused, they are implicitly expressing an objection towards our organization of the material. When they enter a dynamic of subversion, they are objecting to what we teach or what we represent. Resistance, therefore, has an academic status, one that should be expected and treated as an important moment for communication between instructor and students. In this, objection will provide the test for how well a specific instructor responds to resistance.

The first weeks of any course are the crucial period for defining the nature and tone of resistance in the classroom. The most important moment is when, for the first time, a student contradicts us. Put yourself in this position. One October morning, a student raises her hand. She is quite brilliant and generally asks very inquisitive questions, which you have always answered patiently. You have created all the conditions to make her feel comfortable about expressing her "confusions" freely. But this time, something is different. Her intervention begins with, "Yes, but…" and the rest of her statement is a strong objection to what you have just said. No mistake, no misunderstanding. She resists, and she is the very first to do so in this course, this year. Her intervention is followed by a short moment of silence. For a few seconds, you could hear a pin drop. Consciously or not, she – and with her, the whole class – is testing you.

This is the moment when the students will make a series of decisions about the level of energy, attention and intellectual curiosity that they will or will not invest in your course. How will they be heard, listened to and answered – all are at stake right now. Will you try to put out the fire or will you joyfully throw on some starter fluid? This moment can be a turning point in the nature of the interactions between you and your class. It will establish whether relations in your class will be open and healthy, or furtive with fire smouldering underneath.

The strategy I propose is simply to put this moment, and every single one that follows, on a pedestal. In front of all the other students, thank this student warmly for introducing a new momentum to the classroom discussion. Lionize the individuals who object the most convincingly and quote them as examples to the others. Let them taste the pedagogical efficacy of being contradicted. Face the objection for what it is, simply a rediscovery of the dialectical essence of reality and an honest attempt to investigate through reflection and debate. Certainly by giving centrality to objections in this way, you might risk burning your fingers with the starter fluid. But the result will be the emergence of a strong and irreversible process whereby confusion and subversion are absorbed in the free expression of resistance in an open forum. Ultimately, in such a classroom, objection will turn to its opposite.

In conclusion, if we try to fight resistance in the classroom the way we do in our social lives, students will fight back, openly or otherwise. But if we respect students' academic freedom and validate their resistance within a process of apprenticeship, then students who resist can become important instruments in the learning process. And since the fundamental goal of our students is neither to prove us wrong nor to fight us, but simply to learn, we have an opportunity to learn how to "command" resistance in the classroom, just as we modestly command the inexorable laws of the raging river by managing to remain in the canoe instead of drowning. The unavoidable fact is that the instructor is powerless (the river controls the canoe, not the opposite), but being powerless does not imply being helpless. So, adapting what Francis Bacon says about nature in *The New Organon*, Book I, Aphorism III, resistance in the classroom to be commanded must be obeyed. The single most important lesson we have to learn as instructors is to obey our resisting students, for they are our best chance of doing our pedagogical work effectively.

Computer-Mediated Communication: Some Thoughts about Extending the Classroom

Mary-Louise Craven

For some instructors, the spectre of on-line communication conjures up images of the virtual university; others see it as an opportunity to augment face-to-face meetings with our students. With class sizes growing, and students working more, we need to look at ways to communicate with our students outside of the strict timetabling options of the university. While this is important now, it will be become more so in the future. Our pedagogical needs determine our communication choices, but the initial decision is whether and to what extent we will rely on computer-mediated communication (CMC). Can we be assured that our students will have adequate access to networked computers and to training sessions? Can we—as instructors—be assured that the extra work involved in CMC will be justified?

Student access is an important concern. While, at York all students have email accounts, can we assume that they all have a networked computer at home, or ready access to campus computers through their college affiliation or Faculty lab, or through central facilities like the Computer-Assisted Writing Centre or general-access drop-in labs? Can we assume they can afford the hook-up charges? Currently, students at York pay a monthly fee for high-speed access; only a few years ago, they did not have to pay for access. In these days of fiscal restraint, this is an example of another cost that is now borne directly by students. And if we do not make it university policy that students have a networked computer when they enrol—and provide financial assistance to those who can't afford one—is it fair to students to demand that they communicate with instructors and each other via computer?

Further, adequate training sessions must be made available for students. Students should not have to rely only on each other for computer support. It is clear that just as there are some guarantees that students will have chairs to sit on in our classes and books to use in the library, we need assurances that electronic resources will be available before we significantly change our curriculum. As well, students need to be warned before they take CMC courses that on-line communication is a significant part of the course and they must be prepared to take responsibility for ensuring their on-line participation.

But then what kind of CMC choices do we have? As can be seen from the following chart, different technologies are possible depending on time and place specifications.

	SYNCHRONOUS	ASYNCHRONOUS
Place dependent	Video conferencing	
Place independent	MUDS/MOOS IRC Chat (on First Class)	Newsgroups - usenet E-mail Listserv Computer conferencing - including Web systems

Clearly, the advantage of communication facilities such as newsgroups, email, listservs, and conferencing (both dedicated programs and programs attached to web pages) is that they allow intructors and students to communicate when and where we want—and they are also relatively easy to use. While the focus of this article will be on these facilities, I will say first a few words about video conferencing, MOOS and "chats."

Video Conferencing

Video conferencing allows you to bring a guest speaker to your class "in person" or to bring classes from different places in contact with each other. But for the present, video conferencing is still a time and place-dependent activity. We may someday see desktop video conferencing, which will make video conferencing less place-dependent, but many students will still have low-tech computers unable to carry video conferences, and universities will undoubtedly continue to have tight budgets. These factors may delay practical uses of desktop video conferencing for academic purposes.

Multi-User Dimension Object-Oriented (MOOS)

MOOS (Multi-User Dimension Object-Oriented) are spin-offs from MUDS (or Multi-user Dimensions), and are a type of text-based virtual reality where players telnet to a site, and are logged onto the same system at the same time. Once you are in a MOO and have assumed your character, you talk to others in the environment, and you use commands to move around and interact with things. MUDS were seen merely as "fantasy games," but recently academics have seen the possibilities of using them for "learning environments." In her piece from the on-line *Computer-Mediated Communication Magazine*, Gurak (1995) notes that each Thursday evening during the fall semester, we would all log in from our separate locations and hold what in many ways resembled a graduate seminar. ... It was a great experience, one that showed me the potentials of using MOOS ... for distance learning.

Chat

More down to earth is the chat function found on both the Internet and dedicated conferencing systems. For instance, in FirstClass, when logged on, you can check to see if others are on-line in both the public space (common to all FirstClass users regardless of which conference they're in), and private space (open only to members of separate conferences). You can "invite" someone to join you in a chat, and if she agrees you can "talk" as long as you want, and others can be invited to join. It can be a little chaotic if there are number of "talkers"; people's messages get posted in their order of typing, not according to the continuity of the conversation. While my experience so far has been that students use this facility mainly for social reasons, there is no reason why students couldn't arrange to meet in the chat area at midnight, say, to go over a group assignment. As a supplement to the more contemplative asynchronous writing that goes on in the main conferences, the synchronous communication of the chat helps students to stay in touch with each other. For students, it can serve the same function as taking a break in a class to talk informally over coffee.

Newsgroups

One could say that an advantage of Usenet newsgroups is that, unlike listservs and conferencing (described below), they are completely outside the control of the instructor. Introducing students to a newsgroup that is relevant to the subject matter of your course can allow them to overhear, and if they want, to enter into, conversations with others interested in the field. It's the most obvious way to extend the classroom, but depending on the newsgroup, it can also prove to be disappointing. There can often be a high ratio of "noise" to real conversation. A way to balance the "openness" of newsgroups is to provide course-specific communication routes.

Electronic Mail

Let's say you want to communicate with your students about administrative matters— due dates, changes in the schedule, etc.—and you want them to be able to contact you for electronic office hours. Electronic mail would certainly suffice. In fact, electronic mail has many features that would make even more extended communication possible. For instance, in a training session, students could be shown how to set up an "alias" including all the members of the class. This will allow you to email to the entire class by using, say, "class" rather than all the individual userids. However, since the alias is not centrally controlled, it will have to be updated by everyone in the class whenever anyone drops out or is added—there is little benefit to be gained if some of the members of the class are outside the communication loop. To keep messages organized, students should use the "reply" function, so messages can be threaded;

however, judicious editing should be done to remove all the headers. Further, students can be trained to use folders to keep their class messages stored together; they need to learn to delete unnecessary messages, and to archive and to search through the messages they need. If you wish to encourage more extensive communication than email provides, it would make sense to use either a listserv or a conferencing system.

Listservs

Listservs (or listprocs) are usually set up for you by a systems operator; once a person is subscribed, she receives all messages sent to the listserv, including any she might send. The virtue of a listserv, over email, is that there is one central list, which can easily be updated. Listservs can be moderated (that is the mail is vetted before being broadcast), but most are unmoderated. Generally listservs are "open" in that anyone in the world could join; since your goal with a class listserv is to serve the communication needs of the class, you might consider closing the listserv membership. Listervs can also be set up to archive past messages which is important for users who join the listserv after it has begun; they can retrieve earlier messages from the archives using a "send" command. Listservs are very good for casual group communication, including broadcasting information to a group and general question-and-answer interactions. But one list is one list, and is limited to what it was designed to do—broadcast to a group. The more organisation you try to introduce into a group activity via listserv, the more work is required of both the listserv administrator and the users. For example, to break the class into smaller groups that need to work together in privacy, you'd need to create a new closed list for each group. Or, to introduce well ordered sub-topics, you would have to rely on the users to use appropriate subject lines and to sort their messages upon receipt. Because of this low level of organisation and the higher degree of effort required by the users, a simpler solution might be to use a conferencing system.

Conferencing Software

The important distinction between email/listerv communication and conferencing software (and newsgroups) is that the former is delivered through electronic mail. The receiver has to sort messages and to keep course-related communication separate from other kinds of email. Conferencing on the other hand was specifically designed for goal-oriented group interaction. Conference users would argue that participating in a conference is qualitatively different from reading email—even when messages are threaded. In a conference, the conversations remain visible, and threads can be checked at any time. For instance, if I started a discussion about "conferences" three weeks ago and I wanted to see if anyone had responded to my message, I would go to my message, and then click on the "next thread" button. The program would allow me to follow everyone's reactions to my comments on conferences. I wouldn't have to read through all the messages to get to my "conversation" or check an archive for messages I've missed. An advantage for the instructor is that conferencing gives her more control: for example, she can create sub-conferences when needed, and add conference members. On the other hand, she also needs to consider the time she will have to devote to conferencing and to ensuring that the students are talking to and learning from each other. An early disadvantage of separate conferencing software was that the users needed client software to access the program. Now, for instance, FirstClass is accessible over the Web; as well, there are a number of conferencing programs for the Web which allow instructors to add conferencing facilities to their course web pages. Thus, the student can access information about the course, and communicate with other class members from the same space. This blurring of previously separate networked computer functions of information retrieval and communication is a big advance.

Finally, the real plus of both listservs and conferencing is that students are communicating through writing. Fulwiler was not writing about on-line communication when he noted: "student writing will improve when student learning does, and student learning will improve when students do more writing" (1985, p. 5), but he could have been. Listservs and conferencing can be set up to encourage students to engage in contemplative writing and to share these ideas with others—a real extension of the classroom.

References

Fulwiler, T. 1985. Writing is everybody's business. *National Forum: Phi Kappa Phi Journal* 64: 21-24.

Gurak, L. 1995. Cybercasting about cyberspace. *Computer-Mediated Communication Magazine* 2 (1): 4. Available on-line: http://www.december.com/cmc/mag/1995/jan/gurak.html.

Study Group Guide for Instructors and Teaching Assistants

Katie Coulthard

The Goal of Study Groups

Students learn best when they are actively involved in the process. Balacheff (1990) argues that mathematical knowledge is not learned passively by internalizing carefully prepared and organized material through lectures or texts, but is constructed by the learner or doer of mathematics through solving problems. Asking students to form small study groups fosters active learning and encourages them to go above and beyond what is being covered in lectures in order to develop their own understanding of course material. Studies reveal that students who work in small groups tend to learn more of what is being taught, retain it longer and are more satisfied with their courses than when they cover the same content in other instructional formats (see, for example, McKeachie *et al.* 1986; Slavin 1980, 1983 and Whitman 1988). Individuals working in a group help each other by constructing explanations and elaborations. Talking and arguing help build connections between prior knowledge and new problems. According to Silver (1982), such activity helps make new information more meaningful.

The goal of study groups is to help students take ownership of course material, to improve their understanding and internalization of course material and to assist them in developing effective learning skills.

Benefits of Study Groups
For the instructor and teaching assistant

- Once you and your students adjust to this new arrangement, more material can be covered in the course because students can cover material outside of class.
- You are seen to be approachable.
- Students can offer useful feedback about how the course is going.
- Your office hours are used more productively because some difficulties are worked out at group meetings.

- In large classes, if homework is assigned as a group project, the amount of grading is reduced and returning students' work can be handled more efficiently and discretely.

For students

- Students can verify with each other any confusing or complex subject material.
- Learning math is more fun.
- Math is better understood and retained.
- Students can learn skills required to be "team players," the skills that more and more employers seek.
- Instructors and teaching assistants are seen as more approachable.
- Students have a chance to engage in dialogue with classmates and therefore more opportunity to make friends; hopefully students will feel less isolated.
- Other students can be a source of encouragement.
- Students will see themselves as tutors or teachers, not just recipients of someone else's knowledge.
- Students experience an increase of confidence in their own mathematical ability.
- Students have the opportunity to learn new study habits from peers.
- In a nutshell, learning math in a study group is more personally relevant and intellectually stimulating than learning on one's own.

Forming Study Groups

As a course requirement

How a group is formed greatly affects its success. Although many researchers and teachers differ in their opinion about the most effective way to form groups, most recommend that a study group should comprise three to six students. Early in the course, take some time in class to form study groups. Forming groups in class demonstrates the value you place on the collaborative process. In small classes, groups can be formed in a variety of ways.

- Have students sit according to where they live (this eliminates the need for long-distance phone calls among students and gives students the opportunity to meet at someone's house).
- Allow students to form their own groups.
- Count students off from one to n, where n is the number of groups you want.

In larger classes, the following strategy works well and can be initiated in the last twenty minutes of a class period.

- Advise students that in the next class you will be asking them to form study groups. Ask them to come to class having selected two separate one-hour time slots during the days when they are on campus when they would be free to meet other students to work in a small group on course material.

- To form groups, divide your lecture room up into segments – for example, Monday morning, Monday afternoon, Wednesday morning, Wednesday afternoon – for classes that meet on these days (students might not be on campus on Tuesday, Thursday or Friday). It's a good idea to draw a plan on the board in case students need to move around to find a group.
- Before you tell students to move and form their groups, give them careful instructions. Tell them that they are shortly going to move to the segment of the room corresponding to when they have an hour free. When they get there, they are to form small groups of three to six students with the same hour in common. Ask them to choose a place for their first meeting and fill out and return to you a form indicating the names of their group members and the time and place of their first group meeting. Tell them that at their first group meeting you would like them to choose a name for their group and a permanent location for future group meetings. (You might consider including this request in your first assignment.)
- Ask students to move and form their groups, and remind them not to leave without submitting their group form to you. This stage will probably take about fifteen minutes, depending on how clear you have been with your initial instructions.

Voluntary study groups

Ask all students who are interested in joining a study group to come to a mini-session about forming study groups. At this mini-session, distribute and discuss the students' study group guide. You can then form groups according to the suggestions above.

Grooming Students for Study Groups

"Groups can't simply be formed and set to task. Students have to be groomed to work together and then encouraged over and over" (Kalman 1995).

- Tell students why you believe that study groups are important. You might wish to say something like, "Research shows that students learn by doing, not just by watching and listening. Study groups will give you a slice of the action."
- Highlight the parts of the student study group guide (Caldwell n.d.) that you think are particularly important.
- Before you get students to form groups, try a warm-up activity (see below). It's important to provide students with the opportunity to hear each other's concerns or anxieties about the course so that they realize they are not alone.

People who are in a strange environment with strangers often feel a sense of isolation. By addressing their concern and hearing that other people feel the same way, they are able to overcome a great deal of their anxiety. They see that other people in the class will listen to them and sympathize with them. The effect is wonderful. By the end of this exercise the students feel relieved and excited about the class. They return with the mind-set that they can work with other students. This process establishes a friendly, open and caring environment. (Panitz 1996)

Warm-Up and Ice-Breaker Activities

Warm-up activities must be designed carefully or they can backfire easily. If you are going to use a warm-up activity, ensure that it will achieve the following goals.

- connect individuals in the class
- connect the students to the subject matter
- increase the students' willingness to engage in intellectual/personal dialogue in class or in study groups.

A good warm-up activity involves students, either in small groups or the whole class, in a serious discussion or activity that relates to the subject or course at hand. The relationship between the discussion or activity and the course should be clear to students. As well, the activity or discussion should draw on students' experience rather than knowledge.

Example

A statistics professor asks her first-year students to get into groups of between five and ten students. While handing out a tape measure to each group, she asks them first to find the height of everyone in their group and then to determine the mean and median heights of their group. In the middle of this activity, the students in groups of four or six hit a snag trying to find the median height. The professor interrupts the activity and relates the problem to all students. She explains how you average the two middle values. Students get back to work. When the last group finishes, the professor asks for the mean and median of each group. She collects the data on the board.

Interestingly, some students measured in inches and others in centimeters. The professor lists these questions:

- If we converted the centimeter data from this group into inches and then calculated the mean, would it be the same as if we converted the centimeter mean into inches?
- From these data how can we find the mean and median of the class?
- How does the fact that we have groups of four, five and six affect how we will use these data to find the mean and median of the class?

The professor then asks the class to get back in their groups to come up with their own questions about the data. After a few minutes the professor asks for questions. In concluding this exercise she says that many of these question will be answered throughout the course. A copy of the students' data set is pinned to the wall and the professor refers to it throughout the course.

In this activity, not only are students getting to know each other, they are working with statistics. The professor has provided her students with a concrete experience to which students can refer later on. Certainly this ice breaker relates to the course, takes students seriously and also emphasizes the importance of groups.

Keeping Study Groups Running

Regardless of whether you are requiring students to form study groups or not, maintaining their effectiveness requires a small amount of effort. The following three lists provide proactive suggestions that help to smooth out or prevent potential bumps along the way.

Getting Feedback on the Success of Study Groups

- Assign One-Minute Papers as you see fit.[1]
- Conduct a mid-semester course evaluation, asking students to list things they like and dislike about the study group format, and what could be done to improve the quality of learning in their study groups.
- Instructors and TAs should compare notes and discuss any concerns they have regarding student participation in study groups. A student might make a legitimate complaint to a TA that the instructor might be able to do something about.
- Keep your ears open during classes. You might overhear students discussing their study groups at the beginning or end of class.
- Drop by some of the study rooms to say hello to your students. This demonstrates that you are taking an interest in them, and you can try to sense the mood of the various study groups. If you make it your first assignment for students to fill out a form listing the group members and telling you the permanent time and location of their study group meetings, you will know exactly where to find your students.
- Come to class early and ask students how their study group is going.

Responding to Problems

- Often One-Minute Papers and course evaluations can be reassuring. Without them, one or two more vocal students making complaints can give the impression that things are going awry when in fact the silent majority are enjoying the current arrangement.
- Just asking the students for their opinion is being responsive. One-Minute Papers and evaluations allow students to vent.
- The things that students dislike are not exactly fun to read or hear, but can offer some good ideas. You might be able to act on such comments without compromising your principles. For example, it might be appropriate to decrease the length of the homework assignments or give students the option of doing a few assignments independently. When you respond positively to some of their suggestions, students will usually meet you half way.

Evaluation

Evaluation reflects what the instructor views as important. Below is a list of suggested ways to evaluate the study group component of your course.

- Use group grades on homework assignments.
- Students can self-evaluate their involvement in their group.

- Use group self-evaluations of their overall progress and group dynamics.

Keep in mind, though, that not everything students do in a course has to be evaluated. Hopefully students will find the group process itself reward enough.

Keeping Track for Next Time

Keep notes on the rough spots as they occur (and they will). These notes will be invaluable the next time you use study groups as they will help you avoid repeating any glitches.

Don't Expect to Win Them All...

In the end, despite my best efforts, some students fail and some who pass continue to resent my putting so much of the burden of their learning on their shoulders. A student once wrote in a course-end evaluation, "Felder really makes us think!" It was on the list of things he disliked. On the other hand, for their complaints about how hard I am on them, my students on the average earn higher grades than they ever did when I just lectured, and many more of them now tell me that after getting through one of my courses they feel confident that they can do anything. So I lose some, but I win a lot more. I can cheerfully live with the tradeoff. (Felder 1995)

In-Class Group Work

I used to be a good lecturer: well-organized, clear, concise and even humorous. I encouraged Q & A and class discussion, through me. Students liked the classes but would comment frequently that when they went home they didn't really understand the material. I could see people's eyes glaze over in class after about ten minutes. I have [now] moved into interactive group learning exclusively in all my classes while still providing direction using schedules, worksheets and test schedules etc. I am very involved in the class in a variety of ways. Students say they look forward to my classes the most. Can you believe it?! I teach classes everyone loves to hate...ALGEBRA! The benefits are enormous...
– Ted Panitz, Department of Mathematics, Cape Cod Community College

The average adult attention span is about twenty minutes. So, on average, students are struggling to stay focused on a lecture less than half way through it. Also, many students get confused at a certain point through a lecture. Anything in the lecture after this point just adds to the confusion. Many students end up taking down notes they do not understand.

A way to solve both these problems is to provide a brief interlude in a lecture where students get a chance to do some of the mathematics. Five-minute group exercises every ten to fifteen minutes, or longer ten-minute activities every twenty minutes, are effective. Below are some activities you might wish to try.

- Conduct spontaneous investigations inspired by a student's question.
- Ask an open-ended, complex question for groups to explore based on what you have just lectured. You might wish to ask the question, get a few comments from students while still sitting as a class and then have them get into their study groups.
- After you have presented a theorem, have students attempt to prove it in their groups (the variety in approaches might astound you!). When you go through the proof, call on students to provide the next step or, after the discussions, make the proof an assignment to be completed either individually or in their groups.
- Have students generate concrete data or observations for a problem you have presented in the lecture. Have each group write its observations on the board to form a class set of data.
- Provide examples at the board and then have groups generalize and conjecture about their observations.
- Administer partner quizzes about the previous lecture.
- Have students make group presentations summarizing the highlights of the last chapter or from their homework.
- When you hand back assignments, ask certain groups to put part of their solutions on the board.

While an activity is going on, it is important to walk among the groups. Doing so gives you the opportunity to see how groups are approaching the exercise, to observe how groups are getting along, to extend students' thinking if need be and to get to know your students.

It is not necessary to take up all the work you give students. In fact, if students come to expect you to take up these intermittent activities, they will not participate as much as they would if you do not.

The above activities give students a break from passive learning. Although you might not get as much material covered as in an uninterrupted lecture, students will come away from your classes with a much deeper understanding of what you have covered. Recall that you no longer have to cover everything; students, equipped with well-designed assignments and clear deadlines, can be responsible for covering certain sections in their study groups.

Common Problems and Possible Solutions[2]

My goal here is to assure you that initial glitches are both common and natural and that they may be a cause for concern but not for panic or discouragement. The trick is knowing how the process works, taking a few precautionary steps to smooth out the bumps, and waiting out the inevitable setbacks until the payoffs start emerging. (Felder 1995)

Below is a list of some of the dysfunctional situations in which a study group can find itself, along with what you can do to help, if asked.

Problem: Lack of interaction

Possible Cause: Lack of experience with learning in groups
Suggestions:

- Have students review their study group guide about how to successfully interact with each other.
- Encourage students to provide feedback on the effectiveness of their interactions. Students need to feel comfortable to switch from talking about math or statistics to talking about groups dynamics. Insist that when students make complaints, they provide suggestions to remedy the problem.
- Have a meeting with the group. Express your concern. Give students a simple, practical exercise. For example, ask a student to present an opinion in a sentence or two and then ask two students to restate the sentence in their own words. Repeat for each student. Or you could ask a student to voice an opinion and then ask another student to disagree with the opinion but without attacking the person.

Possible Cause: The authority of the instructor or TA is overwhelming
Suggestions:

- Talk less. Too many words can overwhelm students.
- Point out your own mistakes. You will seem more human and students will feel more relaxed.
- Refrain from personal comments, sarcasm and threats.
- Refrain from making wide-sweeping proclamations of praise or negative criticism. State your observations without any sort of judgement. If you must praise or criticize, refer to very specific instances. "Your group always seems to be in some sort of a bind" is not helpful, even as a joke. "I noticed an argument between Peter and Monica" would be more likely to get a helpful response.

Possible Cause: Students feel coerced to participate
Suggestions:

- Make it clear to students that the study groups are for their benefit. If their study group isn't serving their needs they should speak up. Reiterate that attendance isn't taken during class and that students' primary obligation is to themselves and to one another, not to you, the university or to some set of rules.
- If possible, do not assign grades for participation in study groups. Students are more likely to attend their meetings if attendance isn't made mandatory. You could meet this idea half way by setting a minimum number of study group sessions students must attend.

Possible Cause: Physical arrangement
Suggestions:

- Make sure that students understand that they should sit facing each other and that no one student feels isolated by the seating arrangement.

- Make sure that the group is not too large. In a group larger than six people, students feel like they are presenting to a crowd instead of sharing with classmates whenever they speak.

Problem: Students are participating unequally

Possible Cause: Intolerance of silence.

Some people feel a strong need to fill in moments of silence with speech. In the same way that nature abhors a vacuum, some people abhor silence in conversations.

Suggestions:

- Have a meeting with the group. Explain the positive role of silence. Silence allows us time to think and collect our thoughts. It allows quieter students the opportunity to enter the conversation.
- Demonstrate your own acceptance of silence. When giving a lecture or talking with a group of students, allow for long pauses in your speech to show you're comfortable with breaks of silence.

Possible Cause: Dominant speakers monopolize the discussion

Suggestion:

- Talk to the dominating speaker privately. Determine why this person is talking so much and if he or she is aware of the problem. Usually, unaware students are simply outgoing by nature. When students are aware of the problem, they usually feel they have not had their point fully appreciated, or feel a need to compete with classmates. In all cases, recognizing these students in this way reduces the need to dominate.

Possible Cause: A student has no interest in speaking.

Some students feel that they learn better by listening than by talking, while some feel that speaking and helping others is too much work.

Suggestion:

- Talk to the withdrawn student about helping others. Explain how you think they could be helpful to the learning of everyone else. Likely the student will feel flattered for being taken aside and will want to contribute a little more.

Problem: Reinforcing misconceptions.

It is quite easy for a group of students to mistakenly agree; for example, that zero over zero cancels to give one, or to assume that an open disk is the same as a disk that is not closed. Who will be around to point out these errors?

Suggestions:

- Drop in on study groups from time to time. Casually ask students what they are working on. Do not stay for more than five minutes.
- Give eight-minute pair quizzes. In a pair quiz, students first attempt the question on their own and then pair up, submitting the best work between the two. Quizzes such as these give the students regular feedback and also wake them up first thing Monday morning!

- Suggest that those who are sensitive to the careless use of language make a practice of requesting clarification.

Notes

This article is an adaptation of a guide written as part of a project to introduce study groups to faculty and teaching assistants in the York University Department of Mathematics and Statistics. The project codirectors were Pat Rogers and Walter Whiteley; the project was funded by a York University Faculty Association Teaching Development Grant and Release-Time Teaching Fellowship. When she wrote this guide, Katie Coulthard (née Caldwell) was an undergraduate student at York University majoring in mathematics and education.

1. See Rogers, Section VI, Part 1, and Section VIII, Part 1.
2. This section is adapted from Tiberius (1990).

References

Balacheff, M. 1990. Towards a problematique for research on mathematics teaching. *Journal for Research in Mathematics Education* 21 (4): 258–72.

Caldwell, Katie. n.d. Study group guide for students. York University. Internet. www.math.yorku.ca/Undergrad/sg_gdst.htm

Felder, R. 1995. Student resistance to group work. Society for Teaching and Learning in Higher Education. Internet. STLHE-L@unb.ca (8 June).

Kalman, C. 1995. Re: Why do so few teachers use group learning? Society for Teaching and Learning in Higher Education. Internet. STLHE-L@unb.ca (6 June).

McKeachie, W.J. *et al.* 1986. *Teaching and learning in the college classroom: A review of the research literature.* Ann Arbor, MI: National Center for Research to Improve Post-Secondary Teaching and Learning, University of Michigan.

Panitz, Ted. 1996. Getting students ready for cooperative learning. Society for Teaching and Learning in Higher Education. Internet. STLHE-L@unb.ca (27 January).

Silver, E.A. 1982. Knowledge organization and mathematical problem solving. In *Mathematical problem solving: Issues in research*, F.K. Lester and J. Garofalo (eds.). Philadelphia: Franklin Institute Press.

Slavin, R.E. 1980. Cooperative learning. *Review of Educational Research* 50 (2): 315–42.

———. 1983. When does cooperative learning increase student achievement? *Psychological Bulletin* 94 (3): 429–45.

Tiberius, Richard. 1990. *Small group teaching: A trouble shooting guide.* Toronto: Ontario Institute for Studies in Education.

Whitman, N.A. 1988. *Peer teaching: To teach is to learn twice.* ASHE-ERIC Higher Education Report No. 4. Washington, DC: Association for the Study of Higher Education.

Warm-Ups:
Lessening Student Anxiety
in the First Class

Rachel Aber Schlesinger

Alienation is a big issue for first-year students at a large university. Teachers need to find ways to reduce the impersonal aspects of this environment for new students and help them feel part of the university community. This process can begin on the first day the class or tutorial meets: warm-ups are an effective way to reduce student alienation (Nell Warren Assoc. 1991).

What are warm-ups...not? They are not lessons in themselves; they are not set to fill a time block; they are not games without a purpose. They are, however, effective catalysts for promoting group dynamics by creating a foundation for engaged class discussions. A good warm-up is geared to the needs and interests of the group and encourages participation and sharing. It can illustrate a point, challenge group members and stimulate problem solving.

Below are some examples of warm-ups that I have found useful in promoting group dynamics. They have been used in classes of different sizes and usually take fifteen to twenty minutes; they are easily adapted to suit different purposes.

Human Treasure Hunt

On the first day of class, I start to develop an atmosphere that will encourage students to reach, to extend and to know themselves and each other. I often begin with climate-setting warm-ups such as a "human treasure hunt." I give each student a sheet with some "find and ask" questions they must use to find people and begin to discover the resources in the room. My goal is for each student to become known by name and for them to talk with each other. Here are some sample questions:

1. Find someone who likes to cook. What is this person's favourite recipe?
2. Find someone who speaks another language. Learn how to say "hello" and one other word in that language.
3. Find someone who wants to change something. What do they want to change?
4. Find someone who has a special goal for learning in this course. What is it?

Party

Another way to begin a new class is to have a "party." Students approach a person they do not know, introduce themselves and take that person over to someone else, in turn introducing them. The students are required to circulate until they have met everyone in the class. I find that learning names at the beginning is a fruitful way to start a new year. Reinforce this for the first few weeks, and you will find that the atmosphere in the group is enhanced just because they know each other.

Limericks

I use limericks to break the ice by grouping students in pairs. At the beginning of the class, I hand out half a limerick to each student. They have to locate their match and then either find out something about each other or perform a task together. Depending on the purpose, the pairs can then remain together or be grouped together to begin other work.

One caution should always be respected. When using a warm-up, students who do not wish to participate should be allowed that right. Warm-ups should be non-threatening and fun and should create an atmosphere that sparks discussion and enhances learning. My experience has proven over and over that when a group develops an energy of its own, student learning and my own teaching are greatly enhanced.

References

Nell Warren Associates. 1991. *The warmup manual: Tools for working with groups*. Toronto: Nell Warren Associates.

Small Is Beautiful: Using Small Groups to Enhance Student Learning

Femida Handy

At the beginning of the final examination in one of my courses last year, I noticed that one of my students was visibly distressed and unable to proceed. I asked her to leave the room with me and offered my help. She told me that she had been assaulted the night before and had, until this moment, been unable to find anyone to talk to about the assault. Shocking as it was to hear her story, what disturbed me more was her difficulty in finding anyone in whom to confide. She was a first-year student from out of town, living off campus. After four months at York, her social contacts were non-existent. My encounter with this student's isolation provided the catalyst for my attempt to change the undergraduate experience of the students in my courses.

Earlier in the term, the Centre for the Support of Teaching had sponsored a lecture by Richard Light, coordinator of the Harvard Assessment Seminars. I was impressed by his findings regarding the undergraduate experience at Harvard, which showed positive benefits to student learning arising from the experience of working in small groups. He also reported an overall increase in satisfaction with the undergraduate experience when students are engaged with others on campus. This engagement is built, in part, around academic work (Light 1990).

I often have reflected on the value of small-group learning and have experimented with small groups in some of my small classes. I was ready to experiment with small groups in my larger classes, not only to enhance student learning but also to increase social interaction among the students. I believe that social interaction should be an integral part of the undergraduate experience, especially for incoming students who are often shepherded into large classes. This is particularly crucial at a large commuter institution such as York University.

Background

The setting for my experiment was two half courses on mathematical methods for economists. As these are required courses, most students who successfully complete the first half of the course in the fall proceed to the second half in the winter, usually with the same instructor. Last year, I taught two sections of the course in the fall, one in the morning and one in the afternoon, with enrolments of fifty-three and sixty-nine, respectively. In the winter term, the corresponding enrolments in the second half of the course were fifty-one and seventy-seven.

Student performance in each half course was based on two class tests and one final exam worth 20, 30 and 50 per cent, respectively. Problems were assigned but not graded. The final exam was common to both sections and the class tests were similar and of comparable difficulty. In the fall term, the grade-point averages were 3.88 (morning) and 3.86 (afternoon), indicating students of similar capabilities on average.

The Experiment

My goal was to establish small working groups in the classroom to facilitate enhanced learning and increased opportunities for social interaction built around academic work. I chose the morning section for my small-group experiment and left the afternoon section as my control group to see whether any quantifiable benefits would be associated with the small-group experience. A simple show of hands in each class revealed that fewer than six students knew more than one person in the class. After announcing my intentions and goals to the morning class, I set aside time in class for the students to form small groups. I explained that the groups were to meet outside of class to work together on the assignments and that each group would be responsible for handing in one set of solutions to the assignment. The assignments were intended to provide students with practice in the techniques taught and were not graded.

At first the students were a little astonished, but their enthusiasm and goodwill were soon evident as they set about the task of forming their groups and sharing telephone numbers. I encouraged students to form their own groups. Most did this readily, although I helped the shy students who had not been able to join a group by themselves. Students were asked to name their group after their favourite mathematician. We formed six groups, named Bernoulli, Descartes, L'Hôpital, Newton, Pascal and Taylor; each group comprised between seven and twelve students.

I encouraged students in the afternoon section to do the same assignments and made solutions available to students in both sections either in class or during tutorials.

What I Found

	Morning Section	Afternoon Section
First test (20%)	B	C+
Second test (30%)	B	C+
Final exam (50%)	D+	D+
Course	C+	C
Grade-point average	4.90	4.59

Average Grades by Section

While the average overall grade for the morning section was better than that for the afternoon section, the average grade in the common final exam was no different. However, there were some notable differences in the distribution of the course grades: more students in the morning section received a grade of B+ or better (27.5 per cent in the morning section compared with 20 per cent in the afternoon section) and there were fewer failures (2 per cent in the morning section compared with almost 12 per cent in the afternoon section).

I noted an increased level of participation in the morning class. Students voiced questions in class that were first discussed in small groups with greater self-confidence and more thought. There was a greater sense of cooperation among students, and "practice" assignments were taken seriously by the great majority. This was significantly different from the afternoon section, where there was little or no evidence that students did the assignments and there was a marked lack of interaction among students in class. (Recall that there was no direct incentive, in terms of grades, for students in either section to do the assignments.)

What the Students Thought

To find out whether the students thought their work in small groups had been worthwhile, I invited them to fill out a one-page questionnaire, which I mailed out after they had received their final grades. I asked them to list what they liked and what they did not like about the experiment. The questionnaire was anonymous and had a response rate of 45 per cent.

There was overwhelming support for the small-group approach. All respondents noted that they had enjoyed the increased social interaction that the small groups provided. Further, they perceived that they had derived definite academic benefit from the experience. Since the assignments were not mandatory, working on them with their peers had provided an incentive to do the assignments. Many of the students made thoughtful recommendations for the future, notably:

- the size of the small groups should be decreased
- time should be set aside in class for small-group interaction
- students should be assigned to groups by me
- assignments should be marked and included in the final grade.

Conclusion

If I were to assess my experiment by the final examination results alone, I could not conclude that the students who were involved in small groups did better than those who were not. Certainly, they did no worse and there were definite qualitative gains for the students. Furthermore, it is debatable whether grades based on tests and exams provide an accurate picture of the learning that took place in the course.

As noted by Rogers (1992), it is not clear whether the impact of non-traditional teaching methods can be evaluated by quantitative means or in the short term. What is more important is to know whether students are responsive to and learn from academic interaction in small groups. If indeed they do, then this, in and of itself, is valuable, for it also creates a sense of community. Furthermore, if students find working in small groups a non-threatening and pleasant way of learning, it is likely that they will enjoy the material more.

What Next?

As I continue to explore the value of small study groups in my classes, there are some new questions I want to answer:

- What is the ideal group size?
- What process should I use to form the groups?
- Can I afford to set aside class time for small-group work?
- What incentives could I put in place to encourage frequent and productive group work?
- How might I assess group assignments?
- Do some groups function significantly better than others? Why?

Furthermore, it will be important to assess whether, and how, different students gain (or lose) from participating in study groups. For example, which students benefit most from small-group study – the marginal, average or superior students? Certainly this initial experience with small groups was positive enough to encourage me to continue the experiment.

This article was first published in February 1994 in Core 4 (4): 1–2.

References

Light, Richard J. 1990. *The Harvard Assessment Seminars: First report. Explorations with students and faculty about teaching, learning, and student life.* Cambridge, MA: Harvard University.

Rogers, Pat. 1992. Transforming mathematics pedagogy. *On Teaching and Learning* 4: 78–98.

Integrating Group Work into our Classes

Jana Vizmuller-Zocco

Any discipline has a central core of proven, basic "truths." At the boundaries of these core areas there are always significant grey areas that constitute the exciting new frontiers of research. Studying alone, students can achieve an understanding of the core areas and might even glimpse the new frontiers. When called upon to discuss these newly learned ideas with other students, and to engage in a purposeful project to apply their knowledge, students are more able to integrate and master core knowledge and understand the excitement of scholarly inquiry into the new frontiers of knowledge. For this reason, I have tried to integrate group work into all of my classes.

Getting students involved in group activities is neither a new pedagogical strategy nor a difficult one, provided that some important matters are dealt with right from the start (Meyers and Jones 1993, 59). There are two places where group work can occur: in class during the scheduled lecture or seminar time and outside the classroom on students' own time. Personally, I find in-class group activity more feasible, especially on a commuter campus where it is difficult for students to get together outside the classroom. Furthermore, allowing students to engage in group work during class time gives me the opportunity to formally integrate the process into my class, thus demonstrating the value I place on students working together. The following are a few examples of how I make group work an integral component of my language and linguistic courses, in classes of twenty to thirty students.

Peer Discussion as a Route to Explaining the Readings

Throughout the course, I regularly devote ten minutes of class time to group discussion of the assigned reading material. Students are expected to come to class prepared with questions about the readings, terminology and definitions or the use of data. These questions are first discussed in small groups of two or three students and then, if a question remains unanswered, it is taken up by the whole class.

This activity strengthens students' understanding of the discipline's terminology and gives me more time to deal with matters of substance in lectures. Students have told me that they are pleased to learn that others have the same concerns about the readings, and that the opportunity to discuss questions in small groups first makes it easier for them to raise questions later in front of the class. They also learn from explaining new terminology to each other and gain a deeper understanding of the readings by discussing unclear points together.

Using Groups To Evaluate Hypotheses

About two or three weeks in advance of the class assigned for this activity, students are presented with a question or theory to explore, for example, "Refute or support Whorf's hypothesis that 'language determines thought' using concrete examples from English and Italian grammar." Students work on this exercise both independently and in small groups of four or more. To facilitate preparation for the group work, individual students are expected to collect concrete linguistic examples independently, analyze them and bring copies of their findings to class. The groups then meet in class to assess the combined data and to formulate a group response to the assigned task. The group chooses a recorder who prepares a written report. Final submission of this assignment includes the group report as well as the individual students' data. Each student receives a grade for the assignment that reflects their individual effort as well as their group grade.

Although students comment very favourably on this activity, one problem I have encountered is that the stronger students tend to dominate the discussion and volunteer more readily for the recording role. This can be modified somewhat if you require students to rotate this role. However, the advantages of this group assignment far outweigh its disadvantages because it provides students with a richer and more varied perspective on the issues involved than they would ever get by working alone.

Grading Group Work

Grading group work is always tricky. One concern is that the weaker students will always have an easy ride, but I do not consider this an overwhelming problem if the learning outcome is successful for both the strong and the weak students. Often, the brighter students will volunteer to write the group assignment and I think this has value because they become positive role models for students who have trouble with the material. In part, I mitigate these concerns by weighting the group work as a relatively small percentage of the overall course grade, usually between 10 and 15 per cent. To date, I have experimented with two different grading strategies, discussed below.

Strategy A: I count only the group projects, based on written assignments done in class. Although the group does the work, one student writes the results and the rest of the group prepares, reads and signs the submission. The length of the submission is guided by the students' reaction to the design of the group activity. Given the time limitations, I never ask for polished results. For example, I might ask for answers to specific questions that go beyond the course work or reactions to striking statements regarding course material. This works best if students have at least fifty minutes to work on a discrete task.

Strategy B: I count individual students' written reports in addition to the group work itself. For example, if 15 per cent is allocated to group work, I allocate 5 per cent of the grade to individual preparation in advance of the group project and 10 per cent to the group project. Before the group work begins, individual written reports are submitted and graded and students are given feedback. This gives students a better idea of where they might improve and can remedy crucial problems before the group work begins. The advantage of this assessment procedure is that it gives me a clearer idea of each individual's performance. I plan to experiment with increasing the balance of individual grades to discover whether this improves both individual and group performance.

One procedure I have not yet tried, but that might have a significant impact on learning, is to count the students' assessments of other groups' assignments. This encourages students to reflect on the criteria for a good project, which, in turn, might improve their ability to critically assess and improve their own work.

Preparation of Tests and Final Examinations

I encourage students to collaborate in groups to prepare for term tests and final examinations. Independently, students are required to prepare their own draft of a term test or final exam and bring it to class for review within their groups. During class, each group develops a final version of the test, choosing the most appropriate questions and discussing the answers. Students must also decide on the relative weighting of each question and marks to be assigned to each answer. Afterwards, each group's test is photocopied and distributed to all students in the class to use in preparing for the test, which I set based on their suggestions. An alternative form of this activity that I have used is to have the groups prepare answers to all of the questions on their own test or on a test prepared by one or all of the other groups.

The main purpose of this activity is to encourage students to review course material from a pragmatic perspective. Formulating test questions becomes more than a mental exercise, since generating solutions follows from generating questions. Having to develop systematic questions about the course also helps students develop a holistic appreciation of the course material.

I use this activity in almost all of my classes. Student reaction is positive. They especially appreciate the chance to discuss answers to their questions with peers and find that this helps them overcome gaps in their understanding of the material.

This activity also empowers students and makes them realize the difficulties inherent in preparing tests and examinations. Nonetheless, and without detracting from their role in its production, I do reserve the right to design the final version of the test because I find that, although students exhibit a great deal of originality and creativity, they tend to focus solely on content-based, factually oriented questions.

In conclusion, some learning objectives are best supported by activities that involve groups of students working together in class. Group work strengthens each student's voice by generating intellectual awareness of both the core material in a discipline and the emerging scholarly frontiers. While I do not see group work as a pedagogical strategy to be used at all times in all courses, it is one of the better techniques at our disposal to pleasantly motivate our students and to painlessly create incentives for those students who need a nudge.

This article was first published in June 1994 in Core 4 (7): 5–6.

References

Meyers, Chet and Thomas B. Jones. 1993. *Promoting active learning: Strategies for the college classroom.* San Francisco: Jossey-Bass.

Scrapbook Presentations: An Exercise in Collaborative Learning

Katherine Bischoping

In thinking over the strengths and weaknesses of my teaching in the first seminar course I taught, I identified two main problems. First, in leading class discussions I found it difficult to gauge students' views on issues and consequently to pose questions that would produce meaningful debates. Small-group discussions sometimes fell flat, as groups reported back to the class that they'd concluded "the same as what the last group said." Second, my expectations that students could make connections between course materials and current events were too high – not because the course materials were particularly difficult, but because students' awareness of current events was low. For example, in a paper on the former Yugoslavia, one student freely interchanged Serbians and Croatians, producing alarmingly confused conclusions.

Scrapbook Presentation System

To address these two issues, I devised a system of group "scrapbook presentations" and student-led discussions that related course materials to media reports of current events. In designing the group work, I took into account students' fear of presentations, as well as the difficulties of group work on a commuter campus where students have little time to meet outside the classroom. The system consists of the following steps (see the sample assignment on page 236):

1. At the beginning of the term, students sign up on a weekly presentation schedule, with two or three presenters each week. They have the option of including their phone numbers on the schedule. The schedule is copied and circulated to the class.
2. In a given week, a group of students finds four recent sources (newspaper, magazine, scholarly journal articles or a summary of a public lecture) related to the course topics.
3. These are mounted in a class scrapbook, which the instructor brings to each class or puts on library reserve. Complete reference information is given for each source.

235

Sample Assignment

Each week a group of two or three students will make a presentation on "Genocide in the News." This presentation has five steps:

1. Use newspapers or news magazines from the week before the presentation to find four articles that discuss genocide, precursors of genocide or the aftermaths of genocide in four different countries. A good place to look for articles is the periodical reading room on the second floor of Scott Library. They have the *Globe and Mail*, *Toronto Star*, *Calgary Herald*, *Vancouver Sun*, *Montreal Gazette* (English), *Le Devoir* (French), *New York Times*, *Jerusalem Post* (English), *Manchester Guardian*, *Christian Science Monitor* and several other publications. Articles that are in "alternative" publications are also welcome. Instead of an article, you can give a one-page summary of a public lecture or presentation focusing on some aspect of genocide. In this case, label the summary with the name of the group member who attended the lecture, the name of the speaker, the title of the talk, the name of the organization that invited the speaker and the date of the talk.

2. In class, enter these in the course scrapbook, labeling each article with the name of the group members who found it, the title and date of the publication and the page number of the article.

3. Give a ten-minute presentation for the class in which you describe the four events. This presentation will be evaluated on a group basis, so it isn't necessary that all group members speak. In doing the presentation it's important to keep in mind that your listeners are probably less familiar than you are with the facts, figures and details contained in the articles. For this reason it's best to focus on the main issues that the articles deal with.

4. Prepare a hand-out that outlines a single, very specific discussion question for the class to take up, as well as a structure for the discussion. Some formats you might consider are:
   - a free-for-all discussion for the whole group
   - a debate between two halves of the class, preceded by some time in which each side can figure out its set of arguments
   - discussions in small groups that then summarize their views to the class as a whole.

5. Lead the discussion (probably about half an hour), trying to draw in as many participants as possible.

4. Group members summarize their four sources in a ten-minute class presentation. Members can divide the presentation work as they like, so that students are not required to speak publicly if they do not wish to.
5. The group distributes a hand-out that poses a discussion question arising from one of the articles.
6. The group chooses a structure for the discussion (for example, a free-for-all, a meeting of small groups that report back to the class as a whole or a debate) and leads the class discussion.
7. Group members each choose one of the articles they have found and write a one-page paper explaining its connection to course materials. (Groups that present early in the term are given additional time to develop a grounding in the course material before they write their papers.)

Method of Evaluation

I first used scrapbook presentations in a twelve-week, 4000-level seminar, "Sociological Understandings of Genocide," with twenty-one students. With small revisions, the presentations were also used in three tutorials ranging in size from nineteen to thirty-two students in a twenty-four-week, 3000-level course, "Population and Society." In the course evaluations, students were asked to respond to the question, "What did you think of the scrapbook presentation system?" Ten "Understandings of Genocide" students and thirty-eight "Population and Society" students responded. Their responses, as well as my impressions, form the basis for evaluating the strengths and weaknesses of scrapbook presentations.

Strengths of Scrapbook Presentations

On the whole, student comments about the scrapbook presentation system were very positive: thirty-three of the forty-eight students made wholly positive statements, thirteen gave mixed evaluations and only two were negative. Although the positive comments were sometimes vague – for example, "good idea," "fun and interesting" – Table 1 shows that the themes students mentioned most frequently corresponded with my goals in developing the system and, incidentally, with similar findings from other studies of collaborative learning.

First, eighteen of the forty-eight students said that the scrapbook presentations were an enjoyable and useful way to promote class discussion and collaborative learning.

> The presentation system is an excellent way to encourage discussion and participation. I enjoy the intellectual discussions of various contemporary subjects.
> ("Population and Society")

> A real boon to tutorials – actually woke up a lot of sleepy students, brought out lots of interesting ideas, allowed students to educate each other – great concept!
> ("Population and Society")

Table 1. Strengths and Weaknesses of the Scrapbook Presentations: Themes in Students' Comments

Strengths	Frequency of Comment
Informative	21
Class participation enhanced	18
Provides a reference source	4
Weaknesses	
Future uses of scrapbook unclear	4
Uses too much tutorial time	4
Dislike presentations/groups	3

Note: themes mentioned by only one or two students are omitted.

The students were generally successful at choosing discussion topics that produced lively debates. Particularly memorable were the discussions in "Population and Society" about euthanasia and about aboriginal land rights, and the debate in "Genocide" about censorship of hate literature. In addition, the students used the opportunity to structure their own learning by choosing topics with which I was unfamiliar or media sources I had not thought pertinent. Thus, one group of "Population and Society" students broadened the course coverage of the Canadian family by bringing in an article about arranged marriages. A group of "Genocide" students used an article from *Ms Magazine* to debate whether the sterilization of Puerto Rican women was genocidal.

Second, students appreciated the information conveyed by the scrapbook presentations. Of the forty-eight students commenting, twenty-one mentioned that the presentations drew connections between current events and course materials in ways that made either (or both) more meaningful and immediate. For example, students commented:

It was good in helping to learn more about population and society. The fact that we were able to relate the lectures and readings to the newspaper articles made it easier to understand the course material. ("Population and Society")

I think it's a good idea, because not only does it stimulate class discussion, but also we become aware of the latest news, for those who don't have time to catch up on the news! ("Population and Society")

I think this is very helpful. You think that genocide is a distant topic of the past. You think specifically of World War Two. But then, based on the fact that the entire class was able to find at least four articles a week, it really makes you stop and think. ("Genocide")

A related advantage, the value of the scrapbook as a reference source, was particularly noted by students in the "Genocide" course; their scrapbook had been placed on reserve in the library: "This system seemed to be an effective one. The scrapbook becomes a source of vast information and looking it up was quite easy."

Finally, an unexpected strength of the presentation system was that it appeared to promote a sense of community among students in the class, not only because of the interactions in the classroom but also because of the list of student telephone numbers circulated early in the term. Almost all of the students in my sections had been willing to provide their phone numbers. When asked in the course evaluation whether the list had been useful, nine of the thirteen students in the "Genocide" class gave a positive response (I did not ask the "Population and Society" students about the value of the list) and some students mentioned to me that they had used it to contact one another about other classes. At a large university where many students feel anonymous, and have reported that its size was the aspect of the university that created the worst impression (Bell 1994), even a small step towards creating a community is valuable.

Weaknesses and Issues Arising From the Scrapbook Presentations

The most common student concerns about the scrapbook presentations were in three areas, each noted by three or four of the forty-eight students. A few students disliked either presentations or group work and said that they would prefer other formats. These are intractable problems because they are inherent in the framework of the assignment. Others were skeptical about whether the scrapbook would be consulted in the future or wondered how others would use it. Course directors using scrapbook presentations in the future therefore might want to respond to these issues early in a course. Finally, several students in "Population and Society" felt that the presentations were interesting, but took too much time from other uses of the tutorial period, such as reviewing lecture materials. Since scheduling presentations also took class time, it might be preferable to schedule them every other week.

I had my own concerns with the scrapbook presentation system. As more experienced educators might have guessed, the difficulties I had leading discussions before I began to use scrapbook presentations were replaced by a new issue once I began to delegate responsibility: what role should I take in order to facilitate students' learning? During the student-led discussions that followed the presentations, I noticed that my role was determined very early, consistent with social psychological research that indicates group interaction patterns become established in just a few minutes (Webster 1975). At the point of transition between presentation and discussion, it was essential that I avoid leading the discussion or choosing speakers, in order for the presenters to assume these responsibilities. Instead, I tried to define my role as a resource person who might suggest strategies (for example, "will you keep a list of people who want to speak?") rather than enacting them. Once the discussion was underway, I would try to take the role of a participant.

However, when problems arose, such as repeated interruptions in a heated debate or continued silence on the part of a student whose first language was not English, I had to decide whether and how to intervene. The real-time interactions of a classroom don't always allow for careful consideration of the changing roles one is playing or their relative pedagogical values. I recommend demarcating the roles students and the instructor will take, explicitly encouraging discussion leaders to draw all students into the discussion and investigating strategies to facilitate the participation of esl students (Kinsella and Sherak 1995). Most importantly, when students take responsibility for a discussion session, instructors should think through the pedagogical implications – for example, are the benefits of having students learn about group process outweighed by the costs to participants if the discussion goes badly?

Conclusion

According to students' assessments, the scrapbook presentations were a highly successful means of engaging the class in lively and informative discussion. The presentations also enhanced the curriculum by enabling students to bring new sources and topics into the classroom and by building a sense of community among students. Scrapbook presentations can be useful tools in areas such as education, environmental studies, political science and mass communications, where current events or their representations are important. The key issues for instructors to consider in using this system are the pedagogical implications of the roles they should take on, particularly during the classroom discussion.

References

Bell, Stephen. 1994. *Faculty of Arts student satisfaction survey: Initial findings.* Toronto: York University, Office of the Dean of Arts.

Kinsella, Kate and Kathy Sherak. 1995. Initiating ESL students to the cooperative college classroom. *Cooperative Learning and College Teaching* 5 (2): 6–10.

Webster, Murray. 1975. *Actions and actors.* Cambridge, MA: Winthrop.

The Field Walk

Jon Caulfield

Guided field walks can be an important component of courses for which on-site observation is suited. For example, in courses I teach that partly centre on the production of urban space, walks are used to illustrate modernist architecture, social housing, deindustrialization, gentrification and many other themes. Abstract ideas become tangible and the interests, values and sentiments immanent in urban forms are made visible.

The tradition of undergraduate field observation in urban study originated in the early decades of the century at the University of Chicago, where students were often directed onto the streets of the city as their classroom. Generation by generation, the practice has endured, its ethos tersely stated by Allan Jacobs (1985): "You can tell a lot about a city by looking" (1). Toronto geographer Edward Relph (1987) terms it "simply watching," mindful that "the best sources of information about landscape are landscapes themselves" (5).

The format I use is derived from an Algonquin Park nature hike I took many summers ago. Walkers received a small booklet at the trailhead that itemized a series of numbered locations along the route and had a few paragraphs of text discussing some feature of the terrain at each site (a small bog, a cluster of fungus, a woodpecker hole). In the city, we have to make our own "trail," so each field guide starts with a map of the route students are asked to follow. It is sometimes fairly labyrinthine, zigzagging down a street, up an alley, then back along the next street nearly to the starting point. A two-hour walk features about fifteen to twenty numbered locations where students are asked to stop, look around and read a numbered passage in a text attached to the map. The text then gives directions to the next numbered site.

The walks usually have a theme. The Don District walk mainly illustrates varieties of city housing – St. Jamestown's massed highrises, renovated townhouses in Don Vale, the Spruce Court housing cooperative. Students see first-hand what their course readings discuss; for example, differences between social housing built in St. Lawrence in the 1970s and in Regent Park the 1950s. This permits class discussion of issues that might otherwise be more elusive (in this case, modernist design that works, modernist design that doesn't, and why). The Spadina District walk centres on processes of community change and on inner-city planning issues. Jane Jacobs's notion (1961) of gradual money (291–317), for example, is illustrated by looking at fresh paint jobs, new eavestroughs and recent roof repairs on houses on the east side of Huron Street below College Street. Across the street are two old apartment buildings that were badly deteriorating two decades ago but were then refurbished by their owners after City Hall lifted the threat of high-density redevelopment from the area. An infusion of public money is also visible; the city repaved the street in the mid-1980s, some sewer work was done a few years ago and a new library has just been built at the corner. An alley between the apartment buildings leads to a laneway where a cluster of modestly renovated houses illustrates the idea of infill housing. At the bottom of the laneway, a church has been renovated as a community centre, an example of adaptive reuse.

The theme and site of the walk are usually introduced by a slide lecture in the preceding class, which helps prepare students for what they will see. This is useful partly because a large number of suburban students have rarely visited anywhere in downtown Toronto other than the Eaton Centre and the Skydome; places such as Kensington Market, Cabbagetown, St. Lawrence and the underground city beneath the office towers are often unknown turf to them.

One feature of the format is that classes do not walk as a unit. I meet them over the course of thirty minutes at a specified rendezvous (as close as possible to a subway stop) and send them on their way in groups of two or three, map and text in hand. This is partly a question of courtesy; the arrival of a horde of university students is unlikely to improve the quality of life for people living or doing business in inner-city neighbourhoods. It is also a matter of pedagogy; students are more attentive to the task when they walk in small groups and are not depending on me to point things out. Sometimes they walk with a friend who is also in the course; on other occasions, an acquaintanceship is struck up among students who were previously strangers. The latter process is a nice by-product of the walks; students can begin to develop a sense of group feeling apart from my presence. After they are on their way, I skip ahead to a couple of key locations along the route (or a coffee shop) to meet them as they arrive and talk with them about what they're seeing.

Students taking a walk can be asked to do more than just follow a guide. For example, they can record specific observations of their own – a kind of sociological scavenger hunt. I have sometimes asked each small group walking in the Spadina District to count and document evidence of different ethnicities they observe; to date, the high number has been twenty-eight. On other occasions, students are asked to take cameras loaded with slide film and record anything they find interesting; at a later class, we look at some of their slides and talk about them.

Field walks raise practical issues. Doing them on class time requires either a three-hour block or a two-hour block at the beginning or end of the day; I try to arrange my courses this way. (If fieldwork in class time is impossible, guides can be distributed and students directed to do a walk on their own time.) Some locales are inhospitable for pedestrian fieldwork. For example, areas of low-density suburban sprawl are not very practical places for guided walks; a colleague with a relatively small class dealt with this problem by renting a large van for a suburban tour. Weather can be infelicitous, although this can sometimes work to pedagogical advantage; students making a field walk in a snowstorm are driven to work together to cope with their situation and go into places they might otherwise bypass (a Chinatown shopping mall, a Parliament Street doughnut shop).

It is important that, once done, walks are connected to other coursework. For example, students in one of my courses are starting independent observational fieldwork projects at the time we make the walks; the walks give them ideas about how to "see" urban places. In other courses, study questions distributed for the next test ask students to illustrate topics and concepts using observations drawn from the walks.

Field walks could be suitable for a variety of courses. Labour studies students might usefully tour Toronto's abandoned industrial zones beside the waterfront and the inner-city rail lines. Political economy students might be asked to contrast the Eaton Centre and Kensington Market. Women's studies courses might compare differences between suburban and inner-city social housing projects as locales for low-income single-parenting. Students studying the sociology of mass society might observe crowd behaviour at the Skydome, on Yonge Street or on the subway at rush hour. Ethnographic observation in inner-city communities might be useful in a number of courses. Fine arts or history students might be asked to visit sites of public art or locales of "heritage preservation." There are many other possibilities.[1] Where walks are appropriate, students often find them a useful method for making connections between the classroom and the world outside.

Notes

1. Thanks to Engin Isin for discussing these examples with me.

References

Jacobs, Allan. 1985. *Looking at cities*. Cambridge, MA: Harvard University Press.
Jacobs, Jane. 1961. *The death and life of great American cities*. New York: Vintage Books.
Relph, Edward. 1987. *The modern urban landscape*. Baltimore: Johns Hopkins University Press.

Teaching with Cases

Deepika Nath

What are Cases and Why do we Use Them?

In professional schools such as the Schulich School of Business, the case studies used are brief descriptions of real situations faced by organizations in day-to-day business dealings. These cases give students a simulated hands-on opportunity to apply their knowledge and experience to problems that arise in the course of business decision-making. They enhance the practical aspect of the program.

This method of teaching works best with smaller groups. A group of twenty to twenty-five students is manageable and can generate a good discussion. Typically, groups large than thirty become difficult to facilitate, since some members of the group might not participate as actively as others. Groups smaller than about ten people also can pose problems in that there might not be the critical mass needed to generate sufficient discussion. This is especially true when the group members are still relatively new to each other.

Goals of a Case Discussion

When using cases as a pedagogical tool, we need to emphasize that there is no right answer. The purpose of a case discussion is two-fold. First, students can practise taking a position and defending it using the information provided in the case and their own experience. Second, and more long term, students must learn to identify critical issues inherent in the case and to separate the problems from the symptoms.

Grading

Grading case discussions is a challenge. I have found that the pressure of a grade forces students to participate, often without adding much of value. Judging what a student contributes to a case analysis is, in fact, quite difficult, since much of the discussion is unplanned and builds on earlier comments. Having experimented with various options, my bias is to leave this activity ungraded. The students who are naturally inclined to be vocal continue to be so and those who prefer to speak only on occasion do not feel compelled to talk. As a result, the class dynamic remains positive, the quality of the discussion is not compromised and the process is a learning one for the students.

Instructors who feel strongly that case studies should be graded need to state up front the criteria that will be used in evaluating the discussion. It also helps if students are informed periodically where they stand and have an opportunity to discuss this with the instructor.

The Role of the Professor

The use of cases encourages a highly interactive method of teaching. The teacher should both serve as a moderator and ensure that the discussion covers all the key issues. As a moderator, the instructor must *listen* and be able to synthesize the ideas put forth in the discussion. At the same time, the instructor must keep the students from digressing into side issues. Playing the role of devil's advocate helps me emphasize the need to justify a position and strengthens students' ability to do so. An important lesson for me was that I often can learn from my students. They often have interesting insights that I have overlooked.

How Do You Prepare for a Case Discussion?

A successful case discussion depends on thorough class preparation by both students and the professor. I consciously steer clear of "solving" the case when I prepare for class. Hence, I am more receptive to ideas put forth in discussion. This precaution also prevents students from trying to read my mind and becoming frustrated in the process. I focus on the facts of the case, key issues and lessons one might derive from the case. Then I let the "solution" develop in class.

Getting a Discussion Going

The initial portion of the case discussion is crucial in setting the tone for the rest of the class and can take many forms. Some people prefer a "cold call" approach. I have found myself quite uncomfortable with this technique, preferring to use a less confrontational approach. To get the discussion going, I normally ask a few factual questions. Most of the students, if they have prepared the case, will respond readily. This helps me set the stage for more probing questions that are directed at identifying issues and instigating the discussion. Following this procedure helps draw out those students who are hesitant to speak out in class and creates a good rapport, engendering trust and confidence.

Maintaining the Momentum of the Discussion

Sometimes in the heat of discussion students go off in tangential directions. While there is no single way of bringing them back on track, a few well-directed questions will often do the trick. I have found that it helps to have a mental image of what I would like the board to look like at the end of the class. Sometimes I have a very elaborate "board plan" in mind, in other cases only a very sketchy framework that develops as the discussion progresses. This board plan – which identifies the key points and issues that have to be covered and not the "solution" to the case – helps me organize the ideas and discussion. It also provides cues to move the discussion along if it appears to be stalling around a particular point. Finally, the board plan assists in clarifying what I want the students to take away from the entire exercise.

One of the early lessons I learned was that the onus of keeping the energy levels high rests with me. I find that when I sit at the back of the class, students keep turning to me for approval of their ideas, which is not the purpose of case discussions. Also, they tend to treat the discussion as fairly informal and exhibit a low level of energy. When I move around the class, the discussion stays highly charged and purposeful. Students no longer direct their comments towards me, developing instead a more interactive exchange among themselves. Meanwhile, I keep track of the various points on the board to build the framework contained in my mental image of the case analysis.

Sometimes I use different techniques to conduct the discussion. Depending on the nature of the case, I might form students into groups to discuss different options to present to the rest of the class. The discussion then develops out of the ideas put forward by the groups. This technique also helps in situations in which individual students are hesitant to put forward their own ideas but can work comfortably within a smaller group. Alternatively, if the case is conducive to a role-playing situation, I encourage this as another way to reinforce the lessons learned and to maintain enthusiasm.

Summary

There is a lot that can be written about teaching with cases (Christensen and Hansen 1987). Much of what succeeds is learned over time through experience. Individual styles vary and what works for one person need not work for another. What is important to remember is that cases should focus on thinking through the problem posed by an interrelated composite of facts and logically defending a decision regarding how to respond. The solution is often secondary; rather, the spotlight should be on the process by which the solution is arrived at and what is learned as a result.

References

Christensen, C. Roland with Abby J. Hansen. 1987. *Teaching and the case method.* Cambridge, MA: Harvard Business School Press.

Stages in Group Dynamics

Rachel Aber Schlesinger

The Class As a Group

Many things happen in a class that are related not only to teaching and learning, but to group process. Is a class a group? Yes, I am sure that the members of a class that meets with regularity are part of a group. Group workers (as teachers, we too are group workers) are aware that groups have a life of their own, where both process and product are important. People in a group react to factors that can interfere with learning. Groups provide support and resources to their members. In every group/ class the following might be familiar: the monopolizer who always wants to talk, the quiet one who never talks, the listener, the one who feels outside the group, the groupies in cliques, the "organizer," the nay-sayer, the fence sitter, the follower and the leader. Just as people have different learning styles, they also have developed, from past experiences, ways of communicating in groups. We can learn to recognize the modes of communication of each member and to use the group to promote better communication skills.

Most groups share a process of group development. Groups exert a force on the individual member and ideally, over time, the active role of the teacher changes as the group takes over and assumes responsibility for its own learning. We all recall classes in which the teacher ended up doing most of the talking, and students tuned out. Using groups allows students to talk, prepare, read and share the responsibility for the learning that takes place.

Stages of the Group Process

Most groups go through phases that overlap, but are distinct. Being aware of these stages can help an instructor prepare to meet the needs of the students.

1. Groups form. In the university, this occurs by choice, by enrolment or by luck. Groups can begin if participants feel they belong. Consider starting off with name

exchanges; everyone should be known by name and should always use each others' names in class.

2. Groups storm. There is often a period in a group, near the beginning, when there are disputes; the class members argue about almost everything: assignments, control of the discussion, participation. Usually this occurs over a short period. It is difficult for many instructors to allow time for the storming stage, but after the initial grumbling, the air is cleared and the work can begin.

3. Groups norm. Eventually students find a way to reach consensus and are ready and able to get to the tasks at hand.

4. Groups perform. Hopefully, for the majority of the term, the members of the class are ready to work. They might continue to dispute some issues, but they are working together to absorb the material and to relate one to another. They share resources, work together and develop confidence.

5. Groups leave. After thirteen or twenty-six weeks, it is time to move on. You know this has been a good group when students are able to maintain contact with one another, often for the length of their university careers, and stay in contact with you as well.

One way to enjoy teaching, I've discovered, is to be aware of alternative approaches to teaching and learning. I begin with what I know and strive to find new ways to involve the class members to enhance their commitment to learning. My experience has proven that groups can have an energy level of their own. The effective instructor learns to be sensitive to that flow, to develop and nurture it. There are great payoffs both in personal development and in learning skills. The group helps me learn about myself, which will, in turn, help me assess my future university learning goals. We are social beings and we learn well with others. Groups allow us to test out ideas, to listen to others, to be listened to and to internalize what we experience.

The Joy of Seminars

Mary Lou McKenna

As instructors, we frequently face disappointment in how students handle reading assignments, seminar presentations and examinations, yet often they receive little guidance in how to prepare for these tasks. While students learn by doing, there is nevertheless a tradeoff in class time wasted or lacklustre discussions and poorly presented seminars. Commercial handbooks are expensive and unlikely to address the precise concerns of students or your particular agenda of expectations. Some instructors solve the problem by eliminating seminar reports from their evaluation schemes, but this doesn't really help the students and merely passes the problem on to future instructors.

A better solution is to offer students the guidance they need in the form of tip sheets that offer practical advice as well as clarifying your expectations in specific terms. It's a matter of providing students early on with some of the inside knowledge that is gradually acquired over three or four years of university study. If you give students a head start, many will run with the ball. It could be a fortuitous coincidence, but the most satisfying set of seminars ever presented in my classes coincided with the first time I issued detailed guidelines on how to do it right. Following are two samples of tip sheets that I hand out to my students to encourage both productive reading and joyful seminars.

Tip Sheet #1: The Joy of Seminars

Although seminar reports can be painful exercises for deliverers and recipients alike, they are meant to be stimulating forums in which students gain experience in oral presentation while bringing their critical skills to bear on a specific topic or text in such a way as to elicit class interest and facilitate discussion. Following are some reminders designed to make this exercise a satisfying experience for everyone involved.

1. Approach the seminar topic as you would an essay: narrow the topic, choose a focus and develop a thesis or point of view that can be supported through specific points and selected illustrations from the text.

2. Your report should have a structure and information should be placed in context. Clarify at the *beginning* what you hope to accomplish with the information you are presenting and what your method of organization will be. It might be helpful to set out areas you have chosen not to address in your report.

3. Organize your discussion into clearly defined stages or categories and signal your audience as you move to a new stage (aim for subtlety; one strategy is to restate in one sentence the point you have established before moving to the next stage).

4. Don't let your report fade away; end with a clear, emphatic restatement of the central issue and your position; where possible, present a thoughtful or provocative question or statement to initiate discussion.

5. Although you are not expected to be an expert, it is important to demonstrate a command of your topic and a thoughtful approach. Define terms that might not be general knowledge and be prepared to clarify aspects of your report or to answer questions. Some discussion with the instructor while preparing your report will ensure that you have an adequate understanding of the topic and relevant terms and concepts. Expecting the instructor to clarify the topic, define terms or answer basic questions during the presentation itself is unprofessional and lets everyone down.

6. To prepare a worthwhile report, it is essential to begin early and allot sufficient time for reading, research and reflection; aim to present the cream of your thought – the wheat separated from the chaff! An effective starting point is the text itself; READ it, jotting down initial impressions of the text and the topic (don't confine your thoughts at this stage; write freely about whatever comes to mind and include questions or concerns that confront you). The primary objective is to establish your own point of view; occasionally the scope or substance of your report can be enhanced with biographical, critical or reference resources if used intelligently, with restraint and as *supports* rather than *substitutes* for your point of view.

7. Hand-outs enable the audience to digest seminar information more efficiently, as well as providing reference material. Following are some types of information that can be conveyed through hand-outs:
   • seminar outline: thesis and main points of discussion
   • definitions, especially lengthy or complex ones
   • text references and excerpts of important passages
   • selected commentaries by authors, reviewers or critics
   • bibliography of sources consulted or recommended.

Tip Sheet #2: Tips on Delivery

1. NEVER read from a prepared text; those of your audience who do not fall asleep will resent this exercise in tedium. Organizing your material in point form on file cards will ensure that you do not present a rambling stream of information no one can follow.

2. Use the recommended edition of the text to provide relevant and accessible page references.

3. Pay attention to the time range specified for your report; a rehearsal will help you gauge the need to expand or condense information as well as identify problem areas.

4. Make eye contact with your classmates; speak to them rather than the instructor. And remember, you set the tone for the class – please bring energy, expression and enthusiasm to your delivery.

The Office Hour:
Not Just Crisis Management

Molly Ungar

The office hour is an ambiguous area in the teaching assistant – student relationship. Some teaching assistants (TAs) see the office hour as the best time to grade written work; others use it as an opportunity to socialize with other TAs; still others regard the office hour as something to be avoided altogether. The problem arises from the fact that this block of time is unstructured and traditionally has not been given a distinct function other than to ensure that the TA is "made available" to the student.

As a result, the office hour is often associated with crisis occasions – some students come to see the TA only when they are in dire need of an extension or when some overwhelming personal matter drives them to a private meeting with the TA. Most students tend to think that they should visit the TA's office only to discuss problems. These problems usually involve negative aspects of coursework: books that cannot be obtained from the library, essay outlines that are unacceptable, essays that have received disappointing grades or frustrating test results. So students often approach the office hour as the time when they are forced to listen to negative criticism of their work, when they are called upon to defend their reasons for thinking they deserved a better grade or when they have to sit through explanations of the TA's marking.

In sum, both TAs and students suffer from an aversion to the office hour. This is no wonder, because the general overtones of punishment, defensiveness and being "called on the carpet" affect all the participants and produce an adversarial relationship. It is up to the TA to rid the office hour of its negative connotations and to encourage a more positive image. The office hour might be a grey area – it is neither a wholly academic nor a wholly social encounter – yet in many ways it is central to the academic experience. The TA is often the only representative of the academic community with whom the student meets face to face, and the TA can do much to socialize, personalize and therefore enrich the academic process. It is through meeting privately with the TA that students learn how to make the transition between the social and the academic dimension of university education.

If teaching assistants are able to see themselves as facilitators and if there is an understanding that some students are more comfortable in a one-on-one environment, there are numerous techniques that can make the office hour more positive and effective. At the beginning of the course, the TA can explain that the function of the office hour is to familiarize the TA with the student as an individual and vice versa. Students can be encouraged to regard a private meeting with the TA as a time when they can discuss ideas or issues that were not brought up in tutorial or that they were not confident of voicing in public.

More structured techniques also can be used. The TA can schedule a compulsory ten minutes of the office hour, over a period of weeks, just to get to know the students in the tutorial. A percentage of the attendance mark can be assigned to this initial meeting. When an assignment is in the planning stages, a percentage of the mark can be allocated for coming to discuss preliminary work with the TA. When an assignment has been completed and handed back to the student, compulsory fifteen-minute visits with the TA can be scheduled to discuss the finished work with all the students in the tutorial, regardless of grade given. Naturally, it is not usually possible to use all these measures in the course of a semester, especially if there are twenty-five or more students in a tutorial, but at least one of these techniques can be used in every course. Scheduled, short meetings with students can go a long way to putting a human dimension into the student-TA relationship.

Encouraging students to discuss their work ahead of time helps to develop organizational approaches to academic work in an informal atmosphere. It might even decrease the possibility that assignments will be done the night before and certainly increases the general quality of completed assignments. The advantage of discussing already-graded work is that it introduces students to the opportunity to reflect on their work and to discuss its strengths and weaknesses with a mind to past and future work. On these occasions, the TA can help students understand their efforts as part of an academic process, rather than a series of hurdles that are approached with anxiety and uncertainty and then set aside with a sigh of relief.

There are more general approaches that can encourage students to make better use of the office hour. The TA can schedule alternate office hours in one of the university cafeterias. If the cafeteria is close to the room where the lecture or the tutorial is held, and if the office hour follows immediately after the class, it is surprising how many unfamiliar faces show up to discuss assignments. Another good thing to remember is to keep visits short. Spending time with one person while long lines of students form at the office door often results in some students never getting to see the TA at that session, and some students never returning. Visits can be longer than fifteen to twenty minutes if no one else is waiting, but if there are other people you need to see, try scheduling another meeting for the next office hour or make an appointment with that student at another mutually agreeable time.

The teaching assistant is the primary agent through whom students can be introduced to the idea that the university is an environment that exists for the exchange of ideas, and the office hour is a crucial part of this dynamic. This was never more clear to me than when a student commented that the exchange of ideas had not been a noticeable part of the student's first year at university. As this student said, "I thought people would be sitting around all over the place discussing things." For that student, "discussing things" had not been part of lecture or tutorial time, nor part of the TA's office hour. For many students, the TA can enlarge the function of the office hour to include communication and enlightenment, not just crisis management.

Negotiating Power in
the Classroom:
The Example of Group Work

Linda Briskin

> In one of my classes, two students who received "A's" on their assignments were asked to read their papers to the rest of the class. When the male student had the floor, he received the undivided attention of the class. However, when the female student read her essay, there was a perceptible change in the classroom environment. The noise level rose considerably. She did not get our undivided attention. She received a clear message that very few students were interested in hearing why she had received an "A." In order to gain control of the class, she turned to the professor for support. None was given. As women in the classroom we are often left talking to ourselves (Fleming *et al.*, Section 1).

Despite teacher desire to focus on course content, especially at university, I would contend that power is always part of the curriculum.[1] Acknowledging the centrality of power to the teaching-learning process not only shifts attention away from the content, but also unsettles certain notions of what constitutes progressive teaching; at the same time, it opens up possibilities for reorganizing classrooms and creates the foundation for vibrant teaching and learning experiences. This article, then, argues in favour of proactive interventionist strategies to deal with power dynamics and demonstrates how the absence of such an approach can undermine even apparently progressive practices, such as collaborative group work.

Proactive interventionist practices bring to consciousness through naming, and openly negotiating about, the power dynamics in the everyday life of the classroom; this strategy takes the social, albeit shifting, meanings of gender, race, class, sexual orientation, ability and age into account. Such an interventionist approach does not seek a resolution but rather looks for empowering rather than disadvantaging ways to deal with the dynamics of power and privilege and to harness these dynamics in the interests of learning and social change.[2]

This proactive approach is in sharp contrast to the conventional wisdom about how to address sexism and racism in the classroom, the central informing vision of which counterposes sexist and racist with non-sexist and non-racist, sometimes called gender and race neutrality. Strategies of gender and race neutrality presuppose the possibility of making gender and race irrelevant. They try to ignore or at least minimize the significance of gender and race; for example, when we assert that it doesn't matter what colour or sex a person is, or when teachers say, "a child is a child" to indicate their sex and colour blindness.[3]

I challenge this belief in the "abstract individual" of liberalism and argue that teachers never teach, for example, a generic engineering student. She is not an engineering student who just happens to be a woman; being a woman is significant to how she is an engineering student, how and what she learns and how we teach her. This is not an essentialist view. It does not assume that there is a transhistorical and unchanging meaning to being a woman; rather, it is historically specific (Riley 1988). So, as a result of the 1989 Montréal Massacre in which fourteen female engineering students were murdered ostensibly because they were feminists, the meaning of being a "woman engineering student" has changed significantly. Similarly, being a woman or a minority teacher in the classroom always has significance: in what we do, how we do it, how we feel about what we do, how students engage with us and how the institution responds to us. I suggest, then, that gender and race neutrality is impossible and that neutrality strategies reproduce privilege. Strategies to increase classroom equity that do not name openly and confront directly such dynamics will not be successful and could even backfire.[4]

Some Reported Attempts to Alter Classroom Power Dynamics

The text and subtext about power are clearly exposed when research on changing classroom dynamics and student reactions to such changes are examined. Barbara Houston (1987) describes a study in which attempts to eliminate gender bias against girls provoked claims of discrimination by the boys.

> When a teacher tries to eliminate gender bias in participation by giving 34 per cent of her attention to girls who constitute one-half the class, the boys protested: "she always asks girls all the questions"; "she doesn't like boys and just listens to girls all the time." In a sexist society boys perceive that two-thirds of the teacher's time is a fair allotment for them, and if it is altered so they receive less, they feel they are discriminated against. And of course they resist, and they protest, and teachers often give in to foster the cooperation that gives the appearance that they are in control of the classroom (141).

In a similar Swedish study, the teacher upsetting the power relations and producing this anger among the boys was so disturbing to the girls that they asked the teacher to return to her original way of teaching, despite the fact that it gave an advantage to the boys (Molloy 1987).

A teacher of a grade-six class in London, Ontario, recounted the following incident.[5] She had read about teachers discriminating against girls; she thought that she did not, but wanted to be sure. She kept track of how much time and attention she gave to boys and girls and discovered that, indeed, she was giving more time to the boys. After only a week of attempting to equalize her attention, she was called into the principal's office. The parents of the boys had called indicating that their sons had been complaining that she didn't like them anymore. She was quite apprehensive about an upcoming meeting with the boys' parents. I suggested that she insist that the parents of the girls also attend.

In these examples, teachers assume that the lack of equal attention to girls is simply a result of teacher error, which can be corrected through care and diligence. The teachers focused on altering their own behaviour by equalizing attention given to the boys and girls. They did not openly take up the dimensions of power that were producing and reproducing patterns of attention within their classrooms and did not engage students in actively interrogating their own behaviours. What they underestimated are the deeply embedded gendered relations of power. Teacher strategies to eliminate gender bias invariably invoke questions of power and make visible the boys' defence of their privilege, their sense of entitlement to more than a fair share of attention and space and their oft refusal to acknowledge organized gender privilege that accrues to them.[6]

In a debate about peace education in Lewis's university classroom (Lewis 1992) that drew connections among patriarchy, violence and political economy (thus making gender power visible), Lewis notes that the men "showed a strong inclination to redirect discussion to notions of world violence as a human and not a gendered problem. By doing so, the men attempted to reappropriate a speaking space for themselves, which they saw to be threatened by my analysis" (175). In this example, the men are trying to shift the discussion from "the margin back to the centre." In the language used by Llyn De Danaan (1990) to make sense of racial power dynamics in the classroom, but that is relevant also to a discussion of gender,[7] she points out that a class that looks

> at society from margin to centre is...disorienting for most white students... Students who have problems with losing centre place can make a transformed classroom problematic...In a classroom where the oblique view is the norm, white students complain of ambiguity, seek "closure," and wish to redefine the agenda (138–40; emphasis added).

Group Work

Group work is one strategic intervention that can highlight practices of power. Many teachers organize group work and collaboration in the hope of providing a more effective learning environment for marginalized voices: some groups are assigned projects or presentations; others operate as break-out groups for short periods of class time. I would argue, however, that collaboration and group work are not in themselves solutions; if the organization of group work does not take account of power dynamics, group work itself can re-inscribe power relations rather than create openings for more inclusive learning.

The composition of work groups is rarely seen to be significant. Many teachers are inclined to divide students randomly, implicitly informed by a non-sexist, non-racist approach that attempts to make gender and race irrelevant. Some might organize groups with equal numbers of women and men, or people of colour and whites. However, the fact that representation does not equal power has been more than demonstrated by research — for example, studies that examine the impact of the presence of a few men in a class of women[8] or the election of male leaders in female-dominated unions. In such instances, even the numerical domination of women does not necessarily translate into power.

An interventionist approach begins by naming the problematic of power that exists in work groups and then negotiating with students about the composition of groups. The discussion itself about group practices is an important learning moment, especially if marginalized voices are able to articulate their concerns.[9]

In making an argument, then, for the possible use of same-sex or same-race work groups (and, by extension, depending on the context, same-sex or -race classes and perhaps schools), it is important to stress that, in the current historical context, this strategy is different from imposed segregation and from separation based on essentialist difference; rather, it rests on the recognition of differences in power.[10] In this regard it is interesting to trace the shifting discourse on coeducation. Linda Eyre (1991) studies home economics, which was excluded from coeducation until the 1970s, when "feminist concerns about women's equality and the role of schooling in the sexual division of labour' (193) led to the promotion of home economics as a coeducational subject. Her study of "balancing the ratio of female and male students" in home economics concludes that coeducation has "not fulfilled its promise as a solution to gender inequality in schools" (193). It is in this historical trajectory that discussions of single-sex or -race education must be situated. Single-sex work groups, for example, can be a strategy for revealing gendered relations of power and for empowering girls and women to resist them, on the one hand, and, on the other, a context in which their learning can be facilitated.[11]

Research suggests that under many circumstances mixed-gender work groups reproduce existing power dynamics.[12] The report of the American Association of University Women (1992), *How Schools Shortchange Girls*, provides a comprehensive review of the literature. It is worth quoting at some length:

> Researchers have found that the majority of elementary students preferred single-sex work groups...[D]ifferent communication patterns of males and females can be an obstacle to effective cross-gender relationships. Females are more indirect in speech, relying often on questioning, while more direct males are more likely to make declarative statements or even to interrupt. Research indicates that boys in small groups are more likely to receive requested help from girls; girls' requests, on the other hand, are more likely to be ignored by boys...Male students may choose to show their social dominance by not readily talking with females. Not only are the challenges to cross-gender cooperation significant, but cooperative learning as cur-

rently implemented may not be powerful enough to overcome these obstacles. Some research indicates that the infrequent use of small, unstructured work groups is not effective in reducing gender stereotypes, and in fact, increases stereotyping. Groups often provide boys with leadership opportunities that increase their self-esteem. Females are often seen as followers and are less likely to want to work in mixed-sex groups in future. Another study indicates a decrease in female achievement when females are placed in mixed-sex groups (72–73).

Pat Mahoney "claims that one of the most noticeable features of a mixed sex group is the huge amount of time and energy which the boys exert in denying the girls' academic ability" (reported in Reay 1990, 39). In the integrated home-economics classroom, Eyre (1991) found that both girls and boys tended to gravitate towards same-sex work groups. Given the behaviour of the boys, she found the girls' choice more than understandable:

Classroom observations day after day showed that a group of boys not only dominated student — teacher interaction, but they also corrected, interrupted and ridiculed girls and quieter boys and woman teachers. Whereas the silence or the laughter of most girls and quieter boys had the effect of giving power to the dominant boys, those who tried to break this control were subjected to further abuse. Girls had good reasons for segregating themselves from boys (215).

Indeed, evidence suggests that same-sex work groups are effective for girls. Diane Reay (1990) reports on the success of such an initiative in the inner-London school where she taught. She says,

I had the happy experience of seeing a transformation in the girls...As their confidence began to grow, peer group interaction back in the mixed classroom was affected...Tina, one of the girls, wrote in her end of term report..."I've learnt not to put up with the boys putting me down. I tell them to shut up and get on with their work" (42).

Reay finds that girls-only groups work "as a bridge to competence and assertiveness in mixed sex groups, and...[provide] possibilities which allow girls' self-concepts to develop to the stage where they, alongside the boys, can take on the role of initiators" (40). Significantly, the boys' responses to the project were not nearly so positive. "In direct contrast to the girls, many of the boys felt they had learnt nothing about themselves" (43). Reay concludes that "we were left with the inevitable conundrum – should we provide girls with the discrimination they need if the result is a wave of male anger and resentment from the boys?" (44) Despite the fact that the girls' school achievements and self-confidence increased dramatically and that "boys' attempts to sabotage extra resourcing for girls has been documented elsewhere," the school did not continue the girls' project.

A project in Denmark (Kruse 1992) that alternates children between single-sex and coeducational settings had success not only with the girls but also with the boys:

Some of the girls admitted to having missed the boys, their cheek and outspokenness…but the girls now recognized how their classes used to be dominated by boys and realized their own part in letting them…(92–93) Back in the co-educational setting…the girls openly struggled for more space and mounted fierce reactions to the boys' dominant behaviour. The boys were irritated but showed more respect for the girls than they had done earlier…Boys who wish to associate or chose to work with girls no longer got teased by other boys! (96)

Reay's report does not describe the work done with the boys in single-sex settings, but the Danish project stresses the importance of the single-sex settings for boys and, in particular, the critical role of the male teacher, who had a proactive agenda for taking up masculine sex-role patterns and expectations with the boys. Kruse also points out that, from a strategic point of view, "focusing only on girls will result in imposing on them the whole responsibility for change, and it will underpin the assumption that 'boys are boys' and therefore cannot change" (90).[13] Although I am sympathetic to the need to re-educate boys, I am concerned that the power dimensions in the relationships between girls and boys could be lost in the view that both sexes equally need re-education. This kind of "humanism" can hide the power dynamics that heavily favour boys.

The success of active interventions into power dynamics through the strategy of separate work groups is in sharp contrast to the problems that arose when teachers focused on altering their own behaviour by equalizing attention given to the boys and girls, and did not engage students in actively interrogating their own behaviours. Linda Eyre's study (1991) of the integrated home-economics class shows that despite the challenge to certain sex-role stereotypes in that context, "gender as a social relation of power" continued to operate when unchallenged. She discusses two suggestive examples. As a classroom observer, she noticed that the boys' talk was frequently homophobic and misogynist. Teachers were explicit about "making light of" such talk and using "diversionary tactics" (213):

Though teachers showed concern about the amount of noise the boys were making, they did not usually address the content of the boys' talk…By suggesting that such talk should be kept private, or reserved for the locker room, and by not being explicit about the content, teachers may inadvertently have condoned the content of the boys' talk (206).

In another example, Eyre describes instances where teachers drew attention to the silence of the girls and tried to encourage them to speak. However, the teachers did not address the reasons for the girls' silence. Eyre concludes that "although this approach [the teacher's prompting of the girls] sometimes initiated a response from girls, it made a problem of girls' quietness rather than of boys' dominance and inability to listen" (210). I would suggest that without a proactive interventionist approach towards speaking and silence, gendered power dynamics will be reinforced.

In arguing for the strategic use of separate-sex or separate-race groups, a word of caution is necessary. I am not suggesting that inside of these groups power dynamics among students are eliminated. Instead, other dimensions of power – around race or ethnicity, for example, in a single-sex group – can emerge as significant. In the research undertaken by Kruse (1992), separate classes for boys revealed much about the power dynamics among boys that had been submerged in the coeducational classroom.

Let me end with a discussion of an incident recounted to me by a male high-school teacher.[14] While showing a video about violence against women to a grade-ten class, sexist outbursts by some of the male students forced the teacher to stop the video. He tried to discuss the outbursts with the class but, in his assessment, the discussion was derailed by a girl who said that she didn't see any problem with the boys' behaviour. At a distance the history of that particular classroom is unavailable; we do not know, for example, if student bonding against the teacher was invoked. The motivations of the young woman are also opaque; we do not have access to her version of the incident or her understanding of her own agency. Yet it is possible to imagine that she rightly understands that her currency is dependent on the boys' approval (not the approval of the teacher) and so she seeks an alliance with them.

The power of the young woman to derail the discussion also merits analysis. Why would her voice carry such weight when so much evidence underscores the difficulties girls and women have gaining access to authority in classrooms? In this instance, her voice operated to reinscribe patriarchal norms; perhaps this is why it had the impact it did. Would it have been possible for a male student to derail the discussion in this way? Probably not.[15] How difficult, perhaps even dangerous, would it have been for a female student to challenge the boys' outbursts, even with the teacher's support? In such a situation, young women are placed in a difficult position.

However, had the teacher immediately divided the groups by sex and asked them to discuss the outbursts, the girls might have been provided with the space and context to develop a collective voice with enough confidence to challenge the boys. This proactive intervention into the classroom's power dynamics might have helped to overcome their individual powerlessness.

This example suggests that work groups that take account of classroom power dynamics also might have an impact on patterns of speaking and silence; the route to speaking for the marginalized could be collective and not individual. Speaking and silence tend to be understood as a function of individuals, but it could be that alliances among students can strengthen and secure those voices in what are fundamentally unsafe classrooms. Ellsworth (1992) calls for "affinity groups" (which occur outside of class time):

> Dialogue…is impossible in the culture at large,…because power relations between raced, classed, and gendered students and teachers are unjust. The injustice of these relations, and the way in which those injunctions distort communication, cannot be overcome in a classroom, no matter how committed the teacher and students (108)…[A]ffinity groups were necessary for working against the way current histori-

cal configurations of oppressions were reproduced in class. They provided some participants with safer home bases...Once we acknowledged the existence, necessity and value of these affinity groups, we began to see our task not as one of building democratic dialogue between free and equal individuals, but of building a coalition among the multiple, shifting, intersecting, and sometimes contradictory groups carrying unequal weights of legitimacy within the culture and the classroom (109).

Conclusion

Precisely because proactive interventions into power dynamics are about power, teachers, especially those who themselves are marginal, who take power up and on might face a lot of resistance. Naming the practices of power can be very unsettling for those who benefit from them, and even for those who do not benefit but have developed a comfortable acceptance of and familiarity with them.

It could be that for some teachers, isolated in single classrooms, it is impossible (perhaps even foolhardy) to try to unsettle such dynamics. These difficulties underscore the need for collective and institutional-level intervention. That part of university culture that looks upon discussions of teaching with suspicion needs to be challenged; in particular, the tendency to draw sharp lines between teaching practices and course content in such a way that issues of teaching and certainly issues of power are marginalized. Not only do teachers need to reexamine the practices of power in classrooms, but they also need to push for institutional policies that will address issues of power in the classroom and systemic patterns of discrimination, and for extensive training and retraining of teachers to better understand these issues. Such changes will provide institutional support for those groups of teachers and students who are isolated and marginalized in individual classrooms, as well as a foundation for changing the climate and practices of education, for what is learned, who learns it and how.

A version of this article was published in Canadian Woman Studies (winter 1998). Reprinted here with permission.

Notes

This article is part of a larger piece entitled "Negotiating Power and Silence in the Class: A Strategic Approach." I would like to acknowledge the way that this perspective has been clarified and deepened for me through interactions with the participants and audiences of workshops and lectures I have given at Dalhousie University, McMaster University, York University, the Toronto Board of Education, the Women's

Fora of Goteborg, Linkoping and Uppsala Universities, and at Kvinnofolkhogskolan in Sweden. I acknowledge my debt to the many engaged students I have had the opportunity to work with, especially in my fourth-year seminar on feminist thought. I would also like to thank Rebecca Coulter, Harriet Friedmann, Nadia Habib, Didi Khyatt, Roxana Ng and Daphne Read for critical and instructive feedback on earlier drafts of this paper.

1. For an elaboration of the forms of power that operate in the classroom, see "Power in the Classroom" in Section I.

2. It is certainly the case that strategic responses to power dynamics in the classroom must be contextually and historically located. It is not insignificant that I have done most of my teaching in inner-city high schools in Montréal, at Sheridan College in the working-class community of Brampton and at York University, perhaps the university with the most heterogenous student population. In all instances, I taught about gender issues, often in the context of mainstream English, writing or social science courses and sometimes in women's studies courses. I would argue that power is always operating in classrooms, but the dimensions of power with the most resonance will vary historically and contextually; further, there is clearly a range of effective strategic responses to such dynamics.

3. For a more detailed analysis of the limits of "non-sexism," see Feminist Pedagogy: Teaching and Learning Liberation (Briskin 1990–94).

4. Sarita Srivastava (1994) draws the same conclusion about antiracist workshops: "Although the facilitator/producer was skilled, by not explicitly addressing power relations within the workshop, she implicitly reinforced them" (108).

5. This incident was described to me after a talk I gave at the University of Western Ontario in March 1990.

6. One of the best examples of this defence of privilege is in the discussion of affirmative action and the claims by white men of reverse discrimination, as well as by the whole discourse on political correctness, which has significantly undermined attempts to change the power dynamics in universities.

7. I am ambivalent about the use of the metaphor of centre and margin. The danger in this somewhat static dualism is that it assumes not only the notion of a centre, but also implicitly suggests what occupies, and perhaps what should occupy, the centre (white, male, heterosexual, the West). Furthermore, it implies a certain relation between margin and centre – a privileging of the centre over the margin. We need language that problematizes the connection, interrogates the assumption of the marginality of the margin and recognizes that what is understood as centre and margin is always in process and constituted in struggle.

8. For example, in a study by Craig and Sherif (1986) "the major finding was that men were more influential than women when there were 1 man and 3 women present…" (463). The study concluded that "men have been found to be more influential when in a minority of one than in other conditions. There is also some indication that when men are not influential it is their choice, and thus, they are still really in control of the situation…[I]t is clear that a man is more influential in a minority, which has strong implications for men moving into traditionally female occupations and businesses. They may, in fact, be given more than an equal say compared to the women in the group" (465). In a suggestive study, Janice Newton (1995) found that even in situations of anonymity (through a computerized interactive file), the presence of a few male students in the course changed patterns of interaction and made "women less willing to relate course material to their personal experiences" (150).

9. In a meeting to plan sessions on pedagogy at another university where I was invited to speak about power in the classroom, I raised the issue about how we should break up the larger group and pointed out the difficulties of doing it randomly. The tenured faculty member on the committee thought we should do it randomly since she did not think there were any significant power issues in the group (which would be composed of women who identified as feminist, both graduate students and faculty). The graduate student on the committee hesitantly disagreed, pointing out that she thought many of her peers would feel uncomfortable speaking openly with the faculty. The faculty member was quite surprised, but the decision to organize groups by "status" created an opening for graduate students to articulate a wide range of concerns.

10. There is a growing interest in single-sex schooling for girls. The all-girls and specifically feminist Linden School has recently opened in Toronto, and Kinesis (May 1995) reports that a pilot project with girls-only classes is operating at Earl Grey School in Winnipeg. There has been extensive debate in the Toronto Board

of Education about the possibility of "black-focused schools" and the board had recently launched the Triangle Program for lesbian and gay youth at the Oasis Alternative Secondary School.

11. I make a similar kind of argument about "separate organizing" by union women. See "Union Women and Separate Organizing" (1993).

12. I have seen little research on this issue done with university students, except anecdotal material that focuses on women's studies. The lack of research on teaching practices at university reflects the marginalization of pedagogy.

13. A recent debate on boys has occurred in the pages of *The Gen* (March 1994), a publication from the Equity Network of the Department of Employment Education and Training in Australia. The debate has identified a growing concern that a focus on programs for boys will divert resources from the already slim budgets of girls' programs, but also a recognition that "the way the boys behave, particularly violent boys, impinges on girls' self esteem and girls' futures." This last comment is from Cheryl Vardon, the chair of the Taskforce for the Education of Girls. The article continues, "This philosophy is embodied in the Taskforce's terms of reference, one of which is to provide advice on the education of boys as it relates to the education of girls." Vardon says, "It's very important for us to analyse the impact of boys' behaviour on girls and in doing that we'll look at programs for boys which actually improve things for girls." In the April 1994 issue of *The Gen*, teacher Jackie Werner comments, "Girls have been encouraged to develop a growing sense of their rights, and skills to help them access those rights. However, there has not been the same officially sanctioned pressure on boys to change their behaviour correspondingly. Nor has there been the support for those boys who were developing non-stereotyped behaviour patterns. Girls have been encouraged and supported to be more assertive and to develop leadership skills, but boys have not been getting the same encouragement to be better listeners, more self aware, more sensitive or more nurturing…One outcome of this imbalance in programs provided at the institutional level is that girls are once more placed in the traditional role of being responsible for the nature of their interactions with male peers;…they are left to fight the battles themselves with their male peers…"

14. This incident was described to me at a workshop I ran (with Roxana Ng) for the Toronto Board of Education in 1993.

15. A comparison can be made to the differential impact of women and men who speak against feminism: how much more impact antifeminist *women's* voices have in the current historical context.

References

American Association of University Women and the Wellesley College Centre for Research on Women. 1992. *How schools shortchange girls*.

Briskin, Linda. 1990–94. *Feminist pedagogy: Teaching and learning liberation*. Ottawa: Canadian Research Institute for the Advancement of Women.

———. 1993. Union women and separate organizing. In *Women challenging unions: Feminism, democracy and militancy*, Linda Briskin and Patricia McDermott (eds.), 89–108. Toronto: University of Toronto Press.

Craig, Jane and Carolyn Sherif. 1986. The effectiveness of men and women in problem solving groups as a function of group gender composition. *Sex Roles* 14 (7/8): 453–66.

De Danaan, Llyn. 1990. Centre to margin: Dynamics in a global classroom. *Women's Studies Quarterly* (1/2): 135–44.

Ellsworth, Elizabeth. 1992. Why doesn't this feel empowering? Working through the repressive myths of critical pedagogy. *In Feminisms and critical pedagogy*, Carmen Luke and Jennifer Gore (eds.), 90–119. New York: Routledge.

Eyre, Linda. 1991. Gender relations in the classroom: A fresh look at coeducation. In *Women and education*, 2nd ed., Jane Gaskell and Arlene McLaren (eds.), 193–219. Calgary: Detselig Enterprises.

Houston, Barbara. 1987. Should public education be gender-free? In *Women and men*, Greta Nemiroff (ed.), 359–69. Toronto: Fitzhenry and Whiteside.

Kruse, Anne-Mette. 1992. "…We have learnt not to just sit back, twiddle our thumbs and let them take over:" Single sex settings and the development of a pedagogy for girls and a pedagogy for boys in Danish schools. *Gender and Education* 4 (1/2): 81–103.

Lewis, Magda. 1992. Interrupting patriarchy: Politics, resistance and transformation in the feminist classroom. In *Feminisms and critical pedagogy*, Carmen Luke and Jennifer Gore (eds.), 167–91. New York: Routledge.

Molloy, Gunilla. 1987. "Men killarna ar sa sura pa oss…" Om ett larorikt forsok med varannan-frage-metoden. *Krut* 4: 50–53, 82.

Newton, Janice. 1995. What is feminist pedagogy anyway? Distinctions in content and process. In *Teaching women's history: Challenges and solutions*, ed. Bettina Bradbury, Ruby Heap, Franca Iacovetta, Kathryn McPherson, Bina Mehta, Cecilia Morgan and Joan Sangster, 135–45. Athabasca, AB: Athabasca University Press.

Reay, Diane. 1990. Girls' groups as a component of anti-sexist practice—one primary school's experience. *Gender and Education* 2 (1): 37–48.

Riley, Denise. 1988. *Am I that name?: Feminism and the category of "women" in history*. University of Minnesota.

Srivastava, Sarita. 1994. Voyeurism and vulnerability: Critiquing the power relations of anti-racist workshops. *Canadian Woman Studies* 14 (2): 105–09.

Section VII:
Assignments and Evaluation

While the previous section focused on teaching and learning activities during class time, important learning occurs outside the classroom, while students prepare for class, work on assignments or talk about course material during an office visit or with friends. How a faculty member designs these out-of-class activities can be crucial for student success.

Part 1 of this section deals with reading. The first step, of course, is always the challenge of getting students to read. Broomhead's article offers a number of strategies for encouraging students to read, including suggestions for how to respond if no one has done the reading. Greene describes how he uses a checklist to encourage students to read. The two subsequent articles shift the focus to the challenge of how to engage students with the substance of the reading material. In "Telling a Book by Its Cover," Godard explores students' first impressions of titles and cover illustrations of lesbian novels, showing us how to work with these judgements and impressions to discover how meaning is created. Similarly, the Golby article demonstrates how the use of leading questions can take students beyond their first impressions to a deeper understanding of a text.

Part 2 focuses on research essays and writing assignments. The cornerstone article by Brown talks about the crucial importance of sequencing assignments or breaking up complex tasks into smaller, more manageable component parts. This promotes the development of the skills needed to complete a larger research paper and it also has the added advantage of creating early opportunities to give students feedback on how to improve their work. The Rehner article describes how writing and learning groups can improve the writing skills of students in a large course. Rehner formed students into small groups that worked with an essay tutor. She concludes that this kind of group work not only reinforced the students' critical skills, it also diminished the alienation of students in a large class or tutorial. The Braaksma article offers a librarian's perspective on research essays and urges closer collaboration between faculty and librarians in assignment design to build appropriate critical thinking skills into students' research strategies. The Jones article makes useful suggestions about how a graduate student assigned to run a tutorial, though not in charge of designing the course assignments, can nonetheless promote and develop students' writing skills. The role of a writing centre figures prominently in several of the above articles. Clearly, many of our colleagues have found these centres to be a useful adjunct to their teaching. A second article by Rehner describes what happens when a student uses a writing centre and why the interaction between student and writing instructor differs from the interaction that occurs when a course instructor and a student meet to discuss the student's work in a course.

Having addressed reading and writing assignments, we next turn to evaluation and grading in Part 3. The Greenwald article discusses research on grading and argues forcefully for a shift in focus from correcting mistakes to asking the student to "help me understand what you are trying to say." Offering a number of suggestions to improve the way we respond to student writing, Greenwald argues that with proper feedback, we can influence the quality of students' writing. Yoshioka's article confronts issues of grading in mathematics. He addresses how to grade fairly, efficiently and in a manner that motivates students to try difficult problems instead of giving up. The final two articles, by Bunch and Carpenter, share a similar theme: how to give students flexibility and a voice in determining the nature of assignments and the way in which they want to be graded. Both highlight the significant advantages of students taking responsibility for this aspect of their learning. Indeed, these strategies may increasingly make sense as mounting student debt forces more students to commit their out-of-class time to part-time or even full-time work.

When No One Has Done the Reading...

Janet Broomhead

It can wreck classes. It manifests itself in class discussions when no one participates. It is apparent in essays and exams. If no one has done the reading, a tutorial drags on for a very long time.

In preparing this article, I discovered that there are probably as many approaches to getting students to do reading assignments as there are teachers. While methods vary, our goal is common – we want students to want to read. Here, then, are a bunch of carrots (and a couple of sticks).

How To Get Students To Do the Assigned Reading

- Choose readings appropriate for your students. Select works that illustrate the main ideas of the course and are interesting to read. With works rife with jargon and writing styles that can discourage the undergraduate reader, be prepared to work with your students to develop their appreciation of this material.
- Introduce the reading. Explain your rationale for choosing the text and its relevance to the key concepts of the course. Tell students why you like the selection.
- Set up the assignment so that the student will be successful. For example, assign questions that guide the reader through the text. Over time, students should develop and employ this strategy on their own.
- Assign a question on the reading and collect responses at the beginning of the next class. Grade them either satisfactory or unsatisfactory with this single criterion: Has the student shown that she or he has read the material? Accumulated responses can form the basis of a participation grade. (Unlike other evaluative techniques, this system rewards the student for completing the reading assignment, not for finding the right answer to an assigned question).
- "Cold call" with caution. This questioning practice can be embarrassing for students even when they have done the reading and can undermine the

groundwork of trust you have fostered in your classroom. The approach works well after students have had an opportunity to develop and share their ideas with their peers through think-write-pair-discuss.[1]

What To Do in a Tutorial When No One Has Done the Reading

You've tried the techniques listed above (and numerous innovations of your own). Even so, a day arrives when no one has done the reading...

- Stop. If no one has read the assignment, give students class time to read or designate small groups to tackle larger texts collaboratively.
- If some students are prepared for class, you might try the fishbowl technique: students who have done the reading form a circle and discuss the text. The remaining students encircle the discussion group and listen in on the ideas discussed. By the next class, students in the outer circle must hand in a report on the key concepts addressed in the discussion.
- As a last resort, some instructors have cancelled their tutorials when no one is prepared for class. The least positive, this drastic measure is needed only once to communicate the seriousness of unread assignments.

This article was first published in January 1994 in Core 4 (3): 1.

Notes

1. See "Dead Silence..." by Pat Rogers in Section VI, Part 2.

A Strategy for Encouraging Students To Do Readings

Ian Greene

In several of my fourth-year seminar classes, I have experimented with what I call the checklist approach for encouraging students to do the required and suggested readings for each class. Each week at the beginning of the seminar, I pass around a checklist with the students' names along the left-hand side and all the required and suggested readings for that week along the top. It is quite easy to generate each week's checklist. I have a list of my students in my computer. (I usually download these from the university student information system, but someone without such a facility could simply create a list.) I also have my course outline in my computer, from which I can extract each week's readings for the line across the top of the page. Generating the new list for each week takes only a few minutes and students are asked to indicate beside their names whether they have 1) carefully read the item, 2) skimmed the item or 3) not read the item at all.

I tell students that I expect them to at least skim all items and to read the required readings carefully most of the time. However, I do not demand perfection. It takes about ten minutes for the sheet to circulate back to me and I use the results to pitch the level of the remainder of the class. Inevitably, at the first week's class most students have not done the readings and are thoroughly embarrassed. At this point some politeness and diplomacy on my part help to keep the students' trust. I usually admit that as an undergraduate student I often didn't complete readings. At the same time, I tell my students that I wish that I had done them since I would have gotten more out of my classes and would have avoided much time in last-minute cramming.

At subsequent seminar classes I find that all students have read thoroughly at least one of the readings and have skimmed most of the rest. The level of seminar discussion then becomes quite satisfactory. Student evaluations always indicate that the students learned more from the seminar than most of their other classes because they had done the readings.

I have also experimented with using the results of these checklists to assist me in determining the participation grade. The advantage is that I have an objective way of assigning some of the points for participation. The disadvantage is that the calculation can be time consuming and some students always worry that their peers might have exaggerated the extent to which they "carefully read" the readings. My experimentation continues.

This article was first published in 1994 in Core 4 (3): 2–3.

Telling a Book by
Its Cover

Barbara Godard

"You can't tell a book by its cover," according to the old proverb. Many people do, however. In the 1950s, some women looked on paperback stands for covers featuring two women. This was the coded design of the lesbian pulp romance. Students also respond to titles, covers, dust jackets and prefaces when they decide how much time and effort to put into their course texts. I propose that we work *with* students' tendency to judge these overt signals, as a means to critically introduce controversial topics and engage students in how meanings are formed. My example here is lesbian material in a "mainstream" classroom. The strategy, however, could be adapted to any kind of textual material, verbal or visual.

Most teaching in the university is concerned, directly or indirectly, with ideologies. A system of values, which orders events or speech in particular relationships, gives a "fact" or "object of knowledge" certain claims to truth. Not everyone responds to the same claims: people are placed differently in respect to value systems. These differences are what are at stake in producing knowledge in the university classroom. A critical pedagogy explores those values implicated in the production of knowledge and frequently exposes the contradictions embedded in facts, opposing ways of presenting facts and the tension between a text's values and students' values.

Finding ways to encourage students to reflect on these issues becomes a formidable challenge, especially when we want students to consider value systems that might contradict their own. Many students want clear standards, not questions and ambiguity. Some come to university to gain a BA as a passport to social acceptance. If course texts challenge their social norms and ask them to question the social values they strive to acquire, learning becomes a risky undertaking. Material considered marginal from the perspective of the students' value system could incite resistance, which can manifest to differing degrees. Students preselect courses based on a course title and reading lists. Those who sign up for a course with the word "lesbian" in the title or in the title of required texts presumably have overcome the greatest resistance. Yet they can still avoid dealing with material they find disturbing by staying away from classes that discuss it or by attending class without reading the troubling texts.

My strategy for addressing this ambiguous response to potentially threatening material is to explore students' resistance to the material. My class examines how a text addresses its implied reader, considering how this places readers in different positions in respect to its "knowledge." The students' hesitation is a given – a focus for analysis – rather than a matter for blame. How is the reader positioned? Who is included? Who is excluded? What sort of knowledge or experience does this text presuppose? Do these assumptions privilege some readers over others? What are the implications of these differences? Who are the "we" invoked in this preface? What sort of contract is established with the reader or viewer? These questions can lead to more extended discussion. Through critical attention to the covers, dust jackets, cover blurbs, prefaces and dedications of texts, we question how the boundaries of texts are established, turning inwards to synthesize contents and outwards to engage potential audiences. As hinges, they mediate, make bridges or offer invitations to which some might respond more readily than others.

Covers for different editions initiate productive discussion since they immediately broach the possibility of different readings of a text. Comparing the two covers of Joy Kogawa's Obasan (1981), students distinguished between the Japanese character and words printed as poetic lines on the hardcover edition, and the photographic image of a small Japanese girl with her face pressed to a misty windowpane on the paperback. The hardback cover addresses readers familiar with Kogawa's poetry, inviting them to focus on the language of the novel; the paperback cover invokes feelings of loss and longing, asking readers to connect with the emotions of the child and to focus on the novel as personal quest. Students recognized this "framing" as a marketing strategy that targets different audiences: an elite "literary" public on the one hand and a popular audience on the other. Once the initial observation of different modes of address has been broached, students can explore how this framing shapes readers' responses through analysis and discussion of its implications for different kinds of reading.

Lesbian texts might threaten students since they have implications that might call students' lives into question, striking at the heart of the gendered distribution of power. A comparison of two texts can encourage students to recognize the stakes involved. Jovette Marchessault's *Lesbian Triptych* (1985) and Jane Rule's *The Desert of the Heart* (1964), both fictions about lesbian confrontation with the conventions or norms of straight society, expose and contest the norm of compulsory heterosexuality. Students find it easier to read *The Desert of the Heart*. Titles have much to do with this. Since both books share a similar critique of conventions, the differences in the framing and rhetorical mode of the texts become central. Rule's gentle irony and parody of the traditional "love story" contrast with Marchessault's satiric denunciation of religious and educational institutions, with their perpetuation of symbolic motherhood as the norm for women. Analysis of the texts and of their implications within differing historical periods and cultures will take up much of the class time.

We begin, however, with a focus on the covers. One student might comment on the impact the cover has had on other people. Taking *Lesbian Triptych* to work with her, she finds herself addressed by her fellow workers, who ask what she is reading. Although she has taken other course books with her, no one has ever asked her about them before. The student carrying the book is subjected to the gaze of social surveillance. Mere knowledge of lesbian cultures might make one vulnerable to losing an apartment or a job. The title of the book attracts attention by its directness and obliges people to situate themselves immediately in relation to the implied content. We discuss how a title's provocative character polarizes responses. The threat the gaze poses for heterosexual and lesbian readers is different in degree, though both are subject to exclusion. Students offer other narratives of their reaction to this textual object, including those of their hesitation about buying or reading it. This leads to questions about what has made them hesitate and how they have internalized social norms of heterosexuality. Depending on whether they are "out" or not, lesbian students might offer counter-narratives of their pleasure in buying and reading the text. Silence here would be a point to note. It could generate a discussion of systemic homophobia: how women are positioned as good or bad, subject for reward or punishment, in the binaries of this gendered value system.

The class then examines the illustrations. While the title seemingly invites a complicit audience and the reader presumed to have knowledge of lesbian experience, the cover illustrations are less explicit. Indeed, they seem ambiguous to many. Hand drawn in the shape of a three-panelled stained-glass window, they feature a cow, a number of sheep in diagonal lines and a ball of wool with a knitting needle. Only the last of these evokes a specifically feminine image. The others are seemingly neutral. A reader of Gertrude Stein might view the picture of the cow as a code for lesbian erotica. The docile sheep who all follow the leader in a straight line might be read only after the fact as a symbol for compulsory heterosexuality. So too is the ironic use Marchessault makes of the symbol of domesticity, the knitting needle, as abortionist's instrument accessible only with hindsight. Discussion of the different kinds of knowledge needed to read the cover spills over into an analysis of the book itself. The cover offers a contradictory invitation: the threat or shock of the title's explicit address to lesbian-identified readers is moderated by illustrations seemingly addressing general or feminine readers. Nonetheless, the double meaning of the cow positions readers differentially with respect to a tradition of lesbian writing, for some readers have greater knowledge than others. This extra knowledge might be revealed or concealed. The cover positions readers without directly soliciting voyeurism of the lesbian as "exotic other," whose "secrets" are to be unveiled.

This stands in contrast to the cover of Rule's novel. Rule's novel features two figures, which are barely distinguishable as female. The cover of the first edition is faintly evocative of the code of lesbian pulp romances – faintly, because it is hard to distinguish whether the stick figure in the background is male or female. The absence of detail breaks that code to address general readers. Students are asked what they see in these images. The figure in the foreground is presumed to be female because of the long hair. The face, with only black slits or shadows as eyes, is turned forwards, not gazing back at the other figure. In relation to the title, this design suggests that the novel is concerned more with isolation and separation than with affairs of the heart. It deals with both, however, moving from one to the other in what has become a classical "coming out" narrative. In doing so, the narrative focuses on a heterosexual woman discovering her homoerotic tendencies, including heterosexual women in approaching the subject, and hinting at a generalized homosexuality, without disturbing the veils or secrets.

These themes are maintained in the cover blurb, which announces that "Miss Rule does not shirk an issue which a few years ago would have scarcely even seen the light of day." Secret there is, but what? Homosexuality unseen is "invisible," figured within an "epistemology of the closet." In its absence, heterosexuality asserts its power to define the normal, the good. The blurb glances away from the more explicit classic pulp cover announcing "the love that dare not speak its name." While the cover of The *Desert of the Heart* promises a love story and scandal, it is indeterminate about the parties involved. Book reviews commented on its "perverted good taste." Such ambiguity of address and ironic play with romance convention implicates many readers in the novel, keeping them until the unconventional ending. Reading this is a game of hide and seek, very different from Marchessault's book, which announces its perspective and demands that readers take a stand. Consideration of these different styles of address leads to discussion of differences within lesbian cultural politics, complicated by the different generations and languages of the writers. Students discover that lesbianism is by no means a unified or unchanging category.

From the covers, attention turns to the "reading scenes" within the texts. Marchessault's characters read the Bible, especially Genesis, and respond with impertinent questions. They read between the lines of newspaper reports of unsolved violence against women and denounce them as "lies." These are the manoeuvres of a resisting reader, working with supplemental knowledge against the grain of the text. In contrast, Rule presents reading as seduction. The cartoonist's character reveals her "inner self," her lesbian love, to the hitherto heterosexual woman by inviting her to read a book of her unpublished cartoons titled *Eve's Apple*. These cartoons are not described but left to readers' imaginations. Lesbian and heterosexual readers will do so differently. This blank crucially constructs differential positions in respect to knowledge, for it constitutes simultaneously a gesture of exposure and concealment. The secrecy implies inclusiveness, while hardening the boundaries between lesbian and heterosexual.

These "reading scenes" model a variety of ways for readers to interact with texts. They draw attention to how reading relies on knowledge of literary and social conventions and how different interpretive communities hold divergent knowledges. They illustrate how historically irreducible interests divide and define communities, and the interconnection of social categories, personal understanding and language (or representation and interpretation) – none a reflection of the other. Resistance is the site at which the stakes of power make themselves felt. Resistance is not something that should be set aside in the classroom. Rather, it can be developed into a method of resisting reading.

At its best, this focus on the cover – which presumes that students have read no further, yet might not have read the cover thoroughly – will launch a discussion in which the informed students' comments encourage the reluctant students to read the entire book for themselves. In my experience, some students write essays on the texts they have first resisted reading. As a teaching strategy, "telling a book by its cover" need not be restricted to use in English courses or with controversial or difficult material. These techniques could be used with texts in any discipline, using the covers, tables of contents, prefaces, etc., to initiate discussion of the basic parameters and presuppositions of a discipline. In such a case, the classroom goal of getting students to engage intellectually, emotionally and critically with challenging material has been met.

References

Kogawa, Joy. 1981. *Obasan*. Toronto: Lester and Orpen Dennys.
Marchessault, Jovette. 1985. *Lesbian triptych*. Toronto: Women's Press.
Rule, Jane. 1964. *The desert of the heart*. Toronto: Macmillan.

The Sherlock Holmes Approach to Critical Reading (Or How To Help Students Become Good "Detextives")

Kenneth Golby

Our culture worships speed and our breakneck academic pace mirrors this addiction all too well. One of the results of this is that the majority of our students read poorly; that is, they read to find out "what happens" (or in some disciplines to extract a few key principles) and ignore almost everything else they could learn if they read with greater awareness. McCluhan's suggestion that the medium is the message goes largely unheeded by most of our students and consequently few of them read critically. What follows is a brief description of one exercise I use at the beginning of a third-year course (taught in Spanish) in stylistic analysis to help students become good "detextives," to see more and become better readers.

In searching for ways to help students increase their awareness, I remembered spending two winters many years ago in a Gestalt therapy group led by Dr. Harvey Freedman of the University of Toronto. One of Dr. Freedman's many valuable dicta was that, no matter what the issue at hand, the lesson to be learned was simply (and of course it's never simple) to increase one's awareness. This principle has been invaluable in all my teaching and is particularly apposite in the aforementioned course.

When I begin by announcing that this course is designed to help students experience texts more richly than they do at present, most are intrigued, some are surprised (after all, isn't stylistic analysis akin to algebra?) and a few are doubtless offended by the suggestion that they are less than perfect readers. I suggest, *à la* Roland Barthes, that texts do not contain a single truth, but rather a number of equally valid readings and that collectively we can see much more than any one of us alone. As a way of gently pointing out our usual lack of awareness, I ask how many of them are aware of the beating of their own heart, of the colour of the eyes of the student next to them, of the pressure of their own bodies against the chair in which they are sitting, of the number of windows in the room (assuming we're lucky enough to be in a room that actually has windows), of their own breathing, etc.

Next I hand out copies of a laconic sixteen-line poem by the Spanish poet Federico García Lorca and ask them to spend three or four minutes reading it as carefully as they can. When the reading period is up the fun begins. I strive to give no answers or interpretations (although of course the questions reveal my own interests and biases) but to formulate questions that will enable (the word is important) students to realize how much they do not see and subsequently to begin to see more and more. What follows is by no means an exhaustive list, but perhaps it will give some idea of the process.

First come questions relating to point of view: Is this a panorama or a scene glimpsed through a microscope? Does the narrator view what he sees from within or without? Is the poem narrated in the past tense or in the present? What does the reader see on his or her mental screen? Is there action or is this a static scene? What about tastes, smells, sounds, tactile sensations? What patterns of associations are triggered? What are the stimuli for these reactions, Dr. Watson?

How does the syntax affect us? Does it differ from everyday speech? In what ways? Do the nouns refer to concrete things or abstractions? What are the rhythms like? What is the effect of the shift in rhythm between lines eight and nine? Given that the repetition at the end of the opening two lines does not provide any additional information, does it have any other function? Do the several references to round objects have any relationship to the circular nature of the poem and what does this suggest about the theme? Lines three and eight are identical except for the last word. Is this significant?

Cultural information also can be adduced. Some students will know that the Cordoba referred to is in Andalusia, not in Argentina, and that it was once the centre of a vibrant Moslem culture and therefore calls up nostalgic echoes of a long-gone exotic world. A question about the repetition of the exclamation "¡ay!" will spark someone to tell the class that this is the refrain of much flamenco song, that Gypsy art suffused with death, longing and suffering.

Words are not just associative triggers, they also have shape, form and sound. It is a linguistic commonplace that when asked which of the words "loomool" or "takat" they associate with the accompanying shapes,

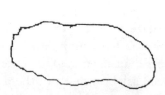 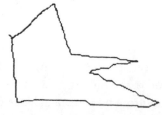

speakers of a wide variety of languages invariably associate the former word with the smooth shape and the latter with the jagged one. Hence, in literary studies at least, it is productive to ask about the effect of the patterns created by the repetition of particular vowels and consonants.

This entire exercise takes only ten or fifteen minutes, but it always produces expressions of pleased astonishment. Students inevitably express surprise at how little they saw at first and at how much they now see after responding to the questions. I always emphasize that *they* are doing the seeing and that *they* are the "detextives" who, with regular practice, can learn to be active readers who see more and more of the richness of any given text. Patient detective work allowed Sherlock Holmes to solve seemingly mystifying crimes. Leading questions can help our students begin to formulate their own questions, to take on increasing responsibility for their own learning and to go on enriching their intellects and their lives. As with many clichés, there is much truth in the saying that the best thing we can teach our students is that they need us to learn that they don't need us.

Sequencing Assignments

James Brown

My tutoring of students at York University's Centre for Academic Writing has made me very aware of the fact that writing assignments that seem relatively straightforward to us can be difficult for even bright students. The writing of an essay involves a very complicated series of processes. Students might perform poorly in the general task only because they run into some hurdle early in the process and just do not have, or know how to apply, the particular strategy that would allow them to overcome it. Sometimes the hurdle arises not so much because they lack a specific cognitive skill but because they do not understand the general context for the assignment, the set of assumptions that underlies writing in an academic culture.

Some Principles of Sequenced Assignments

Designing an assignment sequence is a technique I learned through York's Critical Skills Program (currently housed in the Faculty of Arts Centre for Academic Writing). One of the principles on which this program operates, in at least some classes, is that the intellectual skills – in terms of reading, writing and thinking – that are at the heart of the discipline should be explicitly taught. One way of supporting students in learning a particular genre, such as the research essay, and the cognitive skills associated with the process of its production is to break this process down into component parts and to make each part a separate assignment. Students can then be guided through a sequence of assignments, each designed to develop particular skills, and get feedback from the instructor at each stage.

Designing a Sequenced Assignment: An Example

To design this process-based sequence of assignments for my fourth-year English course, I first tried to think out, on the basis of my own experience in my discipline, a typical process of inquiry. I decided that the first step involves inventing an issue on which other scholars have written and that remains in dispute. The next step entails assembling the texts, generally those of a canonical author, that are relevant to the issue. These "primary" texts are then read from the point of view determined by the issue and with a view to generating an initial or tentative interpretation of the texts in terms of the narrow frame of interest determined by that issue. The next step involves reading secondary sources reflecting the knowledge of the discipline, with a view to figuring out their implications for, and solutions to, the problem. The results of this secondary research are then synthesized with the original interpretation of the text (see the example of a sequenced assignment that follows this article).

The academic model I've just described is, of course, too "staged"; the real process of doing literary research is much more recursive. For instance, someone working within the discipline would, at the time of inventing an issue, already know many of the relevant secondary sources and, in fact, would probably not be able to formulate a meaningful issue without such knowledge. Certainly my model of the process is an analytical construct, but I've found it to be a useful one, even for fourth-year students, whose sense of the relationship between literary criticism and the primary "canonical" texts is often vague and troubled. On the basis of this model, I designed the following sequence of assignments, which I present below in the form I give to my students.

The main advantage of sequencing assignments in this way is that it allows me to intervene in the process of students' writing and to provide direction as they go through that process. There are several other advantages as well. By arranging for students to read secondary sources only after they have formed a tentative view of the issue in a primary text, I have managed to encourage my students to read critics critically, not as a source of information about the primary text, but rather as a source of thoughtful opinion. I also encourage students to argue against at least some of the critics and to sense the "constructedness" of what these authorities propose as knowledge.

"Stage two" of the assignment promotes collaborative learning. It gives students an opportunity to write for an audience other than the instructor in the course: they write for their fellow students. Also, students write in a context in which their audience has a real need for what they produce. In general, it is a good idea to give students opportunities to create different modes of discourse – this one is expository, not argumentative – and to write for a variety of audiences. Sequencing assignments in this fashion helps students to develop their abilities to sense and operate within the constraints of different kinds of writing situations.

An Example of a Sequenced Assignment

Stage One: Research Exercise

What is the relationship between the state of "innocence" and that of "experience" in Blake's *Songs of Innocence and Experience*?

Our first classes will be largely devoted to a research exercise on the question above. This question will be the focus of our seminar discussions and the focus of some collaborative research, which we will conduct in the library. The research will be guided through three linked exercises and this whole process will be a kind of "dry run" for your final research paper. I will both respond to and evaluate your progress at each stage of the process.

Stage Two: Interpretation

Based just on your reading of Blake's *Songs of Innocence and Experience*, you will write an argumentative essay, first stating your position on the research question and then some arguments in support of it. Our class discussion of the Songs will precede and should inform your interpretation.

Due: third class

Length: 1500 words

Stage Three: Secondary Sources/Published Criticism

Each member of the class will write a one-page summary of one journal article or one chapter of a scholarly book that deals with the relationship between "innocence" and "experience." We will go to the library as a class to review the research process and to locate a range of relevant secondary sources. Each member of the class will choose a different article or book chapter and produce the one-page summary. I will reproduce these summaries and everyone will receive a copy of all summaries for the next stage.

Due: fifth class

Length: 250 words

Stage Four: Synthesis

Use the summaries to get a sense of the range of critical opinion on the subject of your original paper. Read a number of the books and articles, rethinking your original interpretation of Blake's text. Rewrite the original paper, taking into account my response to the first version and the criticism you've subsequently read. Use the secondary sources critically: feel free to argue against them on the basis of the primary text as well as to draw on them for authority and support for your interpretation.

Due: eighth class

Length 2500 words

An Experiment in Writing and Learning Groups

Jan Rehner

As teachers, many of us encourage our students to collaborate with each other to enhance their learning process, but sometimes overlook similar opportunities for collaboration ourselves. Happily, the experiment in student writing and learning groups that a colleague and I initiated in 1993 suggests that sharing resources and expertise across teaching units can lead to mutual advantage.

The idea for the writing/learning groups came from a Society for Teaching and Learning in Higher Education conference session given by faculty and students from the writing centre at Trent University. They outlined a model for establishing small writing groups among students enroled in the same communications course. Groups met every two weeks or so with a facilitator at the writing centre to complete a series of writing-to-learn exercises linked to course content. Participation in the groups was a graded component of the course and the course director worked closely with the writing centre in suggesting and designing writing topics.

Inspired by the Trent experience, Fran Cohen and I decided to adapt that model on an informal basis to a first-year humanities course, a team taught course with approximately 150 students divided among five tutorials. We decided on a modest experiment involving two of these tutorials: we invited students to form writing/learning groups of four with, ideally, two students from Fran's tutorial joining with two students from mine. In this way, we felt that students could compare their learning experiences and discover ways in which tutorials, even in the same course, set their own agendas and develop their own emphases.

To form the groups, Fran and I asked students who wanted to participate to hand in a sheet with their name and telephone number, listing in order of preference three hours during the week when they would be available to meet. Ten groups were formed on this basis and each was assigned a writing instructor. Since the writing instructors were already experts at facilitating discussions, diagnosing writing problems and developing strategies for solving them, Fran and I were confident about setting very flexible guidelines for their writing/learning sessions. Essentially, we were content as long as the students were engaged with some aspect of the course, such as analyzing assignments, comparing lecture notes, applying theory to course readings or learning to edit drafts. Rather than set specific tasks, we wanted each group to identify and pursue its own writing and learning priorities.

It was left to the group members to contact each other and make appointments directly with their tutors, following the same procedures at the centre as for individual students. Students were free to meet as often or as little as they wanted or needed, but to provide incentive, Fran and I agreed to reward those students meeting with their tutors eight times over the course of the year with a bonus of five marks.

At the end of the academic year, based on informal and formal student evaluations, we found that the writing/learning groups were a success. The students told us that they reaped a variety of rewards, including better understanding of course content, and learning and applying some essential critical skills. In approaching writing assignments and in discussing the writing process, they learned a wide range of strategies. They helped each other generate focused questions about the course and often brought those questions into the classroom. Most importantly, they had a forum for learning about the course outside the classroom, a forum that allowed them to take more risks, be more honest about problems and be more supportive of each other.

Instructors from the Centre for Academic Writing also enjoyed the small-group dynamics and felt that the teaching of some writing tasks, such as determining the subject and purpose of an essay, was enhanced when working with several students rather than one-on-one. Similarly, Fran and I both found that our tutorials were more cohesive and that our good and average students improved because of their group involvement. The writing/learning groups did not perform miracles; suddenly converting uninterested students into active learners. They did, however, provide an effective structure for helping motivated first-year students learn about thinking and writing strategies and about how they can help each other continue to learn outside the classroom.

To illustrate this effectiveness, I want to tell the story of one student in particular – I'll call her Sally – whose experience convinced me to continue using writing/learning groups in my humanities course. Sally was a member of a writing group that agreed to be videotaped analyzing the first essay assignment. When I watched the tape, I could see and hear how alienated Sally was. She complained about not understanding course material and about how "at sea" she felt with material outside her major discipline. She expressed anxiety about writing and about grades. Gradually, as the discussion progressed, she became silent. Other group members and the writing instructor noticed her painful frustration and tried to encourage her, suggesting strategies she might use to begin writing. Sally's first essay earned a C+, but I was still worried about her sense of not belonging in the course. In tutorials, she often seemed more skeptical than curious and she seldom offered any interpretations or ideas of her own.

Then, as Sally's group continued to meet, I noticed a change. She made friends with other members of her group. She began to answer, rather than only ask, questions. Occasionally, she even challenged or offered a qualification of comments from other students. She was excited by the topic for her major paper, a topic her group had helped her select and focus. Sally's major paper earned a B+ and she finished the course with enthusiasm and much-improved confidence in herself to meet academic challenges.

As Sally herself told me, her participation in the writing/learning group transformed her experience in the course and might even have transformed her first-year experience at York University. Instead of drifting and possibly drowning in a tutorial of thirty-three students, she found a lifeline in a group of five. Clearly, the groups do not have the same effect on everyone nor are they necessary to everyone, but Sally's story gains in relevance as we watch our classes grow larger. Good things amid increasingly difficult circumstances are more likely to happen when course instructors, writing instructors and students combine their strengths to reinforce the learning process. Course instructors help the Centre for Academic Writing by setting up the groups according to the times available for tutoring and by providing guidelines; writing instructors help course instructors by reinforcing essential critical skills and by keeping attendance records for the groups. Students, in intensive and interactive ways, learn to help themselves and their peers write and think clearly about course material.

Paper Chase: The Sequel

Betty Braaksma

Each academic year, instructors and librarians see a new crop of students who arrive at university with few or no skills in library literature searching. Yet most instructors expect that their students will be able to do a literature search to find sources for essays or other assignments. The successful undergraduate literature search is a complex process involving several levels of skill and judgement. The widespread use of diverse information retrieval technologies complicates the process even more. For students whose only previous experience in library research might have been using the clippings files in their high-school library, an academic library can be an intimidating place. In spite of the importance of library research and its complexity, most students do not get any kind of formal instruction in it and acquire the necessary skills through trial and error. How successful are they?

Faculty Survey Results

A faculty survey done in 1992 by York University librarian Anita Cannon shows that most York instructors were dissatisfied with their students' research skills, particularly at the first- and second-year levels. The survey further showed that faculty strongly support the idea of library instruction and that the majority feel that it is very useful to their students. This is very encouraging to librarians, particularly those who devote a great deal of their time to giving library instruction classes. But despite the survey findings, York's Scott Library's instruction statistics year after year show a consistent pattern: only 10 to 20 per cent of undergraduate students actually attend in-library instruction classes given by a librarian. What happens to the other 80 to 90 per cent of new undergraduates?

Ineffective Library Assignments

One possible answer, as indicated by the survey results, is that a significant number of instructors rely on library assignments or quizzes to act as the library instruction component of their courses. The usual intent of these quizzes is to familiarize the students with the physical layout of the library and also to expose them to the literature of the discipline. Oddly, from my perspective, even though these are library-based assignments, they are usually designed without any input from librarians. I believe that this is to the detriment of the quality of the assignment. Many quizzes focus largely on physical orientation or take a scavenger-hunt approach, with little or no explanation as to *why* students have to use these resources, *how* they have to use them or *when* it is appropriate to do so. Sad to say, quite a few quizzes are out of date (students are asked to look at the microfiche catalogue), inaccurate (students are asked to find sources that York Libraries do not own) or inappropriate (students are asked to count the number of nails in the sculptures in Scott Reference).

Librarians often are given no advance warning of impending quizzes or assignments, nor are they given copies of the assignments beforehand. Students usually have no previous orientation to the library or its resources and so do not even know where to begin when they cross the threshold. The result is that students and librarians alike are frustrated by the whole process. Students are turned off by this initial library experience and view the business of literature searching with the trepidation most of us reserve for major dental work. In addition to learning that literature searching is unpleasant and to be avoided at all costs, they learn that it is something outside of their course work, an "extra" that they have to find time for somehow.

Contemporary Research on Library Instruction

The library-science research literature has shown a marked departure in the past five years from results-driven, resource-based, mechanical methods of instruction to those using critical thinking techniques, active learning and other strategies designed to teach students the methodology and logic of literature searching, rather than the memorization of the resources to be used. Equipped with these skills, students should be able to translate their essay questions or assignments into concepts that in turn can be used to find appropriate subject headings or keywords in catalogues, CD-ROM databases or periodical indices. Students also should be able to understand the connections between indices or catalogues and the literature to which they point, as well as the processes involved in using resources effectively. The same skills that allow them to formulate good search strategies also help them to be better able to choose appropriate sources of information.

For example, an unskilled student assigned to write an essay on the effect of television violence on young children could overlook a book entitled *Media and Early Development* simply because it does not literally echo the essay topic. A student taught to think critically should recognize that the term "media" might well include television and that "development" used in this sense will probably be about children rather than economics or real estate.

The objective of the new emphasis on method rather than memorization in library instruction is to encourage students to be informed, independent and critical users of information resources. Quite simply, it helps them make good choices. As information retrieval technologies expand our access to resources, it becomes even more crucial for students to understand what the computers are presenting to them. Many students have an alarmingly uncritical attitude towards computerized information resources, which ultimately costs them in terms of time and the value of the information they are getting. A young man I recently helped at Scott Reference did a CD-ROM search that generated 1,079 citations. He had already spent an hour scrolling through half of them and had extracted exactly six that he could use before he came to me for assistance. He had unquestioningly accepted the omnipotence of the computer and did not know how to further refine his search, or even if the database he was using was appropriate to his needs. This scenario is played out hundreds of times each day, in each of our libraries, not just with CD-ROMS, but with Yorkline, CiteLine, periodical indexes, journals and books.

Developing Effective Library Assignments

How do we, as instructors and librarians, equip our students with the critical skills necessary to survive the literature search? Library instruction classes are a good beginning and I would urge each faculty member to promote the basic library workshops at Scott Library to their students, or to get in touch with the library instruction coordinator at the branch they deal with. However, I realize that not all instructors can take each of their classes to the library, nor does the library have the resources to hold classes for every section of every first- or second-year course.

This brings us back to the question of the library assignment. Many instructors have chosen this method as a way to get their students into the library without having to commit time to a formal library instruction class. This can be an effective approach, but only if done thoughtfully. Library assignments at the university level should be the result of a collaborative effort between the librarian and the instructor, with the common objective being the enhancement of student research skills. The faculty member knows the discipline; the librarian knows the system. Together they can fashion meaningful library assignments that can help students lose some of their fear of libraries and foster an appreciation of the complexities and rewards of doing library research. Most importantly, students should come away with an understanding of the *process* of doing library research and realize that these critical thinking skills can be applied not only to the library collections at York, but to a variety of spheres.

A library *quiz* that emphasizes orientation to the building or the memorization of specific sources does not encourage the development of these critical thinking skills. Rather, it encourages rote learning, memorization of limited resources, dependence on librarians or classmates for answers and avoidance of such tasks in future. A library *assignment* that allows the student to experience the enjoyment of the hunt, the satisfaction of the find and the excitement of discovery will go a long way to inspiring good scholarship.

Working with Students' Writing

Miriam Jones

Responding to students' writing is among the most challenging tasks facing a teaching assistant or inexperienced instructor. We all know the intense frustration of trying to make sense of the fractured prose of students who we know are interested in the class and are doing the readings, yet who lack the skills to articulate their understanding. When facing their papers, how do we begin to address the tangle of difficulties that compete for our attention? Teaching assistants trying to complete a graduate program have probably all felt a conflict between the time spent on their studies and the time spent teaching. We also have to decide how much time we can afford to spend marking essays and working with individual students. In meeting the seemingly overwhelming needs of our students, many likely have been tempted to jettison the syllabus and spend several classes on basic writing skills.

If we recognize a responsibility to our students who are less skilled in writing, we must indicate our interest to them and give them avenues to pursue on their own, in addition to working with them ourselves. We must not blindly conflate writing skills with diligence or intelligence; if we take a more pragmatic approach to writing and demystify the process for our students, they, in turn, will be less inclined to think of writing competency as an inexplicable talent bestowed from above and more as an achievable goal. Below are some guidelines that teaching assistants might find useful.

In Your Classroom

1. Do not assume that students know things. You need to spell out your expectations, especially to first- and second-year students.
2. Recommend reference books or appropriate style guides. See if you can convince your course director to add one of these titles to the required reading.
3. Provide detailed, written guidelines for assignments. Most essay questions I have seen emphasize the material, with little guidance about how to approach it. Focus on the processes that you would like your students to follow.

4. Explain general terms such as "analytical" and "organized." To some students these are just an empty mantra. They need to see concrete examples. (This is also a useful exercise for the tutor, as these terms are not easy to define.)

5. Be specific about how you will be marking the assignment. Explain your criteria to the class orally and consider making up a "response sheet" that breaks down the mark into such categories as research, writing etc., and their appropriate subcategories. This targets areas in need of improvement and highlights areas of achievement that might otherwise go unnoticed. Better yet, distribute this in advance when the essay assignment is distributed.

6. If you design your own assignments for your tutorial group, or at least participate in the design, make your topics directive, yet allow some scope for the more confident students. Try to include a component that bolsters the skill or process you would like to emphasize, such as research skills or close reading. Remember that you cannot teach students to do everything – read, write, research, analyze – at once.

7. Take class time to walk your students through developing a thesis and making a basic outline for an essay.

8. Consider breaking up the assignment into stages: for example thesis, outline, draft and final product.[1] Frequently students' problems result from starting at the end rather than the beginning of this process.

9. Often a student will have difficulties with an assignment that seem to be about writing (incoherence; lack of focus or development) but originate elsewhere. For instance, don't assume that your students know how to do research, especially first- and second-year students. Give them basic information about conducting research in the field. Also, many campus libraries provide introductory tours. Consider arranging one during tutorial time.

10. Consider having your students read each others' essays and give feedback. Clarifying their thoughts for a peer is an excellent way to help them towards a more focused paper.

11. As with any skill, the best way to improve is practise, practise, practise! Consider giving your students brief writing exercises at the beginning of class (five to fifteen minutes) that will be handed in but either not marked or considered as part of the participation grade. If we can work to remove the connection between writing and judgement and help our students explore the possibilities writing has for creativity, communication and clarifying thinking, we will go a long way to lessening their resistance.

Some of these suggestions initially might seem time consuming, but once you have them in place, you will appreciate the benefits of reading smoother, clearer essays and your students will experience more satisfaction with their work in your class and elsewhere. Of course, we must recognize the reality that we cannot spend as much time with each student as they might need, and so we must help them pursue other avenues on their own.

Student Services on Campus

1. At the beginning of the term, tell your students about any services your campus has to help students with their writing (for example, at York University we have the Faculty of Arts Centre for Academic Writing and the Atkinson College Essay Tutoring Centre, which provide one-on-one tutoring, various mini-courses and other services). Your students will ignore you. Tell them again when you hand out the first assignment and stress the importance of signing up early so that they can have more than one hurried appointment the day before the assignment is due. Many writing problems have little to do with grammar and syntax and everything to do with development of thesis and organization. Ideally students should visit a writing tutor shortly after receiving the assignment to toss around ideas about their thesis and various possible approaches they could take, well before they ever put pen to paper. However, most of your students will still ignore you until they get their first assignment back. Recommend the service again; many will now listen.

2. You can, of course, indicate more strongly to individual students that they should consider taking advantage of writing services on campus to develop their writing skills. To demonstrate your commitment to this goal, you could offer to negotiate due dates with students who are seeing tutors. This is especially important now that many writing centres are stretched to capacity and students can routinely wait two weeks or more for an appointment.

3. Some campuses provide a drop-in tutoring service. Students do not need to book these appointments in advance; they simply drop by the writing centre and visit a tutor from a rotating roster for brief quarter-hour appointments. In cases where your students have specific, manageable problems, you could suggest a drop-in appointment.

4. Some writing centres offer mini-courses, usually one to four sessions each, on specific skills such as developing an argument, proper referencing or structuring a sentence. Contact your campus writing centre for a full listing of courses to publicize in your class.

I would like to make it clear that most writing centres do not offer remedial services; they work with students at all skill levels. Anyone can improve their writing; I am certain that most of you reading this have highly developed writing skills yet routinely share your own writing with a trusted friend or colleague before you finalize it. We need to help our students learn that there is no stigma attached to visiting a writing centre.

Teaching Assistants and Writing Centres

1. You could request that an instructor from your writing centre come into your class and offer either a general session on improving essays or a specific discussion of how to approach the next assignment in your class.

2. Instructors can divide their classes into small groups and arrange to have each of these groups regularly visit a writing tutor to discuss class assignments, as part of the course requirements.[2] Under the present constraints, this is a practical and effective use of teaching resources.

3. You could attend any mini-courses that are offered to learn how writing instructors tackle the teaching of particular skills.

4. Many centres have amassed a considerable library of books and articles that address teaching writing, from current pedagogical theory to practical how-tos. Check out what is available there and in the campus library.

5. Take advantage of any professional development your campus has to offer. Even senior tutors can benefit immensely from sharing ideas. Many graduate programs are offering more training in teaching – a necessity in an increasingly competitive job market – and it is time well spent.

As classes grow larger and resources more stretched, our students will need us more than ever, while perversely, we will have less time to share with each of them. As tutors we must be committed to teaching students writing skills and we must work to find creative ways to fulfil this commitment in difficult times.

This is a revised version of an article that originally appeared in March 1995 in Core 5 (2): 8, 11.

Notes

Thanks to Susan Cohen at the Faculty of Arts Centre for Academic Writing for her comments on the original article. Many of these suggestions grow from the ideas of colleagues at York, particularly those in the Centre for Academic Writing.

1. See the article by James Brown, "Sequencing Assignments," in Section VII, Part 2.

2. For an example of how this works see Jan Rehner's "An Experiment in Writing and Learning Groups" earlier in this section.

What Happens After You Say, "Please Go to the Writing Centre"?

Jan Rehner

Many of my colleagues outside the York University Faculty of Arts Centre for Academic Writing sometimes confess that they have no clear image of what happens once their students enrol for one-on-one writing instruction. How, they ask, does one-on-one teaching differ from the individual conferences they often hold with students during office hours? Why, they wonder, do some students already enroled at the centre still hand in flawed assignments, and how can course directors and writing instructors work together to help students articulate their ideas in clear and persuasive ways?

Perhaps context is the most significant difference between one-on-one tutoring sessions and the individual conferences that many faculty have with students in their discipline courses. While instructors and students in the latter instance share a frame of reference grounded in the content of a particular course, the context of the writing instructor is grounded in the writing process as it applies to all of the student's courses. For example, while students in my own courses will often use office hours to ask me to clarify a particular assignment or read an initial thesis, their questions are invariably focused on how to express the content of the single course we share and on determining what I will be looking for when I evaluate their papers.

At the Centre for Academic Writing, however, I am very seldom dealing with my own assignments and I am not likely to be grading the final essay produced. Thus students can be much freer in expressing their concerns about writing for a particular course (or instructor), about the differences between writing a history paper and an English paper and about the individualized process they actually engage in when they write.

The foregrounding of the writing process is also, I think, vital to the special context provided by one-on-one tutoring. Students who come to me at the centre expect me to be an expert in writing; they do not necessarily expect me to be an expert in sociology or philosophy or geography. In other words, I can help the student learn strategies for generating ideas, for developing their ideas in analytical ways and for communicating their ideas clearly, but the student is essentially the "expert" in terms of content. This shift in status can be extremely empowering for students, but while it happens often and almost necessarily in one-on-one tutoring, it seldom happens during individual conferences with students in my own course. I teach the course; I grade their papers. No matter how earnestly I try to empower them, to convince them that I know the content of the course but not their interpretations of it, that structural reality of grading their papers remains.

It is also much more difficult to foreground process when I am dealing with students in my own course because they know that I know what might be missing in terms of content. So if one of those students brings me a draft and I suggest that the thesis is not clear, the student is often in some doubt as to what that suggestion might mean. Is this a writing problem or a content problem? Do I have problems with how the thesis is phrased or with the argument of the thesis? We all know, of course, how closely form and content overlap, but I find myself inevitably teaching content when I have conferences with the students in my course.

At the writing centre, the student and I still talk about what the student wants to write, but how to write it, discover it or organize it takes precedence more easily because I am not perceived by the student as having a dual and potentially confusing role. In other words, my responsibility, clearly seen by both participants, is to teach a range of writing, reading and thinking strategies that will help the student not only with the assignment at hand but also with future assignments and assignments in other courses and disciplines.

At the Centre for Academic Writing, I need to diagnose the particular process in which a student engages when she or he writes, make that process, with its strengths and weaknesses, explicit to the student, and determine with the student a set of writing priorities and strategies that will help her or him gain more control over, or at least comfort with, that process as it is applied to a range of academic disciplines over a period of time. It would be nice if the writing process were simple or if every student wrote the same way or if every discipline had the same methodology. Then I could be relatively assured that the advice I give to students writing assignments in my own discipline course could be generalized to their other courses.

Since none of this is so, one-on-one instruction tailors writing priorities and problem-solving strategies to individual student needs. This strikes me as a very different teaching task than giving the same general advice about, say, developing a thesis to large numbers of students. What works for one student might not work for another; there are just too many kinds of theses and too many styles for developing one. To help students write clearly and critically in the short time allowed amid all their assignments in all their courses during an academic year, I have to know what strategies they are already using, what is working and what is not working in the writing process, what strategies might need to be learned or altered, which strategies can be transferred across disciplines, and whether the student understands differences in methodology across disciplines.

If I am doing my job and all of this exciting stuff is being communicated, how is it that students enroled at the centre might still be submitting flawed papers to their course instructors? Well, first, and most obviously, it takes time to master the complexities of the writing process. There are no quick fixes. Second, in our teaching at the centre, my colleagues and I usually give priority to high-level thinking tasks such as analysis and organization before discussing patterns of error at the sentence level. For this reason, grammar is usually not a central concern until an individual has satisfactorily completed the larger tasks of an assignment. It would be easy for us to edit such essays but then we would not be teaching students how to write independently nor would we be ensuring that the ownership of the paper remains with the student. Further, in setting writing priorities, it would be irresponsible of me to spend an hour teaching subject – verb agreement if the larger problem experienced by the student was failure to understand the assignment or an inability to develop an argument. The key point here is not to assume that a student's writing is not improving on the evidence of a single paper. It could well be that the essay you are asked to grade, however flawed, is still much better than the first draft seen by the writing instructor.

Finally, remember that students write to learn even though it sometimes seems that they write only so we can measure learning. Students write economics papers to learn how to think like an economist, or philosophy papers to learn about how philosophy works. Course directors and writing instructors are partners in this learning process, each with a particular expertise. Our intentions and our pedagogy should be as clear as possible to each other and to the students. So if you really want to know what happens after you send your students to the writing centre, feel free to drop by, meet some of the instructors and perhaps arrange to observe a few tutoring sessions.

Evaluating Student Writing: Problems and Possibilities

Tom Greenwald

For many of us, evaluating our students' writing is a necessary but often frustrating task. Given the time and energy that we spend commenting on our students' essays, it is understandable that we feel the reward should be greater, that our students should pay more attention to our advice than many seem to do. After all, it is in their own best interests to become better, more effective writers. However, the next batch of essays provides fresh evidence that many of our students possess a virtual immunity to our evaluation of their work. Their writing improves, at best, only marginally.

Some Research Findings

Nancy Sommers (1982), in her article "Responding to Student Writing," investigates why students so frequently fail to heed the advice provided in evaluations of their writing. Her conclusion is disturbing. The fault, she suggests, is not so much a lack of diligence on the part of our students, but a problem with the kind of commentary teachers provide. After reviewing hundreds of essay evaluations, Sommers asserts that there are two primary reasons why students often ignore their teachers' advice: first, teachers display a strong tendency to appropriate their students' text, an action that students perceive as essentially hostile. As well, the comments that teachers make are most often general and not specific to the text, reinforcing the students' sense that the teacher is only interested in correcting the text, not reading it.

In appropriating the student's text, the teacher often sends the message, "Make the changes I want, or else." Because teachers often primarily identify errors in usage, diction and style, the student is left with the strong impression that these sentence-level errors take precedence over the meaning of the text and what the student is attempting to say. As a result, the student comes to see revision as "fixing" mistakes that the teacher has marked, rather than as a process of rethinking, reordering and rewriting the ideas contained in the text.

Second, Sommers notes that most teachers' comments are not specific to the text and, in fact, can be interchanged or simply rubber-stamped from one text to another.

Concerning teachers who write in generalities or provide only abstract commands, she states that

> This uniform code of commands, requests and pleadings demonstrates that the teacher holds a license for vagueness while the student is commanded to be specific...The problem presented by these vague commands is compounded for the students when they are not offered any strategies for carrying out these commands (153).

She later concludes that too frequently "teachers do not respond to student writing with the kind of thoughtful commentary which will help students to engage with the issues they are writing about or which will help them think about their purpose and goals in writing a specific text" (154).

Applying the Research

If Sommers is correct, faculty need to change their methods of evaluating student writing, something much easier said than done. As an instructor at the York University Faculty of Arts Centre for Academic Writing and as the critical skills coordinator for York's Vanier College, I have discussed the evaluation of student writing with many dedicated teachers, and I think we all would agree that changing one's approach to evaluation is a long-term and, on occasion, exasperating process. Sometimes this exasperation is the by-product of a particular approach. For instance, many teachers diligently try to catch every error or mistake in their students' essays. This approach takes a great deal of time, not to mention patience, and usually results in the student feeling utterly overwhelmed by the spectre of all that red ink. Instructors usually realize the limitations of such an approach, but are often uncertain about changing their method.

One way of beginning to alter the "correct mistakes" approach is for the teacher to avoid holding a pen or pencil when reading the essay the first time. With pen in hand, people have a strong tendency to point out each error as it arises, an activity that is guaranteed to distract the reader's attention from whatever "flow" the essay might have. Without a pen, the teacher is more likely to read the essay, to focus on what the student is saying or attempting to say. The result is that the evaluation eventually focuses less on correcting errors and more on those aspects of the essay that interfere with or enhance the reader's understanding of the writer's ideas. When the instructor assumes the role of interested (or confused) reader, the student might well begin to see imperfections in the essay in a different context. The advice the evaluator provides takes on the tone of "help me better understand this idea" rather than "fix this mistake."

While their methods differ, the most effective evaluators approach their students' essays with the same respect they show a colleague in their department whose paper they have been asked to critique. Their comments on student essays tend to be substantive, emphasizing strengths as well as weaknesses. They avoid comments such as "You should know better than to try to get away with this," which students perceive as personal attacks. While these evaluators might draw the writer's attention to a variety of weaknesses, they prioritize their concerns so students can grasp which aspects of their writing require the most urgent attention.

Creating a Grading Checklist

To emphasize their priorities as evaluators, some instructors create a formal checklist of concerns. The checklist places in order of importance the criteria upon which the work is judged so that the students see that a clearly stated thesis, a persuasive argument and an appropriate pattern of organization carry more weight in determining the teacher's response to the essays than, say, spelling errors, a category that might be included near the bottom of the checklist. Such errors are not neglected, but their importance is not overly emphasized either. Once a checklist is constructed, a copy can be returned to students after the instructor has completed the evaluation of the essay. The teacher provides a response to each item of the checklist, but reserves detailed commentary for the areas of most significant concern or praise.

Some instructors have stopped writing on their student's essays entirely. These instructors restrict their comments to a separate sheet of paper, which they later staple or clip to the essay. This approach shows respect for the students' ownership of their texts. It also necessitates that the instructor explain the comments and suggestions in more detail, providing the student with clearer explanations and more specific examples than are usually given when the teacher is writing in the margin of a page. This format allows teachers the space to discuss strategies that students can use to improve their subsequent drafts or essays. By emphasizing useful writing strategies, the teacher helps students who might recognize the same weaknesses in their writing that are so obvious to their instructors, but who have little notion of what they need to do to eliminate or reduce the problem.

Intervening in the Writing Process

Perhaps the most certain way to ensure that students take seriously the evaluations of their writing is for the instructor to comment on the first draft. When students have the opportunity to improve the grade of the essay, they pay much greater attention to their instructor's comments than when the grade is already a *fait accompli*. By intervening in the student's first draft, teachers emphasize writing as a process of gradual discovery, reevaluation and change. This conception about writing is foreign to most students, who struggle to get it "right" the first time.

However, many instructors feel that they do not have time to comment on first drafts. These teachers might consider requiring students to hand in "prewriting guides" before their first drafts. Such guides ask students to respond to specific questions related to their writing process before they start their first drafts. Here are some typical questions that often appear on prewriting guides:

- What are the subject and purpose of your essay?
- What is your working hypothesis?
- What kinds of information do you need and what sources will you use?

- Are there any key terms that need to be defined?
- Do you recognize any biases in your thinking?

The students respond to the questions in writing. If problems in a student's approach to the assignment are revealed, these problems can be addressed while the student is still in a position to make changes that will improve the essay. As well, when such guides are required, students often begin working on their writing assignments sooner, with the result that they have more time later for matters of revision.

Students also can profit from reading over and commenting on one another's first drafts. It must be stressed that teachers who adopt this approach must do so with a great deal of care and planning so that some students do not feel intimidated or threatened by having their work read by other students. Also, students usually need to be coached in how to provide constructive commentary. One method some instructors use is to pair students, have them trade essays and then have each student respond in writing to specific questions constructed to be as informative but non-threatening as possible. For argumentative essays, these questions might be:

- What is the thesis of the essay and where is it located?
- What did you like most about the essay? Explain.
- Where did you need more information? Explain.

Each student reads his or her partner's first draft, writes a response to the questions and gives the response to the partner. If class time is made available, they can discuss one another's critique. Students then use the responses of their partners to help them determine what they need to revise in the next draft. As well, many students find that constructively evaluating someone else's writing makes it easier for them to examine their own writing from a more detached perspective.

Audience Considerations

A hugely important variable in essay evaluation is the essay assignment itself. Vague assignments contribute massively to a student's writing difficulties. As faculty, when we write articles, we usually start with a clear sense of the task at hand, with knowledge of our audience's needs and expectations, and with a fairly accurate notion of the criteria upon which our audience will judge our work. We write "across" to peers and sometimes "down" to novices. How often do we write "up" to an audience who, we perceive, knows more than we can ever hope to learn? Yet we often provide our students with little help in dealing with any of these crucial considerations.

Essay assignments that provide students with a clearly defined task, a specific audience, and the criteria upon which the essay will be evaluated not only help nurture effective writing, but in fact make such writing possible. For instance, confusion concerning the audience's needs can lead to incomprehensible prose. Students fail to explain sufficiently an idea because they assume that their audience, the teacher, is a godlike figure who knows everything already and can thus make sense of even the most incoherent abstractions. Yet when these same students are asked to write to an audience of peers, the need for greater explanation and clarification might appear much more obvious.

The "audience" for student essays can take many imaginative forms if the instructor decides to set up the assignment in such a manner. For instance, the audience could be other students in the class, a stranger looking for something to read in a dentist's office, students attending a conference on a particular topic, a historical figure, a government official, a favourite aunt, the author of a text that the student is required to read, and so on, depending upon the instructor's goals. Expert writers often create a mental picture of their audience and use that conception to help guide the choices that they make when they write. Novice writers usually possess no such strategy and require help developing one.

Making Evaluation Criteria Explicit

Assignments that contain explicit statements of the criteria that the teacher will use to judge the essay promote effective writing. If students understand that the teacher highly values, say, a clear statement of thesis in the introduction and the use of specific examples to support generalizations, they can employ this knowledge in organizing their essays and planning their revisions. We teachers can benefit from this approach, too. In explicitly formulating our central criteria of evaluation, we can clarify for ourselves just what it is that we value most in writing, a process that could help us reconstitute our own goals and expectations. When it is practical to do so, instructors might consider asking students to assist in formulating the criteria upon which their essays will be judged. When students participate in designing the terms of evaluation, they might well accept greater responsibility for meeting the demands of the assignment.

Very few university-level instructors ever receive any training in how to evaluate student writing. Yet our evaluations represent one of our most important tasks as teachers. In considering our approach to evaluation, it is important that we explore all of the factors that influence the quality of the writing we will receive. We have more control over these variables than we sometimes realize. A final point: While many of us are reluctant to adopt the role of "writing teacher" when we evaluate our students' writing, we all have acquired a great deal of knowledge about what constitutes effective writing in our own fields. The task of evaluating our students' writing provides us with an opportunity to stress the role and significance of writing in our disciplines and to promote our students' ability to use writing as a means of discovery and analysis. Our students need this ability if they are to participate actively and productively in the construction of knowledge within our disciplines.

References

Sommers, Nancy. 1982. Responding to student writing. *College Composition and Communication* 33 (May): 153.

Fast, Fair and Constructive: Grading in the Mathematical Sciences

Alan Yoshioka

Fast and Fair

Marking is not mechanical work, unless the format of the assignment is multiple choice. You do need to exercise good judgement. Even in mathematics, there are usually several ways to solve a problem and there could be more than one correct answer. In one workshop I conducted, I asked teaching assistants to mark several sample solutions to a test. Different teaching assistants gave very different grades for identical answers and they all had good reasons for doing so. There is no absolute standard for which you must aim, but there are strategies you can use that will enable you to be fair to each student and consistent in your expectations, and that will save you time in the process.

As with many tasks, you will likely spend much of your time making a few hard decisions and speed through the routine areas. I often take less than fifteen seconds to verify that a half-page solution has all the key points, whereas I might spend five minutes on a solution that uses an alternative method or reveals a conceptual misunderstanding. You can save time and be more consistent by reducing the number of times you have to make tough decisions. The biggest time waster is having to go back and change the grade on something you've already marked. Also, the student might perceive you to be unfair if you scratch out one grade and substitute a lower one.

The most important way to save time and improve fairness is to mark all the answers to a single problem at the same time. I cannot emphasize this point enough. If you mark the whole assignment, one student at a time, there is far too much for you to remember by the time you get to the last few papers, so you will take longer and your grades might not be consistent. As you get tired or hurried at the end of your marking period, you could get increasingly irritable and mark harder, or become more lenient because you can no longer be bothered to watch for every little error. It does not matter very much if one problem is marked harder than another, but it is not fair to mark an arbitrary group of students harder than the rest.

Before grading the students' solutions to a particular problem, work completely through the problem yourself. This is important even when you are grading for another instructor who has provided a sample solution, because it will help you identify potential areas of difficulty. Complete the marking for each problem at a single sitting. This uses your short-term memory efficiently; your decisions will be fresh in your mind while you are marking, and then you will be done with them. Keep a scratch-pad record of your precedents for allocating and deducting marks. The next student who gives the same answer can be assigned the same mark almost automatically.

Once you are ready to begin reading through the solutions to a particular problem, it helps to first subdivide them by making a quick pass through the entire stack, sorting them on the basis of similarity of approach, and from best to worst. I call this "grading sideways." Begin with the best solutions for, as Graff (n.d.) writes,

> this saves the problem decisions until last, when I've gotten thoroughly familiar with all the possible mistakes the student can make. If you use sequential grading, Murphy's Law will ensure that the first paper you pick will be done in some weird manner, and you'll lose a lot of time trying to determine whether or not it was a valid method (n.p.).

Grading sideways avoids having to look back through the stack to change grades and is a big time saver.

My final suggestion is to reduce the number of decisions you have to make by limiting the possible outcomes; one way I do this is by marking each question out of five instead of ten. In the long run, provided you are consistent, the difference between seven and eight out of ten marks on one question on one assignment isn't worth the time and the agony it takes to make the distinction.

Making Criticism Constructive

Almost invariably, people who are fearful about mathematics or science have become so because of negative experiences they've had with the subject. You can ease their discomfort by encouraging your students in many ways.

1. Though you should not be afraid to point out errors, do look for something positive and give it a check mark, especially in a very poor answer.
2. Be specific about what's wrong. A big red X is generally not helpful to the student unless the error is an obvious computational one. Try to pinpoint where the student went wrong and check mark the last correct step. If you know there is an error but can't figure out where it is, say so.
3. Protect students' privacy by writing their overall assignment grade on an inside page.
4. Be concrete. If a student is confused about a concept, it is more helpful to give a concrete analogy than, for instance, to state the rule or theorem that has been violated. So, for example, suppose a student writes:

$$\frac{a}{b} + \frac{c}{d} = \frac{a + c}{b + d}$$

One response might be to insert the correct algebraic relationship, but a more helpful and thought-provoking response for the student might be to ask whether it is also true that

$$\frac{1}{2} + \frac{1}{4} = \frac{2}{6}$$

5. Consider adopting an additive marking scheme. Do you tend to grant points for correct steps, or deduct points for errors? The deduction approach – which I still use to some degree – creates an incentive for students to gloss over tricky points. The additive approach, on the other hand, encourages students to show all their thinking and allows you to identify and clarify their points of confusion. This can be a positive learning experience for the students, but it will not happen if they are deliberately vague or sketchy to avoid having marks deducted.

6. Grant partial credit. Many students who do not know the complete answer to a question will freeze and leave it blank. They often underestimate how much they understand about the problem and say they don't know where to start. The only thing they learn from that experience is helplessness. When a student leaves a question blank, I give them zero, but remind them that I give at least one point for any honest attempt, even if it is way off. Since I mark most questions out of five points, there is a fair incentive for them to try to get started.

References

Graff, William. n.d. *Fast, equitable grading.* Longview, TX: Le Tourneau College.

An Individualized Approach to Teaching and Evaluation

Gary Bunch

It is seldom that professors have the opportunity to reflect on the nature, organization and intent of their teaching. We often are too close to the task of teaching to see the "me" behind it.

In this short reflection on my teaching I attempt to step back and see the "me" in what I do. I relate my beliefs about the teacher – learner relationship, examine the various roles I play as a teacher and probe the practical meanings of my view of teaching. In this last regard I focus on the evaluative process in teaching. I show why and how I try to include my students in that process and provide information on how they have responded to the way I structure and evaluate my courses.

Before beginning, I should briefly describe the context in which my teaching has been formed. My early career was as a teacher of deaf students at the elementary, secondary and post-secondary levels. When I moved to the university I focused my teaching, research and writing on people with exceptionalities, those to whom learning does not come easily. I believe that much of what I do now is a result of working for years with those who challenged my teaching skills. My past has left indelible marks on my approach to teaching, marks that lead me to agree with Joubert that "to teach is to learn twice."

Let me now reflect on what it is that I have learned twice.

The Teacher–Learner Relationship

I have learned that I do not agree with traditional perceptions of the professor or teacher as the repository of knowledge and of the student as a passive recipient, memorizer, manipulator and regurgitator of knowledge. These perceptions arise from the traditional, or transmission, model of education in which knowledge is controlled by, and doled out by, the teacher. With the current knowledge explosion, the advent of personal computers, the changes in our understanding of human development, the acknowledgement that learning is an individual act, and the recognition that learning is most effective when the individual accepts responsibility for personal learning, the industrial age transmission model of instruction and learning is no longer acceptable. It simply does not work effectively across the wide range of learners at our universities.

What can replace it? I claim no overriding vision of a new model for the teacher–learner relationship. I know, however, what I am attempting to do as a teacher as I struggle to increase the effectiveness of student learning through the courses I design and offer. It is, in truth, a struggle for me since I initially studied teaching under the transmission model, am experienced in it and cannot reject it fully or with ease. To a considerable degree it has played a role in leading me to where I am as a teacher. In fact, if I were to reject it completely, I would be guilty of over-reaction and of throwing out the baby with the bath water. The best I can do is acknowledge that I am a product of certain formative experiences, accept the need to move forward in my teaching and attempt to understand the changing principles and understandings that guide my teaching. Of particular concern in the last regard are my views concerning how the roles of teacher and learner evolve over the duration of a course.

The Framesetter

I consider my role as teacher in any class to change as the course proceeds because the learner changes as the course proceeds. Initially, I work as a framesetter, an individual who lays out the general parameters of subject theory and content. In this capacity I develop certain themes of thought, knowledge and action as I understand them in the field under consideration. In many ways I take a traditional role as transmitter of information to students and attempt to establish a basic familiarity in them with the knowledge base of the area of study. Transmission takes place through lecture, assignment of selected readings, guest speaker presentations, audio/visual resources and discussions. All are aimed at establishing an initial shared base of theory and fact for the two partners in the learning process, the students and the professor. It is necessary to have this shared background so that the partnership has a mutual base from which to function.

Simultaneously, I overtly introduce and attempt to model the notion that learning is a collegial activity with both parties in the process having certain responsibilities. The primary role of the professor is leading the student to awareness of the area of study and fundamental aspects of that area. The primary role of the student is to become familiar with these fundamentals in order to move forward in understanding.

I find that most of my students interpret this difference in roles to mean that the professor talks and they listen. They do not regard learning as a collegial, interactive process. If my concept of education as interaction between colleagues, albeit colleagues with differing roles, is to be actualized, I must order my teaching to lead students to value and desire incisive interaction.

The Guide Colleague

To stimulate interaction I gradually withdraw from the role of purveyor of information to that of a person who, while familiar with existing understandings of a subject area, never ceases examining those understandings in critical-analytical fashion. I attempt to become a guide colleague, one who draws attention to new and different parts of the field in which the student is engaged. I strive to make students realize that not all that is known about an area of study is set in stone and that one of their first tasks is to question knowledge. Students often are somewhere between hesitant and loathe to query what a professor or a book says, but I believe that education cannot proceed unless we critically analyze that which we are learning.

To initiate this questioning stance I emphasize problematic aspects of theory and fact. Discussion and debate, minority points of view and the relationship of theory to practice form the basis of class meetings. A quite specific effort is made to create sets of teacher–student, student–teacher and student–student interactions that probe what we believe to be the corpus of knowledge of the area under consideration.

During this phase I find that definite movement away from reliance on transmission of information from one person to another occurs, though the professor continues to function didactically on occasions when the direction of discussion or debate requires the insertion of specific information. Such occasions occur routinely when discussion evokes alternative, minority interpretations of existing theory or fact, or when the opportunity arises to extend background and detail of accepted theory or fact. A shift has been made, however, in the role of the professor from directly transmitting knowledge to stimulating and guiding learning indirectly.

At the same time the role of the student has begun to evolve towards co-setting the direction and content of learning and, as we will see, taking responsibility for evaluation. The professor continues to take the lead role in the teaching-learning process but at a much-muted level in comparison to the framesetter stage. The student is moving to the fore in terms of increased familiarity with basic theory and fact, confidence in aspects of the area of study and curiosity to know and understand more.

The Mentor Colleague

Finally, I combine the guide function with that of a mentor colleague, among whose responsibilities is that of responding to and commenting on the student colleague's ability to demonstrate his or her developing control of course content. Prosaically, we refer to this as grading assignments. But it is more than the term would suggest. Students take the lead in submitting evidence of their appreciation of theory, fact and issues. This evidence takes the form of formal papers, in-class presentations, debates, videos and other individually negotiated projects. The form of submissions can vary, but any submission must be focused on revealing a student's critical understanding of an aspect of the field under study.

My role at this point is to provide feedback on the content, organization, strength of argument and other aspects of the students' work. I point to ways in which understanding might be furthered and communication of understanding to others might be strengthened. My objective is to lead students to question and strengthen their understandings of the field of study, to become familiar with relevant readings and to develop the desire to provide evidence of their understandings in acceptable, clear and powerful academic style. Throughout the evolutionary process described above I am guided by three key beliefs:

1. Students learn most effectively when they are treated as independent, yet collaborative, learners who participate in making decisions regarding how and what they will study.
2. Learning is enhanced if high standards are set by both the professor and the learners for developing a critical appreciation of the course material.
3. Learners should be permitted and encouraged to demonstrate the strength of their critical appreciation in ways best aligned with their individual learning styles.

Evaluation

All this leads to evaluation, the assessment of demonstrated learning. As I prepare for each course, I lay out in the course outline a series of assignments that I have found will permit students to engage major portions of the theoretical and factual bases of the course. For each I note a percentage value and a due date. Some assignments lead to a minor paper, some to an in-class presentation and others to a major paper. (Collaboration on papers and presentations is permitted.) The option of taking one or more tests is included as well. Sufficient assignments are described to permit each candidate some degree of choice, while meeting all evaluation requirements.

These assignments provide a framework within which students who respond best to structured situations can operate comfortably. The option is there to pursue stated assignments, with specified values, due at specified times. A number of students in each of my classes opt for this structured format for assignments. It fits well with their learning styles and permits them to plan their academic and personal timetables.

Other students welcome opportunities to follow paths not quite so beaten. Such students are permitted and encouraged to design assignments that they believe will satisfy course standards and allow them to work through their personal areas of learning strength. Alternative assignments can be suggested to meet all course requirements except participation in class discussions and other in-class activities. Whereas the majority of student-designed assignments are relatively routine, students have utilized interpretive dance, videos, guest presenters and short dramas as ways of exhibiting their learning in personally meaningful ways. My guideline in this area is that no idea is too creative to receive consideration. It takes students some time to understand the possibilities opened by this guideline. To guard against misinterpretation I make clear early in each course the basic rule that all alternative projects must be discussed with me.

As noted earlier, due dates are given for each instructor-designed assignment, but they are suggestions only. In an attempt to lead students to assume some control, I inform them that all assignments can be submitted at other times as dictated by their individual timetables, with the proviso that the instructor be informed in advance. Students are told as well that choosing an alternative date means that the assignment might be submitted at a time when I have planned for activities other than grading assignments. The logical consequence is not some type of penalty but that the turnaround time and amount of feedback might not be the same as for assignments handed in on the suggested due dates. This is the tradeoff that the student accepts for flexibility in due date. Students are advised of the wisdom of creating a plan for submitting assignments over the full term of the course and of the risk of digging a pit for themselves if they delay doing and submitting assignments. I make clear that I will feel little responsibility for saving students from self-dug pits at the end of the course. Significant numbers of students elect the flexible due date option; not all handle well the responsibility for self-direction that comes with it. That, too, is part of learning.

Students are advised early in each course that percentage values for structured assignments or tests are not inviolate. The option of suggesting alternative percentages is available. In cases where students suggest valuing a single assignment heavily (in my terms, at more than 40 per cent), they are advised of the associated risk and asked for a rationale. In all possible instances, the plans advanced are accepted so long as sufficient work is undertaken to demonstrate appreciation of course content. More heavily weighted assignments should not be misconstrued as opportunity to do less work. The size and value of assignments is not considered as important as the type of assignment and the thought that goes into completing it. I find that few students suggest realignment of percentage values by more than five or ten per cent, but the positive reaction that I get for this particular type of student input amazes me every year.

These short discussions indicate that students can determine how they will provide evidence of their learning, that they can dictate the timing of assignment submissions and that they have some control over the value of assignments. Each of these is taken a step further by permitting students to change their minds on type of assignment, timing of submission and value up to the point of actual submission, or, in the case of tests, to the point of seeing the test questions. I believe that there should be room for second thoughts without penalty. I also believe that the most effective learning is reached through giving the student as much ownership of effort and outcome as possible. The pedantry of the traditional teacher-centred classroom model, in my view, fetters learning for a goodly number of students. Education is more about minimizing fetters around learning than arbitrary regulations and instructor convenience.

Student Misinterpretation

The degree of flexibility I design into my teaching is not without its dangers. I find that a limited number of students mistake flexibility, individualization and friendliness for a lack of standards. The quality of product I demand as evidence of understanding most often dispels this notion, shocking a few students and motivating a fair number of others. Some students are weak in making effective use of their time and run into the danger of leaving too much work to the end of the course. The structured due date system helps some of these students. I kept track of the records of all students and frequently remind the class that some are busily digging the pits I warned them of earlier. Those who lag far behind I see individually and point out the danger they are facing. Some students ask to have the value of an assignment increased or decreased after they have received their grade. I congratulate them on their courage and creativity and say "No." Word quickly gets around that once a student has chosen a particular path, the prof will not clear a new one for him or her unless a valid reason such as illness or family misfortune creates the necessity.

Student Participation in the Evaluation Process

I encourage student participation in grading in a number of ways. I give the option of peer evaluations for all presentations. In some classes the allocation of the presentation grade is divided evenly between the instructor and the peer group. In others, where the presentation value is modest, peers grade alone. In all instances those making a presentation can take part in their evaluation. My rationale is that no one else knows the learning and effort associated with a presentation as well as the presenters. I find that students approach evaluation of peers seriously and follow the grading guidelines (Figure 1) that I have designed with care. I find as well that peer evaluations and my own are closely similar, with mine a trifle less appreciative of the strength of presentations.

Students are involved in determining their class participation grade as well. As instructor I am able to note such things as attendance patterns, contribution to class discussion and consultations outside of class. Only the student is aware of participation in terms of concentration during class, outside readings, discussions of class topic with others and amount of study. Blending the two views creates a wide-ranging, collegial analysis of this element of the course. This is a technique I continue to ponder. The majority of students rate their participation quite highly, and I wonder if we have a difference in standards in this area or simply a difference in viewpoints, with one side keeping a keener eye on the eventual course grade. On this point I continue to believe that the value of involving students in their evaluation and in exhibiting trust outweighs any negative aspects.

Tracking

The procedures described above require careful individual tracking. To assist in this I provide an individual assignment choice form to each student (Figure 2). Students have access to these forms at each class and between classes by appointment. They are required to keep the form updated in terms of assignments chosen or contemplated, value of assignments and dates for submission. Each of these elements can be changed prior to submission to meet individual timetables, student perceptions of the quality of their work and other factors. I review the assignment choice forms weekly. My experience is that this approach to assignments requires an additional commitment of time. The additional record keeping and student consultations are rewarded by the quality of student learning.

Figure 1. Presentation: Peer Evaluation Form

Presenters: _____

Grades: A+   A   B+   B   C+   C   D+   D   E   F
Each category may be graded or the presentation as a whole may be graded.

CATEGORY	Grade	Comments
CLARITY:	_____	_____
Clear discussion of topic.		_____
		_____
MOTIVATION/INTEREST	_____	_____
Ability to hold audience.		_____
		_____
ORGANIZATION	_____	_____
Parts of seminar interrelated well.		_____
		_____
CONTENT	_____	_____
Advanced student knowledge of topic.		_____
		_____
RELEVANCE	_____	_____
On topic. Linkage of theory and practice.		_____
		_____
RESEARCH	_____	_____
Wide-ranging grasp of topics and resources.		_____
		_____
HAND-OUT	_____	_____
Clear review of seminar. Valuable for future use.		_____
		_____
TOTAL GRADE	_____	

Figure 2. Individual Assignment Choices

NAME: _____

Structured Assignments

1. Field experience. Interview with an individual labeled with   30% _____
   an exceptionality. Focus on societal barriers to community
   acceptance. Critically analyze information obtained and
   relate to lectures, readings, research.
   Due: October 30

2. Field experience. Critical review of an agency offering   30% _____
   services to individuals with a particular exceptionality.
   Focus on objectives of agency and ability to attain them
   given resources and philosophy. Obtain client views.
   Due: January 15

3. Term paper. A formal academic paper examining a   40% _____
   selected exceptionality. Include historical review. Focus
   on societal barriers and assists. Look to appropriate
   societal responses to barriers. Include critical analysis.
   Due: March 12

4. Test #1. A take-home test focused on major dynamics   15% _____
   of lectures and readings.
   Due: October 30

5. Test #2. A take-home test focused on major dynamics   15% _____
   of lectures and readings.
   Due: January 15

Optional Activities

1. Student-suggested alternate assignment.   _____%

2. Student-suggested alternate assignment.   _____%

Notes: 1. All alternate assignments must be negotiated with course director.
       2. Changes to original choices must be cleared with course director.
       3. One assignment must be completed in fall term.
       4. Due dates are suggested only. Other hand-in times to be cleared
          with course director.

Student Reaction

All the above is premised on the assumption that the teaching-learning process is an interactive collegial undertaking that proceeds most powerfully when the learner is able to take ownership of personal learning. At the university level "learning" is a process between adults where one has teaching and evaluative responsibilities and the other has responsibility for learning and demonstration of learning. The professor is charged with provision of an environment that reaches out to individual learners in ways that encourage independence and maximize the quality of the learning experience. Additionally, in any course there are things to be experienced beyond the theory and fact of a discipline. Learning about oneself is one of them. In the courses that I teach, these three areas – theory, fact and self – form a triumvirate at the base of course design.

How do the students feel? In preparation for this discussion, I asked members of one of my classes to let me know anonymously what they thought of the format of the class. The following are some of the remarks they offered.

[This class] has given me the chance to excel at my own rate and has allowed me the ability to choose what I feel I am most interested in within the field of exceptionality [the course focus], therefore allowing me to concentrate my efforts on areas I enjoy. When you are given the freedom to choose an area of study, I believe the learning experience will prove more rewarding.

[The class] gives students opportunity to be creative by letting them choose subjects..., giving the challenge to notice material covered in class when we are out in the community.

[The] evaluation procedure allows for students to express and build on their strengths and interests. Flexibility on choices of assignments and due dates allows students to take responsibility for their own learning and permits a reasonable amount of time for research. Expectations are very high and yet this appears to evoke superior products from students.

[The] marking scheme works well for all types of students because it offers the stability that some need (topics, grades, dates) and the *total* flexibility that others need. For me, it has been such a *relief* this year, that I can shape the course to suit me. By now I know how I do best, and how to manage my time.

In my mind, much of what I do in teaching and evaluation can be defined as the development of collegial mentorship. I believe that learning should be a collegial relationship whatever the age and ability of the learner and whatever the topic. I attempt to activate that collegiality despite tuggings that I feel at times to assume the power that the role of professor can give. The tuggings are quite strong when my time is rushed and the occasional student pushes against the boundaries of my flexibility.

However, the years that I have spent with students who experience exceptional challenge in learning, as well as with regular students, have persuaded me that the most powerful learning for all occurs under conditions of mutual respect, student choice and involvement, and flexibility. The interest, application and learning of the majority of my students reinforce me in my approach to teaching and evaluation and encourage me to continue to refine them.

The Norwegian Motivator, or How I Make Grading Work for Me and My Students

Ken Carpenter

There's a story, perhaps apocryphal, about the introduction of medicare in Scandinavia. In one country, let us say Norway, the government gave doctors a range of different methods for receiving payment and all doctors were allowed individually to choose ones for themselves. Another country, let us say Sweden, announced one payment plan to be applied to all doctors alike. Only one country's doctors went on strike. Which one it would be is entirely predictable.

Perhaps the Norwegian doctors were too busy mulling over the various schemes to work up sufficient irritation to fuel a strike, but as teachers we can recognize a more important aspect of their experience. By the very act of choosing their own scheme – on the basis of their own needs and preferences – the Norwegian doctors came to identify with the medicare program. What they identified with they were motivated to make succeed.

For the past twenty-five years and more I have patterned the assignments in all the classes that I teach (in the faculties of Arts, Fine Arts and Graduate Studies) on the principle that a primary task of *teachers* (it might be best to pass a self-denying ordinance and never say "faculty members") is to ensure that their students can identify with the assignments. At the core of my method is the multi-option "commitment sheet" (Figure 1) that allows each of the students to choose *on an individual basis* how they wish to be graded. It's important that the different plans are seen to entail different kinds of work.

To ensure that this procedure is believable to the students, I take class time to emphasize that I take pleasure in their success and want to set things up so that they can make the best use of their particular abilities and do well in the course. I *do* promise not to "curve" them down if the class does well as a whole. (I *don't* promise not to escalate the rigour of the class as we go along.) I also counsel them not to allow the option of choosing to paralyze them – it's out of that concern that I label the hand-out "commitment sheet" and set an initial deadline for choosing.

Figure 1. Commitment Sheet

This course has a three-option grading scheme; the bottom portion of this form is to be submitted by the last class in September. You will be allowed to change your plan at any time (subject only to deadlines) if you wish – just give me a note saying you're doing so.

PLAN I*	One essay (due Dec. 14)	50%
	Two tests (late Oct., Dec.)	50% (25% each)
		100% of course work
PLAN II	Two four- or five-page "reports"	
	(due Nov. 11 and Dec. 16)	50% (25% each)
	End-of-term test**	50%
		100% of course work
PLAN III	Three one-hour tests	33⅓% each
		100% of course work

*The late-October test (Plan I) covers syllabus topics 1–3; the December test covers topics 4–7. Each is one hour long.

**The end-of-term test (Plan II) covers all topics and is two hours long.

— — — — — — — — — (Detach here) — — — — — — — — — —

Economics 3120.03: Please keep a record of the plan you have chosen.

NAME _____

I have chosen PLAN _____

Two parallel actions are extremely important: I allow students to choose the dates for their term test by majority vote ("It is not my position to tell students when they can do their best work – you tell me") and I regularly tell the students that they are more capable than they think.

The costs of this procedure are not great and the returns over the years have been considerable. The main cost is that one class might be lost to an alternative test, although, if one of the plans is less popular than the others, students might be happy to schedule a test outside of regular class times. There is also the time required to make up extra essay topics and test papers. For a teacher thinking in terms of the long run and the accumulation of "human capital," that is, a bank of test and essay questions, this is by no means prohibitive.

The principal benefit is that students' attitudes change substantially. I get numerous comments to the effect that, "We wish all our classes were like this"; "We work much harder for this class than we do for other classes because we know we can excel if we really work and think"; "It feels good to know that our teacher expects us to be successful"; "I would have hated the other assignments, but I was engrossed in mine." The satisfaction this brings to all parties is not to be underestimated. A secondary benefit is that students are more willing to accept rigorous demands; this is especially so if they are reminded on occasion that rigour helps to maintain *their* reputations.

University teachers can maintain rigorous standards and at the same time establish a community of interests uniting students and teacher in the classroom. The commitment sheet or "Norwegian motivator" method is only one of many procedures that can work to this end, but it has been highly successful for me. I would never go without it.

Section VIII:
Developing and Assessing
Your Teaching

Part 1 of this section opens with informal tools for assessing and developing your teaching. The first four articles describe simple, informal classroom assessment techniques you can use to determine whether students have learned core material. The Newton article provides a brief overview of the nature of classroom assessment techniques and the different ways that they can be used. Following that is an article by Aldridge and Merrens that speak of the usefulness of the "One-Minute Paper" in different disciplinary settings. A second article by Newton urges faculty to use increasingly more challenging questions in One-Minute Papers to encourage higher levels of intellectual skill development among students.

While those first articles suggest simple techniques that a teacher could readily use to assess learning in a given class, the subsequent articles in this section focus on the evaluation of a course. Part 2 addresses formative course evaluations. The Everett article distinguishes between year-end assessments, or summative evaluations, and formative evaluation surveys that are carried out midway through a course. He applauds the value of formative evaluation surveys since the teacher gets the feedback in time to make changes during the course. Alternative types of formative evaluations are described in the articles by Lang, who uses a student feedback committee, and by McKenna, who solicits student feedback in a variety of ways throughout the course.

Part 3 focuses on peer pairing, a collegial way to evaluate and develop your teaching. The Sbrizzi article describes the basic logic of peer pairing, in which partners observe each other's teaching, consult with students and give each other feedback. Though Sbrizzi describes a model that works with institutional support, two colleagues could easily follow this model's guidelines without institutional intervention. The article by Whalen *et al.* describes in detail how peer pairing worked for a group of colleagues in French studies. The benefits of peer pairing accrued not only to the faculty members: students' awareness of the peer-pairing process enhanced the learning atmosphere of the class as students came to appreciate that their input was valued.

The last two parts of this section include guides developed by York University's Senate Committee on Teaching and Learning: the Teaching Evaluation Guide (Part 4) and the Teaching Documentation Guide (Part 5). The Evaluation Guide offers useful advice and guidance for those wishing to develop and improve their teaching using a range of formative and summative methodologies for evaluating teaching effectiveness. Likewise, the Documentation Guide offers assistance with documenting the variety and complexity of an individual's teaching contributions. In combination, the guides promote good teaching by encouraging systematic teaching contributions and reflective practice among university teachers at all stages of their academic careers.

Improving Student Learning Through Feedback: Classroom Assessment Techniques

Janice Newton

In 1990, I had the good fortune of attending a week-long workshop on Classroom Assessment Techniques, based on the work of Patricia Cross and Tom Angelo.[1] Though I was familiar with many of the teaching techniques presented at the workshop, the logic of classroom assessment was new to me and I found it a compelling approach to thinking about teaching and improving student learning in my classes. After the workshop, I found myself thinking about teaching in entirely new ways and was inspired to adapt existing assessment techniques and develop some new ones for my political science classes.[2]

Classroom assessment differs from what most of us would call teaching techniques. It responds to the core challenge of teaching: when we teach something, how do we know the students "got it"? Often that question is answered by a midterm examination or test, but by then it is too late to address the gap between what we thought we taught and what the students actually learned. Classroom assessment techniques respond to this problem. These simple, easy-to-administer techniques can be used throughout any course. Typically, in a variety of ways, they ask students to demonstrate their understanding of what was just taught. Each classroom assessment technique usually embodies the following traits:

- It solicits only information that will help you, or the students, do a better job.
- It is anonymous (usually).
- It is ungraded (usually).
- It should be easy for students to complete and for you to assess.
- The aggregate results are always given back to the class.

Student responses are collected to measure what was learned in a particular segment of a course or class. While individual students might be curious to see whether their understanding fell in line with that of the rest of the class, the overall class pattern of what was or was not learned is of more interest to the instructor than any individual response.

Classroom assessment techniques can be wonderful ways to make lectures more participatory and they can promote active learning in any class setting, from a large lecture with three hundred students to a small graduate seminar.[3] Rather than waiting until the midterm test, we can use an assessment technique in the middle of a lecture; for example, to see if the students understood an important concept discussed in that lecture. It is crucial, however, that we do not stop at this point. Once we have gleaned information about what students have learned, we must summarize the students' responses and report them back to the class as soon as possible.

This feedback process does two crucial things. First, it engages students in an ongoing reflection on whether they are understanding course material and it encourages them to self-monitor their own learning regularly. This creates opportunities for students to act immediately on gaps in their learning, rather than waiting for the midterm to get such feedback, at which point it is often too late for the student to recover lost ground. Second, if there is a significant gap between what I thought I taught and what the students can demonstrate that they learned, then I am forced to reconsider how I initially delivered, organized or presented the course material. Because the feedback is immediate, usually collected in one class and summarized in the next, I have the opportunity to teach the material in a different way in response to the gaps in student learning.

Rather than relying on impressionistic measures, such as the looks of interest in students' faces as I lecture or the responses of the few students who do talk in class, this method gives me a concrete measure of the success of my teaching – based soundly on what students have or have not learned. The genius of classroom assessment, I believe, is this recursive quality that keeps both students and faculty truly focused on whether students are learning the course material. Students are drawn into the process of regularly monitoring their own learning in the course and faculty are challenged to continually adjust and tailor their teaching in response to student learning.

The three articles that follow discuss variations of the assessment technique called the "One-Minute Paper." This has become a popular technique because it is easy to use and can be adapted readily to any class size or subject. A variation on this is, "What was the muddiest point in today's lecture?," which helps identify segments of a class that need clarification. I have also adapted the "Background Knowledge Probe," which I use in the first class of an "Introduction to Politics" course. I design about twenty questions on areas of background knowledge that I might expect to take for granted in preparing lectures for the course: general political history, institutional knowledge, terminology, etc. Students are asked to indicate whether they have never heard of the term, are somewhat familiar with it but not too sure or whether they understand it clearly and could explain it to a friend. Based on the results of this background knowledge probe, I can adapt the course outline and lectures according to areas of acknowledged weakness and strength in students' background knowledge.

This is but a small sampling of the range of techniques assembled by Pat Cross and Tom Angelo. In their book you will find a wealth of ideas for classroom assessment techniques, some more complex and difficult than others, but with some imagination, many of the techniques can be adapted readily for use in your own courses. It is worth the effort to improve student learning in your classes.

Notes

1. For examples of the techniques discussed at the workshop see Cross and Angelo (1988).
2. For an example of one assessment technique I developed to deal with the problem of plagiarism, see the article "Plagiarism and the Challenge of Essay Writing: Learning From Our Students" in Section V.
3. See the Rogers article, "Improving Student Learning in Lectures," in Section VI, Part 1.

References

Cross, Patricia K. and Thomas A. Angelo. 1988. *Classroom assessment techniques: A handbook for faculty.* Ann Arbour, MI: National Center for Research to Improve Postsecondary Teaching and Learning.

The One-Minute Paper ...
Two Success Stories

Keith Aldridge and Roy Merrens

The two stories that follow were contributed to Core, York's Newsletter on University Teaching, in reaction to the publication of an article describing the One-Minute Paper[1]. Each story documents the unexpected nature of the feedback the technique can elicit from students and the power this gives the instructors to modify their teaching.

Roy Merrens:

What I've been reading recently about the One-Minute Paper finally convinced me I really had to try it. The notion of a cheap and simple tool that offered instant feedback, for both students and teacher, was irresistible. I decided to use a One-Minute paper during a two-hour class session in which I was planning to present some especially important material. The purpose of the lecture component was, in fact, to identify and elaborate upon two ideas central to the entire course.

I made the two points in what was, I thought, a remarkably lucid lecture presentation. I distributed scrap paper and asked the students to take a minute to jot down, anonymously, in just a sentence or two, the two main points of the lecture. I then collected and read their responses. The results were revealing indeed – to the students as well as to me. The most revealing response read as follows:

> Professor Merrens:
> I don't want to come across as a "smart ass" but I really don't know what your message is. I think an overhead or some other (sic) would be better in getting your message across. Instead, I have been watching the sunlight move across the wall behind you. It honestly seems more interesting. It moves about one cm every one and a half minutes. I never really noticed it before but it is sort of interesting.

...A salutary reminder, among other things, of the fact that I can't draw reassuring conclusions about my effectiveness as a teacher from the interested expressions on the faces of the students.

Keith Aldridge:

At the first meeting of my Introductory Earth and Atmospheric Science course last fall, I asked my 149 students to take a single sheet of paper and write on it, in one or two sentences, their response to the following questions:

- What was the main point of my lecture today?
- What point was least clearly made?

I informed the students that their papers would be collected at the end of the lecture and I would respond to their comments in the next lecture. They seemed visibly to brighten at the thought of really having a chance to affect the proceedings rather than filling in a form at the end of the term and not realizing any benefits themselves from their comments. Neither the students nor I appreciated how revealing and literally clarifying this new procedure would be as the course unfolded.

My first experience with the One-Minute Paper revealed that most of the class had never heard of a concept called 'angular momentum' even though I had mentioned it at least a dozen times in the lecture. So I put together a small demonstration for the next lecture and gave a short tutorial on this important idea. The students seemed to appreciate this and it was a pleasant reward to find that day's One-Minute Papers said so. This began our exchange through anonymous notes that generated a new rapport between the students and me.

Sometimes I was able to predict with great certainty that I would get a flood of notes when I had not given enough time to a more complex idea. But more often, I received notes that surprised me. I recall one student whose English was weak and who spoke very softly but often asked questions. The questions were usually good ones too. Notes began to arrive saying that I had spent too much time answering his questions and besides the other students couldn't hear his questions. I realised that I had been thinking too much about my answers to this student's questions and not enough about the other students, so I began to repeat his questions so the others would benefit too. More notes, in the same handwriting, that I was still spending too much time with that 'foreign guy' – I winced, remembering there were downsides to anonymity.

Notes

1. For a revised version of the article that inspired these stories see Rogers, "Improving Student Learning in Lectures," in Section VI, Part 1. Keith Aldridge's article was originally published in January 1992 in *Core* 2 (2) and Roy Merrens' article in October 1992 in *Core* 3(2).

Developing the
One-Minute Paper

Janice Newton

In its most basic form, the question for the One-Minute Paper is usually brief and focused: "What was the most important point you learned in today's lecture?"; "What was the muddiest point?"; or "Do you have any outstanding questions?" Cross and Angelo (1988, 148–50) provide a good summary of the One-Minute Paper and argue that it is one of the easiest and most effective of classroom assessment techniques.[1] However, they also encourage faculty to "adapt" classroom assessment techniques such as the One-Minute Paper to suit their specific needs, and many faculty have done so.

For example, Kloss (1993) varied the nature of the question, its timing and its focus. At the outset of a class he asked students to write about what they found difficult or confusing in the week's readings. He quickly reviewed these responses while students worked on other tasks, then began his lecture by clarifying important points raised in the students' responses.[2] In its variety of forms, this simple technique for soliciting anonymous feedback is a wonderful way for us to satisfy – even in large lectures – one of the criterion that is known to promote learning: it encourages students to become active learners.

I believe that we can further the students' active role by progressively increasing the level of difficulty of questions posed by the One-Minute Paper. The question, "What was the most important point?" encourages a particular kind of intellectual activity: the ability to understand and repeat what was just said. In light of research on stages of intellectual growth and development, this reflects a relatively low level of intellectual skill.[3] This level of skill is certainly important, perhaps especially at the outset of a course or when introducing new concepts, but we should not be limited to this kind of question. If we do not move beyond this level of question, our students might be content with a relatively passive intellectual role in our courses. We might encourage students' belief that important ideas are generated by others, in this case the professor or authors of the texts, and that their role is to absorb the wisdom of experts

326

and regurgitate it on demand. I believe that if we appropriately increase the level of difficulty of our questions over the duration of a course, we can help our students achieve higher levels of intellectual development.

As we increase the intellectual challenge of our questions, we encourage students to be more engaged and reflective in our lectures. For example, once you have established that students understand a basic concept, you might ask, "How would you apply this concept to a real situation?" or "How would you relate this concept to other course material?" thereby challenging students to relate the concept to new situations or to connect it with other parts of the course. This compels them to call upon their own knowledge and relate it to the lecture material, thus increasing understanding and recall of the concept. If the class, on the whole, can think of reasonable examples, we can be assured that they understood the lecture material. If many students are unable to think of examples or applications, we can consider altering our approach in the next lecture, using examples from students' responses to clarify the concept or providing further guidance for those students who had trouble moving to this new stage of intellectual development. We will still have gleaned important information about what students have learned, but these different questions will have generated some important supplemental benefits.

Progressively increasing the level of difficulty of our questions communicates a different set of expectations. As our questions move beyond the challenge of absorbing and repeating course material, we train students to become more active thinkers in the classroom, accustomed to deploying their own wonder and curiosity: "What do I think of this?" "How might this idea be useful?" "Can this idea help explain other things I have studied?" Though not every student will be able to respond to higher-level questions initially, and some might require a longer period of time for reflection, nonetheless the exercise creates an opportunity for students to practise these skills in an ungraded forum. In the anonymous safety of the One-Minute Paper, we communicate to students our confidence in their growing abilities to engage with course material and see it as relevant to themselves and the world they are coming to know through their studies.

Another advantage is that more advanced questions create a unique opportunity for us to encourage students to value and respect each others' ideas. When I use One-Minute Papers in my course on public policy, I often ask for examples from current events to illustrate a particular point I am covering in the lecture. Invariably, some students in the class come up with terrific ideas that might not have occurred to me, and I enjoy reading these responses back to the class. I am impressed with how this simple technique elicits original thought from the students and stimulates interest. It provides a regular opportunity for me to encourage students to value each others' ideas and see themselves as generators of knowledge.

If some students' responses to these more complex questions are confused, they need not feel isolated. You have an opportunity to respond immediately to their concerns in the subsequent class by clarifying the material, suggesting helpful readings or using responses generated by other students to help illustrate important points. The key is immediate feedback; for after all, this is a form of dialogue between you and your students. At the first opportunity, I give the class a summary of their responses and address important outstanding questions that emerged from their responses. Students whose questions I am unable to address in class are encouraged to speak with me at the end of the lecture or during my office hours. If the material is important, I might type up the most common student responses, include my own comments, and make this available for the class to consult. These student responses become a wonderful supplement to lecture notes, and in stimulating recall of course content, they provide a terrific review for tests and exams.

In summary, by using a broad range of questions in the One-Minute Paper we still glean the same valuable information about student learning in our classes. If students can apply an important point covered in a lecture to something that falls within their scope of knowledge, or if they can connect it to other ideas discussed in the course, then you can be satisfied that they understand your most important point. But these more sophisticated questions also communicate a higher level of expectations to your students. It is a way of saying to your students, "I don't just want you to repeat what I said, I want you to be able to use these ideas." You are encouraging them to engage in a dialogue with you and other students, a dialogue in which their ideas count, their curiosity and knowledge are valued and they can help illuminate the course for other students.

Notes

1. This technique has gained widespread popularity through the Harvard Assessment Seminars (Light 1990, 35–38).

2. While Kloss's technique (1988) works for a relatively small class, you could use this technique in a larger class by sampling a few student responses. For examples of variations on the One-Minute Paper, see Olmstead (1991), Cottell (1991), Mosteller (1989), Rogers (1991), Pernecky (1993) and Kort (1991).

3. For two different theoretical discussions of the stage of intellectual development that corresponds to this kind of question, see Belenky's discussion (1986) of received knowledge and Perry's discussion (1970) of dualism. See also the article by Page Westcott, "Student Development: From Problem Solving to Problem Finding," in Section II.

References

Belenky, Mary *et al.* 1986. *Women's ways of knowing.* New York: Basic Books.

Cottell, Philip G. 1991. Classroom research in accounting: Assessing for learning. *New Directions for Teaching and Learning* 46 (summer): 43–54.

Cross, Patricia K. and Thomas A. Angelo. 1988. *Classroom assessment techniques: A handbook for faculty.* Ann Arbour, MI: National Center for Research to Improve Postsecondary Teaching and Learning.

Kloss, Robert J. 1993. Stay in touch, won't you. *College Teaching* 41 (spring): 60–63.

Kort, Melissa Sue. 1991. Re-visioning our teaching: Classroom research and composition. *New Directions for Teaching and Learning* 46 (summer): 35–42.

Light, Richard. 1990. *The Harvard Assessment Seminars.* Cambridge, MA: Harvard University School of Graduate Education.

Mosteller, F. 1989. The muddiest point in the lecture as a feedback device. *On Teaching and Learning* (Harvard-Danforth Center for Teaching and Learning) 3 (April): 10–21.

Olmstead, John. 1991. Using classroom research in a large introductory science class. *New Directions for Teaching and Learning* 46 (summer): 55–65.

Perry, William. 1970. *Forms of intellectual and ethical development in the college years.* New York: Holt, Rhinehart and Winston.

Pernecky, Mark. 1993. Reaction papers enrich economics discussions. *College Teaching* 41 (summer): 89–91.

Rogers, Pat. 1991. Improving student learning. *Core* 2 (1): 1,4.

Part Two: Mid-Course Evaluation

Formative Evaluation Surveys

Bob Everett

Although they are less common than other forms of course surveys, formative evaluation surveys can be extremely effective teaching aids. Formative evaluations conducted during a course provide instructors with opportunities to gauge progress towards course objectives, to encourage student feedback and to reinforce information communicated in outlines and classroom discussions. More than that, they hold out the promise of engaging students and instructors in a constructive dialogue that can advance teaching and learning aspirations while enriching shared experiences in the classroom.

The formative evaluation is one of several types of course and instruction surveys. In some instances, students and instructors are now doing self-evaluations. Teaching is also evaluated by means of independent audits carried out by observers. The most common variety of curriculum and instruction survey is the summative evaluation, one that is typically conducted at the end of a course. Students are asked to reflect on their personal history and assess various aspects of course content, evaluate the quality of teaching and relate the course to their scholarly interests and degree programs. Questionnaire results are usually deeded to instructors, prospective students or the teaching units. At the faculty or departmental level, information gathered in this way could feature in curriculum planning or tenure and promotion decisions.

There are a number of problems associated with summative evaluations. Term's end could find respondents in a state of heightened anxiety or relief. Attendance can be lower than at other stages of a course, and questions might not unlock recollections of the critical early phase. Results are often published selectively, if at all. Teaching units might not have devised course evaluation policies. Comprehensive or university-wide surveys frequently present familiar resource dilemmas of money, means and methods. This can lead to cost-cutting measures, streamlining and over-emphasis on aggregated numbers. Conversely, standard survey forms might not adequately capture the unique teaching and learning situations or the distinct aims of particular courses.

Questionnaire design and data analysis are bound to require some sophistication if results are to be meaningful or if they are circulated.

None of these drawbacks diminishes the inherent value of summative evaluations. Certainly there is little to fear from evaluations and much to gain from their incorporation into teaching strategies. However, these problems do argue in favour of concerted, cooperative efforts to develop appropriate policies governing their use and support. At the same time, some of these limitations can be overcome through the use of formative evaluations.

Formative evaluations complement other forms of evaluation while offering their own special advantages. The single most compelling reason to employ formative evaluations consists of the capacity to impart and receive information while a course is in progress. Instructors and students alike have a chance to clarify approaches and expectations early on. A well-constructed survey yields insights about the adequacy of preparation and presentation of course material, alerting instructors to problems. Students – who tend to participate in formative evaluations with enthusiasm – can communicate any uncertainties or frustrations as well as any positive comments. If the results are compiled and distributed – as they should be – they become the basis for further discussions along these lines.

From the perspective of instructors, the questionnaire itself is a channel for basic communication about the nature and aims of a course. In an ideal world, detailed course outlines and positive reputations would pique interest. Students would be fully prepared for the specific topics, approaches and challenges of a particular course. For a variety of reasons, free and informed course selection is not always possible. Even as the answers identify concerns or difficulties for instructors, the questions themselves convey information to students. Conscientious instructors take great pains to develop outlines, select and assemble readings, and make arrangements with their departments, the libraries and the bookstore. But are there enough books on order? Have the readings been put on reserve? Is the grading scheme clear? A formative evaluation is a timely means of following up on these sorts of practicalities.

There are few hard and fast and rules on how to construct a formative evaluation. In the absence of set guidelines, the precise format is likely to depend on circumstances and an instructor's sense of aspects of the course that ought to be considered. A spirit of openness and a little sound advice are the only indispensable prerequisites. Literature and sample evaluation forms are available at York University's Centre for the Support of Teaching. Similar material – and policies that might exist – might also be on file with the teaching unit. The advice will seem common-sensical, stressing brevity, clarity and simplicity.

In terms of timing, a formative survey generally works best when the rhythms of the course are established and evident but not unalterably fixed. Leave sufficient time for enrolments to settle and wait until key introductory topics have been covered, contacts outside of the classroom have begun and some readings explored. The best time might be in the period between the first explanation of a first assignment and its submission. Some questions can then be aimed at discovering if students have understood the nature of the assignment or if they would like any further guidance.

The questions themselves could range over organizational matters and substantive issues. Asking if students have encountered difficulty making contact is both a way of learning if they are experiencing troubles and a reminder of course director availability. A few sight identifications of reading passages can highlight problems of comprehension while drawing attention to important texts. Leave space for open-ended comments. Based on personal experience, some of the most inspired and beneficial observations come from the opportunity for students to express their own concerns in their own way.

Some cautionary notes are in order. One risk turns on the possibility that an evaluation exercise will raise false expectations by fostering the belief that wholesale changes can be made. Students seldom make this assumption, but the purposes of the exercise should be made clear at the outset. By the same token, if the survey leads to adjustments in the format for weekly tutorial or seminar presentations (to inspire more discussion, for example) it is possible that some students will feel slighted. Few are likely to object to positive initiatives, but it is wise to take extra time to explore the implications in terms of grading and individual workloads.

Facilitating
Student Feedback

Reg Lang

You design the course. You deliver the course. At the end, the students evaluate the course. Along the way, a few of them let you know how things are going. You ask for more comments but few are forthcoming. Result: you receive summative feedback, useful for redesigning the course for a future offering, but you lack formative feedback that will help you improve the current version on a week-by week basis.

Perhaps this experience is typical, perhaps not. It was for me until a few years ago. I found it difficult to find out, as the course progressed, whether and what students were learning. Quizzes and mini-assignments were options but they still left me unsure of how much of my material was getting across to the students and whether it met their learning needs. Such information is important in a program such as ours that emphasizes, especially at the graduate level where I have done most of my teaching, self-directedness based on individual plans of study (Lang 1997).

The 1988 conference of the Society for Teaching and Learning in Higher Education equipped me with a further technique for addressing this problem: the feedback committee. Dr. Andy Farquharson of the University of Victoria's School of Social Work described this approach (1988) to tracking and modifying the process and content of undergraduate courses with approximately fifty students (mine are masters' students in groups of fifteen to twenty). Farquharson uses feedback committees in conjunction with Kolb's Learning Style Inventory and a Group Norms Scale. I often employ the Learning Style Inventory along with the Myers-Briggs Type Indicator to identify students' preferred ways of learning and interacting

Here's how I use feedback committees in my courses. A small group of three or four student volunteers constitutes the feedback committee, which then provides a two-way conduit for ongoing evaluation of the course plus, where appropriate, redesign of its content and the teaching-learning process. This exchange occurs in half-hour meetings with me after class once every two or three weeks. We've experimented with various ways of obtaining feedback from the other students:

333

informal discussion at the end of a class, with me present; "structured critique" forms; and, the one that seems to work best, setting aside ten minutes after key classes (for example, at the end of a section of the course) for feedback committee members to gather input from their colleagues in my absence. Feedback committee members also receive feedback informally throughout the course.

My experience with feedback committees in seventeen courses over the years demonstrates that this approach has several important benefits:

- It "models the understanding that effective learners are those who assume increasing responsibility for the management of their learning" (Farquharson 1988, 6), an important survival skill in today's world.
- It gives me quick feedback on the effectiveness of the instructional process — valuable information for designing upcoming sessions of the course and its future offerings. I've consistently found feedback committee members to be rich sources of ideas for improving learning processes.
- It provides a setting for me to discuss my concerns about the course.
- Sharing views with the students and getting their input eases the pressure that accompanies trying to create an effective learning experience.
- Receiving immediate feedback (yes, even the negative) feels good. At the end of the day I can leave knowing how things went rather than carrying away a nagging feeling that maybe something didn't work, maybe I talked too much, etc.
- The opportunity to give feedback is appreciated by the students. I've often heard, "No one has ever asked me before." As well, they gain a useful interpersonal skill.
- Committee members benefit from being involved in designing and adapting a learning process.

It is essential that the feedback committee's terms of reference be clearly established up front. I clearly state that the committee's existence does not diminish the right of individual students to make their views known to me. I ask them to check whether their concern is shared by their peers; if so, it's a public issue that ought to be raised in a feedback session and if not, they are invited to take it up with me one-to-one. I point out that the committee is neither a vehicle for individual student complaints nor an exercise in co-opting or defusing dissent. I emphasize that as instructor, I retain responsibility for the course; it's up to me to determine whether to act on suggestions that come from the committee. I keep the class informed of my discussions with the feedback committee and give reasons for any decisions I make as a result. Finally, I try not to overdo it; too much feedback can be tiresome for all concerned.

My conclusion is that the feedback committee offers a useful vehicle for instructors and students to take mutual responsibility for creating the best possible course and enhancing the learning experience. The approach works for me and it helps make teaching and the facilitation of learning a more rewarding experience.

References

Farquharson, A. 1988. Experiencing the learner: Three strategies. Paper presented to the Society for Teaching and Learning in Higher Education. McMaster University, June 19.

Lang, Reg. 1997. The plan of study: A pathway to student-centered learning. Paper presented to the Society for Teaching and Learning in Higher Education. University of Regina, June 11–15.

Feedback Strategies

Mary Lou McKenna

For many instructors, year-end evaluations provide the main source of student feedback on course content and on our own performance. Whatever the advantages or limitations of this exercise, two things seem clear: it does not always communicate what is really on students' minds, and communication occurs at a point when opportunity for timely response to student concerns is obviated. Over the past few years I have come to rely on more informal strategies for student feedback, both as a complement to formal evaluations and as compensation in their absence. Though rather simple exercises, they elicit sometimes surprising responses.

In the first or second week of classes, after I have introduced the course and set out my expectations, I ask my students to jot down some information about themselves — their academic/personal background, why they signed up for the course, what their expectations or concerns are or whatever they wish me to know. I remember my own pleasure in a similar exercise when a graduate seminar instructor solicited information on student interests as well as input on course direction. As feedback, this exercise can yield a variety of information and provide a number of benefits.

For a start, it reveals the personality lurking behind the often tentative or impassive expressions of a new class. Though some students reply with the bare minimum of information, others embark on lengthy and personal dialogues with the instructor, identifying the apprehension and excitement they feel as mature students, newcomers to the country, or small-town residents confronting the vastness of York University. Some identify their dreams and plans; others, their fears and difficulties.

Second, the exercise provides a sketch of the class's background and skill level. Students often list previous and current courses related to your own as well as indicating the range of their reading interests. Third, feedback on your presentation of the course is usually forthcoming. In this area, students often comment on the perceived fairness of course requirements and evaluation schemes, whether the course seems interesting, what they hope for in terms of class discussion, which texts or topics they look forward to and what aspects of the course raise concern. For example, I learned in one class that the lone male student felt intimidated by the male-to-female ratio, thus alerting me to the special effort that might be required to make him feel comfortable in the tutorial. In another case, a student expressed her concern about ensuring equal effort in group seminar projects. Clearly, instructor awareness of such concerns is invaluable when the feedback is timely.

Some students will even provide you with a rating on your opening monologue (dialogue?), commenting on whether they were made to feel at ease or intimidated by your demeanor. Indeed, there is no limit to the range of feedback produced by this simple and informal exercise, which at the very least functions as an ice breaker and creates goodwill between you and your students.

The second feedback tool I sometimes employ at year's end is to provide the students with a list of the year's texts and ask them to rate them on interest, relevance and readability. When fifteen out of twenty students tell you they *hated* a particular text, or that NEVER is a good time of year to ask them to read *Gone With the Wind*, it is at the very least food for thought. In the past, I have combined this exercise with a short discussion in which I invite students to comment on course direction, assignments and readings and to recommend changes that they feel would benefit the course in the future. Students seem very willing to express their ideas and respond to directed questioning more thoughtfully than they do to a blank space inviting them to comment on whatever comes to mind. I believe that they appreciate this clear demonstration of the instructor's interest in how the course is run and what kind of experience they have had.

While I am suggesting the use of these feedback strategies at the beginning and end of the course, clearly they can be combined and adapted for use mid-year – say, at the end of the first term –when they will either lend assurance that the course is unfolding as it should or create the incentive for you to rethink your strategy. Using these tools mid-year to evaluate the progress of the course requires both courage and commitment – courage to risk being confronted with less than overwhelming adulation for your approach while you're in the midst of it, and commitment to respond reasonably and in a timely fashion to student concerns.

The formal evaluation remains the avenue through which, with guaranteed anonymity, students can freely express their honest feelings about the course and the instructor. But by giving the students more timely and informal forums for affecting the course environment, and by bringing the evaluation process into the open, you can achieve a more satisfactory course experience for all concerned and diffuse the buildup of negative feelings with which you are sometimes surprised at year's end, while addressing student perceptions in such a way that they can better appreciate future instructors' rationales and motivations.

Part Three: Collegial Consultation

Peer Pairing

Sue Sbrizzi

Peer pairing is a process by which two instructors are teamed for the purpose of providing each other with mutual support and feedback on their teaching effectiveness. It was developed by Joseph Katz and run successfully for several years through the New Jersey Institute of Collegiate Teaching and Learning at Seton Hall University (Katz and Henry 1988). The essence of peer pairing is that the partners take turns, for a set period of time, observing each other teach, conducting student interviews in order to deepen their understanding of how to help each other improve, providing constructive feedback and acting as sounding boards for each other's ideas. The length of time spent working together can vary depending on other commitments. It is more important that the peer partners respect each other and be committed to working together than that they are in the same discipline or have the same teaching goals.

For example, Professor A and Professor B decide to work together for one term. They agree that Professor A will spend the first half of the term observing and providing feedback to Professor B and that their roles will be reversed in the second half of the term.

At the beginning of the agreed period, and before any observations take place, the pair meets to discuss their teaching goals and to establish the ground rules for their work together. In our example, since Professor B is being observed first, she is the one who sets the ground rules for the first observation period. When the pair meets, they develop a list of specific aspects of Professor B's teaching on which she would like Professor A to focus. This list can be extensive or quite limited, but it should always be discussed fully before the observation begins. For example, Professor B might ask Professor A to notice

- student participation: are the students engaged? When do they take notes? Do they ask questions? Do they speak to other students?
- the quality of student responses to questions
- the nature and frequency of her questioning – is there enough variety?

338

- the student's ability to apply course content to problem solving and critical thinking
- her discussion skills
- time management
- her communication skills
- the clarity of her explanations
- discrepancies between her stated course goals, her implicit goals and the student's goals
- the learning environment – is she sensitive to race, class and gender issues?
- where students sit
- distracting mannerisms.

Student Interviews

Continuing with our example, Professor B introduces Professor A to her class and tells them he is conducting research on student learning and will be a regular visitor to the class for the first six weeks of term. Professor A tells the class that he is interested in the students' learning experience and invites them to volunteer to participate in his research. From those who volunteer, he selects a group of about three students whom he will interview regularly, either individually or in a group.

The focus of the student interviews is on what is happening in the class — what works, what doesn't. The results of the interviews, as well as feedback from the classroom observations, are discussed during regular meetings between the pair.

Benefits

While they are being observers, instructors receive useful information on areas of their teaching in which they themselves have expressed an interest. Instructors find that they often learn more about their own teaching when observing someone else teach than they do when being observed because in the observer role they are less defensive and more able to reflect on teaching and learning in a broader context. The interviewing process often changes both partners' views on students and often results in improved instructor–student relations on many levels. Overall, it is valuable and rewarding for both participants in this process to have a colleague who is interested in and supportive of their attempts to improve their teaching.

References

Katz, Joseph and Mildred Henry. 1988. *Turning professors into teachers: A new approach to faculty development and student learning.* New York: Macmillan.

Peer Pairing
in French Studies

Karen Whalen, Louise Morrison, Myriam deBie Waller

The peer-pairing observational model provides a framework on which to base enquiry into the complexities of teacher–student interaction. Regardless of discipline-specific concerns, there are general issues that can be shared by colleagues from any field. Although many peer-pairing experiences successfully involve paired colleagues from different academic units, the instructors in French studies felt that they needed to address specific teaching and learning issues related to second-language teaching. Given the complexity of our task as teachers, it is often impossible to evaluate the effectiveness of our delivery in the classroom. Inviting a colleague to regularly observe our classroom can provide meaningful insight, which is often impossible to obtain in other ways despite our most conscientious efforts.

Furthermore, our perception of what is taking place in the classroom can be far removed from the students' perception of what is taking place. The presence of a friendly and attentive observer allows us to view our classroom from a different perspective; these views otherwise might have gone unnoticed. Such a framework assists us in asking essential questions about the effectiveness of our teaching techniques in terms of the quality of the student learning experience. Perhaps most importantly, the observations of a supportive colleague help us better understand our personal and professional vision of our role as teachers and its subsequent influence on our pedagogical choices. If colleagues are concerned about some aspects of their teaching, peer pairing is a professional development tool that can offer new insights, initiate discussion between peers and provide collegial support and feedback.

A Peer-Pairing Classroom Observational Project

Four instructors in the Department of French Studies attended a CST workshop that described the peer consultation process. These instructors decided to initiate an extensive classroom observational project by agreeing to submit their teaching to intensive self- and peer evaluation over a two-year period. While individual concerns initially motivated participation in the project, all members shared the view that this mode of enquiry provides a powerful tool for understanding the complexity of second-language teaching and learning processes. The subsequent award of a Senate Committee on Teaching and Learning Fellowship provided the release time necessary for carrying out frequent classroom observations and other forms of data collection (videotaping, student interviews, instructor–peer interviews, etc.).

From the start, it was felt that a holistic observational approach at the beginning stages of the project would allow the instructors to better understand who they were as teachers and in what directions they would like to develop further. They subsequently decided to adapt a peer-pairing method of enquiry similar to that described in the preceding article by Sbrizzi.

Steps in the Peer-Pairing Observational Process

In our adaptation of the peer-pairing model, the pairs of colleagues agree to spend an entire academic year observing one another's classes. One instructor takes on an observational role, visiting her colleague's classroom once a week. Six steps in the peer-pairing process can be summarized in the following manner:

1. *Establishing a timetable.* After consulting the "observee's" teaching schedule, the observer and observee agree on a convenient day and time for classroom visits.
2. *Setting the tone and agenda.* An initial meeting with the observer allows the observee to set the agenda and make up a list of issues he would like to reflect upon.
3. *Classroom visits and observations (data collection).* Depending on the class they are observing, some instructors might prefer to observe a series of consecutive classes over a two- or three-week period several times during the year. While each peer-pairing group will make such decisions based on individual and clearly defined objectives, it is nevertheless necessary to observe a class regularly enough that the observer develops a clear understanding of the instructor's objectives and teaching style.
4. *Discussing the observation*: the follow-up meeting. Observer and observee meet after each observation session to discuss that particular class.
5. *Videotaping classroom observation sessions* and discussions between observer and instructor. This procedure provides an additional dimension to the peer-pairing process. For example, it might confirm peer observations or it could serve to identify other teacher and learner behaviours that had not been revealed by the observer.
6. *Soliciting student input.* A) Instructors can distribute questionnaires to gather essential information concerning personal and academic profiles, learning strategy profiles, course evaluation and specific class evaluations. These questionnaires serve to include student perceptions in the data collection process. B) Interviews between the observer and students serve to involve students directly in the ongoing dialogue about the teaching and learning taking place in the classroom.

Furthermore, face-to-face interaction between the students and observer will provide more in-depth and significant data.

What Can Be Learned From Peer-Pairing Observation?

It is inevitable that individual teaching styles reflect who instructors are as real people and that the observer comes with her own perception of her role as a teacher. This exchange between observer and observee can be very productive, especially if they have different teaching styles and can recognize this reality without feeling threatened. The interaction between peers during the follow-up discussion benefits the observee because it often confirms an intuition about teaching style and particular teaching techniques and strategies. In addition, the exchange of ideas increases both parties' awareness of possible approaches to teaching and enables them to trace common areas of concern and interest.

What Was Learned by the French Studies Experience?

While the initial purpose of undertaking the peer-pairing project was to collaborate to improve the teaching and learning taking place in the second-language classroom, the participating instructors addressed a number of questions that evolved with the project. They include questions such as:

- What kinds of activities are used in the language classroom?
- Do these activities have an explicit teaching objective?
- Are students aware of our teaching objectives?
- Do instructors use specific teaching strategies with specific learning objectives in mind?
- Do they get the expected response from students?
- Can we draw some conclusions in terms of learning outcomes?
- Do teachers teach what they think they teach?
- Do students learn what teachers think they learn?
- What types of instructional intervention are most effective?

The ultimate goals of these instructors included:

- categorizing various types of activities initiated by the teacher
- understanding how the teacher feels the students respond to these activities
- understanding how students perceive these teaching-learning activities
- understanding how the observer assesses the students' reaction to these activities.

The extensive data collected at each step of the peer-pairing process allowed the instructors to compare the students' perception of a positive learning experience with that of the instructor and the observer. When these perceptions did not correspond, they were able to explain differences of opinion.

Perhaps one of the most interesting and challenging experiences involved soliciting student input from the very beginning of the academic year. Although some colleagues felt uncomfortable with this step, they soon discovered that their students were a valuable source of information. Given the opportunity and the forum to express themselves in an open and collaborative environment, students were able to articulate ideas and feelings about their learning experience. Encouraging student participation in this enquiry process made them aware that they had an equally important role to play in the classroom. This awareness created a new type of interaction whereby students and instructor regularly reflected on the effectiveness of their teaching and learning strategies. In some cases, peer pairing served as a powerful "atmosphere enhancer" because students came to class knowing that their instructor valued their input. For this reason, it seemed that students were more motivated to learn and more comfortable in both individual and group learning situations.

In terms of concrete ramifications on individual teaching practices, the ongoing dialogue with students allows the instructor to evaluate the effect of teaching style and strategies on student learning. As a result of this valuable feedback, instructors are then able to modify and adapt teaching strategies to the needs and learning styles of their students. The French studies group continues to describe and better understand the teaching-learning process through an interpretive analysis of student–teacher interaction and perceptions.

Teaching Evaluation Guide

Senate Committee on Teaching and Learning
York University

Purpose

This Teaching Evaluation Guide is a companion to the Teaching Documentation Guide produced by the York University Senate Committee on Teaching and Learning in November 1990 and revised in December 1993 (see next article). It is aimed at providing teachers with advice on documenting the variety and complexity of their teaching contributions. This Teaching Evaluation Guide provides teachers with advice on how to document their teaching as part of a systematic program of teaching development. As well, it provides guidance on how teaching might be evaluated fairly and effectively, what characteristics of teaching might be considered and what evaluation methods are best suited for which purpose. Further, the guide provides samples of items that might be suitable for inclusion in evaluation instruments.

Need for the Guide

Teaching is currently evaluated using narrow rather than broadly based criteria. Recent research suggests that if evaluation of teaching is to become less threatening (summative evaluation is in essence judgemental) and more an opportunity for growth and change (that is, formative), then it is essential that faculty and administrators work together to develop procedures that recognize that teaching is a complex and personal activity. Informed judgements can be made only when several techniques are used to provide information from various perspectives on different characteristics of teaching. There is no one source for information and no one technique for gathering it. Techniques need to be sensitive to the particular teaching assignments of the instructor being evaluated and to the context in which the teaching takes place. If multiple perspectives are represented, the conclusions reached will be more credible and consequently of more value to the individual being evaluated.

Current evaluation practices at York vary. In many departments and units, teaching is systematically evaluated, but it is done primarily for summative purposes. Individual instructors are free, if they wish, to use the data so gathered for formative purposes or they can contact the Centre for the Support of Teaching, which provides feedback and teaching analysis aimed at growth, development and improvement. Without denying the value of summative evaluation of teaching, the main purpose of this guide is to motivate committees and individuals to employ more energy and resources in encouraging and engaging in formative evaluation.

What Is Good Teaching?

All evaluation instruments contain implicit assumptions about the characteristics considered to constitute good teaching. These assumptions should be made explicit and indeed should become part of the evaluation process itself in a manner that recognizes teachers' right to be evaluated within the context of their own teaching philosophies and goals. First and foremost, then, "teaching is not right or wrong, good or bad, effective or ineffective in any absolute, fixed or determined sense" (Weimer 1990, 202). Teachers emphasize different domains of learning (cognitive, affective, psychomotor). They work at different sites (classrooms, laboratories, seminar rooms, studios, playing fields, field locations, etc.), using different techniques and resources (lecturing, demonstrating, coaching, facilitating discussions, etc.) with students of diverse backgrounds and levels of preparedness. They also can employ different theories of education and teaching methodologies: feminist, antiracist, critical, humanistic, etc. (adapted from Geis 1977). In one situation, teachers might see their role as transmitting factual information and in another as facilitating discussion and promoting critical thinking.

As variable and diverse as effective teaching might be, generalizations nevertheless can be made about its basic characteristics. Put succinctly, *effective teaching is that activity which brings about the most productive and beneficial learning experience for students and promotes their independence as learners*. Along with the information base of the course, *this experience can include such factors as intellectual growth, change in outlook and attitude towards the discipline and its place in the academic endeavour and improvement in specific skills*; for example, critical reading and writing, oral communication, analysis, synthesis, abstraction and generalization.

The criteria for evaluating teaching can vary with the discipline and within the discipline, depending on the level of the course, the instructor's objectives and style and the teaching methodology employed. Nonetheless, the primary criterion must be improved student learning. Research indicates that the following are some of the characteristics that students, faculty and administrators alike agree are *qualities of effective teaching:*

- ability to motivate student learning and establish a positive learning environment
- providing appropriate challenges

- concern for students' needs and welfare
- sensitivity to students' different learning styles
- fairness in evaluation procedures.

For some methodologies – lecturing, for example – the following could also be indicators of effective teaching:

- organization of subject matter and course
- effective communication skills
- knowledge of and enthusiasm for the subject matter and for teaching
- availability to students
- effective choice of materials
- openness to student concerns and opinions.

Some characteristics are more easily measured than others. Furthermore, since teachers are individuals and teaching styles are personal, it is all the more important to recognize that not everyone will display the same patterns of strengths – excellent teachers could be strong in many areas but not necessarily in all of them.

Formative Evaluation

The purpose of formative evaluation is for instructors to find out what changes they might make in teaching methods or style, course organization or content, evaluation and grading procedures, etc., to improve student learning. Information and feedback are solicited from many sources (self, students, colleagues, consultants) and evaluation is initiated by the instructor. The data gathered are varied and are seen only by the instructor and, if desired, a consultant. Formative evaluation of teaching can be carried out at many points during an instruction period, as illustrated in the case study at the end of this article.

Summative Evaluation

Summative evaluation of teaching, by contrast, is normally conducted by an academic unit at the end of a course for the purpose of assessing performance. This evaluation should involve a variety of techniques, including

- the results of teaching evaluations
- letters from individual students commenting on the effectiveness of the instructor's teaching, quality of the learning experience, and impact on their academic progress
- peer assessments based on classroom visits and reviews of curriculum material, scholarship on teaching and teaching dossier
- evidence of exceptional achievements and contributions in the form of awards, committee work, etc.

There are two critical differences between summative and formative evaluation: the point of initiation and the use to which the information can be put. Summative evaluation is initiated by the unit and is used primarily to assess teaching performance.

Formative evaluation is initiated by the instructor and is used primarily to improve teaching and student learning.

An important note: For the formative evaluation of teaching to be effective and achieve its purpose, it is crucial that the two processes of formative and summative evaluation be kept strictly apart. This means that the information gathered in a program of formative evaluation should not be used in summative evaluations unless volunteered by instructors themselves. It also means that people who have been involved in assisting instructors improve their teaching should not be asked to provide information for summative evaluation purposes.

Overview of Techniques for Evaluating Teaching Effectiveness

This section describes a variety of techniques that teachers can use to evaluate their teaching effectiveness. Which techniques are chosen will depend on the intent of the evaluation. The following techniques are included:

- self-evaluation
- classroom observation
- measures of student achievement
- questionnaires
- letters and individual interviews
- focus groups
- analysis of instructional materials.[1]

Self-Evaluation

Source: Self

Description and Purpose: Self-evaluation can take the form of an informal self-reflection exercise, classroom assessments such as the One-Minute Paper or a formal written appraisal compiled, for example, using the Teaching Documentation Guide. Self-evaluation can be carried out for both formative and summative purposes. For formative purposes, it provides instructors with an opportunity to articulate their teaching philosophy, review their teaching goals and objectives and assess their areas of strength and difficulty. Where available, departmental course evaluation forms or the Teaching Documentation Guide can be used as a checklist to assist in identifying professional areas requiring further development. For summative purposes, self-evaluation can take the form of a teaching dossier.

Benefits: Self-evaluation encourages teachers to become monitors of their own performance and promotes reflective practice. It is an excellent first step in planning a thoughtful and comprehensive teaching development program. Informal self-evaluation involves little formal data collection and takes very little time. A formal written appraisal, such as a teaching dossier, provides a context for assessing data about teacher performance gathered using other methods – this can be especially important in the tenure and promotion process as it puts other types of data in their proper perspective. In addition, a teaching dossier can be sent to colleagues at other institutions for appraisal.

Limitations: Self-evaluation is, by its very nature, biased and can rarely stand alone if used for summative evaluation. Some individuals find it very difficult to engage in critical self-evaluation or to be honest with themselves and others about their difficulties.

Sample items from a self-evaluation form for instructors

For each topic, instructors respond using the scale:
1 I don't believe I need help in this area.
2 This is a low priority for me at this time.
3 I'd like to find out more about this area.
4 I'd like to start doing this as soon as possible.

Effective communication:

a. Giving effective, well-organized lectures with clear goals. 1   2   3   4
b. Having students respond to questions I raise.   1   2   3   4
c. Having students formulate and ask questions related
   to the topic.   1   2   3   4
d. Having students become involved in group discussions. 1   2   3   4

Classroom Observation

Source: Peers (instructors from the same department) and colleagues (instructors from another department)[2]

Description and Purpose: In many respects, classroom observations complement student assessment of teaching. Although peers and colleagues are unlikely to be knowledgeable of the full extent of the teaching situation, they are able to comment on subject matter or teaching methodology from a professional perspective. Before visiting a class, the observer should meet with the instructor to discuss the instructor's teaching philosophy as well as the specific teaching objectives and teaching strategies that will be employed for the session to be observed.

Classroom observation can be carried out for both summative and formative purposes. For summative evaluation, it is desirable that more than one person carry out these observations and that each observer visit more than one class. This will counteract observer bias towards a particular teaching approach and the possibility that an observation takes place on an unusually bad day. These precautions also provide for greater objectivity and hence reliability of the results. To ensure that a full picture of a teacher's strengths and weaknesses is obtained, some observers find checklists useful and some departments might choose to designate the task of making classroom observations to a committee. As the range of activities going on in a class can be overwhelming, some observers find it helpful to focus on specific aspects (for example, presentation and interaction, not content). For this reason, colleagues who are unfamiliar with the content being taught can provide a different perspective than that of the instructor's disciplinary peers.

Classroom observation is especially useful for formative evaluation. In this case, it is important that the results of the observations are confidential and are not also used for summative evaluation. The process of observation in this case should take place over time, allowing the instructor to implement changes, practise improvements and obtain feedback on whether progress has been made. It also can include videotaping the instructor's class. This process is particularly helpful to faculty members who are experimenting with new teaching methods.

A particularly valuable form of classroom observation for formative purposes is peer pairing. With this technique, a pair of instructors provides each other with feedback on their teaching on a rotating basis, each evaluating the other for a period of time (anywhere between two weeks and a year). Each learns from the other and can learn as much in the observing role as when being observed. For guidelines for using this technique, see the previous section of this book.

Benefits: Classroom observations can complete the picture of an instructor's teaching obtained through other less direct methods of evaluation. As well, observations are an important supplement to inconsistent student ratings in situations, for example, where an instructor's teaching is controversial because of experimentation, where non-traditional teaching methods are being used or where other unique situations exist within the classroom context. Peers are better able than students to comment upon the level of difficulty of the material, the relevance of examples chosen, knowledge of subject matter and integration of topics. Colleagues are better able than peers to place the teaching within a wider context and to suggest alternative teaching formats and ways of communicating the material.

Limitations: There are several limitations to using classroom observations for summative purposes. It is costly in terms of faculty time since a number of observations are necessary to ensure reliability and validity of findings. Teachers tend to find observations threatening and they and their students might behave differently when there is an observer present. There is evidence to suggest that peers are relatively generous evaluators in some instances. Since observers vary in their definitions of effective teaching and considerable tact is required in providing feedback on observations, it is desirable that observers receive training before becoming involved in providing formative evaluation. Finally, to protect the integrity of this technique for both formative and summative purposes, it is critical that observations for personnel decisions be kept strictly separate from evaluations for teaching improvement.

> *Sample items to be considered when making a classroom observation*
>
> The following are items that relate to an instructor's flexibility in instructional approach. Items can be rated using an appropriate scale or phrased as questions requiring fuller written responses.
>
> Scaled-response items: Uses appropriate instructional techniques.
> Makes appropriate choices between presentation and discussion.
>
> Written response items: To what degree does the instructor vary the instructional methods for the material presented? What other methods might be more appropriate?

Questionnaires

Source: Students and, in some cases, alumni

Description and Purpose: Student questionnaires and surveys are the most commonly used source of summative evaluation data. In many academic units they are mandatory and in several units they are standardized. For purposes such as tenure and promotion, data should be obtained over time using standardized questionnaires. Information obtained via questionnaires also can be used by individual instructors for improving subsequent incarnations of a course and for identifying areas of strength and weakness in their teaching by comparison to those teaching similar courses. Questionnaires are also useful in a program of formative evaluation if designed and administered by an instructor during a course.

Benefits: The use of mandatory, standardized questionnaires puts all teaching evaluations on a common footing and facilitates comparison among teachers, courses and academic units. The data gathered also serve the purpose of assessing whether the educational goals of the unit are being met. Structured questionnaires are particularly appropriate where there are relatively large numbers of students involved or where there are either several sections of a single course or several courses with similar teaching objectives using similar teaching approaches.

Questionnaires are relatively economical to administer, summarize and interpret. Provided that students are asked to comment only on items with which they have direct experience, student responses on questionnaires have been found to be valid. Research[3] has identified the following eight dimensions of an instructor's teaching as especially important in identifying exemplary teaching:

- stimulation of interest in the course and its subject matter
- preparation and organization
- clarity and understandability
- sensitivity to and concern with students' level of understanding and progress
- clarity of course objectives and requirements

- impact of instruction
- encouragement of questions and discussion
- openness to opinions of others.

While questionnaire forms with open-ended questions are more expensive to administer, they often provide more reliable and useful sources of information in small classes and for the tenure and promotion process. Open-ended questions can provide insight into the numerical ratings.

Limitations: Teachers have such different perspectives, approaches and objectives that a standardized questionnaire cannot adequately or fairly compare their performances. For example, the implicit assumption behind the design of many evaluation forms is that the primary mode of instruction is the lecture. Such a form will be inadequate in evaluating the performance of an instructor who uses collaborative or feminist teaching methods. One way to overcome this limitation and to tailor it to the objectives and approaches of a specific course or instructor is to design an evaluation form with a mandatory core set of questions and space for inserting questions chosen by the instructor.

Recent research on the effects of gender on student ratings suggests that female professors tend to be judged more rigidly than male professors on a variety of dimensions, particularly in questions relating to students' interpersonal experiences with the teacher (for specific details see Basow 1994). Further, there is some evidence to suggest that student evaluations are biased against non-traditional teaching methods and curriculum and teachers from under-represented groups. Extreme caution should therefore be exercised to ensure that the data generated are interpreted in light of other sources of data. Another way to ensure fairness and equity is to ask students to identify the strengths of the instructor's approach as well as weaknesses and to ask for specific suggestions for improvement. Required courses are generally rated lower than elective courses. Care should therefore be taken to create an appropriate context for interpreting the data in comparison with other courses.

Sample items from a student questionnaire

1. Rate the instructor on each of the items below using the following five-point scale:

> 1, Unsatisfactory;   2, Below Average;   3, Average;
>
> 4, Above Average;   5, Outstanding

a. Presents material clearly and effectively.	1	2	3	4	5
b. Responds to concerns raised during class.	1	2	3	4	5
c. Encourages questions and discussion.	1	2	3	4	5

2. Please note what you think the instructor does well in teaching this course and what the instructor could do better. *(Please be very specific):*

Instructor does well:

Instructor could do better:

Measures of Student Achievement

Source: Faculty and appropriate administrators

Description and Purpose: In some courses, a test or examination can measure teaching effectiveness explicitly. Ideally, data collected at the beginning of the course are compared with data collected at the end of the course to measure students' improvement on some relevant scale of knowledge, ability, etc. These profiles of achievement can be a good source of summative evaluation information. They are particularly effective in a situation characterized by large numbers of students or multiple sections working to a common syllabus with a common exam, and where the course goals are very specific.

Benefits: Given similar student entry characteristics and teaching situations, this provides perhaps the most objective evidence of teaching effectiveness.

Limitations: The "sameness" required for this method to be meaningful limits the number of situations in which it can be used. As differences in expectations or student assessment procedures enter the equation, the usefulness of this method for summative evaluation declines. The use of examination results to evaluate teaching can lead to instruction being geared to the exam.

Letters and Individual Interviews

Source: Students, alumni, peers

Description and Purpose: Interviews and letters can be used to obtain greater depth of information for the purpose of improving teaching, or for providing details and examples of an instructor's impact on students for the purposes of teaching award nominations and the tenure and promotion process.

Benefits: Interviews and letters elicit information not readily available through questionnaires or student achievement records. Insights, success stories and thoughtful analyses are often outcomes of an interview or request for a written assessment of an instructor's teaching. Students who are reluctant to give information on a rating scale often respond well to a skilled, probing interviewer.

Limitations: The disadvantage of letters is that the response rate can be quite low. The major disadvantage of interviews is time. Interviews can take about thirty minutes to arrange and approximately one hour to conduct, and another block of time must be allocated to coding and interpretation. A structured interview schedule can be used to eliminate the bias that can result when an untrained interviewer asks questions randomly of different students.

Sample structured interview questions

Explain why you would or would not recommend Professor B's class to a friend.

To what extent do you believe that Professor B's class prepared you for advanced work in the subject?

Probes: Can you explain that in more detail?

Can you give me an example of that?

Can you explain the difficulty that you encountered?

Focus Groups

Source: Students

Description and Purpose: Data gathered in a focus group discussion involving about six to eight students chosen randomly from an instructor's class provide a rich description of an instructor's teaching because these data are based on students' individual opinions as well as their reflections on, and reactions to, the opinions of others.

The discussion is carried out outside of class and preferably is facilitated by a colleague or peer. At the beginning of the group meeting, students are given about five minutes to write independently, describing which teaching behaviours they would like to see the instructor maintain and which they think that the instructor should change or improve. The items generated are then gathered and prioritized under the headings "maintain" and "improve." The facilitator then moves from item to item, alternating between the two columns, asking for clarification and examples to illustrate the points. At the conclusion of the discussion, the facilitator prepares an oral or written report.

Benefits: Data generated in this way provide a very rich description of the strengths and weaknesses of an instructor's teaching and are probably the most effective way to generate constructive criticism as well as positive reinforcement for successful strategies. This can be particularly helpful to instructors who are experiencing problems with their teaching, in which case it is important that the students are selected openly in front of the whole class and in the instructor's absence. This technique also provides useful feedback for instructors who are experimenting with new methodologies or are engaged in a program of self-improvement. This method can be used for summative purposes and provides an important supplement to the quantitative data generated by teaching evaluation forms.

Limitations: The only limitation of this method is that it is time consuming. Training in the use of this technique is recommended and is available through the Centre for the Support of Teaching.

Review of Instructional Materials

Source: Self

Description and Purpose: Instructional materials typically include some of the following:

- course outlines
- examinations
- quizzes
- assignments
- reading lists
- student manuals
- practicum requirements
- various audio-visual materials (overhead transparencies, videos, slides, computer software, etc).

Many academic units require a course outline that highlights teaching objectives along with student performance expectations. The content contained within the resource materials can reflect the quality of thought and effort put into the planning and preparation for teaching. The materials can provide insight into the guidance and supervision provided to students outside the classroom setting. Gathering this material provides the instructor with an opportunity to assemble a teaching dossier, which is an essential component of a tenure and promotion file or teaching award nomination. The portfolio also can be useful to units in upgrading or reforming their curriculum.

Benefits: A review of instructional materials can instigate a professional exchange of information regarding the content being taught and research that might be integrated into the course. The data collected in this way provide a perspective on teaching not obtainable through classroom observations and also can enable an academic unit to maintain a curriculum focus. Evaluation of instructional materials by peers is a more reliable and valid measure of an instructor's teaching effectiveness than is asking students to assess the course materials.

Limitations: This initiative is time consuming and costly. It is also open to individual bias and so a standing committee within an academic unit could provide a formal, consistent and systematic approach to carrying out this initiative.

Case Study: Formative Evaluation in Practice

The case that follows is fictitious. It has been devised to give the reader a practical illustration of how this guide, and the evaluation strategies outlined, might be used by an instructor to devise a systematic program of teaching development and improvement.

Joseph Wilson is a prominent scholar of Canadian studies who has spent most of his working life teaching at a small university in Britain. Late in his career, he moves to Canada to be closer to his wife's family, and obtains a position as a professor of political science at a large urban university. On arrival in Canada, he learns that he is scheduled to teach, among other courses, a first-year half-course entitled "Canadian Politics." He is alarmed to learn that the enrolment in his class is expected to be about eighty-five students. Jo is confident of the subject matter of the course, but because he has never taught a class of this size before, he is less confident of his teaching abilities. For years he has taught only small graduate seminars or given individual tutorials to undergraduates. Earlier in the summer he had received a copy of the Teaching Evaluation Guide, which he has read, and he resolves to use its suggestions.

"Canadian Politics" is a multisection course, most aspects of which are prescribed by the course coordinator. Jo has no choice over the course syllabus or the textbook and there is a common final examination. He can, however, cover the course topics in the order he prefers and choose his own supplementary reading materials and in-course evaluation procedures (quizzes, midterm examination, participation marks, etc.).

In the weeks before the course begins, Jo spends some time preparing to teach. He drafts a detailed course outline containing a week-by-week schedule of the topics he will cover. He selects the supplementary readings, obtains copyright permission and has course kits made up for purchase by the students. Finally, he prepares detailed scripts for each of his three-hour lectures. The week before his first class, Jo confirms that the course enrolment is still around eighty-five and visits the lecture theatre. The room appears to be satisfactory. It has 120 tablet armchairs, two large chalkboards and a projection screen. Jo decides to order an overhead projector for each class.

Week 1. Jo begins teaching and soon gets into the swing of things. This being his first experience teaching a large class, he is very sensitive to the classroom atmosphere. He notices, for example, that although the students are very attentive at the start of the class, after the first thirty minutes or so of the lecture their attention has wandered: feet and papers are shuffled, whispered conversations take place and some students stare blankly into space. Even after the break, the students seem less engaged. Jo is concerned about this. It is a real dilemma – if he carries on with his scripted lecture he can see that many students will learn little, but if he abandons the script he might not cover the required material.

Jo has started the self-evaluation process. At the moment this is at the informal stage – he has recognized a problem and wants to deal with it.

Week 2. In the hope that the first class was atypical, Jo ploughs on with his second scripted lecture. The same thing happens. Although the students are physically present, he can see that he has lost them before the first half of the lecture is over and he knows that the second half of the class will be wasted if he continues in the same vein. In desperation, he ends his lecture and calls a break.

While the students are on their break, Jo goes to the blackboard and writes down the following:

Please answer the following questions:
1. Name one thing you like about the course.
2. Name one thing you dislike about the course.
3. Name one thing you would change in this course.
Submit your answers anonymously to me, in writing, now!

When the students return, he asks them to respond to the questions and gives them about two minutes to do so.

Jo is using a simple, but highly effective, classroom assessment instrument (the One-Minute Paper) designed to elicit student opinion about the course.[4]

After collecting the One-Minute Papers, Jo realizes that there is not enough time to go through his prepared lecture, so he summarizes the main points he would have covered and asks the students to read the relevant chapter in the textbook. To his surprise, the students seem much more attentive and receptive to this than to his prepared lecture. When he reads the replies from the One-Minute Papers, a consensus emerges along the following lines:

1. Things I like about the course: Course director seems very organized, competent, knowledgeable and enthusiastic about subject.
2. Things I dislike about the course: Lecture format very dry; textbook not well related to subject; no opportunity for discussion; class too big.
3. Things I would change: Have a smaller class; allow more time for discussion and student participation.

On the basis of this feedback, Jo decides it would be helpful to talk things over with a colleague more experienced with teaching large numbers of students, so he visits the Centre for the Support of Teaching. They suggest that he observe a class of a colleague from the Faculty of Law who is known for her expertise in participatory teaching methods. An appointment is made with Lorna Brown for two weeks ahead. In the meantime, Jo is advised to keep using the One-Minute Paper to break the lecture up and get feedback on student understanding of the material. It is also suggested that, since he is comfortable with the material he is teaching, he could improve his lectures considerably by talking to the students using notes in point form as a guide, rather than reading to them verbatim from his prepared scripts.

Jo has now obtained some insight into what might be causing the problems he perceives with his teaching and has responded by seeking the advice and support of a colleague (a resource person from the Centre for the Support of Teaching or a colleague from another department).

Week 3. Jo begins his next class by thanking the students for their comments on the One-Minute Papers. Briefly, he reports on his findings and tells the students that he will be doing what he can in the following weeks to respond to their concerns. He is concerned that students might not have learned the subject matter that he had not explicitly covered in the last lecture. Accordingly, he begins by assigning the following in-class exercise:

> Imagine you bump into an old school friend at the airport. Your friend is doing a degree in philosophy at the University of Western Ontario and is curious when she learns that you are doing your BA in political science. She asks impatiently, "What's all this controversy about Québec separating? Why is this happening?" Your friend has only a few minutes before she has to rush off to catch her plane. Recognizing that you are talking informally to an educated person and have only five minutes, explain in writing the growth of separation in Québec.

Jo is using a "five-minute writing exercise," through which he achieves two goals: first, he can assess students' understanding of a topic (a "student test of achievement") and second, he is allowing an opportunity for students to practise their writing and communication skills. Coincidentally, he is responding to the students who said they find the lecture format too dry and called for more participation in the class.

Casual conversation during the coffee break informs him that the quiz came as a surprise to many students despite the fact that he had warned them in the first class that he might do this from time to time. For those students who had not done the assigned reading and thus performed poorly on the exercise, this exercise underscored the fact that the readings were an integral part of the course and that Jo was serious about the homework he assigned.

Reading the papers after the class, Jo finds to his delight that not only had most students done the assigned reading, they had also understood the general idea of his topic, and most seemed able to communicate effectively in writing. Some students demonstrated a variety of writing problems and to them Jo recommended a visit to the appropriate writing centre to obtain assistance.

Week 4. By arrangement through the Centre for the Support of Teaching two weeks earlier, Jo observes a class taught by Lorna Brown. After discussing the class with Lorna he decides to try out some of the techniques he observed in her class. He has already experimented successfully with talking from point-form notes rather than detailed scripts, but now he decides to try a format where he makes a short presentation of key topics and then the whole class participates in a case-study analysis.

Observing a colleague teach is a powerful way to gain confidence in experimenting with new teaching methods.

Jo tries this new method and enjoys the experience. Some students are still lost, but most become active and more interested participants. After a couple of weeks, Jo is becoming confident. His enthusiasm for this approach impresses one of his colleagues, who agrees to attend his next class and videotape it for him. After the class, Jo and his colleague discuss the course materials he is using and agree that they work well.

Jo has used a peer to evaluate his teaching both through classroom observation and review of course materials. The videotape of his class will also enable others to benefit from Jo's experiences and will provide Jo with a useful source of further self-evaluation.

Week 7. Jo administers his midterm test. By this time, Jo has become so excited about his approach to teaching that he sets an unusually challenging exam and most of his students do badly. To understand why this happened, Jo sets up a meeting with five of his students chosen at random.

Jo has used a student test of achievement (again) and has set up a student focus group discussion to help him understand why the test results were so poor.

The discussion shows clearly that there was a lack of correspondence between the expectations of the test and what had been covered in the course and assigned readings. Jo remedies this by setting a make-up test for all students who wished to upgrade their marks.

Once again, the evaluation process has identified a problem in Jo's teaching and he has responded to it.

The course proceeds with its ups and downs. At the end of the course the students write the common final exam. Jo is pleased when he learns that his students do well compared to students in other sections.

A student test of achievement has shown superior performance in this section. Providing the allocation of students to course sections was made in a random fashion, and since the final examination was common to all sections, this could be taken, within the context of other evaluation data, to support an argument that the teaching in this section of the course was more effective than in other sections.

Prior to the final exam, all students were asked to complete a departmental course evaluation questionnaire. Seventy of Jo's original students return the questionnaire. The quantitative responses of Jo's students are tabulated in the chart below.

End-of-year student evaluation results

	Poor	Fair	Average	Good	Excellent
The course textbook is	2	40	20	8	0
The course materials are	0	10	40	15	5
The course director's organization was	0	0	25	35	10
The course director's presentation was	0	0	25	35	10
The assignments and grading were	5	10	10	35	10
My overall assessment of the instructor is	0	0	30	35	5

A standard course evaluation questionnaire (highly structured) shows results that are better than average in all categories that are under the control of the teacher.

The only category to score below average (the choice of textbook) was beyond the control of the teacher. In addition to the quantitative assessments, students were also encouraged to write comments on the back of the forms. Jo reads these carefully and notes that, in addition to the difficulties he had identified for himself during the course, more than one student commented on the fact that he moves about too much while teaching, and this is distracting. However, many of the students also take this opportunity to praise Jo for his performance. Students seemed to be particularly impressed by the trouble Jo went to during the course to evaluate his performance and his adaptability when faced with a problem.

Jo has now used an open-ended student questionnaire to evaluate his teaching. Although it is too late to make any further changes in this course, the summative information gathered in this way can be used to improve his teaching in subsequent courses.

As a result of this experience, Jo resolves to do the following:

1. To approach the course coordinator with a view to selecting a more appropriate textbook.
2. To recommend a smaller class size.
3. To learn more about interactive teaching techniques such as case study methods and small-group discussion.
4. To use a greater variety of teaching approaches in future teaching assignments.
5. To continue to incorporate student feedback into his teaching activities.

Jo completes his teaching experience with a final stage of self-evaluation. This will enable him to build on his experiences and grow as a teacher.

Notes

1. This section borrows from Centra (1987).

2. At York, a faculty member can also work with a member of the Centre for the Support of Teaching's Teaching and Learning with Colleagues Network, but note that members of the network are not available to observe classes for the purpose of summative evaluation.

3. See, for example, *The Teaching Professor* 8 (4): 3–4.

4. For a discussion of the One-Minute Paper and the variety of uses to which it can be put, see the articles in Section VIII, Part 1.

References

Armstrong, H. 1990. *The Centennial College professional growth system.* Toronto: Centennial College.

Basow, Susan A. 1994. Student ratings of professor are not gender blind.
http://www.awm-math.org/articles/newsletter/199409/basow.html

Centra, John, *et al.* 1987. *A guide to evaluating teaching for promotion and tenure.* Akron, MA: Copley Publishing Group.

Geis, George L. 1977. Evaluation: Definitions, problems and strategies. In *Teaching is important,* C. Knapper *et al* (eds.). Toronto: Clarke Irwin in association with CAUT.

Weimer, Mary Ellen. 1990. *Improving college teaching.* San Francisco: Jossey-Bass.

Teaching Documentation Guide
Senate Committee on Teaching and Learning
York University

Purpose

This document is designed to provide guidance in assembling material to document an instructor's teaching achievements for use in tenure and promotions submissions, teaching award nominations, applications for leave fellowships and teaching development grants, merit competitions and job applications and transfers. In addition, the guide can contribute to good teaching by stimulating self-analysis and self-development as a teacher.[1]

For tenure and promotion, this guide is intended to reduce the uncertainty inherent in compiling this documentation so that initiating units, working in close collaboration with the candidate, can assemble and organize the items for inclusion in the file. A file cogently and thoroughly documenting teaching will assist units in putting forward the strongest case for tenure and promotion.

Need for the Guide

There is a common perception that teaching is not easily evaluated, whereas research achievements are fairly easy to assess. This guide is designed to counteract that perception and provide users with an easy-to-use template for presenting evidence of teaching accomplishments. Undoubtedly, documenting teaching activities does require considerable effort and planning. As well, if it is not well done, your teaching might not get the credit it deserves, and a tenure and promotion committee, in turn, might not have the evidence to enable it to give good teaching as much weight as good research. Unfortunately, it might not be at all clear, particularly to new teachers, how to go about documenting teaching achievements.

Scope of the Guide

The guide is intended to be as comprehensive as possible to provide you with a wide range of options for documenting your teaching. Consider the unique elements of your teaching style, the subject matter you teach and other concerns (such as the type of course, the level and the number of students) and then select the items from the guide that are most relevant to your teaching. If a particular activity has not been listed but you think it is relevant to your teaching responsibilities, you should include it. Furthermore, you should not feel obliged to include in your documentation every item described in this guide.

Suggestions for Proceeding

What follows are suggestions for items that might be included in your teaching dossier, your curriculum vitae (CV) and/or your tenure and promotion file. A teaching dossier provides a description of your approach to teaching and an elaboration of some of the items on your CV that best illustrate your teaching practices and achievements. The teaching section of your CV contains a comprehensive listing of your teaching activities and achievements. The teaching section of a tenure and promotion file, compiled by the initiating unit, consists primarily of assessment letters from colleagues and students and summaries of teaching evaluations. The teaching dossier – or an excerpt, depending on its length – might be included in the teaching section of your tenure and promotion file, or appended to it, to provide a context within which your teaching performance can be evaluated.

1. Ideally, you should begin gathering and retaining information that pertains to your teaching from the first day of your first teaching assignment. When making decisions about what to retain and what to discard, remember that it is better to err on the side of saving too much than to risk destroying material that could prove useful later. Keep copies of all items you refer to in your teaching documentation, such as examination outlines, original copies of course evaluations (unless they are kept by your unit), letters from chairpersons or students, samples of students' work, etc. These materials will not necessarily be included on your CV or in your teaching dossier, but should be retained by you in case "original" evidence is required. There should be a sentence in your CV assuring the reader that such material is available.

2. It might be helpful to consult your departmental mission statement (where possible), the university's academic plan, the sections on teaching in the senate tenure and promotion documents (at York, the blue book and orange book) or other relevant documents to identify the goals, priorities and expectations of the university concerning teaching and teaching excellence.

3. Examine the Summary of Teaching Contributions (below) and select those areas and items that are most applicable to your teaching. Prepare a list of statements about your accomplishments in each area.

4. In the teaching section of your CV, summarize your teaching contributions. Be sure to include your graduate and undergraduate teaching and your contributions to curriculum and course developments, but also highlight your strengths in other areas, where appropriate, in your teaching unit.

5. What should you do if you have an item that cuts across two categories? Examples include work on departmental curriculum review that could be counted as teaching or as service, or publication of a workbook that could be counted as teaching or as scholarship. While a single activity can have many different aspects that shed light on your performance in different categories, these items should not be listed twice. In such cases, it is best to work with the committee preparing your file to develop an appropriate strategy. This should enable you to decide where to list the item and where to provide a cross-reference (for example, you might list it under service and make reference to it under teaching).

6. You might wish to include as an appendix a few representative samples of materials that illustrate accomplishments referred to in your teaching dossier (for example, an exemplary course outline, unsolicited letters from students or a particularly innovative assignment outline.) A one-page reflection on the samples would enhance their value.

7. The Centre for the Support of Teaching has a collection of materials that support the development of teaching documentation as well as copies of model submissions. These could serve as useful supplements to this guide.

Approach to Teaching

1. Philosophy

You might wish to include a brief description of your teaching philosophy and a statement of your general teaching objectives in your teaching dossier. Examples of statements of objectives from specific course descriptions, including statements concerning the changes you expect or are trying to accomplish in your teaching, also might be included as an appendix.

2. Teaching Practices

Evidence of commitment to teaching can be provided by outlining your teaching strategies and the steps you have taken to evaluate or improve the effectiveness of your classroom teaching. As well, the introduction of innovations in the classroom can illustrate a scholarly approach to your teaching and a commitment to improving instruction. Examples might be included to illustrate the following:

- teaching methods (for example, lecture method, small-group discussions, problem solving, collaborative inquiry, critical-thinking pedagogy, feminist pedagogy, project-based approaches, student presentations, etc.)
- procedures used to evaluate student learning, including an outline of the types of assignments and examination methods, where appropriate
- lists of course materials, special notes, hand-outs, problem sets, laboratory books, computer manuals, etc. if relevant to your teaching methods
- arrangements made to accommodate special students needs
- teaching developments undertaken (course design; curricular changes to include gender, race and class; subject matter; methods of presentation; classroom

processes; evaluation procedures; specially designed assignments; teaching methods geared to developing critical skills; and developments involving teaching resources such as films, computers and other audio-visual material) and, where possible, evidence of the effectiveness and impact of the teaching developments you have undertaken.

3. Professional Development

Professional development includes all steps taken to improve a teacher's effectiveness. The following types of documentation could be included:

- description of steps taken to evaluate and respond to problems arising in a course, and that might inform the redesign of the course
- results of evaluations you have designed for specific courses to provide you with a final assessment of the effectiveness of your teaching
- list of seminars, workshops and conferences on teaching methods attended (internal and external)
- descriptions of any provisions you have made to improve the classroom climate, or your teaching methods, to ensure free and open participation and the comfort of all your students regardless of gender, race, class, sexual orientation or disability of any kind.

Summary of Teaching Contributions

The following items, where applicable, could be included in the teaching section of your CV; you might wish to elaborate on some of them in your dossier. It could be that some of those who will review your teaching performance have little knowledge of your discipline or of the pedagogy appropriate to achieving the teaching objectives in your area.

1. Classroom Teaching

- List the titles and numbers of courses taught, including graduate, undergraduate and reading courses; indicate with asterisks courses you have developed or substantially revised.
- Indicate the number of students in each course and describe your workload, including, where appropriate, the number of teaching assistants assigned to assist you in the course.
- Provide details of other teaching activities, such as supervision of a teaching or research practicum, athletic coaching, field placement supervision, coaching in the performing arts, etc.
- Document teaching that has contributed to the achievement of awards and honours by your students.

2. Supervision

Supervision differs from classroom teaching in a number of respects; for example, it is typically done on a one-to-one basis, there is no set curriculum and it can be extremely time consuming. To allow for an assessment of the extent of your contribution in this area, you might wish to provide data describing the average supervision load in your department.

Documentation of supervision activity should include the names of those supervised and the nature and extent of the supervisory activity. In some cases, it also might be useful to indicate the outcome of the supervision (for example, the thesis title and acceptance date, citation information of a student publication or dates and venues of public performances.) The following list indicates some examples of supervisory activities that might be documented.

a. Graduate Supervision

- PhD dissertation supervision; indicate whether you were the supervisor or a committee member
- Masters' thesis supervision; indicate whether supervisor or committee member
- Supervision of graduate independent study or directed readings.

b. Undergraduate Supervision

- Honours thesis supervision; indicate whether supervisor or committee member
- Supervision of undergraduate independent study or directed readings.

c. Student Achievement

- Supervision that has contributed to publications or conference presentations by students.

3. Teaching Awards or Nominations

Document all teaching awards you have received, including both York (departmental, faculty, university) and external awards. Nominations for awards also can provide an indication of your reputation as a teacher. Where possible, provide information regarding the nature of the award (how many are given, the adjudication procedure, etc.).

4. Teaching-Related Activities

The following local, college-, faculty and university-level activities related to teaching could be included in your CV with appropriate details. (See Suggestions for Proceeding, above.)

a. Departmental Activities

There is a variety of activities that do not take place in the classroom but that do provide important support for teaching within a department. The following list includes some of the activities that can contribute to strengthening departmental teaching. The documentation could include details such as names of committees, dates, the nature of your contribution and the names of committee chairs and collaborators.

i. Membership on Departmental Committees

- List all activities concerned with teaching that you have undertaken as a member of a departmental committee, subcommittee or task force (for example, curriculum development, program review).

ii. Teaching Development Activities

- Providing professional development for teaching assistants (for example, teaching practicum supervision, departmental orientation sessions, sessions that introduce specific techniques)
- Providing professional development for faculty (for example, orientation sessions for new faculty, sessions that introduce teaching techniques or technological developments)
- Observing teaching as part of formal or informal evaluation of teaching effectiveness.

iii. Development of Resources

- Development of department teaching resources (for example, a department computer instruction station, a teaching materials resource centre, a reference map collection).

iv. Development of Awards

- Describe your role in establishing, adjudicating or administering awards or honours for student achievement.

v. Other

- Coordination of multisection, sequenced or interrelated courses
- Organization of departmental retreats.

b. University-Wide Activities

i. Membership on Relevant University Committees

- Senate committees (such as the Academic Policy and Planning Committee, the Committee on Curriculum and Academic Standards and the Committee on Teaching and Learning)
- College and faculty committees (such as academic policy and planning or curriculum committees)
- Other committees, standing or ad hoc, that deal with teaching or matters concerned with teaching.

ii. Cooperation With Other Units and Bodies

- Describe the use that instructors in other departments, colleges, faculties or universities have made of your teaching materials.
- List your involvement in program review of other teaching units.
- List workshops, seminars or invited lectures presented.
- Describe your involvement in providing consultation to instructors in other units on improving teaching effectiveness.
- Include development of widely used course evaluations or other assessment instruments.
- Describe your teaching involvement outside your unit.

5. Publications and Professional Contributions

This section documents your achievements in developing the theory and practice of teaching. All publications on teaching should be included. When listing papers and workshop presentations, it would be helpful to include information about the nature of your audience and your contribution. (See Suggestions for Proceeding, above.)

a. Curriculum Materials

Include details of published and unpublished curriculum materials, textbooks, workbooks, case studies, lab manuals and other classroom materials that you have developed.

b. Research and Professional Contributions

List books (including chapters in books, edited books and special issues of journals), articles (indicate whether refereed, solicited or non-refereed), papers in conference proceedings (indicate whether refereed or non-refereed), bibliographies, newsletters, unpublished conference papers, workshop presentations and unpublished professional reports.

c. Funding

List internal and external research grants and teaching development grants and fellowships received.

Evaluation of Teaching

Listed below are examples of the different types of documentation generally used for evaluating teaching, and that might be included in your teaching dossier. For tenure and promotion purposes the initiating unit generally collects this material.

* summaries of teaching evaluations initiated by your unit, where possible
* results of evaluations that have been initiated by students, where possible
* letters from students selected at random and from students and teaching assistants identified by the candidate
* peer evaluations based on visits to the classroom
* where they exist, objective indicators of student progress, such as proficiency tests or examples of students' work "before" and "after."

The Centre for the Support of Teaching has a collection of materials concerning the preparation of course evaluation instruments. These materials might prove useful to those instructors whose departments do not already routinely evaluate teaching. See also the Senate Committee on Teaching and Learning's Teaching Evaluation Guide.

Notes

1. This Guide was adapted to suit the York University context from Shore *et al* (1986).

References

Shore, Bruce M., *et al* 1986 (revised edition) *The CAUT guide to the teaching dossier: Its preparation and use.* Ottawa: CAUT.

Contributors

Teferi Adem is an Advisor at the Centre for Race and Ethnic Relations at York University.

Robert Adolph is an Associate Professor of Humanities in the Faculty of Arts at York University.

Keith Aldridge is a Professor of Earth and Atmospheric Sciences in the Faculty of Pure and Applied Science at York University.

Dawn Bazely is an Associate Professor of Biology in the Faculty of Pure and Applied Science at York University.

Katherine Bischoping is an Associate Professor of Sociology in the Faculty of Arts at York University.

Betty Braaksma is a former Associate Librarian in the Scott Library at York University.

Pat Bradshaw is an Associate Professor in the Schulich School of Business at York University.

Rae Bridgeman (Anderson), a graduate of the PhD Programme in Social Anthropology, is currently an Assistant Professor in the Faculty of Architecture and Adjunct Professor of Anthropology at the University of Manitoba. She is also a research associate in York's Department of Anthropology.

Linda Briskin is an Associate Professor of Social Science in the Faculty of Arts at York University.

Janet Broomhead, former editorial assistant at York's Centre for the Support of Teaching, is a graduate of the BA Programme in Humanities and English at York University.

James Brown, former Associate Director of York's Centre for the Support of Teaching, currently teaches Business History and Ethics through Calumet College and the Schulich School of Business. He is also Senior Executive Officer in the Office of the Vice President (Administration) at York University.

Jackie Buxton is a PhD candidate in the Graduate Programme in English, and was a member of the Teaching Assistants' Resource Group of York's Centre for the Support of Teaching.

Gary Bunch is a Professor of Education at York University.

Ken Carpenter is an Associate Professor of Economics in the Faculty of Arts and of Visual Arts in the Faculty of Fine Arts at York University.

Jon Caulfield is an Associate Professor of Social Science in the Faculty of Arts at York University.

Sarah Clarke, a graduate of the Ph.D Programme at the Schulich School of Business, is currently living in the United States.

Austin Clarkson is Professor Emeritus of Music in the Faculty of Fine Arts at York University.

Katie Coulthard (Caldwell), a graduate of the BEd Programme in Education and BA Programme in Math, is a high school teacher in the York Region.

Mary-Louise Craven is an Associate Professor of Social Science in the Faculty of Arts at York University.

Myriam deBie Waller is an Associate Lecturer in French Studies in the Faculty of Arts at York University.

Paul Delaney is Associate Lecturer in Physics and Astronomy in the Faculty of Pure and Applied Science at York University.

Annie Dionne was a PhD candidate in York's Graduate Programme in Political Science.

Nick Elson is an Associate Lecturer in Languages, Literatures and Linguistics in the Faculty of Arts at York University.

Bob Everett is an Assistant Secretary of the University and teaches in the Department of Political Science, Faculty of Arts at York University.

M. Brock Fenton is a Professor of Biology in the Faculty of Pure and Applied Science and in the Faculty of Environmental Studies at York University, and former Associate Vice President of Faculties and Research.

Markita Fleming was an undergraduate student at York University.

Jerry Ginsburg is an Associate Professor of History in the Faculty of Arts at York University.

Barbara Godard is an Associate Professor of English in the Faculty of Arts at York University.

Kenneth Golby is an Associate Professor of Languages, Literatures and Linguistics in the Faculty of Arts at York University.

Leslie Green is a Professor of Philosophy in the Faculty of Arts and of Law at Osgoode Hall Law School at York University.

Ian Greene is an Associate Professor of Political Science in the Faculty of Arts at York University.

Tom Greenwald is an Associate Lecturer in the Centre for Academic Writing in the Faculty of Arts at York University.

Femida Handy is an Assistant Professor of Environmental Studies at York University.

Carl E. James is an Associate Professor of Education at York University.

Nancy Johnston, a graduate of York's PhD Programme in English, currently teaches at Ryerson Polytechnic University.

Miriam Jones, a graduate of York's PhD Programme in English, currently teaches at the University of New Brunswick.

Dalton Kehoe is an Associate Professor of Social Science in the Faculty of Arts at York University.

Reg Lang is a Professor in Environmental Studies at York University.

Paul Laurendeau is an Associate Professor of French Studies in the Faculty of Arts at York University.

David Leyton-Brown is Professor of Political Science and former Dean of the Faculty of Graduate Studies at York University.

Mary Lou McKenna is a Writing Instructor in the Centre for Academic Writing, Faculty of Arts at York University.

Kathryn McPherson is an Associate Professor of History in the Faculty of Arts at York University.

Roy Merrens is Professor Emeritus of Geography in the Faculty of Arts at York University.

Louise Morrison is an Associate Lecturer in French Studies in the Faculty of Arts at York University.

Deepika Nath, a former assistant professor at the Schulich School of Business at York University, is currently working for a market research firm in Boston.

Janice Newton is an Associate Professor of Political Science in the Faculty of Arts and former Faculty Associate at the Centre for the Support of Teaching at York University.

Catherine Ng, a graduate of the MBA Programme at the Schulich School of Business, is now teaching in the Department of Management at Hong Kong Polytechnic University.

Hugh Parry is a Professor of Humanities in the Faculty of Arts at York University.

Jan Rehner is an Associate Lecturer in the Centre for Academic Writing, Faculty of Arts at York University.

Pat Rogers is Professor of Education and Mathematics and is Academic Director of the Centre for the Support of Teaching at York University.

Leslie Sanders is Associate Professor of English and Humanities at Atkinson College at York University.

Sue Sbrizzi is Assistant to the Chair of the School of Women's Studies and former Administrative Assistant at York's Centre for the Support of Teaching.

Rachel Aber Schlesinger is an Associate Professor of Social Science in the Faculty of Arts at York University.

John Spencer is an Associate Lecturer in the Centre for Academic Writing, Faculty of Arts at York University and former Faculty Associate at the Centre for the Support of Teaching.

Molly Ungar was a PhD candidate in History at York University, and now lives in Hamilton.

Jana Vizmuller-Zocco is an Associate Professor of Languages, Literature and Linguistics in the Faculty of Arts at York University.

Elizabeth Watson is an Associate Librarian in the Business and Government Publications Library at the Schulich School of Business at York University.

Page Westcott is Professor Emeritus of Psychology at Glendon College at York University.

Karen Whalen is an Associate Lecturer in French Studies in the Faculty of Arts, and former Faculty Associate at the Centre for the Support of Teaching.

Marc Wilchesky is Chair of the Counselling and Development Centre at York University.

Margaret Willis is a Writing Instructor in the Centre for Academic Writing, Faculty of Arts at York University.

Alan Yoshioka, a graduate of York's Masters Programme in Environmental Studies, subsequently completed his PhD in the History of Science, Technology and Medicine at Imperial College, University of London. He currently teaches at York and is a researcher for a pharmaceutical company.